Northern Tanzania

with Kilimanjaro & Zanzibar

the Bradt Safari Guide

Philip Briggs

www.bradtguides.com

Bradt Travel Guides Ltd, UK
The Globe Pequot Press Inc, USA

edition
1

Northern Tanzania
The Big 5

Lion
Panthera leo (AZ)
page 259

Black rhino
Diceros bicornis (AZ)
page 269

African buffalo
Syncerus caffer (AZ)
page 269

African elephant
Loxodonta africana (AZ)
page 268

Leopard
Panthera pardus (AZ)
page 259

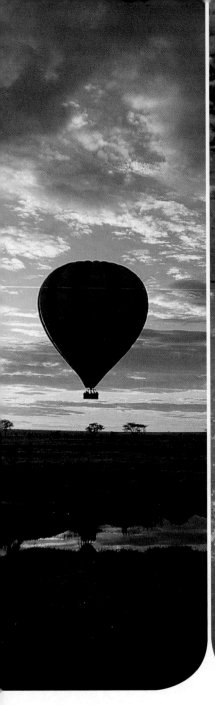

above left **Barabaig traditional dancing** (AZ)
pages 172–3

below **Maasai women preparing for ceremony** (AZ)
pages 190–1

above right **Hadza hunter** (AZ)
pages 185–8

centre right **Hadza woman and child** (AZ)
pages 185–8

above **Serengeti sunset** (ET)
pages 209–24

centre **Ngorongoro Crater:
dining in style** (CC)
pages 197–208

below **Wa-Arusha homestead
on the slopes of Mount Meru**
(AZ) page 90

above **Climbing Kilimanjaro** (AZ)
pages 149–59

centre **Summit of Kilimanjaro** (CH)
pages 149–59

below **Zanzibar Stone Town and dhow** (AZ)
pages 242–51

Author and Contributors

AUTHOR

Philip Briggs is a travel writer specialising in Africa. Raised in South Africa, where he still lives, Philip first visited east Africa in 1986 and has since spent an average of six months annually exploring the highways and back roads of the continent. His first Bradt Travel Guide, to South Africa, was published in 1991, and he has subsequently written or co-authored Bradt guides to Tanzania, Uganda, Ethiopia, Malawi, Mozambique, Ghana and Rwanda. Philip has contributed to numerous other books and magazines about Africa, and he writes a column for independent travellers for the magazine *Travel Africa*.

CONTRIBUTORS

Ariadne Van Zandbergen, who took most of the photographs in this book and did much of the research for sections on Kilimanjaro and Ol Doinyo Lengai, is a Belgian-born freelance photographer who first travelled through Africa from Morocco to South Africa in 1994–95 and is now resident in Johannesburg. She has visited more than 25 African countries and her photographs have appeared in numerous travel and wildlife guides, coffee-table books, magazines, newspapers, maps and pamphlets.

Chris McIntyre is the author of Bradt's *Zanzibar: The Bradt Travel Guide*, which has been thoroughly revised and expanded for a new sixth edition. He is well known for having written successive Bradt guides on Namibia, Botswana and Zambia for many years. Chris also writes and photographs for various UK magazines and assorted broadsheet papers, and also runs the UK tour operator, Expert Africa, who are leading specialists in organising individual and small-group trips to much of southern and east Africa.

Emma Thomson is an editorial assistant at Bradt Travel Guides. She spent a summer living with the Rangi, Chagga and Maasai communities in northern Tanzania, where she became a trustee of the Arusha-based NGO, Serian UK (*www.aangserian.org.uk*), established to promote and preserve indigenous peoples.

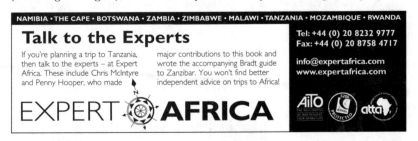

First published February 2006
Reprinted December 2006

Bradt Travel Guides Ltd
23 High Street, Chalfont St Peter, Bucks SL9 9QE, England
www.bradtguides.com
Published in the USA by The Globe Pequot Press Inc, 246 Goose Lane,
PO Box 480, Guilford, Connecticut 06437-0480

Text copyright © 2006 Philip Briggs
Maps copyright © 2006 Bradt Travel Guides Ltd
Illustrations © 2006 Individual photographers and artists

British Library Cataloguing in Publication Data
A catalogue record for this book is available from the British Library

ISBN-10: 1 84162 146 3
ISBN-13: 978 1 84162 146 3

Photographs
Front cover: Cheetah and cubs, *Acynonix jubatus* (Ariadne Van Zandbergen)
Back cover Maasai warrior (AZ) pages 190–1, Burchell's zebra (AZ) page 269
Title page Impala (AZ) page 267, Dhow, Zanzibar (AZ), Lion (AZ) page 259
Text: Ariadne Van Zandbergen (AZ), Nick Garbutt (NG), Emma Thomson (ET),
Catherine Harlow (CH), CCAfrica (CC)

Illustrations Annabel Milne
Maps Steve Munns, Terence Crump

Typeset from the author's disc by Wakewing, High Wycombe
Printed and bound in Italy by Legoprint SpA, Trento

PUBLISHER'S FOREWORD

The first Bradt travel guide was written in 1974 by George and Hilary Bradt on a river barge floating down a tributary of the Amazon. In the 1980s and '90s the focus shifted away from hiking to broader-based guides covering new destinations – usually the first to be published about these places. In the 21st century Bradt continues to publish such ground-breaking guides, as well as others to established holiday destinations, incorporating in-depth information on culture and natural history with the nuts and bolts of where to stay and what to see.

Bradt authors support responsible travel, and provide advice not only on minimum impact but also on how to give something back through local charities. In this way a true synergy is achieved between the traveller and local communities.

* * *

Thirty years ago George and I spent two fruitless days trying to hitchhike through the Serengeti. We were also bitten to distraction by mosquitoes in Mto wa Mbu ('River of Mosquitoes') and arrested in Tabora because, the official said, it was illegal to take photographs in Tanzania without a permit. George sourly wrote in *Backpacker's Africa* (1977): 'We hope someday it will all come together and be the most enlightened and productive country in Africa, but that's not going to happen for a while.' It's happened. The Northern Safari Circuit in Tanzania is widely considered to be the best in east Africa, with an excellent infrastructure and some of the most friendly and welcoming people in Africa. In the introduction of his full-length guide to Tanzania, Philip wrote: 'I've visited most corners of Tanzania … and I have to confess that were my time in the country limited to a couple of weeks, then my first priorities would undoubtedly be the Serengeti, Ngorongoro and Zanzibar. They are very special places.' In his tenth Bradt guide Philip has been able to indulge himself – and his fans – with the detailed descriptions that these special places deserve.

Hilary Bradt

23 High Street, Chalfont St Peter, Bucks SL9 9QE, England
☏ 01753 893444   f 01753 892333
e info@bradtguides.com   www.bradtguides.com

Contents

LIST OF MAPS

For key to map symbols see page VI

Acknowledgements

I received an enormous amount of assistance and support during the course of researching this book, and would like to express my gratitude to the following for services rendered: Barbara Cole and Victor Shao of Safari Makers; Peter Lindstrom of Hoopoe Adventure Tours; Gibson Maasai and Ronny Bender of Tanzania Adventures; Roselyne Mariki of Great African Safaris; Bonny Mudahama of Air Tanzania; and the staff and management of the great many lodges that accommodated us during the course of the research trip.

My greatest debt, as ever, is to my wife, travel companion and photographic collaborator Ariadne Van Zandbergen. My ongoing gratitude goes to those whose efforts have been acknowledged in various editions of my companion book, *Tanzania: The Bradt Travel Guide*.

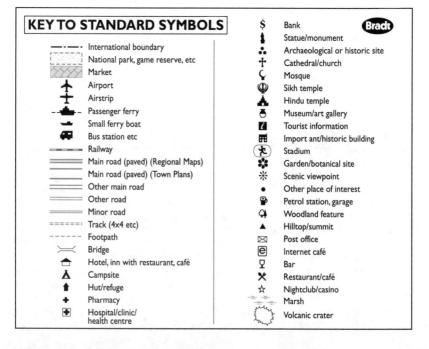

KEY TO STANDARD SYMBOLS

— · — · International boundary	$ Bank
National park, game reserve, etc	Statue/monument
Market	∴ Archaeological or historic site
✈ Airport	† Cathedral/church
✈ Airstrip	ℭ Mosque
Passenger ferry	☪ Sikh temple
Small ferry boat	Hindu temple
🚌 Bus station etc	Museum/art gallery
Railway	Tourist information
Main road (paved) (Regional Maps)	Import ant/historic building
Main road (paved) (Town Plans)	🏃 Stadium
Other main road	✿ Garden/botanical site
Other road	❋ Scenic viewpoint
Minor road	• Other place of interest
====== Track (4x4 etc)	Petrol station, garage
- - - - - Footpath	Woodland feature
⌣ Bridge	▲ Hilltop/summit
🏠 Hotel, inn with restaurant, café	⊠ Post office
▲ Campsite	℮ Internet café
⬆ Hut/refuge	Ⴤ Bar
✚ Pharmacy	✗ Restaurant/café
⊞ Hospital/clinic/ health centre	☆ Nightclub/casino
	Marsh
	Volcanic crater

Bradt

Introduction

Tanzania is a statistician's dream. Within its borders lie Africa's highest and fifth-highest mountains, the world's largest intact volcanic caldera, what is widely agreed to be Africa's greatest national park, as well as the lion's share of the continent's most expansive lake. Yet this vast east Africa country also boasts a litany of evocative place names to touch the heart of any poet: Kilimanjaro, Serengeti, Ngorongoro Crater, Olduvai Gorge, Lake Victoria, Zanzibar, the Indian Ocean, the Great Rift Valley, the Maasai Steppes ...

More remarkable still is that this enviable list of landmarks – with the exception of offshore Zanzibar – is concentrated within a mere 10% of the country's surface area abutting the border with Kenya. And here too, bookended by Lake Victoria in the west and Kilimanjaro in the east, a bloc of contiguous national parks, game reserves and other conservation areas forms what is almost certainly the most expansive safari circuit in Africa, and arguably the finest.

At the heart of this near-pristine ecosystem lies the Serengeti National Park and adjacent Ngorongoro Conservation Area, possibly the most publicised pair of game reserves in the world. And justifiably so: the Serengeti Plains host Africa's greatest wildlife spectacle, the annual migration of perhaps two million wildebeest and zebra, while also supporting remarkably dense populations of predators such as lion, cheetah, leopard and spotted hyena. The floor of the spectacular Ngorongoro Crater is if anything even more densely packed with large mammals, and is the best place in east Africa to see the endangered black rhino.

Less celebrated components of this safari circuit include Lake Manyara and Tarangire national parks, the former protecting a shallow but expansive lake on the Rift Valley floor, the latter a tract of dry acacia woodland notable for its innumerable ancient baobabs and dense elephant population. Then there is the caustic expanse of alkaline water known as Lake Natron, breeding site to millions of flamingoes. There is east Africa's most active volcano, the fiery Ol Doinyo Lengai. There is remote Lake Eyasi, its hinterland home to the region's last remaining hunter-gatherers. And dotted amid the savanna, there is jungle-covered Rubondo Island on Lake Victoria, lush montane forest in Arusha National Park, and sodden groundwater forest rising from the shores of lakes Duluti and Manyara. And, when the clouds lift, towering above the twin safari capitals of Arusha and Moshi stand the jagged peaks of Mount Meru and the even taller Kilimanjaro itself.

In short, northern Tanzania is the Africa you have always dreamed about: vast plains teeming with wild animals; rainforests alive with cackling birds and monkeys; Kilimanjaro's snow-capped peak rising dramatically above the flat scrubland; colourful Maasai herding their cattle alongside herds of grazing wildebeest; perfect palm-lined beaches lapped by the clear warm waters of the Indian Ocean stretching as far as the eye can see – all supported by a tourist infrastructure that has recovered from an immediate post-independence economic freefall to rank as one of the finest anywhere in Africa.

Northern Tanzania has always boasted an incomparable natural abundance. And these days it is serviced by a selection of genuinely world-class game lodges, bush camps and beach resorts. But travel isn't simply about ticking off the sights in comfort. When you spend time in a country, your feelings towards it are determined more than anything by the mood of its inhabitants. And I have no hesitation in saying that, on this level, my affection for Tanzania is greater than for any other African country I have visited. Tanzania is an oasis of peace and egalitarianism in a continent stoked up with political and tribal tensions, its social mood embodying all that I respect in African culture. Its people, as a rule, are polite and courteous, yet also warm and sincere, both among themselves and in their dealings with foreigners.

The one thing I can say with near certainty is that you will enjoy Tanzania. Whether you decide to stick to the conventional Serengeti–Ngorongoro–Zanzibar tourist circuit or strike out to the more offbeat likes of lakes Natron and Eyasi; whether you visit the mysterious rock art of Kolo or track chimps through the remote forests of Rubondo Island, you will find Tanzania to be a truly wonderful country.

FEEDBACK REQUEST

Every effort has been made to ensure that the details contained within this book are as accurate and up to date as possible. Inevitably, however, things move on. Any information regarding such changes, or relating to your experiences in northern Tanzania – good or bad – would be very gratefully received. Such feedback is invaluable when compiling further editions. Send your comments to Philip Briggs at Bradt Travel Guides, 23 High Street, Chalfont St Peter, Bucks SL9 9QE, England; email: info@bradtguides.com.

Part One

General Information

TANZANIA AT A GLANCE

Location East Africa, between 1° and 11°45'S, and 29°20' and 40°35'E
Size 945,166km²
Climate Tropical along coast; temperate in the highlands
Status Republic
Ruling party Chama Cha Mapinduzi (CCM)
President Jakaya Kikwete
Population 3,762,000 (2004 estimate)
Life expectancy at birth 46
Capital Dodoma
Largest city Dar es Salaam
Major exports Coffee, cotton, cashew nuts, sisal, tobacco, tea, diamonds, gold
Languages Official languages KiSwahili, English; over 100 regional variations
Religion 30% Christian, 35% Muslim, 35% indigenous beliefs; Zanzibar 99% Muslim
Currency Tanzanian shilling (Tsh)
Exchange rate £1 = Tsh2,070, US$1 = Tsh1,167, €1 = Tsh1,404 (December 2004)
International telephone code +255
Time GMT + 3 hours
Electrical voltage 230v 60Hz. Round or square three-pinned British-style plugs
Weights and measures Metric
Flag Blue and green, with diagonal black-and-yellow stripe
Public holidays 1 January, 12 January, 5 February, 26 April, 1 May, 7 July, 8 August, 14 October, 9 December, 25–26 December. See also page 58.

Background Information

FACTS AND FIGURES
Size and location
The United Republic of Tanzania came into being in 1964 when Tanganyika on the African mainland united with the offshore state of Zanzibar, the latter comprised of the Indian Ocean islands of Unguja (Zanzibar) and Pemba. It lies on the east African coast between 1° and 11°45'S and 29°20' and 40°35'E, and is bordered by Kenya and Uganda to the north, Rwanda, Burundi and the Democratic Republic of the Congo to the west, and Zambia, Malawi and Mozambique to the south. The country extends over 945,166km² (364,929 square miles), making it one of the largest countries in sub-Saharan Africa, covering a greater area than Kenya and Uganda combined. To place this in a European context, Tanzania is more than four times the size of Britain, while in an American context it's about 1.5 times the size of Texas.

This book concentrates mostly on the northeast of Tanzania, running southward from the Kenyan border to a latitude of around 4°, and between 31.5° and 37.5° east, a total area of around 120,000km², about half the size of Britain.

Capital
Dodoma was earmarked as the future capital of Tanzania in 1973. It has subsequently displaced Dar es Salaam as the official national capital, and is also where all parliamentary sessions are held. Some government departments, however, are still based in Dar es Salaam, which remains the most important and largest city in the country, and is the site of the main international airport, many diplomatic missions to Tanzania, and most large businesses. The main commercial centre and unofficial safari capital of northern Tanzania is the town of Arusha at the southern base of Mount Meru.

Population
The total population of Tanzania is estimated at between 35 and 40 million. The most densely populated rural areas tend to be the highlands, especially those around Lake Nyasa and Mount Kilimanjaro, and the coast. The country's largest city is Dar es Salaam, whose population, estimated at 2.5 million in 2002, exceeds that of the country's next 10 largest towns combined. The only northern Tanzanian towns with a population in excess of 100,000 are Arusha, Moshi and Mwanza.

There are roughly 120 tribes in Tanzania, each speaking their own language, and none of which exceeds 10% of the country's total population. The most numerically significant tribes are the Sukuma of Lake Victoria, Haya of northwest Tanzania, Chagga of Kilimanjaro, Nyamwezi of Tabora, Makonde of the Mozambique border area, Hehe of Iringa and Gogo of Dodoma.

Administrative regions

Tanzania is divided into 21 administrative regions, each with a local administrative capital. These are listed below in descending order of population density.

Government

The ruling party of Tanzania since independence has been Chama Cha Mapinduzi (CCM). Up until 1995, Tanzania was a one-party state, under the presidency of Julius Nyerere and, after his retirement in 1985, Ali Hassan Mwinyi. Tanzania held its first multi-party election in late 1995, when the CCM was returned to power with an overwhelming majority under President Benjamin Mkapa, the country's present leader.

The most recent election, in December 2005, saw the CCM returned to power under Jakaya Kikwete, Mkapa having served his maximum of two presidential terms.

Economy

Immediately after independence, Tanzania became one of the most dedicated socialist states in Africa, and its economy suffered badly as a result of a sequence of well-intentioned but misconceived or poorly managed economic policies. By the mid-1980s, Tanzania ranked among the five poorest countries in the world. The subsequent swing towards a free-market economy, making the country more attractive to investors, has resulted in dramatic improvement, and Tanzania today – while hardly wealthy – has managed to ascend out of the list of the world's 20 poorest countries. The mainstay of the economy is agriculture, and most rural Tanzanians are subsistence farmers who might also grow a few crops for sale. The

ADMINISTRATIVE REGIONS

Region	Capital	Population (millions)	Area (km²)	People per km²
Dar es Salaam	Dar es Salaam	2.6	1,393	1,870
Zanzibar & Pemba	Zanzibar	1.0	2,460	406
Mwanza	Mwanza	3.0	19,592	153
Kilimanjaro	Moshi	1.8	13,309	135
Mtwara	Mtwara	1.4	16,707	83
Mara	Musoma	1.5	19,566	76
Tanga	Tanga	2.0	26,808	75
Kagera	Bukoba	2.1	28,388	74
Shinyanga	Shinyanga	2.8	50,781	55
Dodoma	Dodoma	2.0	41,311	48
Mbeya	Mbeya	2.4	60,350	40
Kigoma	Kigoma	1.4	37,037	38
Iringa	Iringa	1.9	56,864	33
Pwani	Bagamoyo	1.0	32,407	31
Morogoro	Morogoro	1.9	70,799	29
Arusha	Arusha	2.1	82,306	25
Singida	Singida	1.2	49,341	24
Tabora	Tabora	1.7	76,151	22
Ruvuma	Songea	1.2	63,498	18
Rukwa	Sumbawanga	1.1	68,635	16
Lindi	Lindi	1.0	66,046	15

TRADITIONAL MUSICAL INSTRUMENTS

Tanzania's tribal diversity has meant that a vast array of very different – and, for that matter, very similar – traditional musical instruments are employed around the country under a bemusing number of local names. Broadly speaking, however, all but a handful of these variants can be placed in one of five distinct categories that conform to the classes of musical instrument used in Europe and the rest of the world.

The traditional music of many Tanzanian cultures is given its melodic drive by a *marimba* (also called a *mbira*), a type of instrument that is unique to Africa but could be regarded as a more percussive variant of the familiar keyboard instruments. The basic design of all *marimbas* consists of a number of metal or wooden keys whose sound is amplified by a hollow resonating box. *Marimbas* vary greatly in size from one region to the next. Popular with several pastoralist tribes of the Rift Valley and environs are small hand-held boxes with 6–10 metal keys that are plucked by the musician. In other areas, organ-sized instruments with 50 or more keys are placed on the ground and beaten with sticks, like drums. The Gogo of the Dodoma region are famed for their *marimba* orchestras consisting of several instruments that beat out a complex interweave of melodies and rhythms.

The most purely melodic of Tanzanian instruments is the zeze, the local equivalent to the guitar or fiddle, used throughout the country under a variety of names. The basic zeze design consists of between one and five strings running along a wooden neck that terminates in an open resonating gourd. The musician rubs a bow fiddle-like across the strings, while manipulating their tone with the fingers of his other hand, generally without any other instrumental accompaniment, but sometimes as part of an orchestra. Less widespread stringed instruments include the zither-like *enanga* of the Lake Tanganyika region and similar *bango* and *kinubi* of the coast, all of which are plucked like harps rather than stroked with a bow, to produce more defined melodic lines than the zeze.

The most important percussive instrument in African music is the drum, of which numerous local variations are found. Almost identical in structure and role to their European equivalent, most African drums are made by tightly stretching a membrane of animal hide across a section of hollowed tree trunk. A common and widespread type of drum, which is known in most areas as a *msondo* and is often reserved for important rituals, can be up to 1m tall and is held between the drummer's legs.

Percussive backing is also often provided by a variety of instruments known technically as idiophones. Traditionally, these might include the maraca-like *manyanga*, a shaker made by filling a gourd with dry seeds, as well as metal bells and bamboo scrapers. A modern variant on the above is the *chupa*: a glass cold-drink bottle scraped with a piece of tin or a stick.

Finally, in certain areas, horned instruments are also used, often to supply a fanfare at ceremonial occasions. These generally consist of a modified animal horn with a blowing hole cut into its side, through which the musician manipulates the pitch using different mouth movements.

Readers with an interest in traditional music are pointed towards an excellent but difficult-to-locate booklet *The Traditional Musical Instruments of Tanzania*, written by Lewis and Makala (Music Conservatoire of Tanzania, 1990), and the primary source of this box.

SWAHILI NAMES

In KiSwahili, a member of a tribal group is given an M- prefix, the tribe itself gets a Wa- prefix, the language gets a Ki- prefix, and the traditional homeland gets a U- prefix. For example, a Mgogo person is a member of the Wagogo tribe who will speak Kigogo and live in Ugogo. The Wa- prefix is commonly but erratically used in English books; the M- and Ki- prefixes are rarely used, except in the case of KiSwahili, while the U- prefix is almost always used. There are no apparent standards; in many books the Swahili are referred to as just the Swahili while non-Swahili tribes get the Wa- prefix. I have decided to drop most of these prefixes: it seems as illogical to refer to non-Swahili people by their KiSwahili name when you are writing in English as it would be to refer to the French by their English name in a German book. I have, however, referred to the Swahili language as KiSwahili on occasion. I also refer to tribal areas – as Tanzanians do – with the U- prefix, and readers can assume that any place name starting with U has this implication; in other words that Usukuma is the home of the Sukuma and Unyamwezi the home of the Nyamwezi.

country's major exports are traditionally coffee, cotton, cashew nuts, sisal, tobacco, tea and diamonds, but gold – Tanzania is now the third-largest gold producer in Africa after South Africa and Ghana – and a unique gem called tanzanite are of increasing importance to the export economy. Zanzibar and Pemba are important clove producers. The tourist industry that practically collapsed in the mid-1980s has grown steadily during the last decade or so. Over the past few years, more than 500,000 visitors annually have generated up to US$750 million annually in foreign revenue, a fivefold increase since 1990.

Languages

More than 100 different languages are spoken across Tanzania, but the official languages are KiSwahili and English. Until recently, very little English was spoken outside of the larger towns, but this is changing rapidly, and visitors can be confident that almost anybody involved in the tourist industry will speak passable English. KiSwahili, indigenous to the coast, spread through the region along the 19th-century caravan routes, and is today spoken as a second language by the vast majority of Tanzanians.

HISTORY

Tanzania has a rich and fascinating history, but much of the detail is highly elusive. Specialist works often contradict each other to such an extent that it is difficult to tell where fact ends and speculation begins, while broader or more popular accounts are commonly riddled with obvious inaccuracies. This is partly because there are huge gaps in the known facts; partly because much of the available information is scattered in out-of-print or difficult-to-find books; and partly because once an inaccuracy gets into print it tends to spread like a virus through other written works. For whatever reason, there is not, so far as I am aware, one concise, comprehensive and reliable book about Tanzanian history in print.

The following account attempts to provide a reasonably comprehensive and readable overview of the country's history. It is, to the best of my knowledge, as accurate as the known facts will allow, but at times I have had to decide for myself the most probable truth among a mass of contradictions, and I have speculated freely where speculation seems to be the order of the day. My goals are to stimulate the visitor's interest in Tanzanian history, and to give easy access to information that would have greatly enhanced my formative travels in Tanzania. Many of the subjects touched on in this general history are given more elaborate treatment elsewhere in the book, under regional history sections or in tinted boxes.

Prehistory of the interior

The part of the Rift Valley passing through Ethiopia, Kenya and northern Tanzania is almost certainly where modern human beings and their hominid ancestors evolved. Hominids are generally divided into two genera, called *Australopithecus* and *Homo*, the former extinct for at least a million years, and the latter now represented by only one species – *Homo sapiens* (modern man). The paucity of hominid fossils collected before the 1960s meant that for many years it was assumed the most common Australopithecine fossil, *A. africanus*, had evolved directly into the genus *Homo* and was thus man's oldest identifiable ancestor.

This neat linear theory of human evolution became blurred when Richard and Mary Leakey, who were excavating Olduvai Gorge in northern Tanzania, discovered that at least two Australopithecine species had existed. Carbon dating and the skeletal structure of the two species indicated that the older *A. robustus* had less in common with modern man than its more lightly built ancestor *A. africanus*, implying that the *Australopithecus* line was not ancestral to the *Homo* line at all. This hypothesis was confirmed in 1972 with the discovery of a two-million-year-old skull of a previously undescribed species *Homo habilis* at Lake Turkana in Kenya, providing conclusive evidence that *Australopithecus* and *Homo* species had lived alongside each other for at least one million years. As more fossils have come to light, including older examples of *Homo erectus* (the direct ancestor of modern humans), it has become clear that several different hominid species existed alongside each other in the Rift Valley until perhaps half a million years ago.

In 1974, Donald Johansen discovered an almost complete hominid skeleton in the Danakil region of northern Ethiopia. Named Lucy (the song 'Lucy in the Sky with Diamonds' was playing in camp shortly after the discovery), this turned out to be the fossil of a 3.5-million-year-old Australopithecine of an entirely new species dubbed *A. afarensis*. Lucy's anatomy demonstrated that bipedal hominids (or rather semi-bipedal, since the length of Lucy's arms suggest she would have been as comfortable swinging through the trees as she would have been on a morning jog) had evolved much earlier than previously assumed.

In the 1960s it was widely thought that humans and apes diverged around 20 million years ago. Recent DNA evidence has shown, however, that modern man and chimpanzees are far more closely related than previously assumed – to the extent that less biased observers might place us in the same genus. It is now thought that the hominid and chimpanzee evolutionary lines diverged from a common ancestor between four and six million years ago. In 2001, it was announced that the candidate for the so-called 'missing link' between humans and chimps had been discovered in northern Ethiopia: the fossilised remains of a 5.8-million-year-old hominid that has been assigned to a new genus *Arpipithecus*, with clear affiliations with both chimpanzees and humans.

The immediate ancestor of modern man is *Homo erectus*, which appeared about 1.5 million years ago. *Homo erectus* was the first hominid to surmount the barrier of the Sahara and spread into Europe and Asia, and is credited with the discovery of fire and the first use of stone tools and recognisable speech. Although modern man, *Homo sapiens*, has been around for at least half a million years, only in the last 10,000 years have the African races recognised today more or less taken their modern form. Up until about 1000BC, east Africa was populated exclusively by hunter-gatherers with a physiology, culture and language similar to the modern-day Khoisan (or Bushmen) of southern Africa. Rock art accredited to these hunter-gatherers is found throughout east Africa, most notably in the Kondoa-Irangi region of central Tanzania.

The pastoralist and agricultural lifestyles that were pioneered in the Nile Delta in about 5000BC spread to parts of sub-Saharan Africa by 2000BC, most notably to the Cushitic-speaking people of the Ethiopian Highlands and the Bantu-speakers of west Africa. Cushitic-speakers first drifted into Tanzania in about 1000BC, closely followed by Bantu-speakers. Familiar with Iron Age technology, these migrants would have soon dominated the local hunter-gatherers. By AD1000, most of Tanzania was populated by Bantu-speakers, with Cushitic-speaking pockets in areas such as the Ngorongoro Highlands.

There is no detailed information about the Tanzanian interior prior to 1500, and even after that details are sketchy. Except for the Lake Victoria region, which supported large authoritarian kingdoms similar to those in Uganda, much of the Tanzanian interior is too dry to support large concentrations of people. In most of Tanzania, an informal system of *ntemi* chiefs emerged. The *ntemi* system, though structured, seems to have been flexible and benevolent. The chiefs were served by a council and performed a role that was as much advisory as it was authoritarian. By the 19th century there are estimated to have been more than 200 *ntemi* chiefs in western and central Tanzania, each with about 1,000 subjects.

The *ntemi* system was shattered when southern Tanzania was invaded by Ngoni exiles from what is now South Africa, refugees from the rampantly militaristic Zulu Kingdom moulded by Shaka in the early 19th century. The Ngoni entered southern Tanzania in about 1840, bringing with them the revolutionary Zulu military tactics based on horseshoe formations and a short stabbing-spear. The new arrivals attacked the resident tribes, destroying communities and leaving survivors no option but to turn to banditry. Their tactics were observed and adopted by the more astute *ntemi* chiefs, who needed to protect themselves, but had to forge larger kingdoms to do so. The situation was exacerbated by the growing presence of Arab slave traders. Tribes controlling the areas that caravan routes went through were able to extract taxes from the slavers and to find work with them as porters or organising slave raids. This situation was exploited by several chiefs, most notably Mirambo of Unyamwezi and Mkwawa of the Uhehe, charismatic leaders who dominated the interior in the late 19th century.

The coast to 1800

There have been links between the Tanzanian coast and the rest of the world for millennia, but only the barest sketch is possible of events before AD1000. The ancient Egyptians believed their ancestors came from a southerly land called Punt. In about 2500BC an explorer called Sahare sailed off in search of this mysterious land. Sahare returned laden with ivory, ebony and myrrh, a booty that suggests he had landed somewhere on the east African coast. There is no suggestion that Egypt traded regularly with Punt, but they did visit it again. Interestingly, an engraving of the Queen of Punt, made after an expedition in 1493BC, shows her to have distinctly Khoisan features. The Phoenicians first explored the coast in about 600BC. According to the 1st-century *Periplus of the Ancient Sea* they traded with a town called Rhapta, which is thought to have lain upriver of a major estuary, possibly the Pangani or the Rufiji Delta.

Bantu-speakers arrived at the coast about 2,000 years ago. It seems likely they had trade links with the Roman Empire: Rhapta gets a name check in Ptolemy's

4th-century *Geography*, and a few 4th-century Roman coins have been found at the coast. The fact that the Romans knew of Kilimanjaro, and of the great lakes of the interior, raises some interesting questions. One hypothesis is that the coastal Bantu-speakers were running trade routes into the interior and that these collapsed at the same time as the Roman Empire, presumably as a result of the sudden dearth of trade partners. This notion is attractive and not implausible, but the evidence seems rather flimsy. The Romans could simply have gleaned the information from Bantu-speakers who had arrived at the coast recently enough to have some knowledge of the interior.

Historians have a clearer picture of events on the coast from about AD 1000, by which time trade between the coast and the Persian Gulf was well established. The earliest known Islamic buildings on the coast, which stand on Manda Island off Kenya, have been dated to the 9th century AD. Items sold to Arab ships at this time included ivory, ebony and spices, while a variety of oriental and Arabic goods were imported for the use of wealthy traders. The dominant item of export, however, was gold, mined in the Great Zimbabwe region, transported to the coast at Sofala (in modern-day Mozambique) via the Zambezi Valley, then shipped by local traders to Mogadishu, where it was sold to the Arab boats. The common assumption that Swahili language and culture was a direct result of Arab traders mixing with local Bantu-speakers is probably inaccurate. KiSwahili is a Bantu language, and although it did spread along the coast in the 11th century, most of the Arabic words that have entered the language did so at a later date. The driving force behind a common coastal language and culture was almost certainly not the direct trade with Arabs, but rather the internal trade between Sofala and Mogadishu.

More than 30 Swahili city-states sprung up along the east Africa coast between the 13th and 15th centuries, a large number of which were in modern-day Tanzania. This period is known as the Shirazi era after the sultans who ruled these city-states, most of whom claimed descent from the Shiraz region of Persia. Each city-state had its own sultan; they rarely interfered in each other's business. The Islamic faith was widespread during this period, and many Arabic influences crept into coastal architecture. Cities were centred on a great mosque, normally constructed in rock and coral. It has long been assumed that the many Arabs who settled on the coast before and during the Shirazi era controlled the trade locally, but this notion has been questioned in recent years. Contemporary descriptions of the city-states suggest that Africans formed the bulk of the population. It is possible that some African traders claimed Shirazi descent in order to boost their standing both locally and with Shirazi ships.

In the mid-13th century, probably due to improvements in Arab navigation and ship construction, the centre of the gold trade moved southward from Mogadishu to the small island of Kilwa. Kilwa represented the peak of the Shirazi period. It had a population of 10,000 and operated its own mint, the first in sub-equatorial Saharan Africa. The multi-domed mosque on Kilwa was the largest and most splendid anywhere on the coast, while another building, now known as Husuni Kubwa, was a gargantuan palace, complete with audience courts, several ornate balconies, and even a swimming pool.

Although Mombasa had possibly superseded Kilwa in importance by the end of the 15th century, coastal trade was still booming. It came to an abrupt halt in 1505, however, when the Portuguese captured Mombasa, and several other coastal towns, Kilwa included, were razed. Under Portuguese control the gold trade collapsed and the coastal economy stagnated. It was dealt a further blow in the late 16th century when a mysterious tribe of cannibals called the Zimba swept up the coast to ransack several cities and eat their inhabitants before being defeated by a mixed Portuguese and local army near Malindi in modern-day Kenya.

In 1698, an Arabic naval force under the Sultan of Oman captured Fort Jesus, the Portuguese stronghold in Mombasa, paving the way for the eventual Omani takeover of the coast north of modern-day Mtwara. Rivalries between the new Omani and the old Shirazi dynasties soon surfaced, and in 1728 a group of Shirazi sultans went so far as to conspire with their old oppressors, the Portuguese, to overthrow Fort Jesus. The Omani recaptured the fort a year later. For the next 100 years an uneasy peace gripped the coast, which was nominally under Omani rule, but dominated in economic terms by the Shirazi Sultan of Mombasa.

Slavery and exploration in the 19th century

The 19th century was a period of rapid change in Tanzania, with stronger links established between the coast and the interior as well as between east Africa and Europe. Over the first half of the 19th century, the most important figure locally was Sultan Seyyid Said of Oman, who ruled from 1804 to 1854. Prior to 1804, Britain had signed a treaty with Oman, and relations between the two powers intensified in the wake of the Napoleonic Wars, since the British did not want to see the coast fall into French hands. In 1827, Said's small but efficient navy captured Mombasa and overthrew its Shirazi sultan, to assert unambiguous control over the whole coast, with strong British support.

Having captured Mombasa, Sultan Said chose Zanzibar as his east African base, partly because of its proximity to Bagamoyo (the terminus of a caravan route to Lake Tanganyika since 1823) and partly because it was more secure against attacks from the sea or the interior than any mainland port. Said's commercial involvement with Zanzibar began in 1827 when he set up a number of clove plantations there, with scant regard for the land claims of local inhabitants. Said and his fellow Arabs had come to totally dominate all aspects of commerce on the island by 1840, the year in which the sultan permanently relocated his personal capital from Oman to Zanzibar.

The extent of the east African slave trade prior to 1827 is unclear. It certainly existed, but was never as important as the gold or ivory trade. In part, this was because the traditional centre of slave trading had always been west Africa, which was far closer than the Indian Ocean to the main markets of the Americas. In the early 19th century, however, the British curbed the slave trade out of west Africa, leaving the way open for Said and his cronies. By 1839, over 40,000 slaves were being sold from Zanzibar annually. These came from two sources: the central caravan route between Bagamoyo and the Lake Tanganyika region, and a southern route between Kilwa Kivinje and Lake Nyasa.

The effects of the slave trade on the interior were numerous. The Nyamwezi of the Tabora region and the Yua of Nyasa became very powerful by serving as porters along the caravan routes and organising slave raids and ivory hunts. Weaker tribes were devastated. Villages were ransacked; the able-bodied men and women were taken away while the young and old were left to die. Hundreds of thousands of slaves were sold in the mid-19th century. Nobody knows how many more died of disease or exhaustion between being captured and reaching the coast. Another long-term effect of the slave trade was that it formed the driving force behind the second great expansion of KiSwahili, which became the lingua franca along caravan routes.

Europeans knew little about the African interior in 1850. The first Europeans to see Kilimanjaro (Rebmann in 1848) and Mount Kenya (Krapf in 1849) were ridiculed for their reports of snow on the Equator. The Arab traders must have had

ADVICE FOR DISABLED TRAVELLERS
Gordon Rattray (www.able-travel.com)
Despite the fact that some of the upmarket lodges have accessible rooms, and a few operators claim to have adapted vehicles, Tanzania does not yet have the infrastructure to make a disabled safari a 'walk in the park'.

In general, wheelchair users and less ambulant people will need to compromise and improvise. On the plus side, African people are used to dealing with problems and disability is common, so you will have no shortage of help and useful advice.

- **Vehicle transfers** Safari vehicles are higher than normal cars, making transfers more difficult. Drivers/guides are normally happy to help, but are not trained in this skill, so you must thoroughly explain your needs and stay in control of the situation.
- **Seating** Because distances are large and roads are often bumpy, you need to be extra vigilant to avoid pressure wounds. Place your own pressure-relieving wheelchair cushion on top of (or instead of) the original cushion and, if necessary, pad around knees and elbows.
- **Bathrooms** Occasionally (more by accident than through design), showers and toilets are wheelchair accessible. Where this is not the case, be prepared to be carried again, or do your ablutions in the bedroom!
- **Health** Doctors will know about 'everyday' illnesses, but you must understand and be able to explain your own medical requirements. African hospitals are often basic, so if possible, take all necessary medication and equipment with you. It is advisable to pack this in your hand luggage during the flight in case your main luggage becomes lost.

an intimate knowledge of many parts of the interior that intrigued Europeans, but, oddly, at least in hindsight, nobody seems to have thought to ask them. In 1855, a German missionary, James Erhardt, produced a map of Africa, based on third-hand Arab accounts, which showed a large slug-shaped lake in the heart of the continent. Known as the Slug Map, it was wildly inaccurate, yet it did serve to fan interest in a mystery that had tickled geographers since Roman times: the source of the Nile.

The men most responsible for opening up the east African interior to Europeans were David Livingstone, Richard Burton, John Speke and, later, Henry Stanley. Livingstone, who came from a poor Scots background and left school at the age of ten, educated himself to become a doctor and a missionary. He arrived in the Cape in 1841 to work in the Kuruman Mission, but, overcome by the enormity of the task of converting Africa to Christianity, he decided he would be of greater service opening up the continent so that other missionaries could follow. Livingstone was the first European to cross the Kalahari Desert, the first to cross Africa from west to east and the first to see Victoria Falls. In 1858, Livingstone stumbled across Africa's third-largest lake, Nyasa. Later in the same year, on a quest for the source of the Nile funded by the Royal Geographical Society, Burton and Speke were the first Europeans to see Lake Tanganyika, and Speke continued north to Lake Victoria. Speke returned to the northern shore of Lake Victoria in 1863 and concluded – correctly, though it would be many years before the theory gained wide acceptance – that Ripon Falls in modern-day Uganda formed the source of the Nile.

Livingstone had ample opportunity during his wanderings to witness the slave caravans at first hand. Sickened by what he saw – the human bondage, the destruction of entire villages, and the corpses abandoned by the traders – he became an outspoken critic of the trade. He believed the only way to curb it was to open up Africa to the three Cs: Christianity, Commerce and Civilisation. Though not an imperialist by nature, Livingstone had seen enough of the famine and misery caused by the slavers and the Ngoni in the Nyasa area to believe the only solution was for Britain to colonise eastern Africa.

In 1867, Livingstone set off from Mikindani to spend the last six years of his life wandering between the great lakes, making notes on the slave trade and trying to settle the Nile debate. He believed the source of the Nile to be Lake Bangweulu (in northern Zambia), from which the mighty Lualaba River flowed. In 1872, while recovering from illness at Ujiji, Livingstone was met by Henry Stanley and became the recipient of perhaps the most famous words ever spoken in Africa: 'Dr Livingstone, I presume.' Livingstone died near Lake Bangweulu in 1873. His heart was removed and buried by his porters, who then carried his cured body over 1,500km via Tabora to Bagamoyo, a voyage as remarkable as any undertaken by the European explorers.

Livingstone's quest to end the slave trade met with little success during his lifetime, but his death and highly emotional funeral at Westminster Abbey seem to have acted as a catalyst. Missions were built in his name all over the Nyasa region, while industrialists such as William Mackinnon and the Muir brothers invested in schemes to open Africa to commerce (which Livingstone had always believed was the key to putting the slavers out of business).

In the year Livingstone died, John Kirk was made the British Consul in Zanzibar. Kirk had travelled with Livingstone on his 1856–62 trip to Nyasa. Deeply affected by what he saw, he had since spent years on Zanzibar hoping to find a way to end the slave trade. In 1873, the British navy blockaded the island and Kirk offered Sultan Barghash full protection against foreign powers if he banned the slave trade. Barghash agreed. The slave market was closed and an Anglican church built over it. Within ten years of Livingstone's death, the volume of slaves was a fraction of what it had been in the 1860s. Caravans reverted to ivory as their principal trade, while many of the coastal traders started up rubber and sugar plantations, which turned out to be just as lucrative as their former trade. Nevertheless, a clandestine slave trade continued on the mainland for some years – 12,000 slaves were sold at Kilwa in 1875 – and even into the 20th century, only to be fully eradicated in 1918, when Britain took control of Tanganyika.

The partitioning of east Africa
The so-called scramble for Africa was entered into with mixed motives, erratic enthusiasm and an almost total lack of premeditation by the powers involved. Britain, the major beneficiary of the scramble, already enjoyed a degree of influence on Zanzibar, one that arguably approached informal colonisation, and it was quite happy to maintain this mutually agreeable relationship unaltered. Furthermore, the British government at the time, led by Lord Salisbury, was broadly opposed to the taking of African colonies. The scramble was initiated by two events. The first, the decision of King Leopold of Belgium to colonise the Congo Basin, had little direct bearing on events in Tanzania. The partitioning of east Africa was a direct result of an about-face by the German premier, Bismarck, who had previously shown no enthusiasm for acquiring colonies and probably developed an interest in Africa in the hope of acquiring pawns to use in negotiations with Britain and France.

In 1884, a young German metaphysician called Carl Peters arrived inauspiciously on Zanzibar, then made his way to the mainland to sign a series of treaties with local chiefs. The authenticity of these treaties is questionable, but when Bismarck announced claims to a large area between the Pangani and Rufiji rivers, it was enough to set the British government into a mild panic. Britain had plans to expand the Sultanate of Zanzibar, its informal colony, to include the fertile lands around Kilimanjaro. Worse, large parts of the area claimed by Germany were already part of the sultanate. Not only was Britain morally bound to protect these, it also did not want to surrender control of Zanzibar's annual import/export turnover of two million pounds.

Despite pressure put on the British government by John Kirk, angry that his promises to Barghash would not be honoured, there was little option but to negotiate with Germany. A partition was agreed in 1886, identical to the modern border between Kenya and Tanzania. (You may read that Kilimanjaro was part of the British territory before Queen Victoria gave it to her cousin, the Kaiser, as a birthday present. This amusing story, possibly dreamed up by a Victorian satirist to reflect the arbitrariness of the scramble, is complete fabrication.) In April 1888, the Sultan of Zanzibar unwillingly agreed to lease Germany the coastal strip south of the Umba River. Germany mandated this area to Carl Peters' German East Africa Company (GEAC), which placed agencies at most of the coastal settlements north of Dar es Salaam. These agents demanded heavy taxes from traders and were encouraged to behave high-handedly in their dealings with locals.

The GEAC's honeymoon was short. Emil Zalewski, the Pangani agent, ordered the sultan's representative, the Wali, to report to him. When the Wali refused, Zalewski had him arrested and sent away on a German war boat. In September 1888, a sugar plantation owner called Abushiri Ibn Salim led an uprising against the GEAC. Except for Dar es Salaam and Bagamoyo, both protected by German war boats, the GEAC agents were either killed or driven away. A horde of 20,000 men gathered on the coast, including 6,000 Shambaa who refused to relinquish their right to claim tax from caravans passing the Usambara. In November, the mission at Dar es Salaam was attacked. Three priests were killed and the rest captured. The coast was in chaos until April 1889 when the Kaiser's troops invaded Abushiri's camp and forced him to surrender. The German government hanged Abushiri in Pangani; they withdrew the GEAC's mandate and banned Peters from ever setting foot in the area.

The 1886 agreement only created the single line of partition north of Kilimanjaro. By 1890, Germany had claimed an area north of Witu, including Lamu, and there was concern in Britain that they might try to claim the rich agricultural land around Lake Victoria, thereby surrounding Britain's territory. Undeterred by the debacle at Pangani (and with a nod and a wink from Bismarck), Carl Peters decided to force the issue. He slipped through Lamu and in May 1890, after a murderous jaunt across British territory, he signed a treaty with the King of Buganda entitling Germany to most of what is now southern Uganda. This time, however, Peters' plans were frustrated. Bismarck had resigned in March of the same year and his replacement, Von Kaprivi, wanted to maintain good relations with Salisbury's government. In any case, Henry Stanley had signed a similar treaty with the Buganda when he passed through the area in 1888 on his way from rescuing the Emin Pasha in Equatoria.

Germany had its eye on Heligoland, a small but strategic North Sea island that had been seized by Britain from Denmark in 1807. To some extent, German interest in Africa had always been related to the bargaining power it would give them in Europe. In 1890, Salisbury and Von Kaprivi knocked out the agreement that created the modern borders of mainland Tanzania (with the exception of modern-day Burundi and Rwanda, German territory until after World War I). In exchange for an island of less than 1km² in extent, Salisbury was guaranteed protectorateship over Zanzibar and handed the German block north of Witu, and Germany relinquished any claims it might have had to what are today Uganda and Malawi.

German East Africa

The period of German rule was not a happy one. In 1891, Carl Peters was appointed governor. Peters had already proved himself an unsavoury and unsympathetic character: he boasted freely of enjoying killing Africans and, under the guise of the GEAC, his lack of diplomacy had already instigated one uprising. Furthermore, the 1890s were plagued by a series of natural disasters: a rinderpest epidemic at the start of the decade, followed by an outbreak of smallpox, and a destructive plague of locusts. A series of droughts brought famine and disease in their wake. Many previously settled areas reverted to bush, causing the spread of tsetse fly and sleeping sickness. The population of Tanganyika is thought to have decreased significantly between 1890 and 1914.

It took Peters a decade to gain full control of the colony. The main area of conflict was in the vast central plateau where, led by Mkwawa, the Hehe had become the dominant tribe. In 1891, the Hehe ambushed a German battalion led by Emil Zalewski. They killed or wounded more than half Zalewski's men, and made off with his armoury. Mkwawa fortified his capital near Iringa, but the Germans razed it in 1894. Mkwawa was forced to resort to guerrilla tactics, which he used with some success until 1898, when he shot himself rather than face capture by the Germans.

TRIBES

The word 'tribe' has fallen out of vogue in recent years, and I must confess that for several years I rigorously avoided the use of it in my writing. It has, I feel, rather colonial connotations, something to which I'm perhaps overly sensitive having lived most of my life in South Africa. Some African intellectuals have argued that it is derogatory, too, in so far as it is typically applied in a belittling sense to non-European cultures, where words such as 'nation' might be applied to their European equivalent.

All well and good to dispense with the word tribe, at least until you set about looking for a meaningful substitute. 'Nation', for instance, seems appropriate when applied in a historical sense to a large and cohesive centralised entity such as the Zulu or Hehe, but rather less so when you're talking about smaller and more loosely affiliated tribes. Furthermore, in any modern sense, Tanzania itself is a nation (and proud if it), just as are Britain or Germany, so that describing, for instance, the modern Chagga as a nation would feel as inaccurate and contrived as referring to, say, the Liverpudlian or Berliner nation.

It would be inaccurate, too, to refer to most African tribes in purely ethnic, cultural or linguistic terms. Any or all of these factors might come into play in shaping a tribal identity, without in any sense defining it. All modern tribes contain individuals with a diverse ethnic stock, simply through intermarriage. Most modern Ngoni, for instance, belong to that tribe through their ancestors having been assimilated into it, not because all or even any of their ancestors were necessarily members of the Ngoni band who migrated up from South Africa in the 19th century. And, for sure, when the original Bantu-speaking people moved into present-day Tanzania thousands of years ago, local people with an entirely different ethnic background would have been assimilated into the newly established communities. Likewise, the linguistic and cultural differences between two neighbouring tribes are often very slight, and may be no more significant than dialectal or other regional differences within either tribe. The Maasai and Samburu, for instance, share a long common history, are

Germany was determined to make the colony self-sufficient. Sugar and rubber were well established on parts of the coast; coffee was planted in the Kilimanjaro region, a major base for settlers; and cotton grew well around Lake Victoria. The colony's leading crop export, sisal, was grown throughout the rest of the country. In 1902, Peters decided that the southeast should be given over to cotton plantations. This was an ill-considered move: the soils were not suitable for the crop and the scheme was bound to cause great hardship. It also led to the infamous and ultimately rather tragic Maji-Maji rebellion, which proved to be perhaps the most decisive event in the colony during German rule.

Carl Peters was fired from the colonial service in 1906. He believed his African mistress had slept with his manservant, so he flogged her close to death then hanged them both. His successor introduced a series of laws protecting Africans from mistreatment. To the disgust of the settler community, he created an incentive-based scheme for African farmers. This made it worth their while to grow cash crops and allowed the colony's exports to triple in the period leading up to World War I.

When war broke out in Europe, east Africa also became involved. In the early stages of the war, German troops entered southern Kenya to cut off the Uganda Railway. Britain responded with an abortive attempt to capture Tanga. The balance of power was roughly even until Jan Smuts led the Allied forces into German

of essentially the same ethnic stock, speak the same language, and are culturally almost indistinguishable. Yet they perceive themselves to be distinct tribes, and are perceived as such by outsiders.

A few years ago, in mild desperation, I settled on the suitably nebulous term ethno-linguistic group as a substitute for tribe. Clumsy, ugly and verging on the meaningless it might be, but it does sound impressively authoritative, without pinning itself exclusively on ethnicity, language or culture as a defining element, and it positively oozes political correctness. It's also, well, a little bit silly! Just as Tanzanians are unselfconscious about referring to themselves as black and to *wazungu* as white, so too do they talk about their tribe without batting an eyelid. For goodness sake, at every other local hotel in Tanzania, visitors are required to fill in the 'Tribe' column in the standard-issue guesthouse visitors' book! And if it's good enough for Tanzanians, well, who am I to get precious about it?

More than that, it strikes me that even in an African nation as united as Tanzania certainly is, the role of tribe in shaping the identity of an individual has no real equivalent in most Western societies. We may love – or indeed loathe – our home town, we might fight to the death for our loved ones, we might shed tears when our football team loses or our favourite pop group disbands, but we have no equivalent to the African notion of tribe. True enough, tribalism is often cited as the scourge of modern Africa, and when taken to fanatical extremes that's a fair assessment, yet to damn it entirely would be rather like damning English football, or its supporters, because of the actions of a fanatical extreme. Tribalism is an integral part of African society, and pussyfooting around it through an overdeveloped sense of political correctness strikes me as more belittling than being open about it.

So, in case you hadn't gathered, Tanzania's 120 ethno-lingual-cultural groupings are tribes for this edition of the guide, a decision that will hold at least for so long as I'm expected to fill in my tribe – whatever that might be – every time I check into a Tanzanian guesthouse!

territory in 1916. By January 1918, the Allies had captured most of German East Africa and the German commander, Von Lettow, retreated into Mozambique. The war disrupted food production, and a serious famine ensued. This was particularly devastating in the Dodoma region. The country was taken over by the League of Nations. The Ruanda-Urundi District, now the states of Rwanda and Burundi, was mandated to Belgium. The rest of the country was renamed Tanganyika and mandated to Britain.

Tanganyika

The period of British rule between the wars was largely uneventful. Tanganyika was never heavily settled by Europeans so the indigenous populace had more opportunity for self-reliance than it did in many colonies. Nevertheless, settlers were favoured in the agricultural field, as were Asians in commerce. The Land Ordinance Act of 1923 secured some land rights for Africans; otherwise they were repeatedly forced into grand but misconceived agricultural schemes. The most notorious of these, the Groundnut Scheme of 1947, was an attempt to convert the southeast of the country into a large-scale mechanised groundnut producer. The scheme failed through a complete lack of understanding of local conditions; it caused a great deal of hardship locally and cost British taxpayers millions of pounds. On a political level, a system of indirect rule based around local government encouraged African leaders to focus on local rivalries rather than national issues between the wars. A low-key national movement called the TAA was formed in 1929, but it was as much a cultural as a political organisation.

Although it was not directly involved in World War II, Tanganyika was profoundly affected by it. The country benefited economically. It saw no combat so food production continued as normal, while international food prices rocketed. Tanganyika's trade revenue increased sixfold between 1939 and 1949. World War II was a major force in the rise of African nationalism. Almost 100,000 Tanganyikans fought for the Allies. The exposure to other countries and cultures made it difficult for them to return home as second-class citizens. They had fought for non-racism and democracy in Europe, yet were victims of racist and non-democratic policies in their own country.

The dominant figure in the post-war politics of Tanganyika/Tanzania was Julius Nyerere. Schooled at a mission near Lake Victoria, he went on to university in Uganda and gained a master's degree in Edinburgh. After returning to Tanzania in 1952, Nyerere became involved in the TAA. This evolved into the more political and nationalist TANU in 1954. Nyerere became the president of TANU at the age of 32. By supporting rural Africans on grass-roots issues and advocating self-government as the answer to their grievances, TANU gained a strong national following. By the mid-1950s, Britain and the UN were looking at a way of moving Tanganyika towards greater self-government, though over a far longer time-scale than TANU envisaged. The British governor, Sir Edward Twining, favoured a multi-racial system that would give equal representation to whites, blacks and Asians. TANU agreed to an election along these lines, albeit with major reservations. Twining created his own 'African party', the UTC.

In the 1958 election, there were three seats per constituency, one for each racial group. Electors could vote for all three seats, so in addition to putting forward candidates for the black seats, TANU indicated their preferred candidates in the white and Asian seats. Candidates backed by TANU won 67% of the vote; the UTC did not win a single seat. Twining's successor, Sir Richard Turnball, rewarded TANU by scrapping the multi-racial system in favour of open elections. In the democratic election of 1960, TANU won all but one seat. In May 1961,

Tanganyika attained self-government and Nyerere was made Prime Minister. Tanganyika attained full independence on 9 December 1961. Not one life had been taken in the process. Britain granted Zanzibar full independence in December 1963. A month later the Arab government was toppled and in April 1964 the two countries combined to form Tanzania.

Tanzania

At the very core of Tanzania's post-independence achievements and failures lies the figure of Julius Nyerere, who ruled Tanzania until his retirement in 1985. In his own country, where he remains highly respected, Nyerere is called *Mwalimu* – the teacher. In the West, he is a controversial figure, often portrayed as a dangerous socialist who irreparably damaged his country. This image of Nyerere doesn't bear scrutiny. He made mistakes and was intolerant of criticism – at one point Tanzania had more political prisoners than South Africa – but he is also one of the few genuine statesmen to have emerged from Africa, a force for positive change both in his own country and in a wider African context.

In 1962, TANU came into power with little policy other than their attained goal of independence. Tanganyika was the poorest and least economically developed country in east Africa, and one of the poorest in the world. Nyerere's first concerns were to better the lot of rural Africans and to prevent the creation of a money-grabbing elite. The country was made a one-party state, but had an election system which, by African standards, was relatively democratic. Tanzania pursued a policy of non-alignment, but the government's socialist policies and Nyerere's outspoken views alienated most Western leaders. Close bonds were formed with socialist powers, most significantly China, who built the Tanzam Railway (completed in 1975).

Relations with Britain soured in 1965. Nyerere condemned the British government's tacit acceptance of the Unilateral Declaration of Independence (UDI) in Rhodesia. In return, Britain cut off all aid to Tanzania. Nyerere also gave considerable vocal support to disenfranchised Africans in South Africa, Mozambique and Angola. The ANC and Frelimo both operated from Tanzania in the 1960s.

Nyerere's international concerns were not confined to white-supremacism. In 1975, Tanzania pulled out of an Organisation of African Unity (OAU) conference in Idi Amin's Uganda saying: 'The refusal to protest against African crimes against Africans is bad enough ... but ... by meeting in Kampala ... the OAU are giving respectability to one of the most murderous regimes in Africa.' Tanzania gave refuge to several Ugandans, including the former president Milton Obote and the current president Yoweri Museveni. Amin occupied part of northwest Tanzania in October 1978, and bombed Bukoba and Musoma. In 1979, Tanzania retaliated by invading Uganda and toppling Amin. Other African leaders condemned Tanzania for this action, despite Amin having been the initial aggressor. Ousting Amin drained Tanzania's financial resources, but it never received any financial compensation, either from the West, or from any other African country.

At the time of independence, most rural Tanzanians lived in scattered communities. This made it difficult for the government to provide such amenities as clinics and schools and to organise a productive agricultural scheme. In 1967, Nyerere embarked on a policy he called villagisation. Rural people were encouraged to form *Ujamaa* (familyhood) villages and collective farms. The scheme met with some small-scale success in the mid-1970s, so in 1975 Nyerere decided to forcibly re-settle people who had not yet formed villages. By the end of the year 65% of rural Tanzanians lived in *Ujamaa* villages. In many areas, however, water supplies were inadequate to support a village. The resultant mess, exacerbated by one of Tanzania's regular droughts, ended further villagisation. *Ujamaa* is often considered to have been an unmitigated disaster. It did not achieve what it was meant to, but it did help the government improve education and health care. Most reliable sources claim it did little long-term damage to agricultural productivity.

By the late 1970s Tanzania's economy was a mess. There were several contributory factors: drought, *Ujamaa*, rising fuel prices, the border closure with Kenya, lack of foreign aid, bureaucracy and corruption in state-run institutions, and the cost of the Uganda episode. After his re-election in 1980 Nyerere announced he would retire at the end of that five-year term. In 1985, Ali Hassan Mwinyi succeeded Nyerere as prime minister. Nyerere remained chairman of the CCM, the party formed when TANU merged with the Zanzibari ASP in 1975, until 1990.

Under President Mwinyi, Tanzania moved away from socialism. In June 1986, in alliance with the IMF, a three-year Economic Recovery Plan was implemented. This included freeing up the exchange rate and encouraging private enterprise. Since then Tanzania has achieved an annual growth rate of around 4% (in real terms). Many locals complain that the only result they have seen is greater inflation. In 1990 attempts were made to rout corruption from the civil service, with surprisingly positive results. The first multi-party election took place in October 1995. The CCM was returned to power with a majority of around 75% under the leadership of Benjamin Mpaka, who stood down in December 2005 following the country's third multi-party election. This, once again, was won by the CCM, which polled more than 80% of the 11.3 million votes under its new leader, Jakaya Kikwete.

Now into its fifth decade of independence, most of Tanzania still suffers from the tribal problems it had at the outset. Nyerere's great achievement is the tremendous sense of national unity he created by making KiSwahili the national language, by banning tribal leaders, by forcing government officials to work away from the area in which they grew up, and by his own example. Things look better for Tanzania now than they have at any time since independence. It remains one of the world's least-developed countries, but most sources agree that the economic situation of the average Tanzanian has improved greatly since independence, as have adult literacy rates and health care. Tanzania's remarkable political stability and its increasingly pragmatic economic policies form a positive basis for future growth.

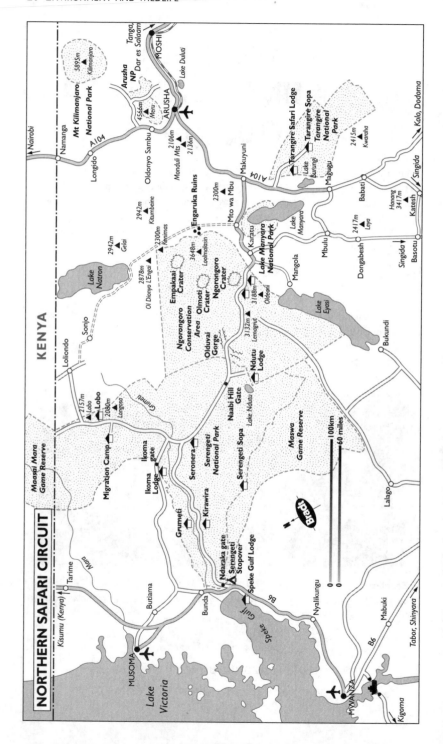

Environment and Wildlife

There are plenty of good reasons to visit northern Tanzania – the beautiful coastline, fascinating history and magnificent scenery – but for most people one attraction overwhelms all others, and that is the wildlife. Tanzania is Africa's prime game-viewing country, best known for the deservedly well-publicised Serengeti and Ngorongoro Crater, highlights in a mosaic of national parks and other conservation areas that cover almost 25% of the country and protect an estimated 20% of Africa's large mammals.

GEOGRAPHY

The bulk of east Africa is made up of a vast, flat plateau rising from a narrow coastal belt to an average height of about 1,500m. This plateau is broken dramatically by the 20-million-year-old Great Rift Valley, which cuts a trough up to 2,000m deep through the African continent from the Dead Sea to Mozambique. The main branch of the Rift Valley bisects Tanzania. A western branch of the Rift Valley forms the Tanzania–Congo border. Lakes Natron, Manyara, Eyasi and Nyasa/Malawi are all in the main rift, Lake Tanganyika lies in the western branch, and Lake Victoria lies on an elevated plateau between them.

East Africa's highest mountains (with the exception of the Ruwenzori Mountains in Uganda) are volcanic in origin, created by the same forces that caused the Rift Valley. Kilimanjaro is the most recent of these: it started to form about one million years ago, and was still growing as recently as 100,000 years ago. Mount Meru is older. Ngorongoro Crater is the collapsed caldera of a volcano that would once have been as high as Kilimanjaro is today. The only active volcano in Tanzania, Ol Doinyo Lengai, rises from the rift floor to the north of Ngorongoro.

Habitats and vegetation

The bulk of Tanzania is covered in open grassland, savanna (lightly wooded grassland) and woodland. The Serengeti Plains are an archetypal African savanna: grassland interspersed with trees of the acacia family – which are typically quite short, lightly foliated and thorny. Many have a flat-topped appearance. An atypical acacia, the yellow fever tree, is one of Africa's most striking trees. It is relatively large, has yellow bark and is often associated with water. Combretum is another family of trees typical of many savanna habitats. The dry savanna of central Tanzania can be so barren during the dry season that it resembles semi-desert.

Woodland differs from forest in lacking an interlocking canopy. The most extensive woodland in Tanzania is in the *miombo* belt, which stretches from southern and western Tanzania to Zimbabwe. *Miombo* woodland typically grows on infertile soil, and is dominated by broad-leafed *brachystegia* trees. You may come across the term mixed woodland: this refers to woodland with a mix of *brachystegia*,

AMANI AND THE EASTERN ARC MOUNTAINS

The phrase Eastern Arc was coined by Dr Jon Lovett as recently as the mid-1980s to encompass a string of 13 ancient east African mountain ranges which, despite being physically isolated from each other, share a very similar geomorphology and ecology. Aside from the Taita Hills in southern Kenya, the crystalline ranges of the Eastern Arc all lie within eastern Tanzania, where – as their name implies – they form a rough crescent running from Pare in the north to Udzungwa and Mahenge in the south. The oldest mountains in east Africa, they formed at least 100 million years ago, along a fault running to the east of the more geologically recent Rift Valley.

The extensive rainforests of the Eastern Arc date back more than 30 million years to a time when Africa was part of a much larger landmass known as Gondwanaland. And, during drier and colder climatic periods when most African rainforests retreated, the Eastern Arc forests flourished thanks to a continuous westerly wind that blew in moisture from the Indian Ocean. It was during one such phase, about ten million years ago, that the Eastern Arc forests became isolated from the lowland rainforests of western and central Africa. More recently, probably, each of the individual forested ranges of the Eastern Arc became a discrete geographical entity, transforming the Eastern Arc into an archipelago of forested islands jutting out from an ocean of low-lying savanna.

Following a pattern characteristic of true islands, the isolated, ancient forests of the Eastern Arc host an assemblage of endemic taxa with few peers anywhere on the planet. The best known of these endemics is the African violet *Saintpaulia ionantha*, first collected in 1892 by Baron Walter von Saint Paul Illaire and now one of the world's most popular perennial pot plants, generating a global trade worth tens of millions of US dollars. In the two Usambara ranges alone, more than 2,850 plant species have been identified, a list that includes 680 types of tree, a greater tally than that of North America and Europe combined. At least 16 plant genera and 75 vertebrate species – including 10 birds and 11 mammals – are endemic to the forests of the Eastern Arc, as are literally thousands of invertebrates. Little wonder, then, that the Eastern Arc Mountains have recently been classified as one of the world's 20 most important biodiversity hotspots, and are frequently referred to as the Galápagos of Africa.

The Eastern Arc endemics fall into two broad categories: old endemics that show little divergence from relict evolutionary lineages, and new endemics representing recently evolved lineages. A clear example of a 'living fossil' in the former category is the giant elephant shrew of the suborder Rhynchocyonidae, represented by three similar species almost identical in structure to more widespread 20-million-year-old fossils of their ancestors. The origins of new endemics are more variable. Some, such as the African violets, probably evolved from an ancestral stock blown across the ocean from Madagascar in a freak cyclone. Others, including many of the birds and flying insects, are essentially locally adapted variants on similar species found in neighbouring savannas or in other forests in east Africa. And four of the endemic birds show sufficient affiliations to Asian species to suggest they may have arrived in Africa at a time when moister coastal vegetation formed a passage around the Arabian peninsula.

The forests of the Eastern Arc Mountains vary greatly in their extent. The natural forest on the vast Udzungwa range extends over some 2,000km², and has yielded previously undescribed bird species and three new monkey taxa in recent years. By contrast, Kenya's Taita Hills retain a mere 6km² of forest. After

Udzungwa, the most significant ranges in terms of biodiversity are the East Usambara and Uluguru, though the Nguru and Rubeho mountains remain relatively unexplored in scientific terms.

The Eastern Arc forests are of great interest to birdwatchers as the core of the so-called Tanzania-Malawi Mountains Endemic Bird Area (EBA). Of 37 described range-restricted bird species endemic to this EBA, all but five occur in Tanzania, and half are confined to the country. In terms of avian diversity, the Udzungwa Mountains are by far the most significant range in the EBA, but Amani Nature Reserve in the Eastern Usambara has the edge over Udzungwa in terms of ease of access to prime birding areas and affordable facilities. The individual distribution patterns of several range-restricted bird species provides clear evidence of the mountains' pseudo-island ecology, with several species widespread on one particular range but absent from other apparently suitable ones. The Usambara akalat, for instance, is confined to the Western Usambara, while Loveridge's sunbird and the Uluguru bush-shrike are unique to the Uluguru Mountains. The most remarkable distribution pattern, however, is that of the long-billed tailorbird or apalis, a poorly known forest-fringe species confined to two ranges situated an incredible 2,000km apart – the Eastern Usambara in northern Tanzania and Mount Namuli in central Mozambique. Stranger still is the case of the Udzungwa partridge: this evolutionary relict, discovered as recently as 1991 and known only from the Udzungwa and Rubeho mountains, evidently has stronger genetic affiliations to the Asian hill partridges than to any other African bird!

For nature lovers, the most accessible and rewarding Eastern Arc add-on to a northern Tanzanian safari is the underrated Amani Nature Reserve in the Eastern Usambara, whose bird checklist of 340 species includes 12 that are globally threatened and 19 endemic to the Eastern Arc Mountains or the east African coastal biome. Formally opened in 1997, this reserve, centred on a former German agricultural research station, protects almost 10,000ha of relatively undisturbed forest. Some of the most productive birdwatching is to be had around Amani village. One of the more conspicuous and alluring residents here is the green-headed oriole, while the flowering gardens attract three of four range-restricted sunbirds associated with the Eastern Usambara, and the rare long-billed tailorbird has been discovered breeding at two sites within the village. In addition to the birds, black-and-white colobus and blue monkey are often seen around the village, as is the outsized Zanj elephant shrew.

Nine walking trails ranging from 3 to 12km in length are also on offer. The 10km Konkoro Trail, which can be covered on foot or in a vehicle, is good for African violets, while the shorter Turaco and Mbamole hill trails are recommended for montane forest birds such as Usambara eagle owl, southern banded snake eagle, silvery-cheeked hornbill, half-collared kingfisher, African green ibis, Fischer's turaco, African broadbill, East Coast akalat, white-chested alethe, Kenrick's and Waller's starlings, and several forest flycatchers.

Amani lies about six to seven hours' drive from Moshi or Arusha via Muheza on the Tanga road. Entrance to Amani Nature Reserve costs US$30 per person, which – unlike national park fees – is a one-off payment no matter how long you spend in the reserve. The daily guide fee is US$8 per person. Twenty per cent of all fees paid will go towards the development of local communities. Basic but comfortable accommodation is available for around US$5 at two guesthouses run by the nature reserve, as are meals. Camping is permitted too. For more details contact the project management at 053 264 6907 or usambara@twiga.com.

acacia and other species. Many woodland habitats are characterised by an abundance of baobab trees.

True closed canopy forest covers less than 1% of Tanzania's surface area, but it is the country's most ecologically diverse habitat, represented along the northern circuit by the montane forests of Kilimanjaro, Meru, Ngorongoro Crater rim and various lesser mountains, as well as the groundwater forests around Lake Duluti and in Lake Manyara. Other interesting but localised vegetation types are mangrove swamps (common along the coast, particularly around Kilwa) and the heath and moorland found on the higher slopes of Kilimanjaro and Meru.

AFRICAN CONSERVATION

The plight of the mountain gorilla, rhinoceros and elephant has made African conservation a household concern in the West. Despite this, few Westerners have any grasp of the issues. What follows is certainly opinionated, and probably simplistic, but does attempt to clarify the root problem as I see it. You may well disagree...

We all romanticise Africa. An incredible amount of drivel was written about it during the colonial era, and this dominates our perception of the continent. The macho blustering of Hemingway and exaggerated accounts of the Great White Hunters vie in our heads with the nostalgic meandering of *Out of Africa*. For the West, Africa represents wildness and space, vast horizons and shimmering red sunsets; powerful images we do not want shattered by the realities of the 21st century.

It was, of course, European settlers who destroyed the Africa they mythologised. The vast herds that had existed alongside people for millennia were decimated during the colonial era. By the early 1960s, when most of Africa became independent, these herds were by and large restricted to conservation areas that had been set aside by the colonial governments to preserve something of the Africa they loved. Their vision of unspoilt Africa did not include people: when an area was declared a national park, the people who lived there were moved to the fringes. Local people had both hunted and conserved the animals for centuries; now hunting was forbidden and they needed new sources of food.

Areas suitable for national parks are not normally densely populated, since they tend to be relatively infertile. Even if someone succeeded in growing crops on the fringe of an unfenced park, one hungry or angry elephant could wipe out their efforts in the space of minutes. This created a circle of poverty around many game reserves, a scenario that ultimately worked in the interests of ivory and rhino horn traders. People living on the verges of reserves would happily kill an elephant or rhinoceros for what was a fraction of the market price, but a fortune in local terms.

As you are no doubt aware, rhinoceros are close to extinction in most African countries. In Tanzania, there are 20 left in the Ngorongoro Conservation Area and at best a couple of hundred in the Selous. Africa's elephant population is now thought to number about half a million. Tanzania is home to a significant number of these. There are an estimated 60,000 animals in the Selous alone, and probably a similar number scattered across other reserves.

In the late 1980s the elephant situation seemed hopeless. In some reserves, herds had been poached to within 20% of their size ten years previously. In the Selous, up to 20,000 were killed in a two-year period. Most African

MAIN CONSERVATION AREAS

Almost half of Tanzania's national parks are located in northern Tanzania, from the big names of the Serengeti National Park and Ngorongoro Conservation Area to several less well-known parks and reserves. Here, too, is the dominant grandeur of Mount Kilimanjaro National Park. All the national parks receive detailed coverage in the main part of the guide, as do any other conservation areas that are reasonably accessible, and some that are not. The following potted descriptions are intended to provide an introductory overview to the north's most significant and accessible conservation areas, not to replicate the more extended descriptions in the main body of the guide. The list starts with the Serengeti and runs roughly clockwise from there.

governments lacked the finance to arrest this process; in some cases they also lacked the will, with strong rumours of corruption and the involvement of government officials. Anti-poaching units armed with old-fashioned rifles were fighting bands of poachers armed with AK47s, and losing. In 1988, I was driven through a part of Kenya's Tsavo East National Park, one of the worst-hit reserves, where less than a quarter of its 1972 population of 17,000 animals were left. I saw more elephant corpses than I did live animals; those elephants I did see ran off in terror at the approach of a vehicle.

A moratorium on the world ivory trade was implemented in 1989. There is a wide consensus that this ban has worked in east Africa: elephant numbers increased and, without a market, poaching virtually stopped. Southern African countries want this moratorium to be lifted. Herds in South Africa, Botswana and Zimbabwe are stable and growing, and since elephants are extremely destructive when overpopulated, excess animals were until recently culled. This issue was greatly misrepresented in Britain at least, where emotive and irresponsible newspaper columns and television programmes equated culling with murder. Obviously culling is not the ideal solution, but it is difficult to see a practical alternative when populations become unnaturally high, an almost inevitable reality in the fenced reserves of southern Africa. (The suggestion most often put forward is that the animals could be moved. To the Cotswolds? Or somewhere else where African crops can be trampled?)

It has become evident to many conservationists that a complete change of approach is the only chance for the long-term survival of Africa's large animals. Local people must be included in the process. If they benefit from the reserves, they will side with conservationists; if they do not they will side with the poachers. Attempts must be made to ensure that locals benefit from money raised by the reserves, that they are given meat from culled animals, and that, wherever possible, work is found for them within the reserve. In an increasingly densely populated continent, reserves can only justify their existence if they create local wealth.

Africa does not belong to the West. I see no reason why Africans should conserve their wildlife for the sake of Western aesthetics, unless they perceive it to be in their interest to do so. If some gun-happy soul with a Hemingway fixation is idiot enough to pay enough money to support a village for a year in order that he can hunt an elephant, good. If the meat from an elephant can feed a village for a week, and the money from the sale of the ivory be put back into conservation, good. If we Westerners can drop the idealism and allow Africans to both conserve their wildlife and feed their bellies, only then is there a chance that our grandchildren will be able to see the Africa we want them to.

Serengeti National Park This world-famous national park, notable for its million-strong migratory herds of wildebeest and zebra, is the lynchpin of the popular northern safari circuit. It also harbours large numbers of predators; it is not unusual to see lion, leopard, cheetah, spotted hyena, bat-eared fox and a couple of jackal and mongoose species in the same day. The Serengeti is so vast that any sense of over-crowding in this popular park is restricted to the Seronera area in the southeast. The northern and western Serengeti have more of a wilderness feel, with surprisingly little tourist traffic around, except when the migration passes through them. Numerous lodges and campsites are dotted around the park.

Ngorongoro Conservation Area This dual-use conservation area – inhabited by the Maasai and their cattle as well as wildlife – protects a large part of Ngorongoro Highlands, including the magnificent Ngorongoro Crater, the largest intact caldera in the world. Ngorongoro Crater supports the world's densest population of lions and spotted hyena. It is the last place in Tanzania where black rhinoceros are reasonably easy to see, and is also notable for its magnificent old tuskers, a rare sight today elsewhere in Tanzania. The Ngorongoro Crater is heavily touristed, which does detract from many people's visit. A number of other remote natural landmarks in the Ngorongoro Highlands can be visited by vehicle or on foot. Numerous lodges and campsites are found on the crater rim.

Lake Manyara National Park The most low-key of the triad of reserves situated between Lake Victoria and the main Arusha-Dodoma Road, Lake Manyara has a fabulous situation at the base of the Rift Valley and is a worthy addition to any itinerary taking in the Serengeti and Ngorongoro. The small park's once-famous elephant population suffered badly at the hands of poachers in the 1980s, but it is well on the way to recovery today, and the elephants are perhaps the least jittery anywhere in Tanzania. Manyara is also renowned for its tree-climbing lions, and the large flocks of flamingo that sometimes congregate on the lake. A recent development at Manyara is a number of adventure activities – canoeing, mountain biking, walking and abseiling – run out of the Serena Hotel. There is one lodge in the park, a lovely campsite at the gate, and accommodation to suit all budgets within 5km of the gate.

Tarangire National Park Lying to the east of Lake Manyara, this excellent national park is included on many northern-circuit itineraries. It preserves a classic piece of dry African woodland studded with plentiful baobabs and transected by the perennial Tarangire River. Best known for the prodigious elephant herds that congregate along the river in the dry season, Tarangire also harbours a rich birdlife and such localised antelope species as fringe-eared oryx and gerenuk. Several lodges are to be found in and around the park.

Arusha National Park This underrated but eminently accessible park lies an hour's drive from Arusha town, the northern 'safari capital', and is best known perhaps for protecting Mount Meru, Africa's fifth-tallest peak. Other attractive features include the Momella Lakes, which host large concentrations of waterbirds including flamingoes, and Ngurdoto Crater, a smaller version of Ngorongoro whose jungle-clad slopes harbour a variety of monkeys and forest birds. It can be visited as a day trip from Arusha, but there is a remote lodge on the northern border and a budget campsite on the southern one.

Mount Kilimanjaro National Park Encompassing the two peaks and higher slopes of Africa's highest mountain, Kilimanjaro is of all the country's national parks the least oriented towards game viewing. Thousands of tourists climb it every year, however, to stand on the snow-capped pinnacle of Africa, and to experience the haunting and somewhat other-worldly Afro-montane moorland habitat of the upper slopes. Accommodation within the park is limited to simple mountain huts and campsites, but several lodges lie outside the boundary.

Amani Nature Reserve This reserve in the Eastern Usambara Mountains, inland of Tanga, protects some of the most important montane forest in Tanzania and a wealth of rare and endemic birds, mammals, butterflies and other creatures. Comfortable and inexpensive accommodation is available within the nature reserve, and a good range of walking trails will keep hikers and birdwatchers busy for days. It's easily accessible on public transport, too.

Saadani National Park This proposed national park (likely to be gazetted very soon) is the only savanna reserve in east Africa to be lapped by the shores of the Indian Ocean. As things stand, it is more accurately characterised as a beach retreat with some wildlife around than as a full-blown safari destination. Boat and walking safaris are a bonus, peace and quiet a given, and the beach really is lovely. One excellent lodge lies on the beach.

Jozani Forest Reserve The main stronghold for the rare Kirk's red colobus, endemic to Zanzibar Island, this small forested reserve is well worth the slight effort required to reach it from Zanzibar Stone Town or the beach resorts of the island's east coast.

Rubondo Island National Park This immensely peaceful national park protects a forested island in Lake Victoria, and is well suited for those who want to explore on foot or by boat. Indigenous fauna includes the sitatunga antelope and spotted-necked otter – both surprisingly easily observed – and introduced elephant, giraffe and chimps can also be seen. The island offers good birdwatching and game fishing. An upmarket lodge and national park bandas are found on the island.

WILDLIFE
Mammals
More than 80 large mammal species are resident in Tanzania. On an organised safari your guide will normally be able to identify all the mammals you see. For serious identification purposes (or a better understanding of an animal's lifestyle and habits) it is worth investing in a decent field guide or a book on animal behaviour. Such books are too generalised to give much detail on distribution in any one country, so that the section that follows is best seen as a Tanzania-specific supplement to a field guide. A number of field guides are available (see *Appendix 3*) and are best bought before you get to Tanzania. For details of individual mammals, see *Appendix 1, Wildlife*.

For most first-time safarigoers, a major goal is to tick off the so-called 'Big Five' – and even if doing so wasn't a priority when you first arrived in Tanzania, your conversations with lion-obsessive driver-guides and with other travellers are likely to make it one. Ironically, given its ubiquity in modern game-viewing circles, the term 'Big Five' originated with the hunting fraternity and it refers to those animals considered to be the most dangerous (and thus the best sport) back in the colonial era, namely lion, elephant, buffalo, leopard, and rhino. Of these, the first three are likely to be seen with ease on a safari of any significant duration, but leopard are

ANIMAL TAXONOMY

In this book, I've made widespread use of taxonomic terms such as genus, species and race. Some readers may not be familiar with these terms, so a brief explanation follows.

Taxonomy is the branch of biology concerned with classifying living organisms. It uses a hierarchical system to represent the relationships between different animals. At the top of the hierarchy are kingdoms, phyla, subphyla and classes. All vertebrates belong to the animal kingdom, phylum Chordata, subphylum Vertebrata. There are five vertebrate classes: Mammalia (mammals), Aves (birds), Reptilia (reptiles), Amphibia (amphibians) and Pisces (fish). Within any class, several orders might be divided in turn into families, and depending on the complexity of the order and family various suborders and subfamilies. All baboons, for instance, belong to the Primate order, suborder Catarrhini (monkeys and apes), family Cercopithecoidea (Old World monkeys) and subfamily Cercopithecidae (cheek-pouch monkeys, ie: guenons, baboons and mangabeys).

Taxonomists accord to every living organism a Latin binomial (two-part name) indicating its genus (plural genera) and species. Thus the savanna baboon *Papio cyenephalus* and hamadrayas baboon *Papio hamadrayas* are different species of the genus *Papio*. Some species are further divided into races or subspecies. For instance, taxonomists recognise four races of savanna baboon: yellow baboon, olive baboon, chacma baboon and Guinea baboon. A race is indicated by a trinomial (three-part name), for instance *Papio cyenephalus cyenephalus* for the yellow baboon and *Papio cyenephalus anubis* for the olive baboon. The identical specific and racial designation of *cyenephalus* for the yellow baboon make it the nominate race – a label that has no significance other than that it would most probably have been the first race of that species to be described by taxonomists.

Taxonomic constructs are designed to approximate the real genetic and evolutionary relationships between various living creatures, and on the whole they succeed. But equally the science exists to help *humans* understand a reality that is likely to be more complex and less absolute than any conceptual structure used to contain it. This is particularly the case with speciation – the evolution of two or more distinct species from a common ancestor – a gradual process that might occur over many thousands of generations and lack for any absolute landmarks.

Simplistically, the process of speciation begins when a single population splits into two mutually exclusive breeding units. This can happen as a result of geographic isolation (for instance mountain and lowland gorillas), habitat differences (forest and savanna elephants) or varied migratory patterns (the six races of yellow wagtail intermingle as non-breeding migrants to Africa during the northern winter, but they all have a discrete Palaearctic breeding ground).

more elusive (the most reliable site in northern Tanzania is the Serengeti's Seronera Valley) and the only part of northern Tanzania where black rhino remain reasonably visible is the Ngorongoro Crater.

Birds

Tanzania is a birdwatcher's dream, and it is impossible to do justice to its rich avifauna in the confines of a short introduction. Casual visitors will be stunned at the abundance of birdlife: the brilliantly coloured lilac-breasted rollers and superb starlings, the numerous birds of prey, the giant ostrich, the faintly comic hornbills,

Whatever the reason, the two breeding communities will share an identical gene pool when first they split, but as generations pass they will accumulate a number of small genetic differences and eventually marked racial characteristics. Given long enough, the two populations might even deviate to the point where they wouldn't or couldn't interbreed, even if the barrier that originally divided them was removed.

The taxonomic distinction between a full species and a subspecies or race of that species rests not on how similar the two taxa are in appearance or habit, but on the final point above. Should it be known that two distinct taxa freely interbreed and produce fertile hybrids where their ranges overlap, or it is believed that they would in the event that their ranges did overlap, then they are classified as races of the same species. If not, they are regarded as full species. The six races of yellow wagtail referred to above are all very different in appearance, far more so, for instance, than the several dozen warbler species of the genus Cisticola, but clearly they are able to interbreed, and they must thus be regarded as belonging to the same species. And while this may seem a strange distinction on the face of things, it does make sense when you recall that humans rely mostly on visual recognition, whereas many other creatures are more dependent on other senses. Those pesky cisticolas all look much the same to human observers, but each species has a highly distinctive call and in some cases a display flight that would preclude crossbreeding whether or not it is genetically possible.

The gradual nature of speciation creates grey areas that no arbitrary distinction can cover – at any given moment in time there might exist separate breeding populations of a certain species that have not yet evolved distinct racial characters, or distinct races that are on their way to becoming full species. Furthermore, where no conclusive evidence exists, some taxonomists tend to be habitual 'lumpers' and others eager 'splitters' – respectively inclined to designate any controversial taxa racial or full specific status. For this reason, various field guides often differ in their designation of controversial taxa.

Among African mammals, this is particularly the case with primates, where in some cases up to 20 described taxa are sometimes lumped together as one species and sometimes split into several specific clusters of similar races. The savanna baboon is a case in point. The four races are known to interbreed where their ranges overlap. But they are also all very distinctive in appearance, and several field guides now classify them as different species, so that the olive baboon, for instance, is designated *Papio anubis* as opposed to *Papio cyenephalus anubis*. Such ambiguities can be a source of genuine frustration, particularly for birdwatchers obsessed with ticking 'new' species, but they also serve as a valid reminder that the natural world is and will always be a more complex, mysterious and dynamic entity than any taxonomic construct designed to label it.

the magnificent crowned crane – the list could go on forever. For more dedicated birdwatchers, Tanzania, following an explosion in ornithological knowledge of the country over the past two decades, must now surely rank with the top handful of birding destinations in Africa.

The national checklist, which stood at below 1,000 species in 1980, had risen to 1,130 in 2005, according to a working checklist compiled by Neil and Liz Baker of the Tanzania Bird Atlas Project. This astonishing gain of 13% in 25 years is exaggerated by the Bakers' admitted bias towards splitting controversial species, but it also reflects an unparalleled accumulation of genuine new records. In 1987,

GALAGO DIVERSITY IN TANZANIA

The Prosimian galago family is the modern representative of the most ancient of Africa's extant primate lineages, more closely related to the lemurs of Madagascar than to any other mainland monkeys or apes. With their wide round eyes and agile bodies, they are also – as their alternative name of bushbaby suggests – uniquely endearing creatures, bound to warm the heart of even the least anthropomorphic of observers. And no natural history lover could fail to feel some excitement at the revolution in the taxonomy of the galago family that has taken place over recent years, largely due to research undertaken in the forests of Tanzania by the Nocturnal Primate Research Group of Oxford Brookes University.

In 1975, only six species of galago were recognised by specialists. By 1998, that number had risen to 18, of which ten are confirmed or likely to occur in Tanzania, including three probable endemic species and two with a core range within Tanzania. The reasons behind this explosion of knowledge probably lie in their nocturnal habits, which makes casual identification tricky, particularly in relatively inaccessible forested habitats. Previously biologists based their definition of galago species largely on superficial visual similarities. It has recently been recognised, however, that the distinctive vocal repertoires of different populations, as well as differences in the penile structure, provide a more accurate indicator of whether two populations would or indeed could interbreed given the opportunity – in other words, whether they should be regarded as discrete species.

By comparing the calls, penile structures and DNA of dwarf galago populations around Tanzania, the Nocturnal Primate Research Group has discovered four previously undescribed species since the early 1990s. These are the Mozambique galago Galagoides granti (coastal woodland south of the Rufiji River), Matundu galago Galagoides udzungwensis (Udzungwa Mountains), Mountain galago Galagoides orinus (Uluguru and Usambara mountains) and Rondo galago Galagoides rondoensis. The last of these species, initially thought to be confined to the Rondo Plateau inland of Lindi, has recently been discovered living in the Pugu Hills, right outside the country's largest city! It is not so much possible as certain that further galago species await discovery: in east Africa alone populations that require further study are found in southeast Tanzania, in the isolated forests of Mount Marsabit in northern Kenya, and in the mountains along the northern shores of Lake Nyasa-Malawi.

Simon Bearder of the Nocturnal Primate Research Group argues convincingly that the implications of these fresh discoveries in galago taxonomy might extend to other 'difficult' groups of closely related animals. He points out that our most important sense is vision, which makes it easiest for us to separate species that rely primarily on vision to recognise or attract partners. It becomes more difficult for us to separate animals that attract their mates primarily by sound and scent, more so still if they use senses we do not possess such as ultrasound or electric impulses. 'Such "cryptic" species', Bearder writes, 'are no less valid than any other, but we are easily misled into thinking of them as being much more similar than would be the case if we had their kind of sensitivity. The easiest way for us to distinguish between free-living species is to concentrate on those aspects of the communication system that the animals themselves use to attract partners.'

the Minziro Forest on the Uganda border yielded 17 additions to the national checklist, and at least 60 new species have been recorded since then. Even if one discounts the controversial splits on the working checklist, Tanzania has almost certainly overtaken Kenya (1,080 species) as the African country with the second most varied avifauna.

Virtually anywhere in Tanzania offers good birding, and species of special interest are noted under the relevant site throughout the main body of this guide. In many areas a reasonably competent novice to east African birds could hope to see between 50 and 100 species in a day. Any of the northern reserves are recommended: Arusha and Lake Manyara national parks are both good for forest and water birds; the Serengeti and Tarangire are good for raptors and acacia and grassland species.

Recent new discoveries now place Tanzania second to South Africa for its wealth of endemic birds – species that are unique to the country. At present, 34 endemic species are recognised, including a couple of controversial splits, three species discovered and described in the 1990s, and four that still await formal description. Six of the national endemics are readily observed on the northern safari circuit, but a greater number are restricted to the Eastern Arc Mountains, together with about 20 eastern forest and woodland species whose core range lies within Tanzania. The forests of the Eastern Arc Mountains must therefore rank as the country's most important bird habitat, with the Amani Nature Reserve the most accessible site for seeing some of the Eastern Arc specials.

Field guides are discussed in *Appendix 3*. A comprehensive and regularly updated checklist of Tanzania's birds, together with atlas maps for a growing number of species, is posted on the Tanzania Bird Atlas Project website: www.tanzaniabirdatlas.com. Experienced birders who wish to fill in species cards for the Atlas Project based on their observations are also welcome to contact them through the website.

Brief details of those confirmed and probable endemics likely to be seen on a northern safari follow:

Grey-breasted spurfowl *Francolinus rufopictus* Game bird with distinctive combination of a red mask under which is a white stripe. Confined to the Serengeti and immediate vicinity, where it is common in scattered woodland in the Seronera area.

Tanzanian red-billed hornbill *Tockus ruahae* Recently 'split' from other red-billed hornbills, from which it can be distinguished by the unique combination of a black (not red) face-mask and pale (not black) eyes, this central Tanzanian endemic is a resident of acacia woodland in the Babati-Kondoa and it may also range into Tarangire National Park.

Fischer's lovebird *Agapornis fischeri* Stunning and colourful parrot-like bird with bright red head and white eye, most often first noticed when a flock passes overhead squawking and screeching. Its natural range is centred on the Serengeti, where it is common. A popular caged bird in Europe, a feral population of this lovebird occurs in Naivasha (Kenya) where it regularly interbreeds with the next species.

Yellow-collared lovebird *Agapornis personatus* Another endemic lovebird – with black rather than red head – that has gone feral in Naivasha, Kenya. Naturally confined to the Maasai Steppes and other semi-arid parts of central Tanzania, the yellow-collared lovebird is common in Tarangire National Park.

Beesley's lark *Chersomanes beesleyi* Recently split from the widespread spike-heeled lark, this endangered species is confined to a single population of fewer than 1,000 individuals in short grasslands west of Kilimanjaro.

Ashy starling *Cosmopsarus unicolor* A drab but nevertheless distinctive member of this

WEAVERS

Placed by some authorities in the same family as the closely related sparrows, the weavers of the family Ploceidae are a quintessential part of Africa's natural landscape, common and highly visible in virtually every habitat from rainforest to desert. The name of the family derives from the intricate and elaborate nests – typically but not always a roughly oval ball of dried grass, reeds and twigs – that are built by the dextrous males of most species.

It can be fascinating to watch a male weaver at work. First, a nest site is chosen, usually at the end of a thin hanging branch or frond, which is immediately stripped of leaves to protect against snakes. The weaver then flies back and forth to the site, carrying the building material blade by blade in its heavy beak, first using a few thick strands to hang a skeletal nest from the end of a branch, then gradually completing the structure by interweaving numerous thinner blades of grass into the main frame. Once completed, the nest is subjected to the attention of his chosen partner, who will tear it apart if the result is less than satisfactory, and so the process starts all over again.

All but 12 of the 113 described weaver species are resident on the African mainland or associated islands, with at least 45 represented within Tanzania, all but six of which have a range extending into the north of the country. A full 20 of these Tanzanian species are placed in the genus Ploceus (true weavers), which is surely the most characteristic of all African bird genera. Most of the Ploceus weavers are slightly larger than a sparrow, and display a strong sexual dimorphism. Females are with few exceptions drab buff- or olive-brown birds, with some streaking on the back, and perhaps a hint of yellow on the belly.

Most male Ploceus weavers conform to the basic colour pattern of the 'masked weaver' – predominantly yellow, with streaky back and wings, and a distinct black facial mask, often bordered with orange. Seven Tanzanian weaver species fit this masked weaver prototype more or less absolutely, and a similar number approximate it rather less exactly, for instance by having a chestnut-brown mask, or a full black head, or a black back, or being more chestnut than yellow on the belly. Identification of the masked weavers can be tricky without experience – useful clues are the exact shape of the mask, the presence and extent of the fringing orange, and the colour of the eye and the back.

The golden weavers, of which only four species are present in Tanzania, are also brilliant yellow and/or light orange with some light streaking on the back, but they lack a mask or any other strong distinguishing features. Forest-associated Ploceus weavers, by contrast, tend to have quite different and very striking colour patterns, and although sexually dimorphic, the female is often as boldly marked as the male. The most aberrant among these is Vieillot's black weaver, the males of which are totally black except for their eyes, while the

normally colourful group of birds, the ashy starling is associated with semi-arid parts of central Tanzania. It's common in Tarangire National Park, and can be seen at the southern end of its range in Ruaha National Park.

Rufous-tailed weaver *Histurgops ruficauda* Large, sturdily built weaver of the central savanna, whose scaly feathering, pale eyes and habit of bouncing around boisterously in small flocks could lead to it being mistaken for a type of babbler, albeit one with an unusually large bill. It is a common and visible resident of the Serengeti, Ngorongoro and Tarangire national parks.

extralimital black-billed weaver reverses the prototype by being all black with a yellow face-mask.

Among the more conspicuous *Ploceus* species in northern Tanzania are the Baglafecht, spectacled, vitelline masked, lesser masked and black-headed weavers – for the most part gregarious breeders forming single- or mixed-species colonies of hundreds, sometimes thousands, of pairs, often in reed beds and waterside vegetation. Most weavers don't have a distinctive song, but they compensate with a rowdy jumble of harsh swizzles, rattles and nasal notes that can reach deafening proportions near large colonies. One more cohesive song you will often hear seasonally around weaver colonies is a cyclic 'dee-dee-dee-Diederik', often accelerating to a hysterical crescendo when several birds call at once. This is the call of the Diederik cuckoo, a handsome green-and-white cuckoo that lays its eggs in weaver nests.

Oddly, while most east African *Ploceus* weavers are common, even abundant, in suitable habitats, seven highly localised species are listed as range-restricted, and three are regarded to be of global conservation concern. These include the Taveta palm weaver, which is restricted to the plains immediately below Kilimanjaro and is most common in the West Kilimanjaro-Amboseli area and around Lake Jipe, and the Usambara and Kilombero weavers, both endemic to a limited number of sites in eastern Tanzania.

Most of the colonial weavers, perhaps relying on safety in numbers, build relatively plain nests with a roughly oval shape and an unadorned entrance hole. The nests of certain more solitary weavers, by contrast, are far more elaborate. Several weavers, for instance, protect their nests from egg-eating invaders by attaching tubular entrance tunnels to the base – in the case of the spectacled weaver, sometimes twice as long as the nest itself. The Grosbeak weaver (a peculiar larger-than-average, brown-and-white weaver of reed beds, distinguished by its outsized bill and placed in the monospecific genus *Amblyospiza*), constructs a large and distinctive domed nest, which is supported by a pair of reeds, and woven as precisely as the finest basketwork, with a neat raised entrance hole at the front.

By contrast, the scruffiest nests are built by the various species of sparrow- and buffalo-weaver, relatively drab but highly gregarious dry-country birds that occur throughout northern Tanzania. The most striking bird in the group is the white-headed buffalo-weaver, which despite its name is most easily identified by its unique bright red rump. The endemic rufous-tailed weaver, a close relative of the buffalo-weavers, is a common resident of Tarangire, Serengeti and the Ngorongoro Conservation Area.

Reptiles
Nile crocodile
The order *Crocodilia* dates back at least 150 million years, and fossil forms that lived contemporaneously with dinosaurs are remarkably unchanged from their modern counterparts, of which the Nile crocodile is the largest living reptile, regularly growing to lengths of up to 6m. Widespread throughout Africa, the Nile crocodile was once common in most large rivers and lakes, but it has been exterminated in many areas in the past century – hunted professionally for its

DANGEROUS ANIMALS

The dangers associated with Africa's wild animals have frequently been overstated since the days of the so-called Great White Hunters – who, after all, rather intensified the risk by shooting at animals that are most likely to turn nasty when wounded – and others trying to glamorise their chosen way of life. Contrary to the fanciful notions conjured up by images of rampaging elephants, man-eating lions and psychotic snakes, most wild animals fear us more than we fear them, and their normal response to human contact is to flee. That said, many travel guides have responded to the exaggerated ideas of the dangers associated with wild animals by being overly reassuring. The likelihood of a tourist being attacked by an animal is indeed very low, but it can happen, and there have been a number of fatalities caused by such incidents in recent years, particularly in southern Africa.

The need for caution is greatest near water, particularly around dusk and dawn, when hippos are out grazing. Hippos are responsible for more human fatalities than any other large mammal, not because they are aggressive but because they tend to panic when something comes between them and the safety of the water. If you happen to be that something, then you're unlikely to live to tell the tale. Never consciously walk between a hippo and water, and never walk along riverbanks or through reed beds, especially in overcast weather or at dusk or dawn, unless you are certain that no hippos are present. Watch out, too, for crocodiles. Only a very large crocodile is likely to attack a person, and then only in the water or right on the shore. Near towns and other settlements, you can be fairly sure that any such crocodile will have been consigned to its maker by its potential human prey, so the risk is greatest away from human habitation. It is also near water that you are most likely to unwittingly corner a normally placid terrestrial animal – the waterbuck. The population on Crescent Island in Kenya's Lake Naivasha has acquired a nasty reputation for attacking on close approach, and the riverine-forest-dwelling bushbuck has a reputation as the most dangerous African antelope when cornered.

There are areas where hikers might still stumble across an elephant or a buffalo, the most dangerous of Africa's terrestrial herbivores. Elephants almost invariably mock charge and indulge in some hair-raising trumpeting before they attack in earnest. Provided that you back off at the first sign of unease, they are most unlikely to take further notice of you. If you see them before they see you, give them a wide berth, bearing in mind they are most likely to attack if surprised at close proximity. If an animal charges you, the safest course of action is to head for the nearest tree and climb it. Black rhinos are prone to charging without apparent provocation, but they're too rare in Tanzania to be a cause for concern. Elephants are the only animals to pose a potential danger to a vehicle, and much the same advice applies – if an elephant evidently doesn't want you to pass, then back off and wait until it has crossed the road or moved further away before you try again. In general, it's a good idea to leave your

skin as well as by vengeful local villagers. Contrary to popular legend, Nile crocodiles generally feed mostly on fish, at least where densities are sufficient. They will also prey on drinking or swimming mammals where the opportunity presents itself, dragging their victim under water until it drowns, then storing it under a submerged log or tree until it has decomposed sufficiently for them to

engine running when you are close to an elephant, and you should avoid letting yourself be boxed in between an elephant and another vehicle.

There are campsites in Tanzania where vervet monkeys and baboons have become pests. Feeding these animals is highly irresponsible, since it encourages them to scavenge and may eventually lead to them being shot. Vervet monkeys are too small to progress much beyond being a nuisance, but baboons are very dangerous and have often killed children and maimed adults with their vicious teeth. Do not tease or underestimate them. If primates are hanging around a campsite, and you wander off leaving fruit in your tent, don't expect the tent to be standing when you return. Chimpanzees are also potentially dangerous, but unlikely to be encountered except on a guided forest walk, when there is little risk provided that you obey your guide's instructions at all times.

The dangers associated with large predators are often exaggerated. Most predators stay clear of humans and are only likely to kill accidentally or in self-defence. Lions are arguably the exception, but it is unusual for a lion to attack a human without cause. Should you encounter one on foot, the important thing is not to run, since this is likely to trigger the instinct to give chase. Of the other cats, cheetahs represent no threat and leopards generally attack only when they are cornered. Hyenas are often associated with human settlements, and are potentially very dangerous, but in practice they aren't aggressive towards people and are most likely to slink off into the shadows when disturbed. A slight but real danger when sleeping in the bush without a tent is that a passing hyena or lion might investigate a hairy object sticking out of a sleeping bag, and you might be decapitated through predatorial curiosity. In areas where large predators are still reasonably common, sleeping in a sealed tent practically guarantees your safety – but don't sleep with your head sticking out and don't at any point put meat in the tent.

All manner of venomous snakes occur in Tanzania, but they are unlikely to be encountered since they generally slither away when they sense the seismic vibrations made by a walking person. You should be most alert to snakes on rocky slopes and cliffs, particularly where you risk putting your hand on a ledge that you can't see. Rocky areas are the favoured habitat of the puff adder, which is not an especially venomous snake, but is potentially lethal and unusual in that it won't always move off in response to human foot treads. Wearing good boots when walking in the bush will protect against the 50% of snake bites that occur below the ankle, and long trousers will help deflect bites higher up on the leg, reducing the quantity of venom injected. Lethal snake bites are a rarity (in South Africa, which boasts almost as many venomous snakes as Tanzania, more people are killed by lightning than by snake bites) but some discussion of treatment is included in the section on *Health*, page 59.

When all is said and done, the most dangerous animal in Africa, exponentially a greater threat than everything mentioned above, is the *Anopheles* mosquito, which carries the malaria parasite. Humans – particularly when behind a steering wheel – run them a close second!

eat. A large crocodile is capable of killing a lion or wildebeest, or an adult human for that matter, and in certain areas such as the Mara or Grumeti rivers in the Serengeti, large mammals do form their main prey. Today, large crocodiles are mostly confined to protected areas within Tanzania.

Snakes

A wide variety of snakes are found in Tanzania, though – fortunately, most would agree – they are typically very shy and unlikely to be seen unless actively sought. One of the snakes most likely to be seen on safari is Africa's largest, the rock python, which has a gold-on-black mottled skin and regularly grows to lengths exceeding 5m. Non-venomous, pythons kill their prey by strangulation, wrapping their muscular bodies around it until it cannot breathe, then swallowing it whole and dozing off for a couple of months while it is digested. Pythons feed mainly on small antelopes, large rodents and similar. They are harmless to adult humans, but could conceivably kill a small child. A slumbering python might be encountered almost anywhere in northern Tanzania.

Of the venomous snakes, one of the most commonly encountered is the puff adder, a large, thick resident of savanna and rocky habitats. Although it feeds mainly on rodents, the puff adder will strike when threatened, and it is rightly considered the most dangerous of African snakes, not because it is especially venomous or aggressive, but because its notoriously sluggish disposition means it is more often disturbed than other snakes. The related Gabon viper is possibly the largest African viper, growing up to 2m long, very heavily built, and with a beautiful cryptic, geometric gold, black and brown skin pattern that blends perfectly into the rainforest litter it inhabits. Although highly venomous, it is more placid and less likely to be encountered than the puff adder.

Several cobra species, including the spitting cobra, are present in Tanzania, most with characteristic hoods that they raise when about to strike, though they are all very seldom seen. Another widespread family is the mambas, of which the black mamba – which will only attack when cornered, despite an unfounded reputation for unprovoked aggression – is the largest venomous snake in Africa, measuring up to 3.5m long. Theoretically, the most toxic of Africa's snakes is said to be the boomslang, a variably coloured and, as its name – literally tree-snake – suggests, largely arboreal snake that is reputed not to have accounted for one known human fatality, as it is back-fanged and very non-aggressive.

Most snakes are in fact non-venomous and not even potentially harmful to any other living creature much bigger than a rat. One of the non-venomous snakes in the region is the green tree snake (sometimes mistaken for a boomslang, though the latter is never as green and more often brown), which feeds mostly on amphibians. The mole snake is a common and widespread grey-brown savanna resident that grows up to 2m long, and feeds on moles and other rodents. The remarkable egg-eating snake lives exclusively on bird eggs, dislocating its jaws to swallow the egg whole, then eventually regurgitating the crushed shell in a neat little package. Many snakes will take eggs opportunistically, for which reason large-scale agitation among birds in a tree is often a good indication that a snake (or small bird of prey) is around.

Lizards

All African lizards are harmless to humans, with the arguable exception of the giant monitor lizards, which could in theory inflict a nasty bite if cornered. Two species of monitor occur in east Africa, the water and the savanna, the latter growing up to 2.2m long and occasionally seen in the vicinity of termite mounds, the former slightly smaller but far more regularly observed by tourists, particularly in the vicinity of Lake Victoria. Their size alone might make it possible to fleetingly mistake a monitor for a small crocodile, but their more colourful yellow-dappled skin precludes sustained confusion. Both species are predatorial, feeding on anything from bird eggs to smaller reptiles and mammals, but will also eat carrion opportunistically.

Visitors to Tanzania will soon become familiar with the common house gecko, an endearing bug-eyed, translucent white lizard, which as its name suggests reliably inhabits most houses as well as lodge rooms, scampering up walls and upside-down on the ceiling in pursuit of pesky insects attracted to the lights. Also very common in some lodge grounds are various agama species, distinguished from other common lizards by their relatively large size of around 20-25cm, basking habits, and almost plastic-looking scaling – depending on the species, a combination of blue, purple, orange or red, with the flattened head generally a different colour to the torso. Another common family are the skinks: small, long-tailed lizards, most of which are quite dark and have a few thin black stripes running from head to tail.

Chameleons

Common and widespread in Tanzania, but not easily seen unless they are actively searched for, chameleons are arguably the most intriguing of African reptiles. True chameleons of the family Chamaeleontidae are confined to the Old World, with the most important centre of speciation being the island of Madagascar, to which about half of the world's 120 recognised species are endemic. Aside from two species of chameleon apiece in Asia and Europe, the remainder are distributed across mainland Africa.

Chameleons are best known for their capacity to change colour, a trait that has often been exaggerated in popular literature, and which is generally influenced by mood more than the colour of the background. Some chameleons are more adept at changing colour than others, with the most variable being the common chameleon *Chamaeleo chamaeleon* of the Mediterranean region, with more than 100 colour and pattern variations recorded. Many African chameleons are typically green in colour but will gradually take on a browner hue when they descend from the foliage in more exposed terrain, for instance while crossing a road. Several change colour and pattern far more dramatically when they feel threatened or are confronted by a rival of the same species. Different chameleon species also vary greatly in size, with the largest being Oustalet's chameleon of Madagascar, known to reach a length of almost 80cm.

A remarkable physiological feature common to all true chameleons is their protuberant round eyes, which offer a potential 180° vision on both sides and are able to swivel around independently of each other. Only when one of them isolates a suitably juicy-looking insect will the two eyes focus in the same direction as the chameleon stalks slowly forward until it is close enough to use the other unique weapon in its armoury. This is its sticky-tipped tongue, which is typically about the same length as its body and remains coiled up within its mouth most of the time, to be unleashed in a sudden, blink-and-you'll-miss-it lunge to zap a selected item of prey. In addition to their unique eyes and tongues, many chameleons are adorned with an array of facial casques, flaps, horns and crests that enhance their already somewhat fearsome prehistoric appearance.

In Tanzania, you're most likely to come across a chameleon by chance when it is crossing a road, in which case it should be easy to take a closer look at it, since most chameleons move painfully slowly and deliberately. Chameleons are also often seen on night game drives, when their ghostly nocturnal colouring shows up clearly under a spotlight – as well as making it pretty clear why these strange creatures are regarded with both fear and awe in many local African cultures. More actively, you could ask your guide if they know where to find a chameleon – a few individuals will be resident in most lodge grounds.

The flap-necked chameleon *Chamaeleo delepis* is probably the most regularly observed species of savanna and woodland habitats in east Africa. Often observed crossing roads, the flap-necked chameleon is generally around 15cm long and bright green in colour with few distinctive markings, but individuals might be up to 30cm in length and will turn tan or brown under the right conditions. Another closely related and widespread savanna and woodland species is the similarly sized graceful chameleon *Chamaeleo gracilis*, which is generally yellow-green in colour and often has a white horizontal stripe along its flanks.

Characteristic of east African montane forests, three-horned chameleons form a closely allied species cluster of some taxonomic uncertainty. Typically darker than the savanna chameleons and around 20cm in length, the males of all taxa within this cluster are distinguished by a trio of long nasal horns that project forward from their face. The most widespread three-horned chameleon in Tanzania is *Chamaeleo johnstoni*, while the most localised is the Ngosi three-horned chameleon *Chamaeleo fuelleborni*, confined to the forested slopes of Ngosi Volcano in the Poroto Mountains. Perhaps the most alluring of east Africa's chameleons is the giant chameleon *Chamaeleo melleri*, a bulky dark-green creature with yellow stripes and a small solitary horn, mainly associated with the Eastern Arc forests, where it feeds on small reptiles (including snakes) as well as insects.

Tortoises and terrapins

These peculiar reptiles are unique in being protected by a prototypal suit of armour formed by their heavy exoskeleton. The most common of the terrestrial tortoises in the region is the leopard tortoise, which is named after its gold-and-black mottled shell, can weigh up to 30kg, and has been known to live for more than 50 years in captivity. It is often seen motoring along in the slow lane of game reserve roads in northern Tanzania. Four species of terrapin – essentially the freshwater equivalent of turtles – are resident in east Africa, all somewhat flatter in shape than the tortoises, and generally with a plainer brown shell. They might be seen sunning on rocks close to water or peering out from roadside puddles. The largest is the Nile soft-shelled terrapin, which has a wide, flat shell and in rare instances might reach a length of almost 1m.

Butterflies

Tanzania's wealth of invertebrate life, though largely overlooked by visitors, is perhaps most easily appreciated in the form of butterflies and moths of the order Lepidoptera. Almost 1,000 butterfly species have been recorded in Tanzania, as compared to roughly 650 in the whole of North America, and a mere 56 on the British Isles. Several forests in Tanzania harbour 300 or more butterfly species, and one might easily see a greater selection in the course of a day than one could in a lifetime of exploring the English countryside. Indeed, I've often sat at one roadside pool in an east African forest and watched 10–20 clearly different species converge there over the space of 20 minutes.

The Lepidoptera are placed in the class Insecta, which includes ants, beetles and locusts among others. All insects are distinguished from other invertebrates, such as arachnids (spiders) and crustaceans, by their combination of six legs, a pair of frontal antennae, and a body divided into a distinct head, thorax and abdomen. Insects are the only winged invertebrates, though some primitive orders have never evolved wings, and other more recently evolved orders have discarded them. Most flying insects have two pairs of wings, one of which, as in the case of flies, might have been modified beyond immediate recognition. The butterflies and moths of the order Lepidoptera have two sets of wings and are distinguished from all other insect orders by the tiny ridged wing scales that create their characteristic bright colours.

The most spectacular of all butterflies are the swallowtails of the family Papilionidae, of which roughly 100 species have been identified in Africa. Named for the streamers that trail from the base of their wings, swallowtails are typically large and colourful, and relatively easy to observe when they feed on mammal dung deposited on forest trails and roads. Sadly, this last generalisation doesn't apply to the African giant swallowtail *Papilio antimachus*, a powerful flier that tends to stick at canopy levels and seldom alights on the ground, but the first two certainly do. With a wingspan known to exceed 20cm, this black, orange and green gem is the largest butterfly on the continent, and possibly the world.

The Pieridae is a family of medium-sized butterflies, generally smaller than the swallowtails and with wider wings, of which almost 100 species are present in Tanzania, several as seasonal intra-African migrants. Most species are predominantly white in colour, with some yellow, orange, black or even red and blue markings on the wings. One widespread member of this family is the oddly named angled grass yellow *Eurema desjardini*, which has yellow wings marked by a broad black band, and is likely to be seen in any savanna or forest fringe habitat. The orange and lemon *Eronia leda* also has yellow wings, but with an orange upper tip, and it occurs in open grassland and savanna countrywide.

The most diverse of African butterfly families is the Lycaenidae, which accounts for almost one-third of the continental tally of around 1,500 recorded species. Known also as Gossamer Wings, this varied family consists mostly of small to medium-sized butterflies, with a wingspan of 1–5cm, dull underwings, and brilliant violet blue, copper or rufous-orange upper wings. The larvae of many Lycaenidae species have a symbiotic relationship with ants – they secrete a fluid that is milked by the ants and are thus permitted to shelter in their nests. A striking member of this family is *Hypolycaena hatita*, a small bluish butterfly with long tail streamers, often seen on forest paths throughout Tanzania.

Another well-represented family in Tanzania is the Nymphalidae, a diversely coloured group of small to large butterflies, generally associated with forest edges or interiors. The Nymphalidae are also known as brush-footed butterflies, because their forelegs have evolved into non-functional brush-like structures. One of the more distinctive species is the African blue tiger *Tirumala petiverana*, a large black butterfly with about two dozen blue-white wing spots, often observed in forest paths near puddles or feeding from animal droppings. Another large member of this family is the African queen *Danaus chrysippus*, which has a slow, deliberate flight pattern, orange or brown wings, and is as common in forest edge habitats as it is in cultivated fields or suburbia.

The family Charaxidae, regarded by some authorities to be a subfamily of the Nymphalidae, is represented by roughly 200 African species. Typically large, robust, strong fliers with one or two short tails on each wing, the butterflies in this family vary greatly in coloration, and several species appear to be scarce and localised since they inhabit forest canopies and are seldom observed. Rather less spectacular are the 200–300 grass-skipper species of the family Hersperiidae, most of which are small and rather drably coloured, though some are more attractively marked in black, white and/or yellow. The grass-skippers are regarded to form the evolutionary link between butterflies and the generally more nocturnal moths, represented in Tanzania by several families of which the most impressive are the boldly patterned giant silk-moths of the family Saturniidae.

Practical Information

WHEN TO VISIT

You can visit northern Tanzania at any time of year, as every season has different advantages. For those with the option, there is much to be said for trying to avoid peak tourist seasons, as the parks and other main attractions will be less crowded with tourists. Broadly speaking, tourism arrivals are highest during the Northern hemisphere winter, while the low season runs from the end of the Easter weekend until the end of September, though this is distorted by a surge of tourism over June and July, when the wildebeest migration is on in the Serengeti.

The rainy season between November and April is a good time to visit the Serengeti; it is when the countryside is greenest, and it offers the best birdwatching, with resident species supplemented by a number of Palaearctic and intra-African migrants. April and May are the official low season, with cheaper rates available at most lodges, yet these months still offer great game viewing, especially in the southern Serengeti. The rainy season is hotter than the period May to October, but in most parts of the country this will only be by a matter of a couple of degrees. The seasonal difference in temperature is most noticeable along the humid coast, which can be rather uncomfortable in the hotter months. The wettest months are March and April, when parts of the country may experience storms virtually on a daily basis.

The dry season, in particular March and September, offers the best trekking conditions on Mount Kilimanjaro and Meru. The dry season is the best time for hiking generally, and for travelling in parts of the country with poor roads. Temperatures at the coast tend to be more bearable during the dry season, which is also considerably safer than the wet season in terms of malaria and other mosquito-borne diseases.

Climate

The northern safari circuit as a whole is far cooler than many visitors expect. Lying at an elevation of roughly 2,300m, the Ngorongoro Crater rim in particular tends to be chilly at night and misty in the morning, and it also receives a sufficiently high annual rainfall to support a belt of montane rainforest. The crater floor and Serengeti Plains are warmer but, since they lie above the Rift Valley escarpment at elevations of well over 1,000m, they are far from being oppressively hot. Tarangire and Lake Manyara national parks lie at lower elevations and are considerably warmer, with Tarangire in particular sometimes becoming seriously hot in the afternoon. Both areas cool down after dusk, however, and most visitors to Manyara will sleep at one of the lodges on the cool, breezy escarpment. Alpine conditions and sub-zero temperatures are characteristic of the higher slopes of Mount Meru and especially Kilimanjaro after dark.

Tanzania is too near the Equator to experience the sort of dramatic contrast between summer and winter experienced in much of Europe or North America,

CLIMATE CHARTS
Arusha

	Jan	Feb	Mar	Apr	May	Jun	Jul	Aug	Sep	Oct	Nov	Dec
Max (°C)	29	29	28	25	22	21	20	22	25	27	28	28
Min (°C)	10	12	12	14	11	10	10	9	9	10	10	10
Rain (mm)	50	85	180	350	205	20	10	15	15	20	105	100

Moshi

	Jan	Feb	Mar	Apr	May	Jun	Jul	Aug	Sept	Oct	Nov	Dec
Max (°C)	36	35	34	30	29	29	28	30	31	32	34	34
Min (°C)	15	15	15	16	14	13	12	12	13	14	14	15
Rain (mm)	50	60	120	300	180	50	20	20	20	40	60	50

but the months between October and April are marginally hotter than May to September. The rainy season is generally split into the short rains or *mvuli*, over November and December, and the long rains or *masika* from late February to early May, though the exact timing of these seasons varies considerably from one year to the next. Game viewing in the Ngorongoro Crater and Lake Manyara is not strongly affected by season, and tends to be good at any time of year. The southern Serengeti, the part of the park visited by most tourists, hosts the greatest concentrations of animals between December and March, while the northern and western Serengeti are normally best over May to July and late October to November, when the migration passes through. That said, game viewing in the Serengeti is pretty good at any time of year, and the more remote northern and western areas have the big advantage of being practically bereft of tourists outside of the migration periods. Tarangire National Park has the most seasonal game viewing on the northern circuit, with animal concentrations generally peaking between July and the start of the rains in November or early December.

TOURIST INFORMATION
The Tanzania Tourist Board (TTB) has improved greatly over recent years, and its offices in London, New York, Stockholm, Milan and Frankfurt may be able to supply you with an information pack and leaflets about the country.

There are also Tanzania Tourist Board (TTB) offices in Dar es Salaam and in Arusha. Both are reasonably helpful and well informed when it comes to tourist-class hotels and major tourist attractions, but neither is generally able to offer much help when it comes to more remote destinations. The TTB office in Arusha is a good source of information about the various cultural tourism programmes that have been established in northern Tanzania over the past few years. Its list of registered and blacklisted safari companies is a useful resource for travellers working through cheap safari companies.

Head office PO Box 2485, Dar es Salaam; ☎ 051 111244; f 051 116420; e md@ttb.ud.or.tz
UK Tanzania Tourist Office, 80 Borough High St, London SE1 1LL; ☎ 020 7407 0566
US Tanzania Tourist Office, 210 E 42 St, New York, NY 10017; ☎ 212 986 7124

RED TAPE
Check well in advance that you have a valid **passport** and that it won't expire within six months of the date on which you intend to *leave* Tanzania. Should your

Mwanza

	Jan	Feb	Mar	Apr	May	Jun	Jul	Aug	Sep	Oct	Nov	Dec
Max (°C)	33	34	33	31	31	30	29	29	30	32	32	31
Min (°C)	15	16	16	16	14	13	12	13	15	16	15	15
Rain (mm)	105	110	165	160	100	20	15	25	30	45	105	120

Zanzibar Town

	Jan	Feb	Mar	April	May	June	July	Aug	Sept	Oct	Nov	Dec
Max (°C)	32	32	33	30	29	28	27	28	29	30	31	31
Min (°C)	25	25	26	26	25	24	23	23	23	25	25	26
Rain (mm)	50	65	140	310	290	45	25	25	35	60	180	135

passport be lost or stolen, it will generally be easier to get a replacement if you have a photocopy of the important pages.

If there is any possibility you'll want to drive or hire a vehicle while you're in the country, do organise an **international driving licence**, which you may be asked to produce together with your original licence. Any AA office in a country in which you're licensed to drive will do this for a nominal fee. You may sometimes be asked at the border or international airport for an **international health certificate** showing you've had a yellow fever shot.

For security reasons, it's advisable to detail all your important information on one sheet of paper, photocopy it, and distribute a few copies in your luggage, your money-belt, and among relatives or friends at home. The sort of things you want to include are your travellers' cheque numbers and refund information, travel insurance policy details and 24-hour emergency contact number, passport number, details of relatives or friends to be contacted in an emergency, bank and credit card details, camera and lens serial numbers, etc.

For up-to-the-minute advice on travel in Tanzania, also check www.fco.gov.uk/knowbeforeyougo.

Visas

Visas are required by most visitors to Tanzania, and will cost between US$30 and US$60, depending on your nationality. At the time of writing, nationals of some Commonwealth countries are exempt from visa requirements, as are nationals of the Scandinavian countries and the Republic of Ireland, but such rulings can change, and it would be advisable for all visitors to check the current situation in advance. Since early 1996, British nationals require a visa to enter Tanzania, at a cost of £39 (US$60). It used to be mandatory to buy your visa in advance at a Tanzanian embassy or high commission abroad. It is now possible, however, to obtain a visa on arrival at the airport or at any international border. This is a very straightforward procedure, and no photographs or other documentation is required but the visa must be paid for in hard currency. The visa is normally valid for three months after arriving in the country, and it evidently allows for multiple entries from neighbouring countries (ie: you can cross to any neighbouring country and back within the three-month period on your original visa).

Embassies abroad

There are Tanzanian embassies or high commissions in Angola, Belgium, Britain, Burundi, Canada, China, Congo, Egypt, Ethiopia, France, Germany, Guinea,

India, Japan, Kenya, Mozambique, Namibia, Netherlands, Nigeria, Russia, Rwanda, Sudan, Sweden, Uganda, USA, Zambia and Zimbabwe. Below are the addresses of those you are most likely to need:

Belgium 363 Av Louise, 1050 Brussels; ꜛ 640 6500
Canada 50 Range Rd, Ottawa, Ontario KIN 8JA; ꜛ 232 1500; f 232 5184
Germany Theaterplatz 26, 5300 Bonn; ꜛ 353219; f 358226
Netherlands Prinsessegracht 32, 2514 AP The Hague; ꜛ 070 365 3800–1; direct line: 070 364 6981; f 070 310 6686
Uganda 6 Kagera Rd, PO Box 5750, Kampala; ꜛ 257357
UK High Commission, 43 Hertford St, London W1Y 8DB; ꜛ 020 7499 8951; f 020 7491 9321
US 2139 R St NW, Washington, DC 20008; ꜛ 202 884 1080/939 6125; f 202 797 7408
Zimbabwe Ujamaa House, 23 Baines Av, Harare; ꜛ 721870; direct line: 251 511063; f 724172

Immigration and customs

Once stringently enforced, the official requirements for entering Tanzania are an onward ticket (a ticket out of Tanzania) and sufficient funds (common wisdom is that this is around US$1,000). These days, however, immigration officials seem a lot more relaxed than a few years back; in practice you are most unlikely to be asked about funds provided that you arrive with a return air ticket. Neither ruling is likely to be raised at an overland border. If you will be arriving with less than US$1,000 on your person, a credit card will normally be considered as good as cash or travellers' cheques. Otherwise, assuming that your papers are in order, getting through customs and immigration is usually a straightforward procedure.

GETTING TO TANZANIA
By air

The following airlines fly to Tanzania from Europe or the United Kingdom: Air Tanzania, British Airways, Gulf Air, KLM and Lufthansa. African airlines that fly to Tanzania from elsewhere in Africa include Air Tanzania, Air Zimbabwe, EgyptAir, Ethiopian Airlines, Kenya Airways, Royal Swazi, South African Airways and Zambia Airways.

There are two international airports on the Tanzanian mainland. Dar es Salaam Airport is the normal point of entry for international airlines, which is generally convenient for business travellers, but for tourists Dar es Salaam is usually no more than a point of entry, and many people transfer directly on to flights to elsewhere in the country. Kilimanjaro International Airport, which lies midway between Moshi and Arusha, is the more useful point of entry for tourists, and following recent privatisation this airport is likely to catch on with more international airlines. For the meantime, however, the only prominent airlines that run direct flights to Kilimanjaro from outside of Africa are the national carrier Air Tanzania, Ethiopian Airlines, Kenya Airways and KLM.

Budget travellers looking for flights to east Africa may well find it cheapest to use an airline that takes an indirect route. London is the best place to pick up a cheap ticket; many continental travellers buy their tickets there. It is generally cheaper to fly to Nairobi than to Dar es Salaam, and getting from Nairobi to Arusha by shuttle bus is cheap, simple and quick. Be warned, however, that a high proportion of travellers are robbed in Nairobi, so it isn't the greatest introduction to the continent.

When you fly out of Tanzania, a US$20 airport tax must be paid in hard currency. Many airlines now incorporate this tax into the ticket price, but if you need to pay it directly, do be aware that travellers' cheques are *not* accepted.

Flight specialists
UK
Bridge the World 47 Chalk Farm Rd, Camden Town, London NW1 8AJ; ☎ 020 7911 0900; f 020 7813 3350; e sales@bridgetheworld.com; www.bridgetheworld.com. Targets the independent traveller.

Flight Centre 13 The Broadway, Wimbledon SW19 1PS; ☎ 020 8296 8181; f 020 8296 0808. An independent flight provider with over 450 outlets worldwide. They also have offices in Australia, New Zealand, South Africa and Canada.

Quest Travel 4–10 Richmond Rd, Kingston upon Thames, Surrey KT2 5HL; ☎ 020 8481 4000; f 0870 442 3545. An independent agent that has been in operation for a decade offering competitive prices, specialising in long-haul flights.

STA Travel 6 Wrights Lane, London W8 6TA; ☎ 020 7361 6262l f 0207 937 9570; e enquiries@statravel.co.uk; www.statravel.co.uk. STA has 12 branches in London and 25 or so around the country and at different university sites. STA also has several branches and associate organisations around the world.

Trailfinders 194 Kensington High St, London W8 7RG; ☎ 020 7938 3939; f 020 7938 3305; www.trailfinders.com. Has several offices in the UK. With origins in the discount flight market, Trailfinders now provides a one-stop travel service including visa and passport service, travel clinic and foreign exchange.

Travel Bag 12 High St, Alton, Hants GU34 1BN; ☎ 01420 541441. The London office is at 52 Regent St, London W1R; ☎ 0207 287 5535; f 0207 287 4522; www.travelbag.co.uk. Provides tailor-made flight schedules and holidays for destinations throughout the world.

Travel Mood 214 Edgware Rd, London W2 1DH; ☎ 020 7258 0280; f 020 7258 0180; e sales@travelmood.com; www.travelmood.com. Provides flights and tailor-made holidays.

WEXAS 45–49 Brompton Rd, Knightsbridge, London SW3 1DE; ☎ 020 7589 3315; f 020 7589 8418; e mship@wexas.com; www.wexas.com. More of a club than a travel agent. Membership is around £40 a year, but for frequent fliers the benefits are many.

USA and Canada
Airtech ☎ 212 219 7000; e fly@airtech.com; www.airtech.com. Standby seat broker that also deals in consolidator fares, courier flights and a host of other travel-related services.

Around the World Travel e travel@netfare.net; www.netfare.net. Provides fares for destinations throughout the world.

Council on International Educational Exchange e info@ciee.org; www.ciee.org. Although the Council focuses on work exchange trips, it also has a large travel department.

Council Travel ☎ 1 800 226 8624; www.counciltravel.com. Sells cheap tickets at over 60 offices around the US.

Flight Centre Freephone: 1 888 9675 331; www.flightcentre.ca

STA Travel Freephone: 1 800 781 4040; e go@statravel.com; www.sta-travel.com. Has several branches around the country.

Travel CUTS Toll free on 1 866 246 9762; www.travelcuts.com. A Canadian student-based travel organisation with 60 offices throughout Canada.

Worldtek Travel e info@worldtek.com; www.worldtek.com. Operates a network of rapidly growing travel agencies.

Australia
AusTravel www.austravel.com. There are several offices in Europe and the US, as well as Australia.

Flight Centre Freephone: 133 133; www.flightcentre.com.au

STA Travel ☎ 1300 733 035; www.statravel.com.au

New Zealand
Flight Centre ➲ 0800 2435 44; www.flightcentre.co.nz. A good starting point for cheap air fares.

South Africa
Flight Centre Shop L3, Eastgate Centre, Bradford Rd, Bedfordview, Johannesburg 2008; ➲ 11 622 5634; f 11 622 5642.

Student Travel Centre The Arcade, 62 Mutual Gardens, Corner of Oxford Rd & Tyrwhitt Av, Rosebank, Johannesburg 2196; ➲ 11 447 5551; f 11 447 5775. Linked to the STA network.
Wild Frontiers ➲ 11 702 2035; f 11 468 1955; e wildfront@icon.co.za; www.wildfrontiers.com. Excellent Johannesburg-based operator with years of experience arranging general/ornithological safaris to east Africa, as well as reasonably priced air tickets.

Tour operators
The following overseas companies specialise in Tanzania. Safari specialists in Tanzania are found under their different regions in *Part Two, The Guide*.

UK
Aardvark Safaris ➲ 01980 849160; e mail@aardvarksafaris.com; www.aardvarksafaris.com. Tailored trips to southern and northern Tanzania, including walking safaris.
Abercrombie and Kent ➲ 0845 0700610; e info@abercrombiekent.co.uk; www.abercrombiekent.co.uk. Tailored safaris.
Africa-in-Focus (UK) ➲ 01803 770956; e africainfocus@yahoo.co.uk; www.africa-in-focus.com. Comfortable mobile camping safaris targeting wildlife enthusiasts, photographers and families.
Africa Select ➲ 01670 787646; e pg@africaselect.com; www.africaselect.com. Tailor-made itineraries, including tours to safari and mountain destinations.
Africa Travel Centre ➲ 0845 450 1520; e info@africatravel.co.uk; www.africatravel.co.uk
Alpha Travel ➲ 020 8423 0220; e alpha@alphauk.com; www.arpsafaris.com. Arranges tours with Ranger Safaris in Tanzania.
Baobab – Alternative Roots to Travel ➲ 0870 382 5003; e enquiries@baobabtravel.com; www.baobabtravel.com. An ethical tour operator specialising in eco-tourism in Africa.
Cazenove and Loyd Safaris ➲ 020 7384 2332; e safaris@caz-loyd.com; www.caz-loyd.com
Crusader Travel ➲ 020 8744 0474; e info@crusadertravel.com; www.crusadertravel.com
Expert Africa ➲ 020 8568 4499; e info@expertafrica.com; www.expertafrica.com
Explore Worldwide ➲ 01252 760000; e res@explore.co.uk; www.explore.co.uk
Footloose ➲ 01943 604030; e info@footlooseadventure.co.uk; www.footlooseadventure.co.uk. Tailor-made tours, safaris and treks throughout Tanzania, including Zanzibar.
Gane and Marshall ➲ 020 8445 6000; e holidays@ganeandmarshall.co.uk; www.ganeandmarshall.co.uk
Hartley's Safaris ➲ 01673 861600; e info@hartleys-safaris.co.uk; www.hartleys-safaris.co.uk. Safaris to east and southern Africa, as well as diving and island holidays in the region.
High Places ➲ 0114 275 7500; e treks@highplaces.co.uk; www.highplaces.co.uk
Imagine Africa ➲ 020 7228 5655; e info@imagineafrica.co.uk; www.imagineafrica.co.uk. Safaris on and off the beaten track.
Journeys by Design ➲ 01273 623 790; e will@journeysby design.co.uk; www.journeysbydesign.co.uk
Okavango Tours and Safaris ➲ 020 8343 3283; e info@okavango.com; www.okavango.com. Individually tailored holidays to east and southern Africa.
Phoenix Expeditions ➲ 01509 881818; e info@phoenixexpeditions.co.uk; www.phoenixexpeditions.co.uk

Rainbow Tours ℩ 020 7226 1004; e info@rainbowtours.co.uk; www.rainbowtours.co.uk
Safari Drive ℩ 01488 71140; e info@safaridrive.com; www.safaridrive.com. Self-drive and tailor-made safaris.
Sherpa Expeditions ℩ 020 8577 2717; e sales@sherpa-walking-holidays@co.uk; www.sherpa-walking-holidays@co.uk
Steppes Africa ℩ 01285 880 980; e africa@travelafrica.co.uk; www.travelafrica.co.uk
Tanzania Odyssey ℩ 020 7471 8780; e info@tanzaniaodyssey.com; www.tanzaniaodyssey.com. Tailor-made tours throughout Tanzania.
Tribes Travel ℩ 01728 685971; e bradtanz@tribes.co.uk; www.tribes.co.uk
Wildlife Worldwide ℩ 0845 130 6982; e sales@wildlifeworldwide.com; www.wildlifeworldwide.com
World Odyssey ℩ 01905 731373; e info@world-odyssey.com; www.world-odyssey.com. Tailor-made safaris.

US

Abercrombie and Kent ℩ 1 800 323 7308; www.abercrombiekent.com. A leader in luxury adventure travel.
Adventure Center ℩ 1 800 228 8747; www.adventurecenter.com. Provides safaris, treks, expeditions and active vacations worldwide, with a focus on value. Represents Explore Worldwide.
Baobab Safari Company ℩ 1 800 835 3692; www.baobabsafaris.com
Big Five Tours and Expeditions ℩ 800 244 3483; e info@bigfive.com; www.bigfive.com. Family-owned safari company.
Eco-resorts ℩ 1 866 326 7376; e info@eco-resorts.com; www.eco-resorts.com. A variety of safaris. Part of the booking fee is used to support local communities and the environment.
Ker and Downey USA ℩ 800 423 4236; e safari@kerdowney.com; www.kerdowney.com.
Micato Safaris ℩ 800 642 2861; e info@micato.com; www.micato.com. Family company, based in Nairobi but with an office in New York.
Naipenda Safaris ℩ 1 888 4044499; e jo@naipendasafaris.com; www.naipendasafaris.com
Next Adventure ℩ 1 800 562 7298; e safari@nextadventure.com; www.nextadventure.com. California-based company with strong ties to Tanzania.
Park East ℩ 800 223 6078; e ingo@parkeast.com; www.parkeast.com.
Thomson Safaris ℩ 800 235 0289; e info@thomsonsafaris.com; www.thomsonsafaris.com. Operates innovative safaris throughout the country.
Remote River Expeditions ℩ 1 888 66 FLOAT; e info@remoterivers.com; www.remoterivers.com
United Travel Group ℩ 1 800 223 6486; e info@unitedtravelgroup.com; www.unitedtravelgroup.com. One of the oldest safari companies specialising in Africa.

Europe

Wild Spirit Safari ℩ +33 (0)1 45 74 11 14; e infos@wild-spirit-safari.com; www.wild-spirit-safari.com.

PACKING

There are two simple rules to bear in mind when you decide what to take with you to Tanzania, particularly for those using public transport. Rule one is to bring with you *everything* that you could possibly need and that mightn't be readily available when you need it. Rule two is to carry as little as possible. Somewhat contradictory rules, you might think, and you'd be right – so the key is finding the right balance, something that probably depends on personal experience as much as anything. Worth stressing is that most genuine necessities are surprisingly easy to get hold of in the main centres in Tanzania, and that most of the ingenious gadgets you can buy in camping shops are unlikely to amount to much more than deadweight on the road. If it came to it, you could easily travel in Tanzania with little more than a change of clothes, a few basic toiletries and a medical kit.

Carrying your luggage

Make sure that your suitcase is tough and durable, and that it seals well, so that its contents will survive bumpy, dusty drives to the game reserves. A lock is a good idea, not only for flights, but also for when you leave your case in a hotel room – in our experience, any theft from upmarket hotels in Africa is likely to be casual, and a locked suitcase is unlikely to be tampered with. A daypack will be useful when on safari, and you should be able to pack your luggage in such a manner that any breakable goods can be carried separately in the body of the vehicle and on your lap when necessary – anything like a Walkman or camera will suffer heavily from vibrations on rutted roads. If you are likely to use public transport, then a backpack is the most practical way to carry your luggage.

Camping equipment

If you go on a budget safari or do an organised Kilimanjaro climb, camping equipment will be provided by the company you travel with. Taken together with the limited opportunities for camping outside of the safari circuit, this means that for most travellers a tent will be deadweight in Tanzania. An all-weather sleeping bag is required on Mount Meru or Kilimanjaro, and you may want to bring your own sleeping bag for any camping safari.

Clothes

Assuming that you have the space, you ought to carry at least one change of shirt and underwear for every day you will spend on safari. Organising laundry along the way is a pain in the neck, and the dusty conditions will practically enforce a daily change of clothes. It's a good idea to keep separate one or two shirts for evening use only.

When you select your clothes, remember that jeans are heavy to carry, hot to wear, and slow to dry. Far better to bring light cotton trousers and, if you intend spending a while in montane regions, tracksuit bottoms, which will provide extra cover on chilly nights. Skirts are best made of a light natural fabric such as cotton. T-shirts are lighter and less bulky than proper shirts, though the top pocket of a shirt (particularly if it buttons up) is a good place to carry spending money in markets and bus stations, since it's easier to keep an eye on than trouser pockets. One sweater or sweatshirt will be adequate in most parts of the country, though you will need serious Alpine gear for Kilimanjaro and to a lesser degree Mount Meru.

Socks and underwear *must* be made from natural fabrics. Bear in mind that re-using sweaty undergarments will encourage fungal infections such as athlete's foot, as well as prickly heat in the groin region. Socks and underpants are light and compact enough that it's worth bringing a week's supply. As for footwear, genuine hiking boots are worth considering only if you're a serious off-road hiker, since they are very heavy whether on your feet or in your pack. A good pair of walking shoes, preferably made of leather and with good ankle support, is a good compromise. It's also useful to carry sandals, thongs or other light shoes.

Another factor in deciding what clothes to bring is the sensibilities of Tanzania's large Muslim population, which finds it offensive for a woman to expose her knees or shoulders. It is difficult to make hard and fast rules about what to wear, but some generalisations may help. Shorts are fine at most beach resorts, in game reserves and possibly in Dar es Salaam, Zanzibar Town or Arusha where people are used to tourists. Elsewhere, I wouldn't wear shorts. For women, trousers are frowned upon in some quarters but my impression is that they are viewed as unconventional rather than offensive. The ideal thing to wear is a skirt that covers your knees. A shoulderless T-shirt that exposes your bra – or worse – is unlikely to go down well.

Men, too, should be conscious of what they wear. Shorts seem to be acceptable, but few Tanzanian men wear them and it is considered more respectable to wear trousers. Walking around in a public place without a shirt is totally unacceptable.

Other useful items

Your **toilet bag** should at the very minimum include soap (secured in a plastic bag or soap holder unless you enjoy a soapy toothbrush!), shampoo, toothbrush and toothpaste. This sort of stuff is easy to replace as you go along, so there's no need to bring family-sized packs. Men will probably want a **razor**. Women should carry at least enough **tampons** and/or **sanitary pads** to see them through at least one heavy period, since these items may not always be immediately available. Nobody should forget to bring a **towel**, or to keep handy a roll of **loo paper** which, although widely available at shops and kiosks, cannot always be relied upon to be present where it's most urgently needed.

Other essentials include a **torch**, a **penknife** and a compact **alarm clock** for those early morning starts. You should carry a small **medical kit**, the contents of which are discussed in *Chapter 4*, as are **mosquito nets**. If you wear **contact lenses**, bring all the fluids you need, since they are not available in Tanzania. You might also want to bring a pair of **glasses** to wear on long bus rides, and on safari – many lens wearers suffer badly in dusty conditions. In general, since many people find the intense sun and dry climate irritates their eyes, you might consider reverting to glasses.

Binoculars are essential if you want to get a good look at birds, or to watch distant mammals in game reserves. For most purposes, 7x21 compact binoculars will be fine, though some might prefer 7x35 traditional binoculars for their larger field of vision. Serious birdwatchers will find a 10x magnification more useful, and should definitely carry a good field guide.

MONEY AND BANKING

The unit of currency is the Tanzanian shilling (pronounced *shillingi*), divided into 100 cents. The Tanzanian shilling comes in Tsh10,000, 5,000, 1,000, 500 and 200 denomination bills. It is often very difficult to find change for larger denomination bills, so try always to have a fair spread of notes available. The bulky small denomination coins are worth considerably less than their weight in whatever leaden metal it is that's used to mint them! At the time of writing the exchange rate of roughly US$1 = Tsh1,100 is reasonably stable, but like most African currencies the Tanzanian shilling has steadily devalued against hard currencies in recent years, averaging 10% a year. It is reasonable to expect that a similar trend will persist during the lifespan of this edition. For rates of exchange, see page 2.

Most upmarket hotels and safari companies in Tanzania quote rates in US dollars. Some will also demand payment in this or another prominent hard currency, though some hotels and lodges actually prefer payment in local currency. National park fees and port and airport taxes must be paid in hard currency: this is treated as a foreign exchange transaction, which means that if you don't have the exact amount in US dollar bills or travellers' cheques, you will have to exchange a larger denomination and will receive the change in local currency at a poor exchange rate. In practice, most tourists won't need to pay park fees directly, since they will be included in the safari or lodge price.

The above exceptions noted, most things in Tanzania are best paid for in local currency, including restaurant bills, goods bought at a market or shop, mid-range and budget accommodation, public transport and most other casual purchases. Indeed, most service providers geared towards the local economy will have no facility for accepting any currency other than the Tanzanian shilling.

There are three ways of carrying money: hard currency cash, travellers' cheques or a credit card. My advice is to bring at least as much as you think you'll need in the combination of cash and travellers' cheques, but if possible to also carry a credit card to draw on in an emergency. I would strongly urge any but the most denominationally chauvinistic of backpackers to bring their cash and travellers' cheques in the form of US dollars, and to learn to think and budget in this currency.

From the point of view of security, it's advisable to bring the bulk of your money in the form of travellers' cheques, which can be refunded if they are lost or stolen. Best to use a widely recognised type of travellers' cheque such as American Express or Thomas Cook, and to keep your proof of purchase discrete from the cheques, as well as noting which cheques you have used, in order to facilitate a swift refund should you require one. Buy your travellers' cheques in a healthy mix of denominations, since you may sometimes need to change a small sum only, for instance when you're about to cross into another country. On the other hand, you don't want an impossibly thick wad of cheques. Currency regulations and other complications make it practically impossible to break down a large denomination travellers' cheque into smaller ones in most African countries, so don't bring travellers' cheques in denominations larger than US$100.

In addition to travellers' cheques, you should definitely bring a proportion of your money in hard currency cash, say around US$200 to US$300, since you are bound to hit situations where travellers' cheques won't be accepted, and cash gets a better exchange rate than travellers' cheques, especially large-denomination bills. This would not be much consolation were all your money to be stolen, so I'd strongly advise against bringing cash only, but would suggest that you save what cash you do bring for situations where it will buy you a real advantage. Note that US dollar bills printed before 2000, particularly larger denominations such as US$100 and US$50, may be refused by banks and foreign exchange (forex) bureaux.

Carry your hard currency and travellers' cheques as well as your passport and other important documentation in a money-belt that can be hidden beneath your clothing. Your money-belt should be made of cotton or another natural fabric, and everything inside the belt should be wrapped in plastic to protect it against sweat.

Foreign exchange
Foreign currencies can be changed into Tanzanian shillings at any bank or bureau de change (known locally as forex bureaux). All banks are open from 08.30 to 12.30 on weekdays and in many larger towns they stay open until 15.00. They open from 08.30 to 11.30 on Saturdays. Most private forex bureaux stay open until 16.00 or later. You can normally change money at any time of day at Dar es Salaam's international airport. Most private forex bureaux deal in cash only (sometimes US dollars only), for which reason you'll probably be forced to change your travellers' cheques at a bank. The rate for this is often slightly lower than the cash rate and a small commission is also charged.

Generally, private forex bureaux offer a better rate of exchange than banks, though this is not so much the case as it was a few years ago, and some forex bureaux actually give notably lower rates than the banks. It's worth shopping around before a major transaction. The private bureaux are almost always far quicker for cash transactions than the banks, which might be a more important consideration than a minor discrepancy in the rate they offer. Before you change a large amount of money, check the bank or forex bureau has enough high denomination banknotes, or you'll need a briefcase to carry your local currency. The legalisation of private forex bureaux has killed off the black market that previously thrived in Tanzania. Private individuals may give you a slightly better rate than the banks, but the official rate is so favourable it seems unfair to exploit this. In Dar es Salaam or Arusha you will be offered exceptionally good rates on the street, but if you are stupid or greedy enough to accept these, you can expect to be ripped off. There are plenty of forged US$100 bills floating around Tanzania, and you can assume that anyone who suggests a deal involving a US$100 bill is trying to unload a forgery.

Credit cards
Only a few years ago, credit cards were practically useless in Tanzania. Today, however, most major international credit cards (especially Visa but also MasterCard and American Express) are widely accepted by the better safari operators, in upmarket hotels and, to a lesser extent, in smarter restaurants and upmarket tourist-oriented shops in Dar es Salaam, Arusha, Moshi and Zanzibar Town. They are also accepted in many but certainly not all game lodges and upmarket beach resorts, and in a handful of city hotels elsewhere in the country. Increasingly, carrying a credit card is a viable alternative to cash or travellers' cheques, since it can be used to draw up to Tsh200,000 daily (about US$200) at 24-hour ATMs (autotellers) outside selected banks in Dar es Salaam, Arusha and Mwanza.

Having said that, ATM facilities are not available in other towns as yet. There are still many lodges and beach resorts that only accept payments in cash or travellers' cheques, and you are not permitted to pay park fees and the like with a card. Budget travellers can safely assume that hotels and other facilities within their reach cannot process credit-card payments. Although things are changing, and surprisingly rapidly, I would still tend to carry most of the money you're likely to need in cash or travellers' cheques, and carry a credit card primarily as a backup for emergencies. Tourists on pre-booked holidays will not of course need to carry a vast amount of cash, and can check with their tour operator whether the lodges they are booked into will accept credit-card payments for extras. No matter how long you are travelling, do make sure that you are set up in such a way that you won't need to have money transferred or drafted across to Tanzania.

ITINERARY PLANNING
Tanzania has a well-defined tourist circuit. It would be no exaggeration to say that as many as 90% of visitors divide their time in the country between the northern safari circuit and the island of Zanzibar. If this is what you plan on doing, then any tour operator or safari company in Arusha will be able to put together a package to meet your requirements. A 10–14-day trip is ideal for the Zanzibar/safari combination. You might want to read the section *Organising a safari* before making contact with a tour operator. With Zanzibar, the main decision you need to make in advance is whether you want to be based at a hotel in the old Stone Town, or out on one of the beaches, or a combination of the two. For a short trip to Tanzania, it is advisable to fly between Arusha (the springboard for safaris in northern Tanzania) and Zanzibar. If you are really tight for time, you'll get more out of your safari by flying between lodges. A fly-in safari will also be less tiring than the more normal drive-in safari.

After the northern safari circuit and Zanzibar, Tanzania's main tourist attraction is Kilimanjaro, which is normally climbed over five to seven days. A Kilimanjaro climb is one of those things that you either do or don't want to undertake: for a significant minority of travellers, climbing Kilimanjaro is the main reason for visiting Tanzania, but for the majority it is of little interest. If you want to do a Kili climb, it can be organised in advance through any number of tour operators and safari companies, and there is a lot to be said for arranging the climb through the same operator that organises your safari. As with safaris, it is generally possible to get cheaper prices on the spot. To combine a Kili climb with a few days on safari and a visit to Zanzibar, you would need an absolute minimum of two weeks in the country, and even that would be very tight, allowing for no more than two nights on Zanzibar.

Organising a safari

There are, in essence, four types of safari package on offer: budget camping safaris, standard lodge-based safaris, upmarket camping safaris and fly-in safaris. Budget camping safaris are generally designed to keep costs to a minimum, so they will make use of the cheapest camping options, often outside the national parks, and clients are normally expected to set up their own tents. Most backpackers and volunteers working in Tanzania go on budget camping safaris, though even with these there is a gap between the real shoestring operators, who'll skimp on

THE NORTHERN SAFARI CIRCUIT ON PUBLIC TRANSPORT

The combination of steep national park entrance and camping fees, and the expense of running 4x4 vehicles in northern Tanzania, places the northern safari circuit pretty much out of bounds for travellers on a very tight budget. It is possible, however, to see parts of the circuit relatively cheaply by using public transport and/or hiring vehicles locally.

The most affordable way of traversing the Serengeti National Park is on one of the buses and Land Rovers that run daily along the B142 between Mwanza and Arusha. This route passes through conservation areas for a total of about 250km, firstly the Serengeti's Western Corridor and Seronera Plains, then the plains of the western Ngorongoro Conservation Area and over the Ngorongoro Crater rim. You'd get a good feel of the scenery and landscapes from a bus window, and between November and July you should see plenty of game, including large predators, but of course the vehicle cannot be expected to stop for special sightings. The trip will entail paying US$80 in park entrance fees, over and above the bus fare. In theory, it is possible to make advance arrangements for one of these buses to drop you off at Seronera, and to pick you up at a later stage, but it's difficult to see any reason why anybody would want to do this.

A more satisfying option for travellers who specifically want to see the Serengeti, have time on their hands, and cannot afford a safari of several days' duration, is to approach the park from the western side. This cuts out the long drive and overnight stops coming from Arusha, allowing you to get within 1km of the entrance gate on public transport and to visit the park as a day or overnight trip rather than as part of a longer safari. The best place to set up something like this would be Serengeti Stopover, a private campsite situated right next to the entrance gate to the Serengeti's Western Corridor and alongside the main road between the Lake Victoria ports of Mwanza and

everything, and those operators who offer a sensible compromise between affordability and adequate service.

Most fly-in tourists go on a standard lodge-based safari, which will generally cost around double the price of a similar budget camping safari. For the extra outlay, you get a roof over your head at night, restaurant food and a far higher degree of luxury and comfort. If you decide to go on a lodge safari, the probability is that the operator will decide which lodges you stay at. If you have the choice, however, it's worth noting that the former government 'Wildlife Lodge' chain generally has the best natural settings, but the rooms are relatively basic. The Sopa Lodges are far more luxurious and slightly more expensive, but only the Ngorongoro Sopa Lodge has a setting to compare to its wildlife lodge equivalent. The lodges in the Serena chain are generally the best of the mainstream chain lodges, with modern facilities, good locations and attractive décor.

The above chain lodges are all of the institutionalised 'hotel in the bush' variety, but there are also a number of smaller lodges scattered around the circuit offering accommodation in standing tents and a more intimate bush atmosphere. Many of these, though absolutely superlative, are considerably more expensive than the larger chain lodges – well worth it if you can afford it, but not within everybody's means. Fortunately, there are also a number of tented camps offering a bush atmosphere at rates comparable to the chain lodges – Tarangire Safari Lodge,

Musoma. The Western Corridor itself generally offers good game viewing, particularly when the migration passes through between May and July, and the game-rich Seronera Plains and Campsite are only about two hours' drive from the western entrance gate. Serengeti Stopover charges US$130 per day for a vehicle that can carry up to five people into the park, which means that a day trip would work out at around US$100 per person for two people including park fees, and about US$70 per person for four people. For further details, see page 224.

On the eastern side of the northern safari circuit, affordable local buses run daily from Arusha to Karatu, stopping at the village of Mto wa Mbu near the entrance of Lake Manyara National Park. The Ngorongoro Safari Resort in Karatu rents out 4x4 vehicles seating up to four people, or five at a push, for US$110/120 for a half/full-day visit to Lake Manyara National Park or the Ngorongoro Crater exclusive of entrance fees. Should you want to make advance arrangements, the resort's contact details are included under the *Where to stay* listings for Karatu. Worth noting, too, that safari vehicles are found in abundance in Mto wa Mbu and Karatu, so there's every chance you could make cheaper private arrangements to hire a vehicle for a day. Were you to do something like this, you should be very clear about what the deal covers and how long you will spend in the game reserve – ambiguities at the negotiating stage often result in frayed tempers later in the day.

Hitching into most of the reserves covered in this chapter is pretty much out of the question. Relatively few private vehicles pass this way, and most safari companies forbid their drivers to pick up hitchhikers. In any case, people who have paid for a safari, or who are in a private vehicle loaded with supplies, are unlikely to want to carry freeloaders. Even if you were to catch a lift, you may well get stuck in the Serengeti or Ngorongoro and although you will see little game from a campsite or lodge, you will still have to pay park fees.

Kirurumu Tented Camp and Ndutu Lodge stand out – and these are highly recommended to those seeking a bush experience at a package price.

Camping isn't necessarily a cost-reducing device. Sleeping under canvas and eating under the stars will unquestionably make you feel more integrated into the bush environment than staying in a lodge, and this is where upmarket camping safaris come into play. At the top end of the range, you can organise safaris using private or so-called 'special' campsites, as well as tented lodges, and these will be as luxurious as any lodge safari, with top-quality food, a full team of staff, large tents, portable showers and the like. The cost of a safari like this will depend on your exact requirements, but it will probably cost at least as much as a similar lodge safari. What you are paying for is exclusivity and a real bush experience.

Regular scheduled flights connect all the main reserves in northern Tanzania, and an increasingly high proportion of safari-goers choose to fly around rather than bump along the long, dusty roads that separate the parks. Flying around will be particularly attractive to those who have bad backs or who tire easily, but it is more expensive and does dilute the sense of magic attached to driving through the vast spaces that characterise this region. Fly-in safaris allow you to see far more wildlife in a shorter space of time, because you don't lose hours on the road.

In all categories of safari, the price you are quoted should include the vehicle and driver/guide, fuel, accommodation or camping equipment and fees, meals and park entrance fees. You are expected to tip the driver and cook. Around US$5 per day per party seems to be par, but you should check this with the company. Drivers and cooks are poorly paid; if they have done a good job, be generous.

Group size

One factor that all visitors should consider is the size of the group doing the safari. It is almost invariably cheaper to go on safari as part of a group, but it can also ruin things if the people in that group are not compatible. A group safari will be highly frustrating to those who have a special interest such as birding or serious photography. And, frankly, I think it is unfair to impose this sort of interest on other passengers, who will have little interest in identifying every raptor you drive past, or in waiting for two hours at a lion kill to get the perfect shot. Another consideration is that non-stretch Land Rovers can feel rather cramped with four people in the back, especially when the luggage is in the vehicle, and jostling for head room out of the roof can be a nightmare when four cameras are vying for the best position.

A small proportion of companies – generally the large package tour operators – use minibuses as opposed to conventional 4x4s. In my opinion, minibuses have several disadvantages, notably that the larger group size (typically around eight people) creates more of a package tour atmosphere, and that it is difficult for a large group to take proper advantage of the pop-up roofs which are usually found on safari vehicles. In any event, bouncing around rutted roads in a Land Rover is an integral part of the safari experience – it just wouldn't be the same in a minibus.

Finally, there is the question of aesthetics. Without wishing to wax too lyrical, the thrill of being on safari doesn't derive merely from the animals you see. There is an altogether more elusive and arguably spiritual quality attached to simply being in a place as wild and vast and wonderful as the Serengeti, one that is most easily absorbed in silence, whether you travel on your own or with somebody with whom you feel totally relaxed. It isn't the same when one has to make small talk to new acquaintances, crack the rote jokes about who should be put out of the vehicle to make the lion move, decide democratically when to move on, listen to the driver's educational monotones, and observe social niceties that seem at odds with the surrounding wilderness.

Itinerary

Your itinerary will depend on how much time and money you have, and also the time of year. There are endless options, and most safari companies will put together the package you ask for. They know the ground well and can advise you on what is possible, but may tend to assume you will want to cover as many reserves as possible. This is not always the best approach.

A typical five- or six-day safari takes in Ngorongoro, Serengeti, Manyara and Tarangire. A typical three-day trip takes in all these reserves except for the Serengeti. In the dry season (July to October) there is little game in the Serengeti; most safari companies will suggest you spend more time in Tarangire.

The distances between these reserves are considerable and the roads are poor; you will have a more relaxed trip if you visit fewer reserves. On a five-day safari, I would drop either the Serengeti or Tarangire. To visit all four reserves, six days is just about adequate, seven or more days would be better.

Three days isn't long enough to get a good feel for Tarangire, Manyara and Ngorongoro; four or even five days would be better. The combination of Ngorongoro and Tarangire would make an unhurried three-day safari. If you are limited to two days, you could either visit Tarangire on its own or do a combined trip to Manyara and Ngorongoro. If your budget is really limited, Tarangire can be visited as a day trip from Arusha; it is less than two hours' drive each way.

At the other end of the time scale, there is enough to see and do in the area to warrant a safari of two weeks in duration, or even longer. You could easily spend a few days exploring the Serengeti alone. In a two-week package, you could also visit Lake Natron and Ol Doinyo Lengai, the Kondoa-Irangi rock art and/or the Lake Eyasi area.

Miscellaneous warnings

Malaria is present in most parts of the region, with the notable exception of the Ngorongoro Crater rim, and the normal precautions should be taken. Aside from malaria, there are no serious health risks attached to visiting this area. Tsetse flies are seasonally abundant in well-wooded areas such as Tarangire and the Western Corridor of the Serengeti. Sleeping sickness is not a cause for serious concern, but the flies are sufficiently aggravating that it is worth applying insect repellent to your arms and legs before game drives (though this doesn't always deter tsetse flies) and avoiding the dark clothing that tends to attract them.

Tarangire can be reached via a good tar road, and so too can Lake Manyara and the eastern entrance gate to Ngorongoro Conservation Area. The roads between the Ngorongoro Crater and Serengeti are very rough, for which reason safari-goers with serious back problems or a low tolerance for bumping around in the back of a vehicle might want to consider flying between the reserves. If one member of a safari party has a particular need to avoid being bumped around, they will be best off in the front passenger seat or the central row of seats – the seats above the rear axle tend to soak up the most punishment.

The combination of dust and glare may create problems for those with sensitive eyes. Sunglasses afford some protection against glare and dust, and if you anticipate problems of this sort, then don't forget to pack eye drops. Many people who wear contact lenses suffer in these dusty conditions, so it is a good idea to wear glasses on long drives, assuming that you have a pair. Dust and heat can damage sensitive camera equipment and film, so read over the precautions mentioned in the *Photographic tips* box on pages 56–7.

As is standard practice in many countries, safari drivers earn a commission when their clients buy something from one of the many curio stalls in Mto wa Mbu and elsewhere in the region. There's nothing inherently wrong with this arrangement,

PHOTOGRAPHIC TIPS
Ariadne Van Zandbergen
Equipment
Although with some thought and an eye for composition you can take reasonable photos with a 'point and shoot' camera, you need an SLR camera with one or more lenses if you are at all serious about photography. Wildlife photography will be very frustrating if you don't have at least a 300mm lens. Fixed fast lenses are ideal, but very costly and big. Zoom lenses are easier to change composition easily without changing lenses the whole time. For a small loss of quality, tele-converters are a cheap and compact way to increase magnification: a 300 lens with a 1.4x converter becomes 420mm, and with a 2x it becomes 600mm. Note that tele-converters reduce the speed of your lens by 1.4 and 2 stops respectively. For wildlife photography from a safari vehicle, a solid beanbag, which you can make yourself very cheaply, will be necessary to avoid blurred images and is more useful than a tripod. A clamp with a tripod head screwed on to it can be attached to the vehicle as well.

Film/digital
Digital photography is now the preference of most amateur and professional photographers. The resolution of digital cameras is improving the whole time. For ordinary prints a 6 megapixel camera is fine. For better results and the possibility to enlarge images for professional reproduction, higher resolution is available up to 16 megapixels.

It is important to have enough memory space when photographing on safari. As you tend to shoot a lot of film when photographing wildlife, you tend to fill up memory cards even more quickly because there is no limit and no cost involved. Depending on your level of dedication, I would count on taking at least a hundred, and more probably 200-plus, pictures per day on safari. The number of pictures you can fit on a card depends on the quality you choose. You should calculate how many pictures you can fit on a card and either take enough cards or take a storage drive on to which you can download the cards' content. You can obviously take a laptop which gives the advantage that you can see your pictures properly at the end of each day and edit and delete rejects. If you don't want the extra bulk and weight you can buy a storage device like 'flashtrax' which can read memory cards. These drives come in different capacities up to 80Gb.

Keep in mind that digital camera batteries, computers and other storage devices need charging. Make sure you have all the chargers, cables and converters with you. Most hotels/lodges have charging points, but it will be best

but you might find that your safari driver is very keen to stop at a few stalls along the way. If this isn't what you want, then the onus is on you to make this clear the first time it happens – there's no need to be rude or confrontational, just explain gently that this isn't why you're on safari. Even if you do want to buy curios, don't fall into the obvious trap of assuming that you'll get a better deal buying locally. Many of the curios you see in places like Mto wa Mbu probably found their way there from outside, and they will generally be cheaper in Arusha than they will be at roadside stalls dealing exclusively with tourists.

Travellers on a budget camping safari who want to keep down their extra costs should be aware that drinks, although available at all game lodges, are very

to enquire about this in advance. When camping you might have to rely on charging from the car battery.

If you are shooting print or slide film you should ideally use 50 or 100 ISO film which is fine grained and gives the best colour saturation, but which will need more light, so support in the form of a tripod or beanbag is important.

Dust and heat

Dust and heat are often a problem in Africa. Keep your equipment in a sealed bag, stow films in an airtight container (such as a small cooler bag) and avoid exposing equipment and film to the sun when possible. Digital cameras are prone to collecting dust particles on the sensor which results in spots on the image. The dirt mostly enters the camera when changing lenses, so you should be careful when doing this. To some extent photos can be 'cleaned' up afterwards in Photoshop, but this is time-consuming. You can have your camera sensor professionally cleaned, or you can do this yourself with special brushes and swabs made for this purpose, but note that touching the sensor might cause damage and should only be done with the greatest care.

Light

The light in Africa is much harsher than in Europe or North America, for which reason the most striking outdoor photographs are often taken during the hour or two of 'golden light' after dawn and before sunset. Shooting in low light may enforce the use of very low shutter speeds, in which case a beanbag or tripod will be required to avoid camera shake.

With careful handling, side lighting and back lighting can produce stunning effects, especially in soft light and at sunrise or sunset. Generally, however, it is best to shoot with the sun behind you. When photographing animals or people in the harsh midday sun, images taken in light but even shade are likely to look better than those taken in direct sunlight or patchy shade, since the latter conditions create too much contrast.

Protocol

Except in general street or market scenes, it is unacceptable to photograph people without permission. Expect some people to refuse or to ask for a donation. Don't try to sneak photographs as you might get yourself into trouble, especially where the Maasai are concerned. Even the most willing subject will often pose stiffly when a camera is pointed at them; relax them by making a joke, and take a few shots in quick succession to improve the odds of capturing a natural pose.

expensive. A beer at a lodge will typically cost around US$3-4, as opposed to less than US$1 in a shop or local bar, and prices of sodas are similarly inflated. It is definitely worth stocking up on mineral water in Arusha (at least one 1.5l bottle per person per day), since this will be a lot more expensive on the road. Once in the game reserves, some travellers might feel that it's worth spending the extra money to enjoy the occasional chilled beer or soda at a lodge. Those travellers who don't should ask their driver where to buy drinks to bring back to the campsite – there are bars aimed at drivers near to all the budget safaris' campsites, and the prices are only slightly higher than in Arusha.

Finally, and at risk of stating the obvious, it is both illegal and foolhardy to get out of your safari vehicle in the presence of any wild animal, and especially buffalo, elephant, hippo and lion.

PUBLIC HOLIDAYS

Tourists visiting Tanzania should take note of public holidays, since all banks, forex bureaux and government offices will be closed on these days. In addition to Good Friday, Easter Monday, Idd-ul-Fitr, Islamic New Year and the Prophet's Birthday, which fall on different dates every year, the following public holidays are taken in Tanzania:

1 January	New Year's Day
12 January	Zanzibar Revolution Day
5 February	CCM Day
26 April	Union Day (anniversary of union between Tanganyika and Zanzibar)
1 May	International Workers' Day
7 July	Saba Saba (Peasants') Day
8 August	Nane Nane (Farmers') Day
14 October	Nyerere Memorial Day
9 December	Independence Day
25 December	Christmas Day
26 December	Boxing Day

Health

with Dr Felicity Nicholson and Dr Jane Wilson-Howarth

PREPARATIONS

Preparations to ensure a healthy trip to Tanzania require checks on your immunisation status: it is wise to be up to date on tetanus (ten-yearly), polio (ten-yearly) and diphtheria (ten-yearly), and immunisations against yellow fever, meningococcus, rabies and hepatitis A may also be needed.

Hepatitis A vaccine (Havrix Monodose or Avaxim) comprises two injections given about a year apart. The course costs about £100, but protects for ten years. It is now felt that the vaccine can be used even close to the time of departure and has replaced the old-fashioned gamma globulin. The newer typhoid vaccines (eg: Typhim Vi) last for three years and are about 85% effective. They should be encouraged unless the traveller is leaving within a few days for a trip of a week or less when the vaccine would not be effective in time. Meningitis vaccine (containing strains ACW and Y) is also recommended, especially for trips of more than four weeks (see *Meningitis*). Immunisation against cholera is no longer required for Tanzania, but if you are planning to visit Zanzibar then it is wise to obtain a cholera exemption form from your GP or a travel clinic, as it is sometimes requested. Vaccinations for rabies are advised for travellers visiting more remote areas (see *Rabies*). Hepatitis B vaccination should be considered for longer trips (two months or more) or for those working with children or in situations where contact with blood is likely. Three injections are needed for the best protection and can be given over a three-week period if time is short. Longer schedules give more sustained protection and are therefore preferred if time allows. A BCG vaccination against tuberculosis (TB) may be advised for trips of two months or more.

Ideally you should visit your own doctor or a specialist travel clinic (see pages 62-4) to discuss your requirements about eight weeks before you plan to travel.

Protection from the sun

Give some thought to packing suncream. The incidence of skin cancer is rocketing as Caucasians are travelling more and spending more time exposing themselves to the sun. Keep out of the sun during the middle of the day and, if you must be exposed to the sun, build up gradually from 20 minutes per day. Be especially careful of sun reflected off water and wear a T-shirt and lots of waterproof SPF15 suncream when swimming; snorkelling often leads to scorched backs of the thighs so wear Bermuda shorts. Sun exposure ages the skin and makes people prematurely wrinkly; cover up with long, loose clothes and wear a hat when you can. The glare and the dust can be hard on the eyes, too, so bring UV-protecting sunglasses and, perhaps, a soothing eyebath.

Malaria prevention

There is no vaccine against malaria, but there are other ways to avoid it; since most of Africa is very high risk for malaria, travellers must plan their malaria protection

LONG-HAUL FLIGHTS
Dr Felicity Nicholson

There is growing evidence, albeit circumstantial, that long-haul air travel increases the risk of developing deep vein thrombosis (DVT). This condition is potentially life threatening, but it should be stressed that the danger to the average traveller is slight.

Certain risk factors specific to air travel have been identified. These include immobility, compression of the veins at the back of the knee by the edge of the seat, the decreased air pressure and slightly reduced oxygen in the cabin, and dehydration. Consuming alcohol may exacerbate the situation by increasing fluid loss and encouraging immobility.

In theory everyone is at risk, but those at highest risk are shown below:

- Passengers on journeys of longer than eight hours' duration
- People over 40
- People with heart disease
- People with cancer
- People with clotting disorders
- People who have had recent surgery, especially on the legs
- Women on the pill or other oestrogen therapy
- Women who are pregnant
- People who are very tall (over 6ft/1.8m) or short (under 5ft/1.5m)

A deep vein thrombosis is a clot of blood that forms in the leg veins. Symptoms include swelling and pain in the calf or thigh. The skin may feel hot to touch and

properly. Seek current advice on the best antimalarials to take. If mefloquine (Lariam) is suggested, start this two-and-a-half weeks (three doses) before departure to check that it suits you; stop it immediately if it seems to cause depression or anxiety, visual or hearing disturbances, severe headaches, fits or changes in heart rhythm. Side effects such as nightmares or dizziness are not medical reasons for stopping unless they are sufficiently debilitating or annoying. Anyone who is pregnant, who has suffered fits in the past, has been treated for depression or psychiatric problems, has diabetes controlled by oral therapy or who is epileptic (or who has suffered fits in the past) or has a close blood relative who is epileptic, should avoid mefloquine.

Malarone (proguanil and atovaquone) is a new drug that is almost as effective as mefloquine. It has the advantage of having few side effects and need only be continued for one week after returning. However, it is expensive and because of this tends to be reserved for shorter trips, even though it is licensed for use up to three months. Malarone may not be suitable for everybody (it has yet to receive a licence for children under 40kg in the UK) so advice should be taken from a doctor. Paediatric Malarone for children under 40kg is now available in the UK and is given based on weight. If you intend to use this for your child/children then please know their weight in kilograms before attending your GP or travel clinic.

The antibiotic doxycycline (100mg daily) is a viable alternative when either mefloquine or Malarone are not considered suitable for whatever reason. Like Malarone it can be started one or two days before arrival. Unlike mefloquine, it may also be used in travellers with epilepsy, although certain anti-epileptic medication may make it less effective. Users must be warned about the possibility of allergic skin reactions developing in sunlight which can occur in about 1–3% of people. The

becomes discoloured (light blue-red). A DVT is not dangerous in itself, but if a clot breaks down then it may travel to the lungs (pulmonary embolus). Symptoms of a pulmonary embolus (PE) include chest pain, shortness of breath and coughing up small amounts of blood.

Symptoms of a DVT rarely occur during the flight, and typically occur within three days of arrival, although symptoms of a DVT or PE have been reported up to two weeks later.

Anyone who suspects that they have these symptoms should see a doctor immediately as anticoagulation (blood thinning) treatment can be given.

Prevention of DVT

General measures to reduce the risk of thrombosis are shown below. This advice also applies to long train or bus journeys.

* While waiting to board the plane, try to walk around rather than sit.
* During the flight drink plenty of water (at least two small glasses every hour).
* Avoid excessive tea, coffee and alcohol.
* Perform leg-stretching exercises, such as pointing the toes up and down.
* Move around the cabin when practicable.

If you fit into the high-risk category (see opposite) ask your doctor if it is safe to travel. Additional protective measures such as graded compression stockings, aspirin or low molecular weight heparin can be given. No matter how tall you are, where possible request a seat with extra legroom.

drug should be stopped if this happens. Women using the oral contraceptive should use an additional method of protection for the first four weeks when using doxycycline. It is also unsuitable in pregnancy or for children under 12 years.

Chloroquine and proguanil are no longer considered to be very effective for Tanzania. However, they may still be recommended if no other regime is suitable.

All prophylactic agents should be taken with or after the evening meal, washed down with plenty of fluid and with the exception of Malarone (see above) continued for four weeks after leaving.

Travellers to remote parts would probably be wise to carry a course of treatment to cure malaria. Experts differ on the costs and benefits of self-treatment, but agree that it leads to over-treatment and to many people taking drugs they do not need; yet treatment may save your life. Discuss your trip with a specialist to determine your particular needs and risks, and be sure you understand when and how to take the cure. If you are somewhere remote in a malarial region you probably have to assume that any high fever (over 38°C) for more than a few hours is due to malaria (regardless of any other symptoms) and should seek treatment. Diagnosing malaria is not easy, which is why consulting a doctor is sensible: there are other dangerous causes of fever in Africa, which require different treatments. Presently Malarone or Co-artemether are the favoured regimes, but check for up-to-date advice on the current recommended treatment. And remember malaria may occur anything from seven days into the trip to up to one year after leaving Africa.

The risk of malaria above 1,800m above sea level is low. It is unwise to travel in malarial parts of Africa while pregnant or with children: the risk of malaria in many parts is considerable and these travellers are likely to succumb rapidly to the disease.

In addition to antimalarial medicines, it is important to avoid mosquito bites between dusk and dawn. Pack a DEET-based insect repellent, such as Repel (roll-ons or stick are the least messy preparations for travelling). You also need either a permethrin-impregnated bednet or a permethrin spray so that you can 'treat' bednets in hotels. Permethrin treatment makes even very tatty nets protective and prevents mosquitoes from biting through the impregnated net when you roll against it; it also deters other biters. Putting on long clothes at dusk means you can reduce the amount of repellent you need to put on your skin, but be aware that malaria mosquitoes hunt at ankle level and will bite through socks, so apply repellent under socks too. Travel clinics usually sell a good range of nets, treatment kits and repellents.

TRAVEL CLINICS AND HEALTH INFORMATION

A full list of current travel clinic websites worldwide is available from the International Society of Travel Medicine on www.istm.org. For other journey preparation information, consult www.tripprep.com. Information about various medications may be found on www.emedicine.com. For information on malaria prevention, see www.preventingmalaria.info.

UK

Berkeley Travel Clinic 32 Berkeley St, London W1J 8EL (near Green Park tube station); ℘ 020 7629 6233

Cambridge Travel Clinic 48a Mill Rd, Cambridge CB1 2AS; ℘ 01223 367362; e enquiries@travelcliniccambridge.co.uk; www.travelcliniccambridge.co.uk. Open Tue–Fri 12.00–19.00, Sat 10.00–16.00.

Edinburgh Travel Clinic Regional Infectious Diseases Unit, Ward 41 OPD, Western General Hospital, Crewe Rd South, Edinburgh EH4 2UX; ℘ 0131 537 2822; www.link.med.ed.ac.uk/ridu. Travel helpline (0906 589 0380) open weekdays 09.00–12.00. Provides inoculations and antimalarial prophylaxis, and advises on travel-related health risks.

Fleet Street Travel Clinic 29 Fleet St, London EC4Y 1AA; ℘ 020 7353 5678; www.fleetstreetclinic.com. Vaccinations, travel products and latest advice.

Hospital for Tropical Diseases Travel Clinic Mortimer Market Bldg, Capper St (off

---

MEDICAL FACILITIES IN TANZANIA

Private clinics, hospitals and pharmacies can be found in most large towns, and doctors generally speak fair to fluent English. Consultation fees and laboratory tests are remarkably inexpensive when compared with most Western countries, so if you do fall sick it would be absurd to let financial considerations dissuade you from seeking medical help. Commonly required medicines such as broad-spectrum antibiotics are widely available and cheap throughout the region, as are malaria cures and prophylactics. Quinine and doxycycline, or quinine and fansidar, are best bought in advance – in fact it's advisable to carry all malaria-related tablets on you, and only rely on their availability locally if you need to restock your supplies.

If you are on any medication prior to departure, or you have specific needs relating to a known medical condition (for instance if you are allergic to bee stings or you are prone to attacks of asthma), then you are strongly advised to bring any related drugs and devices with you.

Tottenham Ct Rd), London WC1E 6AU; ⟍ 020 7388 9600; www.thehtd.org. Offers consultations and advice, and is able to provide all necessary drugs and vaccines for travellers. Runs a healthline (⟍ 0906 133 7733) for country-specific information and health hazards. Also stocks nets, water purification equipment and personal protection measures.
Interhealth Worldwide Partnership House, 157 Waterloo Rd, London SE1 8US; ⟍ 020 7902 9000; www.interhealth.org.uk. Competitively priced, one-stop travel health service. All profits go to their affiliated company, InterHealth, which provides health care for overseas workers on Christian projects.
MASTA (Medical Advisory Service for Travellers Abroad) Moorfield Rd, Yeadon LS19 7BN; ⟍ 0870 606 2782; www.masta-travel-health.com. Provides travel health advice, anti-malarials and vaccinations. There are over 25 MASTA pre-travel clinics in Britain; call or check online for the nearest. Clinics also sell mosquito nets, medical kits, insect protection and travel hygiene products.
NHS travel website www.fitfortravel.scot.nhs.uk. Provides country-by-country advice on immunisation and malaria, plus details of recent developments, and a list of relevant health organisations.
Nomad Travel Store/Clinic 3–4 Wellington Terrace, Turnpike Lane, London N8 0PX; ⟍ 020 8889 7014; travel-health line (office hours only) ⟍ 0906 863 3414; e sales@ nomadtravel.co.uk; www.nomadtravel.co.uk. Also at 40 Bernard St, London WC1N 1LJ; ⟍ 020 7833 4114; 52 Grosvenor Gardens, London SW1W 0AG; ⟍ 020 7823 5823; and 43 Queens Rd, Bristol BS8 1QH; ⟍ 0117 922 6567. For health advice, equipment such as mosquito nets and other anti-bug devices, and an excellent range of adventure travel gear.
Trailfinders Travel Clinic 194 Kensington High St, London W8 7RG; ⟍ 020 7938 3999; www.trailfinders.com/clinic.htm
Travelpharm The Travelpharm website, www.travelpharm.com, offers up-to-date guidance on travel-related health and has a range of medications available through their online mini-pharmacy.

Irish Republic
Tropical Medical Bureau Grafton Street Medical Centre, Grafton Bldgs, 34 Grafton St, Dublin 2; ⟍ 1 671 9200; www.tmb.ie. A useful website specific to tropical destinations. Also check website for other bureaux locations throughout Ireland.

USA
Centers for Disease Control 1600 Clifton Rd, Atlanta, GA 30333; ⟍ 800 311 3435; travellers' health hotline 888 232 3299; www.cdc.gov/travel. The central source of travel information in the USA. The invaluable Health Information for International Travel, published annually, is available from the Division of Quarantine at this address.
Connaught Laboratories PO Box 187, Swiftwater, PA 18370; ⟍ 800 822 2463. They will send a free list of specialist tropical-medicine physicians in your state.
IAMAT (International Association for Medical Assistance to Travelers) 1623 Military Rd, 279, Niagara Falls, NY14304-1745; ⟍ 716 754 4883; e info@iamat.org; www.iamat.org. A non-profit organisation that provides lists of English-speaking doctors abroad.
International Medicine Center 920 Frostwood Drive, Suite 670, Houston, TX 77024; ⟍ 713 550 2000; www.traveldoc.com

Canada
IAMAT Suite 1, 1287 St Clair Av W, Toronto, Ontario M6E 1B8; ⟍ 416 652 0137; www.iamat.org
TMVC Suite 314, 1030 W Georgia St, Vancouver BC V6E 2Y3; ⟍ 1 888 288 8682; www.tmvc.com. Private clinic with several outlets in Canada.

Australia, New Zealand, Singapore

IAMAT PO Box 5049, Christchurch 5, New Zealand; www.iamat.org
TMVC ↘ 1300 65 88 44; www.tmvc.com.au. Clinics in Australia, New Zealand and
Singapore, including:
Auckland Canterbury Arcade, 170 Queen St, Auckland; ↘ 9 373 3531
Brisbane 6th floor, 247 Adelaide St, Brisbane, QLD 4000; ↘ 7 3221 9066
Melbourne 393 Little Bourke St, 2nd floor, Melbourne, VIC 3000; ↘ 3 9602 5788
Sydney Dymocks Bldg, 7th floor, 428 George St, Sydney, NSW 2000; ↘ 2 9221 7133

South Africa and Namibia

SAA-Netcare Travel Clinics P Bag X34, Benmore 2010; www.travelclinic.co.za. Clinics
throughout South Africa.
TMVC 113 D F Malan Drive, Roosevelt Park, Johannesburg; ↘ 011 888 7488;
www.tmvc.com.au. Consult website for details of other clinics in South Africa and
Namibia.

Switzerland

IAMAT 57 Chemin des Voirets, 1212 Grand Lancy, Geneva; www.iamat.org

Further reading

Wilson-Howarth, Dr Jane, and Ellis, Dr Matthew *Your Child Abroad: A Travel Health Guide*
Bradt Travel Guides, 2005
Wilson-Howarth, Dr Jane *Bugs, Bites & Bowels* Cadogan, 2006

TREATING TRAVELLERS' DIARRHOEA

Dr Jane Wilson-Howarth

It is dehydration which makes you feel awful during a bout of diarrhoea and
the most important part of treatment is drinking lots of clear fluids. Sachets
of oral rehydration salts give the perfect biochemical mix to replace all that
is pouring out of your bottom but other recipes taste nicer. Any dilute
mixture of sugar and salt in water will do you good: try Coke or orange
squash with a three-finger pinch of salt added to each glass (if you are salt-
depleted you won't taste the salt). Otherwise make a solution of a four-
finger scoop of sugar with a three-finger pinch of salt in a glass of water. Or
add eight level teaspoons of sugar (18g) and one level teaspoon of salt (3g)
to one litre (five cups) of safe water. A squeeze of lemon or orange juice
improves the taste and adds potassium, which is also lost in diarrhoea.
Drink two large glasses after every bowel action, and more if you are
thirsty. These solutions are still absorbed well if you are vomiting, but you
will need to take sips at a time. If you are not eating you need to drink
three litres a day plus whatever is pouring into the toilet. If you feel like
eating, take a bland, high carbohydrate diet. Heavy greasy foods will
probably give you cramps.

If the diarrhoea is bad, or you are passing blood or slime, or you have a
fever, you will probably need antibiotics in addition to fluid replacement. A
single dose of ciprofloxacin (500mg) repeated after 12 hours may be
appropriate. If the diarrhoea is greasy and bulky and is accompanied by
sulphurous (eggy) burps, the likely cause is giardia. This is best treated with
tinidazole (four x 500mg in one dose, repeated seven days later if
symptoms persist).

PERSONAL FIRST-AID KIT

The more I travel, the less I take. My minimal kit contains:

- A good drying antiseptic, eg: iodine or potassium permanganate (don't take antiseptic cream)
- A few small dressings (Band-Aids)
- Suncream
- Insect repellent; malaria tablets; impregnated bednet
- Aspirin or paracetamol
- Antifungal cream (eg: Canesten)
- Ciprofloxacin antibiotic, 500mg x 2 (or norfloxacin) for amoebic dysentery (see below for regime)
- Tinidazole (500mg x 8) for giardia
- Antibiotic eye drops, for sore, 'gritty', stuck-together eyes (conjunctivitis)
- A pair of fine-pointed tweezers (to remove hairy caterpillar hairs, thorns, splinters, coral, etc)
- Condoms or femidoms
- Maybe a malaria treatment kit and thermometer

MAJOR HAZARDS

People new to exotic travel often worry about tropical diseases, but it is accidents that are most likely to carry you off. Road accidents are very common in many parts of Tanzania, so be aware and do what you can to reduce risks: try to travel during daylight hours and refuse to be driven by a drunk. Listen to local advice about areas where violent crime is rife, too.

COMMON MEDICAL PROBLEMS
Travellers' diarrhoea

Travelling in Tanzania carries a fairly high risk of getting a dose of travellers' diarrhoea; perhaps half of all visitors will suffer and the newer you are to exotic travel, the more likely you will be to suffer. By taking precautions against travellers' diarrhoea you will also avoid typhoid, cholera, hepatitis, dysentery, worms, etc. Travellers' diarrhoea and the other faecal-oral diseases come from getting other peoples' faeces in your mouth. This most often happens from cooks not washing their hands after a trip to the toilet, but even if the restaurant cook does not understand basic hygiene you will be safe if your food has been properly cooked and arrives piping hot. The maxim to remind you what you can safely eat is:

PEEL IT, BOIL IT, COOK IT OR FORGET IT.

This means that fruit you have washed and peeled yourself, and hot foods, should be safe but raw foods, cold cooked foods, salads, fruit salads which have been prepared by others, ice cream and ice are all risky. And foods kept lukewarm in hotel buffets are often dangerous. If you are struck, see the box opposite for treatment.

Water sterilisation

It is much rarer to get sick from drinking contaminated water but it happens, so try to drink from safe sources.

Water should have been brought to the boil (even at altitude it only needs to be brought to the boil), or passed through a good bacteriological filter or purified with iodine; chlorine tablets (eg: Puritabs) are also adequate although theoretically less effective and they taste nastier. Mineral water has been found to be contaminated in Tanzania but should be safer than contaminated tap water.

Malaria

Whether or not you are taking malaria tablets, it is important to protect yourself from mosquito bites (see box, *Malaria in Tanzania*, below, and *Malaria prevention*, pages 59–62), so keep your repellent stick or roll-on to hand at all times. Be aware that no prophylactic is 100% protective but those on prophylactics who are unlucky enough to catch malaria are less likely to get rapidly into serious trouble. It is easy and inexpensive to arrange a malaria blood test.

Dengue fever

This mosquito-borne disease may mimic malaria but there is no prophylactic medication available to deal with it. The mosquitoes that carry this virus bite during the daytime, so it is worth applying repellent if you see any mosquitoes around. Symptoms include strong headaches, rashes, excruciating joint and muscle pains and high fever. Dengue fever lasts only for a week or so and is not usually fatal. Complete

MALARIA IN TANZANIA

Along with road accidents, malaria poses the single biggest serious threat to the health of travellers in most parts of tropical Africa, Tanzania included. The Anopheles mosquito which transmits the parasite is most abundant near marshes and still water, where it breeds, and the parasite is most prolific at low altitudes. Parts of Tanzania lying at an altitude of 2,000m or higher (a category that includes the Ngorongoro Crater rim, Mount Kilimanjaro and Meru, and parts of the Eastern Arc Mountains) are regarded to be free of malaria. In mid-altitude locations, malaria is largely but not entirely seasonal, with the highest risk of transmission occurring during the rainy season. Moist and low-lying areas such as the Indian Ocean coast and the hinterland of lakes Tanganyika, Victoria and Nyasa are high risk throughout the year, but the danger is greatest during the rainy season. This localised breakdown might influence what foreigners working in Tanzania do about malaria prevention, but all travellers to Tanzania must assume that they will be exposed to malaria and should take precautions throughout their trip (see page 59 for advice on prophylactic drugs and avoiding mosquito bites).

Even those who take their malaria tablets meticulously and do everything possible to avoid mosquito bites may contract a strain of malaria that is resistant to prophylactic drugs. Untreated malaria is likely to be fatal, but even strains resistant to prophylaxis respond well to prompt treatment. Because of this, your immediate priority upon displaying possible malaria symptoms – which might include any combination of a headache, flu-like aches and pains, a rapid rise in temperature, a general sense of disorientation, and possibly even nausea and diarrhoea – is to establish whether you have malaria.

The blood test for malaria takes ten minutes to produce a result and costs about US$1 in Tanzania. A positive result means that you have malaria. A negative result suggests that you don't have malaria, but bear in mind that the parasite doesn't always show up on a test, particularly when the level of infection is mild or is 'cloaked' by partially effective prophylactics. For this reason, even if you test negative, it would be wise to stay within reach of a laboratory until the symptoms clear up, and to test again after a day or two if they don't. It's worth noting that if you have a fever and the malaria test is negative, you may have typhoid, which should also receive immediate treatment. Where typhoid testing is unavailable, a routine blood test can give a strong indication of this disease.

It is preferable not to attempt self-diagnosis or to start treatment for malaria

rest and paracetamol are the usual treatment; plenty of fluids also help. Some patients are given an intravenous drip to prevent dehydration. It is especially important to protect yourself if you have had dengue fever before, since a second infection with a different strain can result in the potentially fatal dengue haemorrhagic fever.

Insect bites

It is crucial to avoid mosquito bites between dusk and dawn; as the sun is going down, don long clothes and apply repellent on any exposed flesh. This will protect you from malaria, elephantiasis and a range of nasty insect-borne viruses. Otherwise retire to an air-conditioned room or burn mosquito coils (which are widely available and cheap in Tanzania) or sleep under a fan. Coils and fans reduce rather than eliminate bites. During the day it is wise to wear long, loose (preferably 100% cotton) clothes if you are pushing through scrubby country; this will keep ticks off and also tsetse and day-biting Aedes mosquitoes which may spread dengue

before you have tested. There are, however, many places in Tanzania where you will be unable to test for malaria, for instance in the game reserves and in most of the popular hiking areas. With malaria, it is normal enough to go from feeling healthy to having a high fever in the space of a few hours (and it is possible to die from falciparum malaria within 24 hours of the first symptoms). In such circumstances, assume that you have malaria and act accordingly – whatever risks are attached to taking an unnecessary cure are outweighed by the dangers of untreated malaria.

It is imperative to treat malaria promptly. The sooner you take a cure, the less likely you are to become critically ill, and the more ill you become the greater the chance you'll have difficulty holding down the tablets. There is some division about the best treatment for malaria. Currently Malarone or Co-artemethor are considered the best standby treatments, but other regimes such as a quinine/doxycycline course are usually effective. Alternatively quinine and fansidar can be used if doxycycline is unavailable. And if there is no quinine either then fansidar alone can be used. The latter is widely available in Tanzania. One cure that you should avoid is Halfan, which is dangerous, particularly if you are using Lariam as a prophylactic.

In severe cases of malaria, the victim will be unable to hold down medication, at which point they are likely to die unless they are hospitalised immediately and put on a drip. If you or a travelling companion start vomiting after taking your malaria medication, get to a hospital or clinic quickly, ideally a private one. Whatever concerns you might have about African hospitals, they are used to dealing with malaria, and the alternative to hospitalisation is far worse.

Malaria typically takes around two weeks to incubate (minimum time seven days), but it can take much longer, so you should always complete the prophylaxis as recommended after returning home. If you display possible malaria symptoms up to a year later, then get to a doctor immediately and ensure that they are aware you have been exposed to malaria.

Every so often I run into travellers who prefer to acquire resistance to malaria rather than take preventative tablets, or who witter on about homoeopathic cures for this killer disease. That's their prerogative, but they have no place expounding their ill-informed views to others. Travellers to Africa cannot acquire any effective resistance to malaria, and those who don't make use of prophylactic drugs risk their life in a manner that is both foolish and unnecessary.

QUICK TICK REMOVAL

African ticks are not the prolific disease transmitters they are in the Americas, but they may spread Lyme disease, tick-bite fever and a few rarities. Tick-bite fever is a non-serious, flu-like illness, but still worth avoiding. If you get the tick off whole and promptly the chances of disease transmission are reduced to a minimum. Manoeuvre your finger and thumb so that you can pinch the tick's mouthparts, as close to your skin as possible, and slowly and steadily pull away at right angles to your skin. This often hurts. Jerking or twisting will increase the chances of damaging the tick, which in turn increases the chances of disease transmission, as well as leaving the mouthparts behind. Once the tick is off, dowse the little wound with alcohol (local spirit, whisky or similar are excellent) or iodine. An area of spreading redness around the bite site, or a rash or fever coming on a few days or more after the bite, should stimulate a trip to a doctor.

and yellow fever. Tsetse flies hurt when they bite and are attracted to the colour blue; locals will advise on where they are a problem and where they transmit sleeping sickness.

Minute pestilential biting blackflies spread river blindness in some parts of Africa between 190°N and 170°S; the disease is caught close to fast-flowing rivers since flies breed there and the larvae live in rapids. The flies bite during the day but long trousers tucked into socks will help keep them off. Citronella-based natural repellents do not work against them.

Mosquitoes and many other insects are attracted to light. If you are camping, never put a lamp near the opening of your tent, or you will have a swarm of biters waiting to join you when you retire. In hotel rooms, be aware that the longer your light is on, the greater the number of insects will be sharing your accommodation.

Tumbu flies or putsi are a problem where the climate is hot and humid. The adult fly lays her eggs on the soil or on drying laundry and when the eggs come in contact with human flesh (when you put on clothes or lie on a bed) they hatch and bury themselves under the skin. Here they form a crop of 'boils' which each hatches a grub after about eight days, when the inflammation will settle down. In putsi areas either dry your clothes and sheets within a screened house, or dry them in direct sunshine until they are crisp, or iron them.

Jiggers or sandfleas are another flesh-feaster. They latch on if you walk barefoot in contaminated places, and set up home under the skin of the foot, usually at the side of a toenail where they cause a painful, boil-like swelling. They need picking out by a local expert; if the distended flea bursts during eviction the wound should be dowsed in spirit, alcohol or kerosene, otherwise more jiggers will infest you.

Bilharzia or schistosomiasis
with thanks to Dr Vaughan Southgate of the Natural History Museum, London
Bilharzia or schistosomiasis is a disease that commonly afflicts the rural poor of the tropics who repeatedly acquire more and more of these nasty little worm-lodgers. Infected travellers and expatriates generally suffer fewer problems because symptoms will encourage them to seek prompt treatment and they are also exposed to fewer parasites. However, it is still an unpleasant problem that is worth avoiding.

The parasites digest their way through your skin when you wade, bathe or even shower in infested fresh water. Unfortunately, many African lakes, rivers and irrigation canals carry a risk of bilharzia.

The most risky shores will be close to places where infected people use water, wash clothes, etc. Winds disperse the cercariae, though, so they can be blown some distance, perhaps up to 200m from where they entered the water. Scuba-diving off a boat into deep offshore water, then, should be a low-risk activity, but showering in lake water or paddling along a reedy lakeshore near a village is risky.

Although absence of early symptoms does not necessarily mean there is no infection, infected people usually notice symptoms two or more weeks after parasite penetration. Travellers and expatriates will probably experience a fever and often a wheezy cough; local residents do not usually have symptoms. There is now a very good blood test which, if done six weeks or more after likely exposure, will determine whether you need treatment. Since bilharzia can be a nasty illness, avoidance is better than waiting to be cured and it is wise to avoid bathing in high-risk areas.

Avoiding bilharzia

- If you are bathing, swimming, paddling or wading in fresh water which you think may carry a bilharzia risk, try to get out of the water within ten minutes.
- Dry off thoroughly with a towel; rub vigorously.
- Avoid bathing or paddling on shores within 200m of villages or places where people use the water a great deal, especially reedy shores or where there is lots of water weed.
- If your bathing water comes from a risky source, try to ensure that the water is taken from the lake in the early morning and stored snail-free, otherwise it should be filtered or Dettol or Cresol added.
- Bathing early in the morning is safer than bathing in the last half of the day.
- Covering yourself with DEET insect repellent before swimming will protect you.
- If you think that you have been exposed to bilharzia parasites, arrange a screening blood test (your GP can do this) MORE than six weeks after your last possible contact with suspect water.

MARINE DANGERS

Most established tourist beaches in Tanzania can be assumed to be safe for swimming. Elsewhere along the coast, it would be wise to ask local advice before plunging in the water, and to err on the side of caution if no sensible advice is forthcoming, since there is always a possibility of being swept away by strong currents or undertows that cannot be detected until you are actually in the water.

Snorkellers and divers should wear something on their feet to avoid treading on coral reefs, and should never touch the reefs with their bare hands – coral itself can give nasty cuts, and there is a danger of touching a venomous creature camouflaged against the reef. On beaches, never walk barefoot on exposed coral. Even on sandy beaches, people who walk barefoot risk getting coral or urchin spines in their soles or venomous fish spines in their feet.

If you do tread on a venomous fish, soak the foot in hot (but not scalding) water until some time after the pain subsides; this may be for 20–30 minutes in all. Take the foot out of the water to top up; otherwise you may scald it. If the pain returns, re-immerse the foot. Once the venom has been heat-inactivated, get a doctor to check and remove any bits of fish spine in the wound.

Skin infections

Any mosquito bite or small nick in the skin gives an opportunity for bacteria to foil the body's usually excellent defences; it will surprise many travellers how quickly skin infections start in warm humid climates and it is essential to clean and cover even the slightest wound. Creams are not as effective as a good drying antiseptic such as dilute iodine, potassium permanganate (a few crystals in half a cup of water) or crystal (or gentian) violet. One of these should be available in most towns. If the wound starts to throb, or becomes red and the redness starts to spread, or the wound oozes, and especially if you develop a fever, antibiotics will probably be needed: flucloxacillin (250mg four times a day) or cloxacillin (500mg four times a day). For those allergic to penicillin, erythromycin (500mg twice a day) for five days should help. See a doctor if the symptoms do not start to improve in 48 hours.

Fungal infections also get a hold easily in hot moist climates so wear 100% cotton socks and underwear and shower frequently. An itchy rash in the groin or flaking between the toes is likely to be a fungal infection. This needs treatment with an antifungal cream such as Canesten (clotrimazole); if this is not available try Whitfield's ointment (compound benzoic acid ointment) or crystal violet (although this will turn you purple!).

Eye problems

Bacterial conjunctivitis (pink eye) is a common infection in Africa; people who wear contact lenses are most open to this irritating problem. The eyes feel sore and gritty and they will often be stuck closed in the mornings. They will need treatment with antibiotic drops or ointment. Lesser eye irritation should settle with bathing in salt water and keeping the eyes shaded. If an insect flies into your eye, extract it with great care, ensuring you do not crush or damage it otherwise you may get a nastily inflamed eye from toxins secreted by the creature.

Prickly heat

A fine pimply rash on the trunk is likely to be heat rash; cool showers, dabbing dry, and talc will help. Treat the problem by slowing down to a relaxed schedule, wearing only loose, baggy, 100% cotton clothes and sleeping naked under a fan; if it's bad you may need to check into an air-conditioned hotel room for a while.

Meningitis

This is a particularly nasty disease as it can kill within hours of the first symptoms appearing. The telltale symptoms are a combination of a blinding headache (light sensitivity), a blotchy rash and a high fever. Immunisation protects against the most serious bacterial form of meningitis and the tetravalent vaccine ACWY is recommended for Tanzania. Other forms of meningitis exist (usually viral) but there are no vaccines for these. Local papers normally report localised outbreaks. A severe headache and fever should make you run to a doctor immediately. There are also other causes of headache and fever; one of which is typhoid, which occurs in travellers to Tanzania. Seek medical help if you are ill for more than a few days.

Safe sex

Travel is a time when we might enjoy sexual adventures, especially when alcohol reduces inhibitions. Remember that the risks of sexually transmitted infection are high, whether you sleep with fellow travellers or locals. About 40% of HIV infections in British heterosexuals are acquired abroad. Use condoms or femidoms; spermicide pessaries help reduce the risk of transmission. If you notice any genital ulcers or discharge, get treatment promptly since these increase the risk of acquiring HIV.

Rabies

Rabies can be carried by all mammals (beware the village dogs and small monkeys that are used to being fed in the parks) and is passed on to humans through a bite, scratch or a lick of an open wound. You must always assume any animal is rabid (unless personally known to you) and seek medical help as soon as possible. In the interim, scrub the wound with soap and bottled/boiled water, then pour on a strong iodine or alcohol solution. This helps stop the rabies virus entering the body and will guard against wound infections, including tetanus.

If you intend to have contact with animals and/or are likely to be more than 24 hours away from medical help, then pre-exposure vaccination is advised. Ideally three doses should be taken over a minimum of three weeks. Contrary to popular belief, these vaccinations are relatively painless!

If you are exposed as described, treatment should be given as soon as possible, but it is never too late to seek help as the incubation period for rabies can be very long. Those who have not been immunised will need a full course of injections together with rabies immunoglobulin (RIG), but this product is expensive (around US$800) and may be hard to come by. This is another reason why pre-exposure vaccination should be encouraged in travellers who are planning to visit more remote areas!

Tell the doctor if you have had pre-exposure vaccine, as this will change the treatment you receive. And remember that, if you do contract rabies, mortality is 100% and death from rabies is probably one of the worst ways to go!

Snakes

Snakes rarely attack unless provoked, and bites in travellers are unusual. You are less likely to get bitten if you wear stout shoes and long trousers when in the bush. Most snakes are harmless and even venomous species will dispense venom in only about half of their bites. If bitten, then, you are unlikely to have received venom; keeping this fact in mind may help you to stay calm. Many so-called first-aid techniques do more harm than good: cutting into the wound is harmful; tourniquets are dangerous; suction and electrical inactivation devices do not work. The only treatment is antivenom. In the event of a bite which you fear may have been from a venomous snake:

- Try to keep calm – it is likely that no venom has been dispensed.
- Prevent movement of the bitten limb by applying a splint.
- Keep the bitten limb BELOW heart height to slow the spread of any venom.
- If you have a crêpe bandage, bind up as much of the bitten limb as you can, but release the bandage every half-hour.
- Evacuate to a hospital which has antivenom.

And remember:

NEVER give aspirin; you may offer paracetamol, which is safe.
NEVER cut or suck the wound.
DO NOT apply ice packs.
DO NOT apply potassium permanganate.

If the offending snake can be captured without risk of someone else being bitten, take this to show the doctor – but beware since even a decapitated head is able to bite.

Travelling in Tanzania

GETTING AROUND
Air
There has been a tremendous improvement in the network of domestic flights within Tanzania over recent years, especially between major tourist centres. In addition to the national carrier, Air Tanzania, several private airlines now run scheduled flights around Tanzania, most prominently Precision Air, Coastal Travel and Eagle Air. Between them, these carriers offer reliable services to most parts of the country. Scheduled flights operate to Dar es Salaam; Zanzibar, Pemba and Mafia islands; Kilimanjaro International Airport (for Moshi and Arusha); Serengeti (Grumeti and Seronera), Ngorongoro and Lake Manyara; Mwanza, Rubondo Island, Bukoba and Musoma; Tabora and Kigoma; Selous Game Reserve, Ruaha National Park and Mbeya; and Kilwa, Lindi and Mtwara. There are also regular flights between Arusha and Mombasa and Nairobi in Kenya.

Air Tanzania ` 022 211 0245; f 022 211 3114; e commercial@airtanzania.com; www.airtanzania.com. Has a head office on Ohio St in Dar es Salaam and branch offices all around the country.
Coastal Travel ` 022 211 7959/60; f 022 211 8647/7895; e safari@coastal.cc; www.coastal.cc. Based in Dar es Salaam, Coastal has the most extensive domestic flight network in Tanzania, covering most national parks in the north and the south, as well as Arusha, Mwanza, Tanga, Kilwa and all the main Indian Ocean islands. The head office is on Ohio St close to the Royal Palm Hotel.
Precision Air ` 027 250 6903/2818/7319; f 027 250 8204; e information@precisionairtz.com; www.precisionairtz.com. Has offices in Arusha, Dar es Salaam, Mwanza and Zanzibar. The head office is in the Arusha International Conference Centre's Ngorongoro Wing.

Public transport
Good express coach services, typically covering in excess of 60km per hour, connect Arusha and Moshi to Dar es Salaam and Nairobi (Kenya). The Scandinavia Coach company is particularly recommended, approaching if not quite attaining Greyhound-type standards, and with at least one daily service on the country's two most important routes, ie: Dar es Salaam to Arusha and Dar es Salaam to Mbeya. A number of shuttle companies such as Riverside and Impala run twice-daily minibus transfers between Arusha, Moshi and Nairobi. Coaches and shuttles can be booked through reliable tour operators. The alternative to buses on most routes is a *dalla-dalla* – a generic name that seems to encompass practically any light public transport. On the whole, *dalla-dallas* tend to be overcrowded by comparison with buses, and they are more likely to try to overcharge tourists, while the manic driving style results in regular fatal accidents. When you check out bus departure times, be conscious that many Tanzanians will translate Swahili time to English without making the six-hour

conversion – in other words, you might be told that a bus leaves at 11.00 when it actually leaves at 05.00.

Private safaris and car rental

The most normal way of getting around northern Tanzania is on an organised safari by Land Cruiser, Land Rover or any other similarly hardy 4x4 with high clearance. It is standard procedure for safari companies to provide a driver-guide with a fair knowledge of local wildlife and road conditions, as well as some mechanical expertise. Self-drive car hire isn't a particularly attractive or popular option in northern Tanzania, but it is widely available in Zanzibar and Dar es Salaam.

ACCOMMODATION

The volume of hotels in major urban tourist centres such as Zanzibar Town, Arusha, Moshi and Dar es Salaam is quite remarkable. So, too, is the variety in standard and price, which embraces hundreds of simple local guesthouses charging a couple of US dollars a night, as well as fantastic exclusive beach resorts and lodges charging upwards of US$300 per person – and everything in between.

All accommodation listings in this guidebook are placed in one of five categories: exclusive, upmarket, moderate, budget, and camping. The purpose of this categorisation is twofold: to break up long hotel listings that span a wide price range, and to help readers isolate the range of hotels that will best suit their budget and taste. The application of categories is not rigid. Aside from an inevitable element of subjectivity, I have categorised hotels on their feel as much as their rates (the prices are quoted anyway), and this might be influenced by other accommodation in the same place.

Before going into more detail about the different accommodation categories, it's worth noting a few potentially misleading quirks in local hotel-speak. In Swahili, the word *hoteli* refers to a restaurant while what we call a hotel is generally called a lodging, guesthouse or *gesti* – so if you ask a Tanzanian to show you a hotel you might well be taken to an eatery (see *Appendix 2*). Another local quirk is that most Tanzanian hotels in all ranges refer to a room with an en-suite shower and toilet as being self-contained. Finally, at most hotels in the moderate category or below, a single room will as often as not be one with a three-quarter or double bed, while a double room will be what we call a twin, with two single or double beds. 'B&B' refers to bed and breakfast, 'HB' to half-board, 'FB' to full board.

Exclusive

This category does not generally embrace conventional international-style hotels, but rather small and atmospheric beach resorts and game lodges catering to the most exclusive end of the market. Lodges in this category typically consist of no more than 20 accommodation units built and decorated in a style that complements the surrounding environment. The management will generally place a high priority on personalised service and quality food and wine, with the main idea being that guests are exposed to a holistic 24-hour bush or beach experience, rather than just a hotel room and restaurant in a bush/beach location. In several instances, lodges that fall into the exclusive category might be less conventionally luxurious, in terms of air conditioning and the like, than their competitors in the upmarket category. It is the bush experience, not the range of facilities, that lends lodges in this category a quality of exclusivity. Rates are typically upwards of US$250 per person all-inclusive, with substantial discounts offered to operators. This is the category to look at if you want authentic, atmospheric bush or beach accommodation and have few financial restrictions.

EMBASSIES AND DIPLOMATIC MISSIONS

A selection of embassies and high commissions in Dar es Salaam is listed below. Most are open mornings only and not at all at weekends. Typical hours are 09.00 to 12.30, but this varies considerably.

Algeria 34 Ali Hassan Mwinyi Rd; ✆ 022 211 7619; f 022 211 7620
Belgium 5 Ocean Rd, Upanga; ✆ 022 211 2688/3466; f 022 211 7621
Canada 38 Mirambo Close; ✆ 022 211 2831/5; f 022 211 6897
China 2 Kajifcheni Close; ✆ 022 266 7586/694; f 022 266 6353
Denmark Ghana Av; ✆ 022 211 3887/8; f 022 211 6433
Finland Cnr Mirambo St and Garden Av; ✆ 022 211 9170; f 022 211 9173
France Ali Hassan Mwinyi Rd; ✆ 022 266 6021-3; f 022 266 8435
Germany 10th floor, NIC House, Samora Av; ✆ 022 211 7409/15; f 022 211 2944
Greece 64 Upanga Rd; ✆ 022 211 5895; f 022 260 0151
Hungary 204 Chake Chake Rd, Oyster Bay; ✆ 022 266 8573; f 022 266 7214
India 11th Floor, NIC House, Samora Av; ✆ 022 211 7175/6; f 022 211 8761
Indonesia 299 Ali Hassan Mwinyi Rd; ✆ 022 211 9119; f 022 211 5849
Ireland Msasani Rd; ✆ 022 266 0614/2355; f 022 266 7852
Italy 316 Lugalo Rd; ✆ 022 211 5935/6; f 022 211 5938
Japan 1081 Ali Hassan Mwinyi Rd; ✆ 022 211 5827; f 022 211 5830
Netherlands 2nd Floor, ATC Building, Ohio Rd; ✆ 022 211 8566/8; f 022 211 2828
Norway Cnr Mirambo St and Garden Av; ✆ 022 211 3366/3610; f 022 211 8564
Poland 63 Ali Kahn Rd; ✆ 022 211 5271; f 022 211 5812
Romania 11 Ocean Rd, Upanga; ✆ 022 211 5899; f 022 211 3866
Russia 73 Ali Hassan Mwinyi Rd; ✆ 022 266 6005/6; f 022 266 6818
South Africa Mwaya Rd, Msasani; ✆ 022 260 1800; f 022 260 1684
Spain 99B Kinondoni Rd; ✆ 022 266 6936/6018; f 022 266 6938
Sweden Cnr Mirambo St and Garden Av; ✆ 022 211 1235; f 022 211 3420
Switzerland Kinondoni Rd; ✆ 022 266 6008/9; f 022 266 6736
UK Social Security House, Samora Av; ✆ 022 211 7659/94; f 022 211 2951
USA 140 Msese Rd, Kinondoni; ✆ 022 266 6010-5; f 022 266 6701

Upmarket

This category includes most hotels, lodges and resorts that cater almost entirely to the international tourist or business travel market. Hotels in this range would typically be accorded a two- to four-star ranking internationally, and they offer smart accommodation with en-suite facilities, mosquito netting, air conditioning or fans depending on the local climate, and satellite television in cities and some beach resorts. Hotels in this bracket might charge anything from under US$100 to upwards of US$300 for a double room, dependent on quality and location. As a rule, upmarket hotels in areas that see few foreign visitors are far cheaper than equivalent hotels in or around urban tourist centres such as Dar es Salaam or Arusha, which are in turn cheaper than beach hotels and lodges in national parks and game reserves. Room rates for city and beach hotels invariably include breakfast, while at game lodges they will also normally include lunch and dinner. Most package tours and privately booked safaris use accommodation in this range.

Moderate

In Tanzania, as in many African countries, there is often a wide gap in price and standard between the cheapest hotels geared primarily towards tourists and the best hotels geared primarily towards local travellers and budget travellers. For this reason, the moderate bracket is rather more nebulous than other accommodation categories, essentially consisting of hotels which, for one or other reason, couldn't really be classified as upmarket, but equally are too expensive or of too high quality to be considered budget lodgings. Many places listed in this range are superior local hotels that will suffice in lieu of any genuinely upmarket accommodation in a town that sees relatively few tourists. The category also embraces decent lodges or hotels in recognised tourist areas that charge considerably lower rates than their upmarket competitors, but are clearly a notch or two above the budget category. Hotels in this range normally offer comfortable accommodation in self-contained rooms with hot water, fan and possibly satellite television, and they will have decent restaurants and employ a high proportion of English-speaking staff. Prices for moderate city and beach hotels are generally in the US$20–50 range, more in some game reserves. This is the category to look at if you are travelling privately on a limited or low budget and expect a reasonably high but not luxurious standard of accommodation.

Budget

Hotels in this category are aimed largely at the local market and definitely don't approach international standards, but are still reasonably clean and comfortable, and a definite cut above the basic guesthouses that proliferate in most towns. Hotels in this bracket will more often than not have a decent restaurant attached, English-speaking staff, and comfortable rooms with en-suite facilities, running cold or possibly hot water, fans (but not air conditioning) and good mosquito netting. Hotels in this category typically charge around Tsh7,000–10,000 (around US$10) for a self-contained double room, but they may charge as little as Tsh5,000 in relatively out-of-the-way places and closer to US$20 in major tourist centres. This is the category to look at if you are on a limited budget, but want to avoid total squalor!

Camping

There are surprisingly few campsites in Tanzania, and those that do exist tend to be in national parks, where camping costs US$20 per person. Along the coast north of Dar es Salaam and in Moshi and Arusha, several recently opened private sites cater to backpackers and overland trucks. If you ask at moderate hotels in out-of-the-way places, you may sometimes be allowed to camp in their grounds for a small fee.

FOOD AND DRINK
Food

Most tourists will eat 90% of their meals at game lodges or tourist-class hotels, whose kitchens range in standard from adequate to excellent. Game lodges tend to offer a daily set menu with a limited selection, so it is advisable to have your tour operator specify in advance if you are a vegetarian or have other specific dietary requirements. First-time visitors to Africa might take note that most game lodges in and around the national parks have isolated locations, and driving within the parks is neither permitted nor advisable after dark, so that there is no realistic alternative to eating at your lodge. You will rarely be disappointed.

Most game lodges offer the option of a packaged breakfast and/or lunch box, so that their guests can eat on the trot rather than having to base their game-viewing hours around set meal times. The standards of the packed lunches is rather variable (and in some cases pretty awful) but if your first priority is to see wildlife, then taking a breakfast box in particular allows you to be out during the prime game-viewing hours immediately after sunrise. Packed meals must be ordered the night before you need them.

When you are staying in towns such as Arusha and Moshi, there is a fair selection of eating-out options. Indian eateries are particularly numerous in most towns, thanks to the high resident Indian population, and good continental restaurants and pizzerias are also well represented. Seafood is excellent on the coast. A selection of the better restaurants in each town is listed in the main part of the guide.

As for the local cuisine, it tends to consist of a bland stew eaten with one of four staples: rice, chapati, *ugali* or *batoke*. *Ugali* is a stiff maize porridge eaten throughout sub-Saharan Africa. *Batoke* or *matoke* is cooked plantain, served boiled or in a mushy heap. In the Lake Victoria region, *batoke* replaces *ugali* as the staple food. The most common stews are chicken, beef, goat and beans, and the meat is often rather tough. In coastal towns and around the great lakes, whole fried fish is a welcome change. The distinctive Swahili cuisine of the coast makes generous use of coconut milk and is far spicier than other Tanzanian food.

Mandaazi, the local equivalent of doughnuts, are tasty when freshly cooked. They are served at *hotelis* and sold at markets. You can eat cheaply at stalls around markets and bus stations. Goat kebabs, fried chicken, grilled groundnuts and potato chips are often freshly cooked and sold in these places.

Note: KiSwahili names for various foods are given in *Appendix 2*.

Drinks

The most widely drunk beverage is *chai*, a sweet tea where all ingredients are boiled together in a pot. Along the coast *chai* is often flavoured with spices such as ginger. In some places *chai* is served *ya rangi* or black; in others *maziwa* or milky. Sodas such as Coke, Pepsi, Sprite and Fanta are widely available, and normally cost around US$0.30 in outlets geared towards locals, and up to five times that price in tourist-oriented lodges. In large towns you can often get fresh fruit juice. On the coast and

---

TRADITIONAL MBEGE BANANA BEER
Emma Thomson

This party brew is prepared for many different Chagga ceremonies, but it is always drunk from a dried squash plant that has been hollowed out to form an enormous chalice, with the village landlord's clan name engraved upon it. Below is a rough recipe, as the measurements are only approximate.

1kg mashed banana
1 litre water
1kg finger millet

Boil in water until the bananas turn red, and then cover for three days.

Meanwhile, wash the finger millet, cover and leave in a wet, warm and dark place for three to four days until the millet begins to sprout. Then grind the millet into flour.

From this, make porridge by mixing two parts flour to one part water.

Next add ten parts of the boiled banana to one part porridge, mix and cover until the next day.

Let the celebrations begin.

Note The longer you leave it, the stronger the brew.

in some parts of the interior, the most refreshing, healthy and inexpensive drink is coconut milk, sold by street vendors who will decapitate the young coconut of your choice to create a natural cup, from which the juice can be sipped. Tap water in Tanzania is often dodgy, and most travellers try to stick to mineral water, which comes in 1.5l bottles that cost a few hundred shillings in supermarkets in Arusha but are very overpriced at game lodges – it is advisable to stock up with a dozen bottles or so before your safari leaves Arusha.

The two main alcoholic drinks are beer and *konyagi*. *Konyagi* is a spirit made from sugar cane. It tastes a bit strange on its own, but it mixes well and is very cheap. The local Safari lager used to be appalling, but since the national brewery was taken over by South African Breweries a few years ago there has been a dramatic improvement not only in the quality of Safari, but also in the selection of other brands available. Around ten different lager beers are now available, of which Castle, Kilimanjaro and Serengeti seem to be the most popular. All beers come in 500ml bottles and cost anything from US$1 at a local bar to US$5 at the most upmarket hotels. A variety of imported spirits are available in larger towns. South African wines are widely available at lodges and hotels, and they are generally of a high quality and reasonably priced by international standards.

SHOPPING

Until a few years ago it was difficult to buy anything much in Tanzania. One of my most vivid memories of Dar es Salaam in 1986 was walking into a general store where a lone shelf of teaspoons was the only stock. Things have improved greatly since then. In Dar es Salaam and most other large towns a fair range of imported goods is available, though prices are often inflated. If you have any very specific needs – unusual medications or slide film, for instance – bring them with you. Toilet roll, soap, toothpaste, pens, batteries and locally produced food are widely available. Shopping hours are normally between 08.30 and 16.30, with a lunch break between 13.00 and 14.00, but *duka*s, the stalls you see around markets or lining roads, are cheaper than proper shops and stay open for longer hours.

Curios

A variety of items specifically aimed at tourists is available: Makonde carvings, Tingatinga paintings (see box, page 106), batiks, musical instruments, wooden spoons and various soapstone and malachite knick-knacks. The curio shops near the Clock Tower in Arusha are the best places to shop for curios. Prices are competitive and the quality is good. Prices in shops are fixed, but you may be able to negotiate a discount. At curio stalls, haggling is necessary. Unless you are good at this, expect to pay more than you would in a shop. The colourful *vitenge* (the singular of this is *kitenge*) worn by most Tanzanian women can be picked up cheaply at any market in the country.

MEDIA AND COMMUNICATIONS
Newspapers

The English-language *Daily News* and *Daily Guardian* are available in Dar es Salaam and other major towns. They don't carry much international news, but the local news can make interesting reading and the international coverage seems to be steadily improving. The Kenyan *Daily Nation*, available in Dar es Salaam, Arusha and Mwanza, is slightly better. The excellent *East African* is a weekly newspaper published in Kenya but distributed throughout the three countries to which it dedicates roughly equal coverage, ie: Kenya, Tanzania and Uganda. Stalls in Uhuru Avenue, Dar es Salaam sell *Time* and *Newsweek*, as well as a variety of

European, British and American papers. You can sometimes buy the same from vendors around the Clock Tower in Arusha.

Phone calls

If you want to make an international phone call or send a fax, a TCC Extelcomms centre can be found in most large towns. Calls are cheap by international standards, and some Extelcomms centres will receive as well as send faxes. The costlier but more convenient alternative is to phone directly from your lodge or hotel. If you are carrying a mobile phone that receives international calls, the satellite network is pretty good in and around towns but rather less so in more remote parts of the game reserves.

Cell phones

If you bring a cell phone with you from home, it's emphatically worth the minor investment in a Tanzanian SIM card (which costs around US$0.30 and gives you a local number) and airtime cards (available in units of Tsh1,000 to 5,000). International text messages and calls out of Tanzania are seriously cheap: at the time of writing, US$1 will buy you around 20 text messages to anywhere in the world, and international calls work out at around US$1 for 3–4 minutes. By contrast, you can expect to rack up a hefty bill using your home phone number for calls and/or messages, since in most instances these are charged at international rates out of your home country, even when you are phoning home. SIM and airtime cards can be bought at a specialist Vodacom outlet (there are several in Arusha and Moshi) or at numerous other small shops displaying the ubiquitous Vodacom sticker. Network reception is increasingly widespread in northern Tanzania, even in the national parks.

Internet and email

The spread of internet use in Africa has been remarkable over the last half-decade, and the existence of email represents a real communications revolution on a continent where international lines tend to be unreliable and expensive. Internet and email have caught on particularly quickly in Tanzania, where internet cafés are more prolific and affordable than in any other African country I've visited recently. Numerous internet cafés are dotted around major urban tourist centres such as Dar es Salaam, Arusha, Mwanza and Moshi, the servers are generally pretty fast, and rates are very affordable. Internet access is not available in most game reserves and national parks, and the few game lodges that do offer browsing or email services tend to charge very high rates.

INTERACTING WITH TANZANIANS

Tanzania has perhaps the most egalitarian and tolerant mood of any African country that I've visited. As a generalisation, Tanzanians tend to treat visitors with a dignified reserve, something that many Westerners mistake for a stand-offish attitude, but in my opinion is more indicative of a respect both for our culture and their own. Granted, dignified probably won't be the adjective that leaps to mind if your first interaction with Tanzanians comes from the pestilence of touts that hangs around bus stations in Arusha or Moshi, or somewhere similar. But then in most poor countries, you'll find that people who make a living on the fringe of the tourist industry tend be pushy and occasionally confrontational in their dealings – from their perspective, they probably have to be in order to make a living. But I do think that anybody who spends time travelling in Tanzania will recognise the behaviour of touts to be wholly unrepresentative of what is essentially a conservative, unhurried and undemonstrative society.

On the whole, you would have to do something pretty outrageous to commit a serious faux pas in Tanzania. But, like any country, Tanzania does have its rules of etiquette, and while allowances will always be made for tourists, there is some value in ensuring that they are not made too frequently!

General conduct

Perhaps the most important single point of etiquette to be grasped by visitors to Tanzania is the social importance of formal greetings. Tanzanians tend to greet each other elaborately, and if you want to make a good impression on somebody who speaks English, whether they be a waiter or a shop assistant (and especially if they work in a government department), you would do well to follow suit. When you need to ask somebody directions, it is rude to blunder straight into interrogative mode without first exchanging greetings. With Tanzanians who don't speak English, the greeting 'Jambo' delivered with a smile and a nod of the head will be adequate.

Whenever I visit Tanzania after travelling elsewhere in Africa, I am struck afresh by how readily people greet passing strangers, particularly in rural areas. In Tanzania, this greeting doesn't normally take the form of a shrieked *mzungu* (or whatever local term is used for a white person), or a 'give me money', something that you become accustomed to in some African countries. On the contrary, in Tanzania adults will normally greet tourists with a cheerful *Jambo*, and children with a subdued *Shikamu* (a greeting reserved for elders). I find this to be a very charming quality in Tanzanian society, one that is worth reinforcing by learning a few simple Swahili greetings.

Among Tanzanians, it is considered poor taste to display certain emotions publicly. Affection is one such emotion: it is frowned upon for members of the opposite sex to hold hands publicly, and kissing or embracing would be seriously offensive. Oddly, it is quite normal for friends of the same sex to walk around hand in hand. Male travellers who get into a long discussion with a male Tanzanian shouldn't be surprised if that person clasps them by the hand and retains a firm grip on their hand for several minutes. This is a warm gesture, one particularly appropriate when the person wants to make a point with which you might disagree. On the subject of intra-gender relations, homosexuality is as good as taboo in Tanzania, to the extent that it would require some pretty overt behaviour for it to occur to anybody to take offence.

It is also considered bad form to show anger publicly. It is difficult to know where to draw the line here, because many touts positively invite an aggressive response, and I doubt that many people who travel independently in Tanzania will get by without the occasional display of impatience. Frankly, I doubt that many bystanders would take umbrage if you responded to a pushy tout with a display of anger, if only because the tout's behaviour itself goes against the grain of Tanzanian society. By contrast, losing your temper will almost certainly be counterproductive when dealing with obtuse officials, dopey waiters and hotel employees, or unco-operative safari drivers.

Muslim customs

Visitors should be aware of the strong Muslim element in Tanzania, particularly along the coast. In Muslim society, it is insulting to use your left hand to pass or receive something or when shaking hands. If you eat with your fingers, it is also customary to use the right hand only. Even those of us who are naturally right-handed will occasionally need to remind ourselves of this (it may happen, for instance, that you are carrying something in your right hand and so hand money to a shopkeeper with your left). For left-handed travellers, it will require a constant effort. In traditional Muslim societies it is offensive for women to expose their knees or shoulders, a custom that ought to be taken on board by female travellers, especially on parts of the coast where tourists remain a relative novelty.

Tipping and guides

The question of when and when not to tip can be difficult in a foreign country. In Tanzania, it is customary to tip your guide at the end of a safari and/or a Kilimanjaro climb, as well as any cook and porter that accompanies you. A figure of roughly US$5–10 per day is accepted as the benchmark, though it is advisable to check this with your safari company in advance. I see no reason why you shouldn't give a bigger or smaller tip based on the quality of service. Bear in mind, however, that most guides, cooks and porters receive nominal salaries, which means that they are largely dependent on tips for their income. It would be mean not to leave a reasonable tip in any but the most exceptional of circumstances.

In some African countries, it is difficult to travel anywhere without being latched on to by a self-appointed guide, who will often expect a tip over and above any agreed fee. This sort of thing is comparatively unusual in Tanzania, but if you do take on a freelance guide, then it is advisable to clarify in advance that whatever price you agree is final and inclusive of a tip. By contrast, any guide who is given to you by a company should most definitely be tipped, as tips will probably be their main source of income. In Zanzibar and Arusha, a freelance guide may insist upon helping you find a hotel room, in which case they will be given a commission by the hotel, so there is no reason for you to provide an additional tip. In any case, from the guide's point of view, finding you a room is merely the first step in trying to hook you for a safari or a spice tour, or something else that will earn a larger commission.

It is not customary to tip for service in local bars and *hotelis*, though you may sometimes *want* to leave a tip (in fact, given the difficulty of finding change in Tanzania, you may practically be forced into doing this in some circumstances). A tip of 5% would be very acceptable and 10% generous. Generally any restaurant that caters primarily to tourists and to wealthy Tanzania residents will automatically add a service charge to the bill. Since the government claims the lion's share of any formal service charge, it would still be reasonable to reward good service with a genuine tip.

Bargaining

Tourists to Tanzania will sometimes need to bargain over prices, but generally this need exists only in reasonably predictable circumstances, for instance when chartering a private taxi, organising a guide, agreeing a price for a safari or mountain trek, or buying curios and to a lesser extent other market produce. Prices in hotels, restaurants and shops are generally fixed, and overcharging in such places is too unusual for it to be worth challenging a price unless it is blatantly ridiculous.

You may well be overcharged at some point in Tanzania, but it is important to keep this in perspective. After a couple of bad experiences, some travellers start to haggle with everybody from hotel owners to old women selling fruit by the side of the road, often accompanying their negotiations with aggressive accusations of dishonesty. Unfortunately, it is sometimes necessary to fall back on aggressive posturing in order to determine a fair price, but such behaviour is also very unfair on those people who are forthright and honest in their dealings with tourists. It's a question of finding the right balance, or better still looking for other ways of dealing with the problem.

The main instance where bargaining is essential is when buying curios. What should be understood, however, is that the fact a curio seller is open to negotiation does not mean that you were initially being overcharged or ripped off. Curio sellers will generally quote a price knowing full well that you are going to bargain it down (they'd probably be startled if you didn't) and it is not necessary to respond aggressively or in an accusatory manner. It is impossible to say by how much you should bargain the initial price down. Some people say that you should offer half the asking price and be prepared to settle at around two-thirds, but my experience is that curio sellers are far more whimsical than such advice allows for. The sensible approach, if you want to get a feel for prices, is to ask the price of similar items at a few different stalls before you actually contemplate buying anything.

In fruit and vegetable markets and stalls, bargaining is the norm, even between locals, and the most healthy approach to this sort of haggling is to view it as an enjoyable part of the African experience. There will normally be an accepted price band for any particular commodity. To find out what it is, listen to what other people pay and try a few stalls. A ludicrously inflated price will always drop the moment you walk away. When buying fruit and vegetables, a good way to feel out the situation is to ask for a bulk discount or a few extra items thrown in. And bear in mind that when somebody is reluctant to bargain, it may be because they asked a fair price in the first place.

A final point to consider on the subject of overcharging and bargaining is that it is the fact of being overcharged that annoys; the amount itself is generally of little consequence in the wider context of a trip to Tanzania. Without for a moment wanting to suggest that travellers should routinely allow themselves to be overcharged, I do feel there are occasions when we should pause to look at the bigger picture. If you find yourself quibbling over a pittance with an old lady selling a few piles of fruit by the roadside, you might perhaps bear in mind that the notion of a fixed price is a very Western one. When somebody is desperate enough for money, or afraid that their perishable goods might not last another day, it may well be possible to push them down to a lower price than they would normally accept. In such circumstances, I see nothing wrong with erring on the side of generosity.

Women travellers

Women travellers in Tanzania have little to fear on a gender-specific level. Over the years, I've met several women travelling alone in Tanzania, and none had any serious problems in their interactions with locals, aside from the hostility that can be generated by dressing skimpily. Otherwise, an element of flirtation is about the sum of it, perhaps the odd direct proposition, but nothing that cannot be defused by a firm 'no'. And nothing, for that matter, that you wouldn't expect in any Western country, or – probably with a far greater degree of persistence – from many male travellers.

It would be prudent to pay some attention to how you dress in Tanzania, particularly in the more conservative parts of the Swahili coast. In areas where people are used to tourists, they are unlikely to be deeply offended by women travellers wearing shorts or other outfits that might be seen to be provocative. Nevertheless, it still pays to allow for local sensibilities, and under certain circumstances revealing clothes may be perceived to make a statement that's not intended from your side.

More mundanely, tampons are not readily available in smaller towns, though you can easily locate them in Dar es Salaam and Arusha, and in game lodge and hotel gift shops. When travelling in out-of-the-way places, carry enough tampons to see you through to the next time you'll be in a large city, bearing in mind that travelling in the tropics can sometimes cause heavier or more regular periods than normal. Sanitary pads are available in most towns of any size.

CRIME AND SECURITY

Crime exists in Tanzania as it does practically everywhere in the world. There has been a marked increase in crime in Tanzania over recent years, and tourists are inevitably at risk, because they are far richer than most locals, and are conspicuous in their dress, behaviour and (with obvious exceptions) skin colour. For all that, Tanzania remains a lower crime risk than many countries, and the social taboo on theft is such that even a petty criminal is likely to be beaten to death should they be caught in the act. With a bit of care, you would have to be unlucky to suffer from more serious crime while you are in Tanzania.

Mugging

There is nowhere in Tanzania where mugging is as commonplace as it is in, say, Nairobi or Johannesburg, but there are certainly several parts of the country where walking around alone at night would place you at some risk of being mugged. Mugging is generally an urban problem, with the main areas of risk being Dar es Salaam, Arusha and Zanzibar Town. Even in these places, the risk is often localised, so ask local advice at your hotel, since the staff there will generally know of any recent incidents in the immediate vicinity. The best way to ensure that any potential mugging remains an unpleasant incident rather than a complete disaster is to carry as little as you need on your person. If you are mugged in Tanzania, the personal threat is minimal provided that you promptly hand over what is asked for.

Casual theft

The bulk of crime in Tanzania consists of casual theft such as bag-snatching or pickpocketing. This sort of thing is not particularly aimed at tourists (and as a consequence it is not limited to tourist areas), but tourists will be considered fair game. The key to not being pickpocketed is not having anything of value in your pockets; the key to avoiding having things snatched is to avoid having valuables in a place where they could easily be snatched. Most of the following points will be obvious to experienced travellers, but they are worth making:

- Many casual thieves operate in bus stations and markets. Keep a close watch on your belongings in these places, and avoid having loose valuables in your pocket or daypack.
- Keep all your valuables – passport, travellers' cheques, etc – in a money-belt. One you can hide under your clothes has obvious advantages over one of the currently fashionable codpieces that are worn externally.
- Never carry spending money in your money-belt. A normal wallet is fine provided it contains only a moderate sum of money. Better still is a wallet you can hang around your neck. If I plan to visit a risky area such as a busy market, I sometimes wear shorts under my trousers and keep my cash in the pockets of the shorts. In my opinion, it is difficult for somebody to stick a hand in the front pocket of a shirt unobserved, for which reason this is normally my favourite pocket for keeping ready cash.
- Distribute your money throughout your luggage. I always keep the bulk of my foreign currency in my money-belt, but I like to keep some cash and travellers' cheques hidden in various parts of my pack and daypack.
- Many people prefer to carry their money-belt on their person at all times. I think it is far safer to leave it locked away in a bag or safe in your hotel room. It's not impossible for a locked hotel room to be broken into, but I've not heard of it happening in Tanzania, whereas I have met countless people who have been pickpocketed, mugged or had possessions snatched from them on

the street. Circumstances do play a part here: in a large city, I would be far happier with my valuables locked away somewhere, whereas in a game lodge the risk of theft from a room has to be greater than that of theft from your person. One factor to consider is that some travellers' cheque companies won't issue refunds on cheques stolen from a hotel room.

- If you have jewellery that is of high personal or financial value, leave it at home.
- If you are robbed, think twice before you chase the thief, especially if the stolen items are of no great value. An identified thief is likely to be descended on by a mob and quite possibly beaten to death. I have met a few travellers who found themselves in the bizarre position of having to save someone who had just ripped them off.

Documentation

The best insurance against complete disaster is to keep things well documented. If you carry a photocopy of the main page of your passport, you will be issued a new one more promptly. In addition, keep details of your bank, credit card (if you have one), travel insurance policy and camera equipment (including serial numbers).

Keep copies of your travellers' cheque numbers and *a record of which ones you have cashed*, as well as the international refund assistance telephone number and local agent. If all this information fits on one piece of paper, you can keep photocopies on you and with a friend at home.

You will have to report to the police the theft of any item against which you wish to claim insurance.

Security

Tanzania is a very secure country, with a proud record of internal stability since independence. The bombing of the US embassies in Dar es Salaam and Nairobi resulted in large-scale cancellations of US tours to Tanzania in late 1998, despite a mass of evidence that would provide any rational human with greater cause to give a wide birth to US embassies than to cancel a holiday in east Africa. Aside from this, the only part of Tanzania where there is currently a security problem is in the remote tract of Maasailand lying between Lake Natron and the Serengeti. The security situation here is the direct result of the recent incursion of a group of armed Somalis from Kenya, and while it has resulted in several deaths locally, the only effect on tourists to date has been an isolated incident in which a safari vehicle was held up along the road west of Natron. The indications are that this is a short-term problem, and it is unlikely that any responsible safari company would risk taking tourists into this area until it is resolved.

Tanzania shares a western border with the troubled countries of the Congo, Rwanda and Burundi, an area that sees very little tourism. So far as I am aware, the recent civil war in the Congo has had little direct effect on Tanzania, probably because Lake Tanganyika divides the two countries. The Rwanda and Burundi border areas have been overrun with refugees at several points over the last few years, a situation that is of some concern to locals, officials and international aid workers, but has had no effect on parts of Tanzania likely to be visited by tourists.

Part Two

The Guide

Arusha

6

Situated in the fertile southern foothills of Mount Meru, less than 100km from the Kenyan border as the crow flies, the bustling town of Arusha is Tanzania's so-called 'safari capital', the most popular and convenient springboard from which to explore the legendary northern game-viewing circuit. The town is also an important gateway into Tanzania, the first town visited by travellers coming across the border from Nairobi, and the entry point for a growing number of fly-in tourists following the recent privatisation of (and introduction of daily KLM flights to) the nearby Kilimanjaro International Airport.

First impressions of Arusha are that practically *everything* there revolves around the safari industry, a perception that is only reinforced by more prolonged exposure. Wander around the old town centre or backroads north of the stadium, and it can feel like every second person you pass has something to sell, be it a safari, a batik or last week's edition of some or other foreign newspaper, while every other vehicle sports a safari company logo. Bizarrely, many of the passenger vehicles that weave through the streets of Arusha have been converted from safari vehicles – and there is something cheeringly incongruous about the sight of your standard overcrowded *dalla-dalla* driving past with a bunch of heads sticking out of the open-topped roof as if waiting for an elephant to emerge from the nearest alley.

In reality, Arusha's rare economic vitality is buoyed by several contributory factors, not the least of which is its location in the bountiful Mount Meru foothills, whose drizzly sub-montane microclimate nurtures the rich volcanic soil to agricultural profligacy. There is also the proximity of the Mererani Hills, the only known source of the increasingly popular gemstone tanzanite, while a more ephemeral economic boost has been provided by the presence of UN and other NGO personnel linked to the Rwandan War Crimes Tribunal, which took up residence in the Arusha International Conference Centre some years back and shows no signs of leaving just yet. For all this, however, one suspects that the lure of the tourist dollar is primarily responsible for the rural inflow associated with a fiftyfold population growth in Arusha over as many years, from fewer than 10,000 inhabitants in 1955 to an estimated 400,000 today.

Situated at an altitude of around 1,500m in the rainshadow of Mount Meru, Arusha makes for a climatically temperate – and, during the rainy season, often downright soggy – introduction to tropical Africa. The town itself is a pleasant enough place to hang out, and these days it boasts a growing number of trendy bars, restaurants and cafés catering to expatriates, tourists and wealthier locals. Away from these few select spots, however, Arusha remains something of an African everytown, where low-rise colonial-era buildings rub shoulders with a small but gradually increasing number of more modern structures. Indeed, it could be argued that the wealth generated by the safari industry serves to accentuate the vast economic gulf between the haves and have-nots and the spectrum of cultural influences that play havoc with those visitors seeking to pigeonhole the 'Real Africa'.

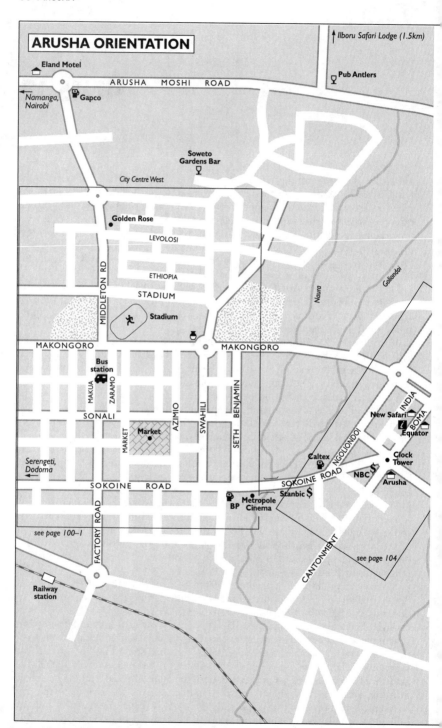

ARUSHA ORIENTATION

Eland Motel

↑ Ilboru Safari Lodge (1.5km)

ARUSHA   MOSHI   ROAD

Pub Antlers

Gapco

← Namanga,
Nairobi

Soweto
Gardens Bar

City Centre West

Golden Rose

LEVOLOSI

ETHIOPIA

MIDDLETON RD

STADIUM

Stadium

MAKONGORO

MAKONGORO

Naura

Goliondoi

Bus
station

MAKUA   ZARAMO

SONALI

MARKET

Market

AZIMIO

SWAHILI

SETH   BENJAMIN

INDIA

New Safari

BOMA

Equator

Caltex

NGOLIONDOI

Clock
Tower

NBC $

Serengeti,
Dodoma ←

SOKOINE   ROAD

SOKOINE ROAD

Stanbic $

Arusha

BP   Metropole
Cinema

FACTORY ROAD

see page 100–1

CANTONMENT

see page 104

Railway
station

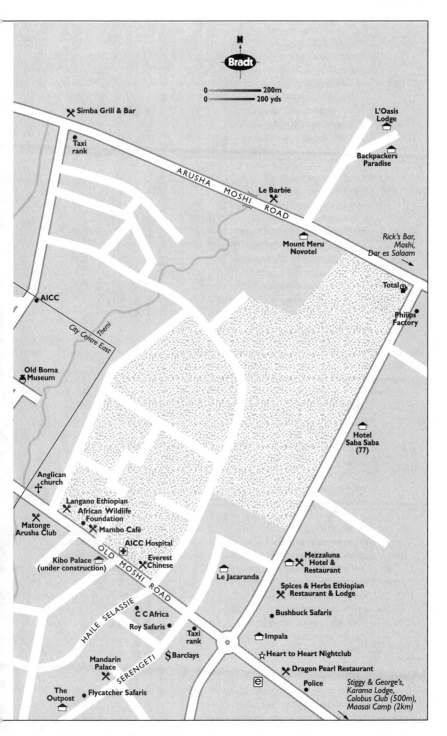

SOME HISTORY

Little is known about the Arusha area prior to the 17th century, when the Bantu-speaking Meru people – migrants from the west with strong linguistic and cultural affinities to the Chagga of Kilimanjaro – settled and farmed the fertile and well-watered northern foothills of Mount Meru. In 1830 or thereabouts, the southern slopes of the mountain verging on the Maasai Steppes were settled by the Arusha, a Maasai subgroup who lost their cattle and territory in one of the internecine battles characteristic of this turbulent period in Maasailand. The Arusha people speak the same Maa language as the plains Maasai and share a similar social structure based around initiated age-sets, but when they settled in the Mount Meru area they forsook their pastoralist roots, turning instead to agriculture as a primary source of subsistence.

The Arusha economy was boosted by the trade in agricultural produce – in particular tobacco – with the closely affiliated Maasai of the plains. The Arusha also became known as reliable providers of food and other provisions for the Arab slave caravans that headed inland from the Pangani and Tanga area towards modern-day Kenya and Lake Victoria. Invigorated by this regular trade, the Arusha had, by 1880, cleared the forested slopes of Mount Meru to an altitude of around 1,600m to make way for cultivation. As their territory expanded, however, the Arusha people increasingly came into contact with their northern neighbours, the Meru, resulting in several territorial skirmishes and frequent cattle raids between the two tribes.

In 1881, prompted by the need to defend their combined territories against the Maasai and other potential attackers, the incumbent warrior age-sets of the Arusha and Meru united to form a formidable military force. Since they were settled on the well-watered slopes of Mount Meru, and their subsistence was not primarily dependent on livestock, the Arusha and Meru people were less affected than the plains pastoralists by the devastating series of droughts and rinderpest epidemics of the 1880s and early 1890s. As a result, the combined army, known as the Talala – the Expansionists – was able to exert considerable influence over neighbouring Maasai and Chagga territories.

The Talala staunchly resisted German attempts to settle in their territory, killing the first missionaries to arrive there and repelling an initial punitive attack by the colonial army. In October 1896, however, the Arusha and Meru were soundly defeated by a military expedition out of Moshi led by Karl Johannes and consisting of 100 German troopers supported by some 5,000 Chagga warriors. In the aftermath of this defeat, the Germans drove home the point by razing hundreds of Arusha and Meru smallholdings, killing the men, confiscating the cattle and repatriating women of Chagga origin to the Kilimanjaro area.

In 1889, the Germans established a permanent settlement – modern-day Arusha town – on the border of Arusha and Maasai territories, and used forced Arusha and Maasai labour to construct the Boma that can still be seen on the north end of Boma Road. Relations between the colonisers and their unwilling subjects remained tense, to say the least. During the construction of the fort, a minor dispute led to some 300 labourers being massacred while

Which is it, then: the colourfully dressed Maasai and Arusha women who sell traditional beadwork on the pavement, the suited businessmen who scurry in and out of the International Conference Centre, or the swaggering, sunglass-shrouded wide-boys who scurry about offering cheap safaris, change money, marijuana ...?

marching peacefully along present-day Boma Road, and several local chiefs from outlying areas were arbitrarily arrested and taken to Moshi to be hanged in the street.

Following the construction of the Boma, Arusha quickly developed into a significant trading and administrative centre, with about two dozen Indian and Arab shops clustered along what is today Boma Road. John Boyes, who visited Arusha in 1903, somewhat fancifully compared the Boma to 'an Aladdin's Palace transported from some fairyland and dropped down in the heart of the tropics'. The town, he wrote, was 'a real oasis in the wilderness' and 'spotlessly clean', while 'the streets [were] laid out with fine sidewalks, separated by the road from a stream of clear water flowing down a cemented gully'.

At the outbreak of World War I, the small German garrison town was of some significance as a local agricultural and trade centre, but it remained something of a backwater by comparison with Moshi, which lay a week's ox-wagon trek distant at the railhead of the Tanga line. Much of the area around Arusha was, however, settled by German farmers, who had forcibly displaced the original Arusha and Meru smallholders. In 1916, British troops captured Arusha and expelled the German farmers, resulting in some resettlement by indigenous farmers, but the German farmland was eventually re-allocated to British and Greek settlers. The British also set aside large tracts of land around Arusha for sisal plantations, which meant that by 1920, less than 20% of the land around Mount Meru was available to local farmers, most of it on dry foothills unsuited to cultivating the local staple of bananas.

Arusha grew steadily between the wars. The settler economy was boosted by the introduction of coffee, sisal and other export crops, and trade links were improved with the construction of road links to Moshi and Nairobi and the opening of the railway line to Moshi and the coast in 1929. Yet the land issues continued to simmer, eventually coming to a head after World War II, with the eviction of thousands of Meru farmers from north of Mount Meru to make way for a peanut production project overseen by 13 white farmers. The peanut project, aside from being a dismal and costly failure, resulted in the pivotal Meru Land Case, which not only caused great embarrassment to the UN Trusteeship Council, but also proved to be an important catalyst to the politicisation of the anti-colonial movement in Tanganyika.

Prior to independence, Arusha remained a relatively small town whose primary role was to service the surrounding agricultural lands. The official census of 1952 placed the urban population at fewer than 8,000 people, of which more than half were of Asian or European stock. The town has, however, grown markedly since independence, attracting large numbers of domestic migrants from surrounding rural areas and beyond. This can be attributed to a number of factors: the town's short-lived but prestigious role as capital of the east African community in the 1960s, the tanzanite mining boom, and perhaps most of all its strategic location as the springboard for the northern safari circuit. The population of Arusha is currently estimated at around 400,000, with up to 250,000 tourists passing through annually!

If nothing else, Arusha is an attractively green town, with its northern skyline – weather permitting – dominated by the imposing hulk of Africa's fifth-highest mountain. And for those who prefer not to stay in the town centre, there are plenty of more rustic options in the immediate area. The 4,556m Mount Meru is the dominant geographical feature in Arusha National Park which, despite its proximity to Arusha and manifold points of interest, attracts little more than a trickle of tourism. Also of interest in the immediate vicinity of Arusha is Lake Duluti, an attractive forest-fringed crater lake that lies immediately south of the Moshi road, and a cluster of attractive farms set on the coffee plantations and forested hills between Arusha and Usa River – many of which offer views to Meru *and* Kilimanjaro on a clear day.

ORIENTATION

Unlike Dar es Salaam or Zanzibar's labyrinthine Stone Town, Arusha is not a difficult town to familiarise yourself with. Its most significant geographical features are the Naura and Goliondoi rivers, which run parallel to each other through the town centre, cutting it into two distinct parts. To the east of the rivers lies the 'old' town centre, a relatively smart area whose main north-south thoroughfares – Boma, India and Goliondoi roads – are lined with upmarket hotels, tourist-friendly restaurants, safari companies, curio shops, banks, bookshops and tourist offices. Major landmarks in this part of town include the Clock Tower, the Old Boma (now a museum) and the Arusha International Conference Centre (AICC).

Connected to the old town centre by Sokoine Road in the south and Makongoro Road in the north, the more bustling modern town centre consists of a tight grid of roads west of the rivers centred on the market and bus station south of the stadium. This area is well equipped with small budget hotels and Indian restaurants, but it boasts few facilities that approach international standards. Similar in feel, though more residential and less commercially orientated, is the suburb of Kaloleni immediately north of the stadium and main bus station.

Another important suburb is Kijenge, which lies to the southeast of the old town centre, and is reached by following Sokoine Road across a bridge over the Themi River to become the Old Moshi Road. Kijenge has a spacious, leafy character and it is dotted with relatively upmarket hotels (notably the Impala) and restaurants, as well as an increasing number of safari company offices.

SAFETY

Arusha can be a daunting prospect on first contact, particularly if you arrive by bus. Competition between budget safari companies is fierce, and 'flycatchers' – the street touts who solicit custom for these companies – know that their best tactic is to hook travellers who don't have a pre-booked safari when they arrive. As a consequence, when you arrive in Arusha by bus you're likely to spend your first few minutes dodging the attention of a dozen yelling touts, all of who will claim to be able to offer you the cheapest safari and room in town. In most cases, the touts probably will show you to a decent room, but allowing this to happen does open the door to your sense of obligation being exploited later in your stay.

Fortunately, once you've run the bus station gauntlet, things do calm down somewhat, though the flock of flycatchers, newspaper vendors and curio sellers who hang around the old town centre can be a nuisance. Unlike in some other parts of Africa, however, it is unusual for such an exchange to descend into something truly unpleasant: most touts here seem capable of taking a good-humoured no for an answer, especially one spoken in Swahili, and they will usually back down at any show of genuine irritation. As for the dodgy moneychangers that sometimes hang around with the touts, don't let the offer of a superior rate sucker you in – changing money on the street in Arusha as elsewhere in Tanzania is a definite no-no!

Such annoyances aside, Arusha is not an especially threatening city, though it is certainly not unheard of for tourists to be mugged after dark. The usual commonsense rules apply: avoid walking around singly or in pairs at night, especially on unlit roads and parks, and avoid carrying valuables on your person or taking out significantly more money than you need for the evening. After dark, the dodgiest part of town for muggings is probably the area east of the Themi River, in particular the quiet, unlit roads between the Arusha and Impala hotels and Mount Meru Novotel. On the whole, Arusha is very safe by day, but do be wary of bag-snatchers and pickpockets in and around the central market.

GETTING THERE AND AWAY
By air
The main local point of entry is Kilimanjaro International Airport (KIA), which lies roughly halfway along the 80km road between Arusha and Moshi, and is connected to Europe by daily KLM flights, eliminating the need to travel to northern Tanzania via Nairobi or Dar es Salaam. Other international carriers that fly to KIA are Kenya Airways, Ethiopian Airlines and South African Airways, while Air Tanzania operates connecting flights there from several destinations via Dar es Salaam, as well as domestic flights to Dar es Salaam, Mwanza, Zanzibar, Pemba, Mafia and Mbeya.

Travellers arriving at or leaving from KIA with Air Tanzania should note that the national carrier offers a free shuttle service between the airport and Arusha connecting with all flights and dropping you at the central hotel of your choice. It's easy enough to locate the shuttle when you arrive at the airport. Leaving Arusha, ask about departure times at the Air Tanzania office on Boma Road. For KLM flights, the Impala Hotel runs a connecting shuttle between KIA and the town centre, but this costs US$10 per person. Taxis are available at the airport. Travellers with odd flight times might think about booking into the excellent KIA Lodge (see page 122), which lies just 1km from the airport.

Aside from Air Tanzania, most other domestic carriers, such as Coastal and Precision Air, fly in and out of the smaller Arusha Airport, which lies about 5km out of town along the Serengeti road. There are daily flights from Arusha to all major airstrips on the northern Tanzania safari circuit, including Manyara, Ngorongoro, Seronera, Grumeti and Lobo, as well as to Dar es Salaam and Zanzibar. There are also regular scheduled flights to the likes of Mwanza, Rubondo Island, Mafia Island and the reserves of the southern safari circuit.

Most tourists flying around Tanzania will have made their flight arrangements in advance through a tour operator, and this is certainly the recommended way of going about things, but it is generally possible to buy tickets from Arusha to major destinations such as Dar es Salaam and Zanzibar at short notice.

By road
A number of companies run express bus services to and from Dar es Salaam. These generally take around 10 hours, stopping only at Moshi to pick up further passengers and at Korogwe for a 20-minute lunch break, and tickets cost US$10–12. Most such buses leave early in the morning, so it is advisable to make enquiries and a booking the afternoon before you want to leave. The best coach at present is the Scandinavia Express, which runs three services daily in either direction, leaving between 07.30 and 08.30 and costing between Tsh11,000 and 18,000 depending on whether you use the normal or luxury service. The office is on Kituoni Road, immediately south of the bus station; ` 027 250 0153. Another recommended company is Dar Express, based on Colonel Middleton Road more

or less opposite the Golden Rose Hotel. This runs three luxury air-conditioned buses daily, leaving at 06.00, 07.30 and 08.15 and taking around eight hours in either direction – tickets cost Tsh14,000. Cheaper bus services between Arusha and Dar es Salaam aren't worth bothering with, as they stop at every town and can take anything from 12 to 15 hours to cover the same distance.

The quickest and most efficient road transport between Arusha and Nairobi are the minibus shuttles run by Riverside, the Impala Hotel and a few other operators. These all leave twice daily in either direction at 08.00 and 14.00, mostly from the parking lot of the Mount Meru Novotel (though you can arrange to be picked up elsewhere) and take around five hours, depending on how quickly you pass through immigration and customs at the Namanga border. Tickets officially cost US$20–25 for non-residents, but more often than not walk-in customers will be permitted to pay the resident's rate of Tsh10–12,000. Tickets for the Impala Shuttle can be bought directly from the Impala Hotel, while those for the Riverside Shuttle can be bought at the Golden Rose (an official pick-up point) or Mount Meru Novotel. Alternatively, tickets for all shuttles can be arranged through any safari operator in Arusha. Another option is to travel to Nairobi with Scandinavia Express (see above), which runs two buses daily, leaving at around 15.00 and costing Tsh10,000.

A steady stream of minibuses and buses connect Moshi and Arusha. I would avoid using minibuses along this route due to the higher incidence of accidents, but they are generally quicker than buses. This trip usually takes between one and two hours. There are also regular buses to other relatively local destinations such as Mto wa Mbu, Karatu, Mbulu, Babati and Kondoa. Most buses and minibuses for destinations along the Nairobi and Moshi/Dar es Salaam road leave from the main bus station near the football stadium, while those for more westerly destinations such as Babati and Karatu leave from the station opposite the Shoprite supermarket.

WHERE TO STAY

This section concentrates on accommodation located within the city limits. It also includes a handful of individual hotels situated along the Old Moshi and Serengeti roads within 5km of the town centre, but excludes the ever-growing assortment of lodges that flank the Moshi road east of the Mount Meru Novotel. All hotels in the latter category are covered in the chapter *Around Arusha*, but it is worth noting that most would make a perfectly viable – and, on the whole, more aesthetically pleasing – alternative to staying in the town itself.

Exclusive (above US$120)

Arusha Coffee Lodge (18 rooms) ☎ 027 254 0630–9; f 027 254 8245; e info@elewana.com; www.elewana.com. Justifiably billed as 'the first truly 5-star hotel in Arusha' when it opened in 2002, the immaculate Arusha Coffee Lodge lays even stronger claims to that accolade following its recent acquisition by Elewana Lodges and subsequent renovations. It is situated about 5km out of town along the Serengeti road, close to Arusha Airport, on what is reputedly the largest coffee estate in Tanzania, with a good view of Mount Meru. Accommodation is in stand-alone split-level chalets distinguished by their elegant Victorian décor, hardwood floors, huge balconies and stunning fireplaces and in-room percolators to provide the true aroma of the coffee estate. Designed around the original plantation houses, the excellent restaurant serves a spit-roasted lunchtime grill and a sumptuous à la carte dinner. Facilities include a swimming pool. *Rooms normally cost US$130/250 sgl/dbl B&B, rising to US$210/350 in peak season (Feb, Jul and Aug) and dropping to US$100/200 in Apr and May.*

THE ARUSHA HOTEL

Symbolic of Arusha's growing significance in the 1920s was the opening of the New Arusha Hotel in lushly wooded grounds formerly occupied by the small town's only hostelry, the small boarding house operated by the Bloom family since the late 1890s. A 1929 government brochure eulogised the newly opened establishment as having 'hot and cold water in all bedrooms, modern sanitation, teak dancing floor, electric light and really excellent food, as well as golf, tennis, big game and bird shooting'. Less complimentary was the description included in Evelyn Waugh's amusingly acerbic travelogue *A Tourist in Africa* in 1960: it 'seeks to attract by the claim to be exactly midway between Cape Town and Cairo... I did not see any African or Indian customers. Dogs howled and scuffled under the window at night. Can I say anything pleasant about this hotel? Yes, it stands in a cool place in a well-kept garden and it stocks some potable South African wines in good conditions.' The New Arusha continued its slide, hosting the likes of John Wayne along the way, until finally it closed for overdue renovations a few years back, to re-open in 2004 as the Arusha Hotel, the only five-star establishment in the city centre.

Arusha Hotel (65 rooms) ⊺ 027 250 7777/8870; m 0744 250777; f 027 250 8889; e gm@newarusha.com; www.arushahotel.com. Giving Arusha Coffee Lodge a close run for its money is the newly renovated and re-opened Arusha Hotel (formerly the New Arusha), which – situated right opposite the Clock Tower – now offers the only 5-star accommodation in central Arusha. Situated in large wooded grounds running down towards the Themi River, this stately hotel has an Edwardian feel about the décor, befitting its status as the oldest hostelry in Arusha, and the spacious rooms all come with satellite TV, netting, in-room internet access, smoke detector, electronic safes and tea- and coffee-making facilities. Air-conditioned and non-smoking rooms are available. Facilities include 24-hour room service, a business centre, several curio shops, 24-hour satellite internet access, a heated swimming pool, 3 bars, 2 restaurants and an airport shuttle service. *Executive rooms US$140/160 sgl/dbl B&B; suites US$250–450.*

Upmarket (US$60–120)

Impala Hotel (150 rooms) ⊺ 027 250 7197/8448; f 027 250 8680/8220; e impala@cybernet.co.tz or impala@habari.co.tz; www.impalahotel.com. The recently expanded and renovated Impala Hotel, situated in Kijenge about 10 minutes' walk from the town centre, is justifiably rated by many tour operators as the best-value hotel in its range in the immediate vicinity of Arusha, and it's certainly one of the largest, busiest and most reliable. Facilities include 4 restaurants variously specialising in Indian, Italian, Chinese and continental cuisine (the Indian is among the best in town), an internet café, a forex bureau offering good rates, a swimming pool, a gift shop, an inexpensive shuttle service to Nairobi as well as to KIA, and an in-house safari operator. The rooms are comfortable and attractively decorated, and have satellite TV, hot showers and a fridge. The only criticism that could be levelled at the Impala is that it is decidedly lacking in character, but taken on its own terms this is recommended as a smooth-running and very reasonably priced hotel. *US$72/83/132 sgl/dbl/triple B&B; HB and FB rates additional US$10 pp per meal. Dbl executive rooms and suites available at a higher rate.*

Mount Meru Novotel (168 rooms) ⊺ 027 250 2711/2; f 027 250 8503/8221; e mountmeruhotel@cybernet.co.tz.; www.novotel.com. Government owned but

DAR ES SALAAM

Situated about 550km southeast of Moshi by road, Dar es Salaam – often referred to as plain 'Dar' – is Tanzania's capital in all but name. With a population estimated at two to three million, it is far and away the country's largest city and most important commercial centre, a lively bustling Indian Ocean port rivalled in regional maritime significance only by Mombasa in Kenya. Unfortunately, however, Dar es Salaam cannot claim to be a tourist centre of any great note. On the contrary, the increasing ease with which one can fly into KIA directly, or fly straight on to Zanzibar or the north after landing at Dar, means that a relatively small proportion of fly-in tourists ever set foot in the city itself.

Whether or not this is a good thing is a matter of opinion. Dar es Salaam is one of those cities that draws extreme reactions from travellers, a real 'love it or hate it' kind of place, and its many detractors would probably regard any Dar-free itinerary through Tanzania to be a highly desirable state of affairs. Personally, however, I enjoy Dar es Salaam more perhaps than any other major east African city, since it boasts all the hustle and bustle of somewhere such as Nairobi, yet has none of that city's underlying aggression or bland architectural modernity.

If nothing else, Dar is imbued with a distinctive sense of place, one derived from the cultural mix of its people and buildings, not to say a torpid coastal humidity that permeates every aspect of day-to-day life. Architecturally, the city boasts German, British, Asian and Arab influences, but it is fundamentally a Swahili city, and beneath the superficial air of hustle, a laid-back and friendly place. People are willing to pass away the time with idle chat and will readily help out strangers, yet tourists are rarely hassled, except in the vicinity of the New Africa Hotel, where a resident brigade of hissing money-changers froths into action every time a *mazungu* walks past.

If you decide to fly into Dar es Salaam, the international airport is situated 13km from the city centre, a 20-minute taxi ride that costs up to US$15 dependent on how hard you bargain. Long-haul buses out of Dar es Salaam almost all leave from the vast Ubungu Bus Station, situated out of town along the Morogoro road, which enforces a special trip out of town to book tickets a day ahead of departure – a taxi from the city centre to Ubungu will cost up to US$6, depending on how receptive the driver is to negotiation. A notable exception to the above is the excellent Scandinavia Express (℩ 022 218 4833/4 or 285 0847/9; m 0811 336625 or 0741 325474; f 022 285 0224; e scandinavia@raha.com), a relatively luxurious coach service whose vehicles leave from a private terminus at the junction of Nyerere and Msimbazi streets on the airport road. These services connect Dar es Salaam to Moshi and Arusha (thrice daily), as well as Nairobi (once daily), Mwanza (once daily) and various towns in the south.

If you need to overnight in Dar, there are plenty of hotels in and around the city to suit all budgets. A few recommendations, in descending order of price and quality, follow:

managed by the French Novotel chain, the Mount Meru Hotel was at one time the only truly international-standard option situated within walking distance of the town centre. Set in large landscaped gardens overlooking the golf course, it remains a reasonably attractive set-up, albeit with a rather bland feel and fuddy-duddy décor by comparison with its newer rivals. It's ideally suited to international business travellers due to its good facilities, which include digital satellite TV in all rooms, a large outdoor swimming pool, a gym, 2 restaurants and an efficient business centre. The large, comfortable rooms

Ras Kutani ☏ 022 213 4802; f 022 211 2794; e selous@twiga.com. Closer in spirit and feel to a bush retreat than a typical beach resort, Ras Kutani is a wonderful small lodge – 12 sleeping units only – situated on a wild and isolated stretch of coast some 35km south of Dar es Salaam. The *bandas*, constructed almost entirely with organic materials, are set in dense coastal woodland overlooking a small mangrove-lined lagoon and a wide sandy beach. Vervet and blue monkeys and prolific birdlife in the woodland are complemented by good snorkelling and fishing in the nearby reefs. Full board accommodation costs US$150–200 pp.

Sea Cliff Hotel ☏ 022 260 0380–7; f 022 260 0476; e information@hotelseacliff.com; www.hotelseacliff.com. Arguably the top hotel within Dar's greater city limits, the Sea Cliff boasts a fabulous seafront location on the Msasani Peninsula, only 15 minutes by taxi from the city centre. Air-conditioned rooms with en-suite showers and satellite TV. US$160–240.

New Africa Hotel Corner Azikiwe & Sokoine Drive. ☏ 022 211 7050/1; f 022 211 6731; e newafricahotel@raha.com. Re-opened in 1998 following total renovation, the New Africa is built on the site of the legendary Kaiserhof, the first hotel to open in Dar es Salaam, during the German era. The New Africa in its most recent incarnation is plush and thoroughly modern, charging US$162/192 for a sgl/dbl room.

Oyster Bay Hotel ☏ 022 260 0352/3/4; f 022 260 0347; e oysterbay-hotel@twiga.com. Set in rambling suburban grounds overlooking a popular bathing beach, this long-serving family-run hotel provides a refreshingly friendly and mildly quirky alternative to the bland internationalism that characterises most other hotels in its price range. It's very decent value at US$120/150 sgl/dbl. A shopping mall with a coffee shop, an internet café and several well-stocked shops is attached.

Protea Hotel Oyster Bay ☏ 022 266 6665; f 022 266 7760; e proteadar@africaonline.co.tz. Particularly recommended to business travellers spending a while in Dar es Salaam, this unique modern complex lies about 2km from the city centre on the road to the Msasani Peninsula. The spacious, air-conditioned units cost US$145–185, and the complex contains a swimming pool and restaurant.

Peacock Hotel ☏ 022 211 4071; f 022 211 7962; e mlangila@twiga.com or reservation@peacockhotel.co.tz. Arguably the best value in its range within the city centre, the Peacock Hotel on Bibi Titi Mohammed Street offers bland but comfortable self-contained rooms with AC, hot water, satellite TV and fridge at a very reasonable US$60/70 sgl/dbl. There is a good restaurant attached.

Palm Beach Hotel ☏ 022 212 2931; f 022 211 9272; e palmbeach@cctz.com. About 20 minutes' walk from the town centre along the Bagamoyo road, this rambling and rather atmospheric hotel is possessed of a time-warped colonial charm that elevates it way above most of the other options in the US$30–40 range.

Econo Lodge ☏ 022 211 6048/9; f 022 211 6053; e econolodge@raha.com; www.econolodge.co.tz. This smart new hotel has a convenient central location off Libya Street, and is outstandingly good value in the budget range. Self-contained rooms with fans cost US$13/18/22 sgl/dbl/triple, while air-conditioned dbls cost US$28.

with en-suite bathrooms and private balconies are now quite reasonably priced. *US$80/100/120 sgl/dbl/triple B&B or US$104/148/192 FB.*

New Safari Hotel (48 rooms) ☏ 027 250 3261/2; e newsafarihotel@habari.co.tz. Recently re-opened after protracted renovations, this long-serving hotel, once popular with the hunting fraternity, now seems more geared towards business travellers, with its convenient – though potentially noisy – central location a few minutes from the AICC and a number of government offices and restaurants. Facilities include a ground-floor internet café and a good restaurant. The large tiled en-suite rooms with digital satellite TV have a modern feel, and seem fair value. *US$70/90 sgl/dbl.*

Karama Lodge (22 rooms) ☎ 027 250 0359; m 0744 745 188; f 27 254 8299; e infro@karama-lodge.com; www.karama-lodge.com. Aptly named after the Swahili word for 'blessing', this fabulous eco-lodge, constructed by Tropical Trails, is remarkable for possessing a genuine bush atmosphere, despite being situated only 3km from central Arusha along the Old Moshi Road. Perched on the small but densely wooded Suye Hill, the lodge was recently extended to consist of 22 stilted wood-and-*makuti* units with Zanzibar-style beds draped in netting, en-suite shower and toilet, and private balcony facing Kilimanjaro. The *brachystegia* woodland in the lodge grounds and adjacent forest reserve harbours a wide range of birds (the localised brown-throated barbet prominent among them) as well as small nocturnal mammals such as bushbaby, genet and civet. The restaurant serves tasty snacks and meals, and offers views to Kilimanjaro and Meru on a clear day. Overall, it's highly recommended as an antidote to the bland city hotels that otherwise characterise Arusha in this price range. *US$79/107 sgl/dbl B&B or US$107/163 FB.*

Ilboru Safari Lodge (16 rooms) ☎ 0744 33796/270357; e ilboru-lodge@habari.co.tz or reservations@ilborusafarilodge.com; www. ilborusafarilodge.com. Situated in large, leafy grounds among the banana plantations that swathe the Mount Meru foothills some 2.5km north of the town centre, this highly regarded owner-managed lodge has been offering good-value accommodation for some years. It's a pleasant and peaceful retreat, centred on a large swimming pool, and the comfortable thatched bungalows are very reasonably priced. *US$59/70 sgl/dbl B&B or US$87/126 FB, with a discount of 10–20% available in low season.*

L'Oasis Lodge (26 rooms) ☎ 027 250 7089; m 0745 749945; f 027 250 7089; e s.broadbent@edi-africa.com; www.loasislodge.com. Set in large green grounds about 500m north of the Moshi Road, along a side road signposted opposite the Mount Meru Novotel, this pleasant lodge has recently undergone some major renovations and expansions, but it retains the rustic feel that has that made it popular. A variety of comfortable en-suite rooms are available, including some attractive stilted bungalows with in-room internet access (10% extra), while other facilities include 2 restaurants and a large bar alongside the swimming pool. *US$65/75/94 sgl/dbl/triple B&B or US$89/123/166 FB – ask for the low-season discount of 20% for direct bookings.*

Hotel Equator (40 rooms) ☎ 027 250 8409/3727/3127; e reservations@newarusha.com. This recently refurbished old hotel on Boma Road, though it falls under the same management as the nearby Arusha Hotel, isn't in quite the same class as its rejuvenated sibling. The rooms are very spacious and well kept, and come with fridge and TV, but – as with so many former government hotels – the fixtures are all very outmoded and the atmosphere is somewhat bland and institutional. Still, it's not bad value, especially if you are looking for a central location. *US$60/70 sgl/dbl B&B.*

Arusha Crown Hotel (38 rooms) ☎ 027 250 8523–4. f 027 254 4162; e info@arushacrownhotel.com; www.arushacrownhotel.com. This gleaming new multi-storey hotel looks decidedly misplaced in the seedy backroads between the bus station and football stadium, a location that might well feel mildly intimidating to the more timid traveller. If you can get past that, it's not a bad option, albeit with zero ambience, and the functional and airy en-suite rooms with tiled floor, digital satellite TV and modern décor seem fair value. The cafeteria-style restaurant on the ground floor has meals for around Tsh5,000. *US$60/65/70 sgl/dbl/twin.*

Moderate (US$30–60)

The Outpost (23 rooms) ☎ 027 250 8405; e info@outposttanzania.com; www.outposttanzania.com. Probably the pick in this range is the welcoming and homely Australian-owned Outpost, which is set in a suburban garden at 37A Serengeti Street and has proved to be consistently popular with travellers seeking the combination of affordability and comfort. Cheap and tasty lunches and dinners are available. To get here from the Clock Tower, head out in the direction of the Impala Hotel for about 1km, then follow a signposted right turn into Serengeti Road, passing the Roy Safaris office, and you'll reach it after another 300m or so. *Bed in a dorm US$21 B&B; self-contained rooms with TV US$36/49 sgl/dbl.*

Hotel Le Jacaranda (9 rooms) ☏ 027 254 4624/4945; e jacaranda@tz2000.com. Situated in the garden suburbs immediately east of the town centre, not far from the Outpost, this converted colonial-era homestead doesn't lack for character, and it is set in prettily overgrown grounds with a mini-golf course and shady restaurant/bar area. The large en-suite rooms all have a 4-poster bed with netting, and seem very acceptable value. *US$45/50/65 dbl/twin/triple.*

Arusha Naaz Hotel (21 rooms) ☏ 027 250 2087/8893; e arushanaaz@yahoo.com. Situated on Sokoine Road close to the Clock Tower, this clean, convenient and secure hotel, once a favourite with budget travellers, now slots more into the moderate category following extensive renovations. The en-suite rooms with net, fan, hot water and digital satellite TV are definitely on the cramped side, but they are still pretty good value. There is a good, inexpensive Indian restaurant on the ground floor and an internet café will open in 2006. *US$30/45 sgl/dbl occupancy.*

Hotel Seventy Seven (aka Hotel Saba Saba – 120 rooms) ☏ 027 254 8052; f 027 254 8407; e hotel77@bol.co.uk; www.seventysevenhotel.netfirms.com. It used to bill itself as 'the largest tourist village in east Africa', it now claims to be the 'Geneva of Africa', and yet one could be forgiven for thinking that the true architectural inspiration for the cheerless concrete quadrangles that comprise the 'new look' (just like the 'old look') Hotel Seventy Seven lay somewhere in Soviet-era Siberia. Hype aside, the rooms are quite comfortable and sensibly priced, and there's a decent garden bar with live 'African beats' music nightly except Mondays but still it is difficult to imagine a more aesthetically confrontational place to start a Tanzanian safari. *US$25/40 sgl/dbl.*

Golden Rose Hotel (40 rooms) ☏ 027 250 7959/8862; m 0741 510696; e info@goldenrosehotel.net; www.goldenrosehotel.net. This well-known landmark on the western side of town, the most central departure point for the Riverside Shuttle to Nairobi, used to be regarded as one of the top hotels in Arusha. Today, however, the small en-suite rooms with TV, fan, net and balcony feel rather timeworn and gloomy, and are indifferent value. *US$36/48 sgl/dbl.*

Hotel AM88 (41 rooms) ☏ 027 250 1773. This comfortable high-rise block on the west side of town is decent vale for those with residence permits, but the 300% mark-up makes it outstandingly poor value for non-residents. *US$40/60.*

Sinka Court Hotel (29 rooms) ☏ 027 250 4961. The new multi-storey hotel in the backroads between the market and the Naura River has cramped but clean en-suite rooms with digital satellite TV. *US$30/30 sgl/dbl; ask nicely and they might let you pay the resident rate (about US$5 cheaper).*

Pallson's Hotel (28 rooms) ☏/f 0744 746292/755850. This long-serving multi-storey hotel has a central location, a short walk south of the bus station on the corner of Market and Sokoine roads. The rather timeworn self-contained rooms, with satellite TV, fan and hot shower, are adequate value. *US$25/30/40 sgl/dbl/triple B&B.*

Budget (US$10–30)

Backpackers' Paradise (12 rooms) ☏ 027 250 7089; m 0745 749945; f 027 250 7089; e s.broadbent@edi-africa.com; www.loasislodge.com. Situated opposite L'Oasis Lodge and under the same management, this offers newcomers to east Africa a comfortable and reasonably affordable suburban retreat with access to the facilities and restaurant at the main lodge. The small tree house-like rooms aren't exactly a bargain, but it's a good, safe choice all the same. *US$15 pp inclusive of a full breakfast.*

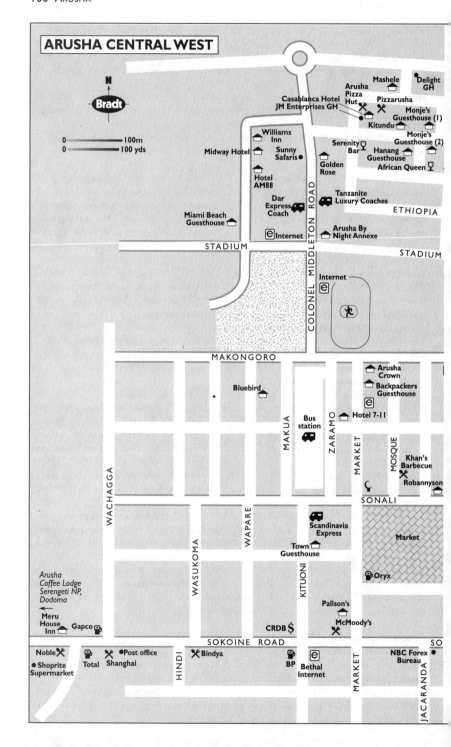

ARUSHA CENTRAL WEST

N

Bradt

0 _____ 100m
0 _____ 100 yds

Mashele
Delight GH
Arusha Pizza Hut
Pizzarusha
Casablanca Hotel
JM Enterprises GH
Monje's Guesthouse (1)
Kitundu
Monje's Guesthouse (2)
Serenity Bar
Hanang Guesthouse
African Queen
Williams Inn
Midway Hotel
Sunny Safaris
Golden Rose
Hotel AM88
Tanzanite Luxury Coaches
ETHIOPIA
Dar Express Coach
COLONEL MIDDLETON ROAD
Miami Beach Guesthouse
Internet
Arusha By Night Annexe
STADIUM
STADIUM
Internet

MAKONGORO

Bluebird
Arusha Crown
Backpackers Guesthouse
Hotel 7-11
MAKUA
Bus station
ZARAMO
MARKET
MOSQUE
Khan's Barbecue
Robannyson
SONALI

WACHAGGA
WAPARE
Scandinavia Express
Town Guesthouse
KITUONI
Market
Oryx

Arusha Coffee Lodge
Serengeti NP, Dodoma
Meru House Inn
Gapco
WASUKOMA
Palison's
McMoody's
CRDB

SOKOINE ROAD

Noble
Shoprite Supermarket
Total
Shanghai
Post office
HINDI
Bindya
BP
Bethal Internet
MARKET
NBC Forex Bureau
JACARANDA
SO

Hotel Fort Des Moines (20 rooms) ✆ 027 250 0277; f 254 8523; e bimel@cybernet.co.tz; www.bimel.co.tz. Pretentious name aside, this clean and reasonably smart new hotel near the market and bus station seems decent enough value. *US$22/28 sgl/dbl.*

Seven Eleven Hotel (16 rooms) ✆ 027 250 1261. Handily located right opposite the main bus station, this small, modestly priced hotel charges US$20 for a comfortable self-contained room with hot shower, irrespective of whether it's sgl or dbl occupancy.

Midway Hotel (32 rooms) ✆ 027 250 2790. Part of a cluster of hotels situated along Corner Road northwest of the stadium, this charges US$15/17 for a clean but spartan sgl/dbl room with en-suite hot shower and TV.

Shoestring and camping

Maasai Camp ✆ 027 250 0359; m 0744 745 188; f 27 254 8299; e info@tropicaltrails.com; www.tropicaltrails.com. Situated about 2km out of town along the Old Moshi Road, Maasai Camp is one of the best campsites in Tanzania, and it also offers simpler accommodation in huts. Facilities include an ablution block with hot water, a pool table, volleyball and a lively 24-hour bar, and an excellent safari company called Tropical Trails is on site. The restaurant is well known for its pizzas, which cost around Tsh4,000. If you're without transport, you can get a taxi here for around Tsh2,000. *Camping US$3 pp, rooms US$7 pp.*

Williams Inn Guesthouse (29 rooms) ✆ 027 250 5378. Conveniently located on Corner Road next to the Midway Hotel, this is one of the best shoestring options in Arusha, charging US$8/10 B&B for a clean en-suite sgl/dbl in which 'women of immoral turpitude are strictly not allowed'!

Kilimanjaro Villa ✆ 027 250 8109. A long-standing backpacker standby situated close to the market and bus station, the Kilimanjaro Villa is nothing special, but it's friendly, clean and reasonably priced. *US$5/7 sgl/dbl using common showers.*

Monje's Guesthouse ✆ 027 250 3060. Arguably the pick of a cluster of bottom-of-the-range guesthouses in the backroads north of the stadium, this quiet, family-run affair actually consists of 3 guesthouses split by a road. All 3 places have clean rooms, friendly staff, hot showers and a vigorously enforced anti-flycatcher policy! *Around Tsh4,000/6,000 sgl/dbl.*

Mashele Guesthouse Worth listing only because a great many travellers are dragged here by a flycatcher, for the sole reason that it's one of the few places that will allow the flycatcher to hang around. And if having to make friends with half the flycatchers in Arusha isn't reason enough to put you off, then reports of theft from the rooms and occasional bar-room brawls probably should be.

Arusha Vision Campsite ✆ 0744 040810/344538. Centrally located alongside the Themi River next to the Equator Hotel, this is a basic but friendly campsite. *US$2 pp to camp with your own tent.*

WHERE TO EAT

Plenty of good restaurants are dotted around Arusha, with many international cuisines represented and most budgets catered for by a number of places. The following is an alphabetical selection of some long-standing favourites and interesting recent additions, but new places open and close frequently, so don't be afraid to try restaurants that aren't listed.

Arusha Naaz Hotel The ground-floor restaurant at this popular central hotel offers a great all-you-can-eat Indian buffet lunch at Tsh4,000.

Café Bamboo Restaurant This homely restaurant on Boma Road serves decent filter coffee, good fruit juices, as well as a huge range of sandwiches, pancakes and other snacks. The home-cooked lunch of the day is a real bargain for around Tsh2,000. It's justifiably packed at lunchtime, but closes up completely in the evenings.

Green Hut House of Burgers Situated on Sokoine Road alongside the Metropole Cinema, the Green Hut serves excellent, inexpensive burgers and other greasy fast food staples and light meals.

Ice Cream Parlour Situated on Sokoine Road, close to Neha Snacks, this bright parlour serves cheap sundaes and cones, as well as other gooey snacks.

Impala Hotel The Indian restaurant in this large hotel is justifiably rated as one of the best in Arusha – and there are 3 other specialist restaurants to choose from if Indian isn't your thing.

Jambo Coffee House & Makuti Garden The coffee house serves arguably the best coffee in town (not that's there is much competition) as well as good cooked breakfasts and light snacks. The adjacent Makuti Garden, set in a green courtyard, is one of the best places in the town centre for evening meals – curries and grills in the Tsh2,500–5,000 range.

Khan's Barbecue Situated in Mosque Street to the north of the market, this singular and popular place has become something of an Arusha institution, functioning as a spare motor parts shop by day and a street barbecue in the evening. It serves fabulous kebabs of beef, chicken and lamb, with a huge selection of salads, naan bread and the like. It's not particularly cheap given its unromantic setting, but the food is great and you can pick and choose what you like. No alcohol is allowed.

Le Barbie Restaurant Situated on the Moshi Road close to the Mount Meru Novotel, this vast and very pleasant *makuti* construction, affiliated to L'Oasis Hotel, serves a good variety of grills and seafood dishes, mostly in the Tsh4,000–5,000 range.

Maasai Camp The bar here has long been a popular evening hangout with expatriates, for the friendly atmosphere and music as much as the pizzas and Mexican dishes.

McMoody's This McDonald's clone on Sokoine Street serves reasonable hamburgers and cheeseburgers for around Tsh2,000 – the plastic décor, like the food, is designed to make fast food junkies feel at home.

Mezzaluna Restaurant Situated close to the Impala Hotel, the Mezzaluna, though closed for renovations in mid-2005, is generally regarded to serve the best Italian food in Arusha. Pizzas are something of a speciality, and they cost around Tsh4,000–5,000. There is an indoor dining room, but weather permitting it's much more pleasant to eat in the spacious thatched garden area.

Milk & Honey Restaurant This new place on Sokoine Road seems to be very popular with locals, serving a variety of Tanzanian, Indian and Western dishes from Tsh1,500 to Tsh4,000.

Noble Restaurant Situated at the west end of Sokoine Road close to the Shoprite supermarket, this cosy Indian restaurant serves a wide variety of Indian and Chinese dishes in the Tsh4,000–5,000 price range, as well as full 3-course meals for Tsh7,000 and a huge selection of fruit juices for around Tsh1,000 each.

Patisserie Centrally located, on Sokoine Road close to the Clock Tower, this popular backpackers' and volunteers' hangout is pretty much unique in Tanzania – a huge range of freshly baked loaves, rolls and pastries, great light meals, fruit juice and filter coffee. The coffee is frequently disappointing, but everything else is excellent. Great for a light (and inexpensive) breakfast or lunchtime snack! Closed in the evenings. Good internet café attached.

Pizzarusha Restaurant Most backpackers who stay in the guesthouses north of the stadium will find themselves eating at this excellent budget eatery opposite the Mashele Guesthouse. Huge tasty meals, ranging from pizzas to curries to steaks, are good value at around Tsh2,500. The atmosphere is great, too – the building is constructed from traditional materials, and the candle-lit tables look into the kitchen, so you can be sure your food is freshly prepared. An internet café is attached. Easily the best-value restaurant in Arusha!

Shamiara Restaurant This excellent Indian eatery on the second floor of Pallson's Hotel has notoriously slow service, but the food is worth the wait – huge and very tasty portions for around Tsh5,000.

Sidewalk Bar This rather cramped new restaurant at the northern end of India Road specialises in filled pitta bread, and also serves a variety of sandwiches, burgers and fruit juices. For vegetarians, the new lunchtime salad buffet on Tuesdays and Thursdays should be a real draw.

Spices & Herbs Restaurant The oldest Ethiopian restaurant in Arusha – actually owned by an Eritrean – lies 1km out of town near the Impala Hotel. If you're already a fan of sub-Saharan Africa's most distinctive cuisine (a spicy meat or vegetarian stew called *kai wat* served with a flat round sour bread called *injera*) you won't need me to persuade you to give this place a try. Vegetarian dishes cost around Tsh2,500 and meat dishes around Tsh4,000. There is sometimes live music.

Steers Situated at the southern end of India Road, this franchise of the popular South African fast food chain serves decent burgers, steak rolls and fried chicken for around Tsh2,000–4,000.

Stiggy's Thai Restaurant Situated on the Old Moshi Road less than 500m past the Impala Hotel, this enjoyably unpretentious restaurant is owned and managed by an Australian–Thai couple whose relaxed informality is matched by their golden touch behind the stove. The Thai and continental cuisine isn't cheap (around Tsh7,000 or more for a main course), but the quality and presentation are up to international standards. Even if you don't want to eat here, the bar has a pool table and is a pleasant place to hang out and meet people. The area is one you'd only want to visit by night in a taxi.

Via Via Restaurant Belgian-owned garden restaurant-cum-bar tucked away behind the Old Boma on the north end of Boma Road. Despite the central location, it has a relaxing

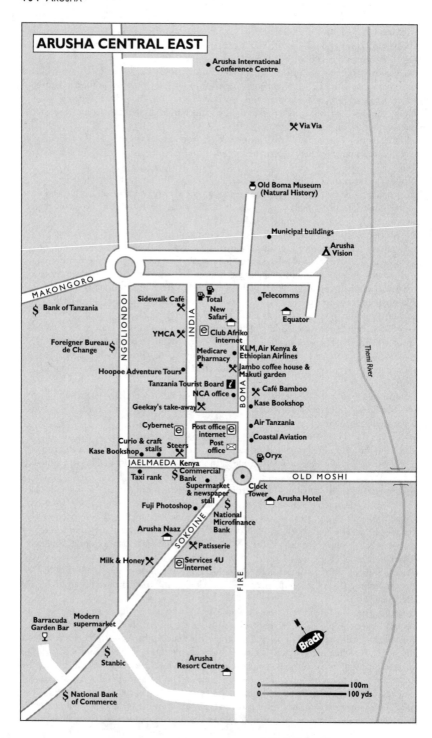

ARUSHA'S MUSEUMS

Two museums are to be found in central Arusha, neither of which could be described as wholly inspirational. The Natural History Museum, housed in the old German Boma on the north end of Boma Road, might more accurately be renamed the Archaeological or Palaeontological Museum. The limited displays – you can walk around the museum in one minute – include a selection of animal and hominid fossils unearthed at Olduvai and Laetoli in the Ngorongoro Conservation Area, as well as life-size models of *Australopithecus* hunter-gatherers at play. Although the museum recently closed for quite some time for renovations, evidence of any such activity was thin on the ground in 2001 when we visited. The museum is open from 09.00 to 17.00 daily and a nominal entrance fee is charged.

The Arusha Declaration Museum, by contrast, is dedicated primarily to Tanzania in the 20th century, with some interesting displays on the colonial period and particular focus on the post-independence Nyerere era. It also contains a few decent ethnographic displays. Diverting rather than essential sightseeing, this museum is located on the northwest side of the Uhuru Monument Circle. Opening hours are 08.30 to 17.30 and entrance costs Tsh1,000.

suburban atmosphere, and probably the best (or at least the most eclectic) selection of music in Arusha. The food's good too – filled baguettes at Tsh1,500 and meals at Tsh2,500. Via Via hosts regular film evenings and cultural events involving artistes from all of Africa, details of which can be obtained if you pop in at lunchtime.

BARS AND NIGHTSPOTS

There has been a notable increase in nightspots around Arusha in recent years. The liveliest at the time of writing is the recently relocated **Colobus Club**, which lies on the Old Moshi Road about 500m past the Impala Hotel, and doubles as disco, snack bar, boozer and pool hall – it keeps going all night over weekends. Opposite the Colobus Club, the more sedate **Stiggy's Thai Restaurant** is a popular drinking spot with expatriates.

There are several decent bars in the same area as the cluster of guesthouses behind the Golden Rose Hotel. The best place to drink in this part of town is **Soweto Gardens**, a relaxed but atmospheric garden bar that normally hosts live bands over the weekends. Other good spots for live Tanzanian music include the outdoor bar at the **Hotel Seventy Seven** (every night except Mondays) and **Rick's Bar** on the Moshi Road.

PRACTICALITIES
Airlines

The offices of the international airlines are mostly dotted along Boma Road in the old town centre. The combined office of Kenya Airways and KLM (✆ *027 254 8062*) is situated alongside the New Safari Hotel, as is that of Ethiopian Airlines (✆ *027 250 6167*), while the combined office of Air Tanzania and South African Airways is closer to the Clock Tower (✆ *027 250 3201*). Domestic carriers include Coastal Travels (*office on Boma Road next to Air Tanzania,* ✆ *027 250 0087*), Precision Air (*office in the Ngorongoro Wing of the AICC,* ✆ *027 250 6903*) and Air Excel (✆ *027 2548429*).

Bookshops

The best bookshop by far is the Bookmark, tucked away off Sokoine Road opposite the Twin Peaks Casino, which stocks a good selection of novels, maps, Africa interest books and travel guides. Also worth trying are the two branches of Kase Book Shop, one on Boma Road next to Café Bamboo and the other on Jael Marda Road next to Steers. A few vendors usually hang around the Clock Tower selling the maps and national park booklets at highly inflated prices, and most of the upmarket hotels also sell a limited selection of reading matter in their curio shops. To buy or exchange second-hand novels, there are a couple of stalls dotted around town, the best of which is the one in the alley connecting Boma and India roads.

TINGATINGA PAINTINGS

The brightly coloured paintings of fabulous creatures you might notice at craft stalls in Arusha and elsewhere in the region are Tingatinga paintings, a school of painting that is unique to Tanzania and named after its founder Edward Tingatinga. The style arose in Dar es Salaam in the early 1960s, when Tingatinga fused the vibrant and popular work of Congolese immigrants with art traditions indigenous to his Makua homeland in the Mozambique border area (a region well known to aficionados of African art as the home of Makonde carving). When Tingatinga died in 1972, the accidental victim of a police shoot-out, his commercial success had already spawned a host of imitators, and shortly after that a formal Tingatinga art co-operative was formed with government backing.

In the early days, Tingatinga and his followers produced fairly simple paintings featuring a large, bold and often rather surreal two-dimensional image of one or other African creature on a monotone background. But as the paintings took off commercially, a greater variety of colours came into play, and a trend developed towards the more complex canvases you see today. Modern Tingatinga paintings typically depict a menagerie of stylised and imaginary birds, fish and mammals against a backdrop of a natural feature such as Kilimanjaro or an abstract panel of dots and whorls. An offshoot style, reputedly initiated by Tingatinga himself, can be seen in the larger, even more detailed canvases that depict a sequence of village or city scenes so busy you could look at them for an hour and still see something fresh.

Tingatinga painters have no pretensions to producing high art. On the contrary, the style has been commercially driven since its inception: even the largest canvases are produced over a matter of days and most painters work limited variations around favourite subjects. It would be missing the point altogether to talk of Tingatinga as traditional African art. With its bold, bright images – tending towards the anthropomorphic, often subtly humorous, always accessible and evocative – Tingatinga might more appropriately be tagged Africa's answer to pop art.

Labels aside, souvenir hunters will find Tingatinga paintings to be a lively, original and surprisingly affordable alternative to the identikit wooden animal carvings that are sold throughout east Africa (and, one suspects, left to gather dust in cupboards all over Europe). Take home a Tingatinga panel, and you'll have a quirky but enduring memento of your African trip, something to hang on your wall and derive pleasure from for years to come.

Craft and curio shops

Arusha is one of the best places in east Africa to buy Makonde carvings, Tingatinga paintings, batiks, Maasai jewellery and other souvenirs. The curio shops are far cheaper than those in Dar es Salaam and their quality and variety are excellent. Most of the curio shops are clustered between the Clock Tower and India Road, though be warned that the outdoor stalls can be full of hassle. One reader has warmly recommended the Craft Shop on Goliondoi Road, which has great items at very reasonable prices, will arrange shipment home if required, and you can look around at leisure without any harassment. The Cultural Heritage Centre, about 3km out of town on the Serengeti road, stocks one of the best selections of curios you'll come across anywhere in Tanzania – it can be visited on the way back from a safari, or as a short taxi trip from Arusha.

Foreign exchange

Various private and bank-related bureaux de change are dotted all around Arusha, and it is worth shopping around to find the best rate for US dollars cash. Many bureaux de change won't accept less widely used international currencies or travellers' cheques, but the National Bank of Commerce on Sokoine Road will, as will the bureau de change at the Impala Hotel. Whatever else you do, don't change money on the streets of Arusha, as you are sure to be ripped off. If you are desperate for local currency outside banking hours, Foreigners Bureau de Change on Goliondoi Road is open seven days a week from 07.00 to 18.30, and later than that you will probably have to ask a safari company or hotel to help you out with a small transaction. Alternatively, the ATMs at the Standard Chartered Bank on Goliondoi Road and the Barclays Bank on Serengeti Road offer a 24-hour withdrawal service of up to around US$200 daily against an international Visa card. American Express is represented by Rickshaw Travels on Sokoine Road near McMoody's.

Internet and email

There are numerous internet cafés dotted all over Arusha, charging a fairly uniform and inexpensive rate that works out at around US$1 per hour's browsing. One of the best – not least because so few people seem to know about it or use it, so access is generally very fast – is the Telecom-run internet café on the first floor of the Post Office building on Boma Road. Also good are the Kremola Internet Café on India Road, the Cybernet Centre on India Road and the internet café in the Patisserie on Sokoine Road. If you're staying in the market or stadium area, the Silver Touch Internet Café on Makongoro Road can be recommended.

Medical

The AICC Hospital on the Old Moshi Road (℡ 027 250 2329) is generally regarded to be the best in Arusha, while the nearby Trinity Clinic on Engira Road (℡ 027 254 4392) can be recommended for malaria and other tests. For further information, consult your hotel reception or safari company.

Newspapers

A selection of local newspapers is available on the day of publication, as is the Kenya Nation, which is generally stronger on international news. You won't need to look for these newspapers, because the vendors who sell them will find you quickly enough. The excellent East African, a weekly newspaper, is available at several newspaper kiosks. The American weeklies Time and Newsweek are widely available in Arusha.

MAKONDE CARVINGS

The Makonde of the Tanzania–Mozambique border area are widely regarded to be the finest traditional sculptors in east Africa, and according to oral tradition the males of this matrilineal society have been practising this craft to woo their women for at least 300 years. Legend has it that this is when the first person on earth, not yet male or female, living alone in the foothills of the Makonde Plateau, carved a piece of wood into the shape of a human figure. The carver left his creation outside his home before he retired for the night, and awoke to find it had been transformed into a living woman. Twice the woman conceived, but both times the child died after three days. Each time, the pair moved higher onto the plateau, believing this would bring them luck. The third child lived, and became the first true Makonde. The mother is regarded to be the spiritual ancestor of all the Makonde, and the legend is sometimes said to be a parable for the difficulty of creation and the necessity to discard unsatisfactory carvings.

In their purest form, the intricate, stylised carvings of the Makonde relate to this ancestral cult of womanhood, and are carried only by men, as a good-luck charm. Traditional carvings almost always depict a female figure, sometimes surrounded by children, and the style was practically unknown outside of Tanzania until a carving workshop was established at Mwenge in suburban Dar es Salaam during the 1950s. Subsequently, like any dynamic art form, Makonde sculpture has been responsive to external influences and subject to changes in fashion, with new styles of carvings becoming increasingly abstract and incorporating wider moral and social themes.

The most rustic of the new styles is the Binadamu sculpture, which depicts traditional scenes such as old men smoking pipes or women fetching water in

Post and telephone

The main post office is on Boma Road facing the Clock Tower. The telecommunications centre further along Boma Road is a good place to make international phone calls and faxes.

Supermarkets

Far and away the best is the new Shoprite on the west end of Sokoine Road. This warehouse-sized representative of a major South African supermarket chain stocks a huge range of imported and local goods (including South African wines at a third the price the hotels charge) and is an excellent place to stock up with whatever goodies you need before you head out on safari.

Swimming

The swimming pools at the Mount Meru Novotel, Ilboru Lodge and Impala Hotel are open to non-residents for a daily fee of Tsh2,000.

Taxis

There are plenty of taxis in Arusha. Good places to pick them up include the market and bus station, the filling station on the junction of Goliondoi Road and the Old Moshi Road, and the open area at the north end of Boma and India roads. A taxi ride within the town centre should cost roughly US$2, though tourists are normally asked a slightly higher price. A taxi ride to somewhere outside the town centre will cost more.

a relatively naturalistic manner. Altogether more eerie and evocative is the Shetani style, in which grotesquely stylised human forms, sometimes with animal-like features, represent the impish and sometimes evil spirits for which the style is named. Many Makonde and other east Africans leave offerings for Shetani sculptures, believing them to be possessed by ancestral spirits. Most elaborate of all are the naturalistic Ujamaa sculptures, which depict many interlocking figures and relate to the collective social policy of Ujamaa fostered by the late President Nyerere. Also known as People Poles or Trees of Life, these statues sometimes incorporate several generations of the carver's family, rising in circular tiers to be up to 2m high. A newer style called Mawingu – the Swahili word for clouds – combines human figures with abstract shapes to represent intellectual or philosophical themes. Today, the finest examples of the genre fetch prices in excess of US$5,000 from international collectors

The Makonde traditionally shape their creations exclusively from *Dalbergia Melanoxylon*, a hardwood tree known locally as *mpingo* and in English as African Blackwood or (misleadingly) African Ebony. The carver – always male – will first saw a block of wood to the required size, then create a rough outline by hacking away excess wood with an instrument called an adze. The carving is all done freehand, with hammers, chisels and rasps used to carve the fine detail, before the final sculpture is sanded and brushed for smoothness. A large Ujamaa sculpture can take several months to complete, with some of the carving – appropriately – being undertaken communally. Traditionally, the craft was more or less hereditary, with sons being apprenticed by their fathers from a young age, and different families tending to work specific subjects related to their own traditions.

Tourist information

The **Tanzania Tourist Board** (TTB) office on Boma Road is refreshingly helpful and well informed. It stocks a useful colour road map of Tanzania as well as a great street plan of Arusha, both given free of charge to tourists, though this doesn't stop the book vendors out on the street from trying to sell the same maps at a very silly price. The TTB has been actively involved in the development of cultural tourism programmes in Ng'iresi, Mulala, Mkuru, Longido, Mto wa Mbu, Usambara, North Pare and South Pare, as well as several projects further afield. The Arusha office stocks informative pamphlets about these programmes, and can help out with information on prices and access. If you want to check out a safari company, the TTB office keeps a regularly updated list of all registered safari and trekking companies, as well as those that are blacklisted.

The head office of **Tanzania National Parks** (TANAPA) recently moved to the new Mwalimu J K Nyerere Conservation Centre about 3km out of town along the Serengeti road, roughly opposite the Cultural Heritage Centre. Contact details are PO Box 3134, Arusha; ＼027 250 1930/4; f 027 250 8216; e tanapa@habari.co.tz.

The **Ngorongoro Conservation Authority** has recently opened an information office on Boma Road close to the Tourist Board office. In addition to some worthwhile displays on the conservation area, it sells a good range of books and booklets about the northern circuit.

The **Immigration Office** on Simeon Road can normally extend visas on the spot.

SAFARI OPERATORS

The list below is by no means definitive, but it provides a good cross-section of the sort of services that are on offer, and except where otherwise noted, it sticks to companies that have maintained high standards over several years. There are, of course, many other good operators in Arusha, but with so many fly-by-night companies around, I prefer to stick to a few select companies in which I have total confidence. This policy may be unfair to other good companies, but my first responsibility is to readers, and it is vindicated by the simple fact that I've only ever received one letter of complaint from a reader who used one of the safari operators recommended in *Tanzania: The Bradt Travel Guide*. The companies listed below generally specialise in safaris on the northern circuit, but most can also set up Kilimanjaro and Meru climbs, fly-in safaris on the southern safari circuit, and excursions to Zanzibar.

Bushbuck Safaris ↘ 027 250 7779/254 4186/254 8924; f 027 254 8293/2954; e bushbuck@yako.habari.co.tz; www.bushbuckltd.com. This reliable company specialises almost exclusively in lodge safaris and was selected for Hilary Clinton's Tanzanian safari a few years ago. Prices and service are relatively upmarket, but not extortionate. It has a large fleet of new and competently maintained 4x4 vehicles, and employs articulate drivers and guides.
CCAfrica ↘ 027 254 8549/8038 or (South Africa) 11 809 4447; e res@ccafrica.co.tz or reservations@ccafrica.com; www.ccafrica.com. This South African organisation, lauded throughout southern Africa for its superlative lodges and commitment to genuine eco-tourism, owns excellent upmarket lodges and tented camps in Ngorongoro, Serengeti and Lake Manyara, as well as on Zanzibar, and it arranges fly-in, drive-in (or mixed) safaris throughout northern Tanzania. It makes no bones about its commitment to high cost, low impact tourism, and its Tanzanian properties are notable for their fine attention to detail, informal and personalised service, well-trained guides and rangers, and general air of exclusivity.
Great African Safaris ↘ 027 254 8163; m 0744 493606, f 0 27 254 4563; e inquiries@greatafricansafaris.com; www.greatafricansafaris.com. This new Tanzanian-run company offers the usual midrange safari options as well as Kili climbs using all routes, and an exciting selection of cultural tourism itineraries to Maasailand, the Usambara Mountains and Marangu.
Hoopoe Adventure Tours ↘ 027 250 7011 or (UK) 01923 255462; f 027 254 8226 or (UK) 1923 255452; e hoopoeUK@aol.com or hoopoesafari@africaonline.co.tz; www.hoopoe.com. One of the most highly regarded safari companies in Arusha, Hoopoe specialises in personalised luxury camping and lodge safaris. It owns tented camps outside of Lake Manyara and Tarangire national parks, as well as a superb private camp in a Maasai concession at Loliondo (to the east of the Serengeti) and another in West Kilimanjaro. Following a recent merger with Tropical Tours, Hoopoe is also one of the best companies to contact with regard to trekking and walking safaris in Natron, the Ngorongoro Highlands, and the game-rich Maasai Plains to the east of the Serengeti. It was recently voted the Best Eco Tourism Operator in the World by the magazine *Condé Nast Traveller*.
Leopard Tours ↘ 027 250 3603/8441-3; f 027 250 8219; e leopard@yako.habari.co.tz; www.leopard-tours.com. One of the largest operators out of Arusha, Leopard Tours specialises in midrange safaris concentrating on the larger lodges and more established game-viewing areas, and offers a highly reliable service to those who want to stick firmly to the beaten track.
Nature Discovery ↘ 027 254 4063/8406; m 0744 400003; e info@naturediscovery.com; www.naturediscovery.com. This eco-friendly operator is widely praised for its high-quality, top-end Kilimanjaro climbs, and it also arranges standard northern circuit safaris as well as trekking expeditions in the Ngorongoro Highlands and elsewhere.

Oreteti Cultural Discovery ℩ +255 (0)745 744 992; e info@oreteti.com;
www.oreteti.com This small, Arusha-based, family company is run by an English woman
and her Maasai husband. They offer personalised cultural and educational programmes,
combining academic lectures and seminars in anthropology with a range of walking tours,
safaris or volunteer work camps. Other activities on offer include visits to Maasai and
Chagga villages, short courses in Maasai beadwork, drumming, dance, cookery and Swahili
hip-hop. 10% of the profit is donated to community-based organisations.
Roy Safaris ℩ 027 250 8010/2115; f 027 254 8892; e roysafaris@intafrica.com;
www.roysafaris.com. Founded in the late 1980s, this dynamic and efficient company has
established itself as a leading operator when it comes to high quality but reasonably priced
budget camping safaris. Vehicles are always in excellent condition and the drivers are
usually competent and knowledgeable. It also offers reasonably priced semi-luxury camping
safaris and lodge safaris.
Safari Makers ℩ 0744 300817/318520; e safarimakers@habari.co.tz;
www.safarimakers.com. Owned and managed by a dynamic hands-on American–
Tanzanian couple, Safari Makers runs competitively priced camping and lodge safaris, and
is one of the few companies in Arusha committed to promoting the various cultural
programmes in communities outside Arusha – a recommended first contact at the budget
to midrange level, and notable for its flexible and responsive management.
Swala Safaris ℩ 057 270 6424; m 0744 300806; f 027 270 8424; e sengo@habari.co.tz or
swala@habari.co.tz. This flexible company provides the standard safari options but also
organises a number of hikes in northern Tanzania and is a good contact for any itinerary
incorporating Lake Natron. Special hiking packages include a 3-day trip to Ol Doinyo
Lengai and Natron, 3 days at Empakaai Crater, a 4-day Rift Valley hike, and a 6-day hike
through the Ngorongoro Highlands to Empakaai.
Sunny Safaris ℩ 027 250 7145; f 027 250 8035; e info@sunnysafaris.com or
sunny@arusha.com; www.sunnysafaris.com. This established company has long offered
the cheapest reliable camping safaris in Arusha, though rates vary depending on season and
group size. Their cheapest safaris won't involve camping in national parks, and you might
find your driver inflexible about doing any excursion that puts extra kilometres on the
clock, but otherwise you will get a thoroughly reliable service, with good vehicles and
drivers. They also organise more upmarket camping safaris and lodge-based safaris at
reasonable rates. The office is opposite the Golden Rose Hotel.
Tanzania Adventure ℩ 0748 448813; e info@tanzania-adventure.com; www.tanzania-
adventure.com. Dynamic new joint German–Tanzania company offering a wide selection
of safaris, including an extensive walking programme in the Ngorongoro Highlands and
Serengeti border areas. Especially recommended to German-speakers.
Thomson Safaris ℩/f 027 250 8551 or (USA) 617 923 0246 or 800 235 0289;
e info@thomsonsafaris.com. Catering primarily to the US market, this company offers
good lodge-based safaris and, based on the number of their vehicles we saw while we were
last on safari, it must be one of the most popular in Arusha – a good contact for Americans
who plan on visiting Tanzania.
Tropical Trails ℩ 027 250 0358; f 027 254 8299; e info@tropicaltrails.com;
www.tropicaltrails.com. Based at Maasai Camp, this is a genuinely eco-friendly company
which arranges standard lodge-based and camping safaris for all budgets, as well as walking
excursions on the fringes of the main national parks, and Kili climbs along the Machame
and Shira routes. Tropical Trails is especially worth contacting if you have unusual
requirements, or you want to get really off the beaten track. They also have some
experience in arranging special one-off charity or group events.

Around Arusha

Arusha's status as Tanzania's safari capital is not in dispute, but, paradoxically, only a small proportion of fly-in safari-goers ever get to spend a night in town. The reason for this is that, unless you're on a tight budget or you actively want an urban base, there is far more to be said for overnighting at one of the more rustic midrange to upmarket lodges that lie within a 50km radius of the town centre – along the Moshi Road towards Kilimanjaro International Airport, and in the vicinity of Arusha National Park.

The main attraction of these out-of-town lodges is arguably the simple fact that they *are* out of town. Don't get me wrong: as these things go, Arusha is a pleasant enough urban centre, neither as intimidating nor as sprawling as Nairobi, say, or Dar es Salaam. But equally, it is difficult to imagine that any first-time safari-goer on their first night in Tanzania would regard the modest urban bustle of Arusha as the fulfilment of their African dream. By contrast, the better out-of-town lodges do manage to project a genuinely African feel, and offer a relatively tranquil introduction to the land of safaris – in most cases capped (weather permitting) by sterling views of Mount Meru and the more distant snow-capped peak of Kilimanjaro.

Most visitors perceive Arusha and its immediate environs to be little more than a convenient overnight staging post *en route* to the great game reserves to its west. But the area is well worth exploring in its own right. The main attraction is undoubtedly Arusha National Park, an underrated conservation area which amply pays back whatever time and effort you choose to invest – be it a quick afternoon game drive, a couple of nights at one of the lodges on its periphery, or the altogether more challenging ascent of the mighty Mount Meru. Also of interest is Lake Duluti, which lies within walking distance of the main road between Arusha town and the eponymous national park, while a number of low-key eco-tourist programmes offer visitors the opportunity to interact with the local Maasai and Wa-Arusha in relatively non-contrived circumstances.

ARUSHA NATIONAL PARK

Only 45 minutes from town, Arusha is the most accessible of northern Tanzania's six national parks, but also, after the remote Rubondo Island, the one that has been most neglected by the safari industry, largely because it offers limited possibilities to see the so-called Big Five. And yet, this one perceived failing aside, Arusha National Park is a quite extraordinary conservation area, and thoroughly worth a visit. A mere 137km^2 in extent, the park boasts a habitat diversity that spans everything from montane rainforest to moist savanna to Alpine moorland, its prodigious fauna includes some 400 bird and several unusual mammal species, while more prominent landmarks include Africa's fifth-highest mountain, a cluster of attractive lakes and a spectacular extinct volcanic crater – all with Kilimanjaro looming large on the eastern skyline.

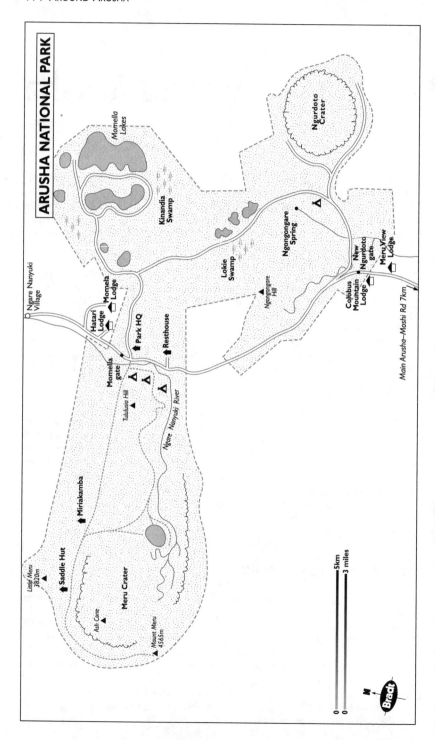

ARUSHA NATIONAL PARK

Ngare Nanyuki Village

Momella Lakes

Kinandia Swamp

Hatari Lodge

Momela Lodge

Park HQ

Resthouse

Momella gate

Tululusia Hill

Ngare Nanyuki River

Miriakamba

Saddle Hut

Little Meru 3820m

Ash Cone

Meru Crater

Mount Meru 4565m

Lokie Swamp

Ngongongare Spring

Ngongongare Hill

Colobus Mountain Lodge

New Ngurdoto gate

Meru View Lodge

Main Arusha–Moshi Rd 7km

Ngurdoto Crater

5km
3 miles

N

Bradt

Arusha National Park's most publicised draw is Mount Meru, whose eastern slopes and 4,566m peak lie within its boundaries. The product of the same volcanic activity that formed the Great Rift Valley 15 to 20 million years ago, Mount Meru attained a height similar to that of Kilimanjaro until 250,000 years ago, when a massive eruption tore out its eastern wall. Meru is regarded as a dormant volcano, since lava flowed from it as recently as 100 years ago, but there is no reason to suppose it will do anything dramatic in the foreseeable future. Though low-key by comparison with nearby Kilimanjaro, Mount Meru is regarded by many as the most rewarding mountain to climb in east Africa, a hike that can be done over three days at a fraction of the cost of a Kilimanjaro climb (see box *Climbing Mount Meru* pages 116–17).

Arusha National Park has much to offer non-hikers. The Ngurdoto Crater is in itself worth the entrance fee, a fully intact 3km-wide, 400m-deep volcanic caldera that has often been described as a mini-Ngorongoro. Tourists are not permitted to descend into the crater, but the viewpoints on the forest-fringed rim over the lush crater floor are fantastic. A large herd of buffalo is resident on the crater floor, and with binoculars it is normally possible to pick up other mammals, such as warthog, baboon and various antelope. Look out, too, for augur buzzard, black eagle and other cliff-associated raptors soaring above the crater. The forests around the crater rim harbour many troops of black-and-white colobus and blue monkey, as well as a good variety of birds including several types of hornbill and the gorgeous Hartlaub's turaco and cinnamon-chested bee-eater.

Another area worth exploring is Momela Lakes to the north of Ngurdoto. Underground streams feed this group of shallow alkaline lakes, and each has a different mineral content and is slightly different in colour. In the late evening and early morning, it is often possible to stand at one of the viewpoints over the lakes and see Kilimanjaro on the eastern horizon and Mount Meru to the west. The lake area is one of the best places in Tanzania for waterbirds: flamingo, pelican, little grebe and a variety of herons, ducks and waders are common. Among the more common mammals around the lakes are hippo, buffalo and waterbuck – the waterbuck population evidently intermediate to the Defassa and common waterbuck races. You should also come across a few pairs of Kirk's dik-dik, an attractively marked small antelope that seems to be less skittish here than it is elsewhere in the country. Other large mammals likely to be seen in Arusha National Park include giraffe, zebra and vervet monkey. Elephants are present but seldom seen, since they tend to stick to the forest zone of Mount Meru, while the only large predators are leopard and spotted hyena.

From a vehicle, most of the park can be seen in a day. The 52-page booklet *Arusha National Park*, available from the National Parks office in Arusha for US$5, contains detailed information on every aspect of the park's ecology and wildlife. An excellent map of Arusha National Park, with a detailed map of the ascent of Mount Meru on the flip, is published by Giovanni Tombazzi in collaboration with Hoopoe Adventure Tours. The standard park entrance fee of US$25 per 24-hour period is charged.

The MBT Snake Park at the entrance to Arusha National Park has been recommended for the good collection of reptiles and intelligent guided tour.

Getting there and away

To reach Arusha National Park from Arusha, you must first follow the surfaced Moshi Road for about 20km until you arrive at a signposted turn-off to the left near Usa River. After about 8km, this dirt road enters the park boundary, where all visitors must pay park entrance fees at a newly constructed main gate. It then runs through the park for another 15km or so to Hatari and Momela lodges, both of which stand immediately outside the northern national park boundary. This road is in fair condition and can normally be driven in an ordinary saloon car, though a 4x4 may be necessary after rain.

The park is normally visited as an easy day trip or overnight trip out of Arusha. Any safari company can organise this. Most companies can also organise a three-day climb up Meru. If you want to organise your own climb or spend some time exploring the park on foot, you will have to find your own way there. You could hire a taxi in Arusha, but it is cheaper to catch a bus or *dalla-dalla* along the Moshi road as far as the turn-off, from where 4x4 vehicles serve as *dalla-dallas* to the village of Ngare Nanyuki about 3km past the northern boundary of the park, passing through the main entrance gate (where fees must be paid) *en route*.

Where to stay
Exclusive
Hatari! (8 rooms) ✆/f 027 255 3456; e marlies@theafricanembassy.com; www.hatarilodge.com. This new owner-managed lodge, situated in a patch of moist yellow fever woodland just outside the Momela Gate, is named after the 1961 film *Hatari!* (*Danger!*), and stands on a property formerly owned by Hardy Kruger, one of the film's co-stars. Accommodation is in large en-suite dbl chalets with king-size beds and tall *makuti*

CLIMBING MOUNT MERU

The Arusha and Meru people deify Mount Meru as a rain god, but it is unlikely that any local person actually climbed to the 4,566m peak prior to Fritz Jaeger's pioneering ascent in 1904. Often overlooked by tourists today because it is 'only' the fifth-highest mountain in Africa, Meru is admittedly no substitute for Kilimanjaro for achievement-orientated travellers. On the other hand, those who climb both mountains invariably enjoy Meru more. Also going in its favour, Meru is less crowded than Kilimanjaro, considerably less expensive to climb, and – although steeper and almost as cold – less likely to engender the health problems associated with Kilimanjaro's greater altitude. Meru is just as interesting as Kilimanjaro from a biological point of view and, because comparatively few people climb it, you are more likely to see forest animals. A lot of big game can be seen on the lower slopes.

Meru can technically be climbed in two days, but three days is normal, allowing time to explore Meru Crater and to look at wildlife and plants. Most people arrange a climb through a safari company in Arusha. The going rate for a three-day hike is around US$250 per person. You can make direct arrangements with park officials at the gate, but won't save much money by doing this. The compulsory armed ranger/guide costs US$20 per day (US$10 park fee and US$10 salary), hut fees are US$20 per night, and there is the usual park entrance fee of US$30 per day. A rescue fee of US$20 per person covers the entire climb. The minimum cost for a three-day climb is therefore US$150 per person, with an additional US$60 to be divided between the climbers. Food and transport must be added to this, and porters cost an additional US$5 per day each.

Meru is very cold at night, and you will need to bring clothing adequate for Alpine conditions. In the rainy season, mountain boots are necessary. At other times, good walking shoes will probably be adequate. The best months to climb are between October and February.

ceilings, while the individualistic décor is an imaginative, colourful blend of a classic African bush feel and a more 'retro' look dating back to the era of the film for which the lodge is named. The common areas – littered with *Hatari!* memorabilia – overlook a swampy area inhabited by buffalo, waterbuck, crowned crane and various other waterbirds. The food is excellent, the service is highly personalised, and there are also stirring views across to nearby Kilimanjaro and Meru. Activities on offer include game drives and walks, canoeing on the Momela Lakes and birdwatching excursions. *US$250 pp FB or US$295 for FB with activities included; 10% discount for direct booking of longer than 3 nights.*

Upmarket

Ngurdoto Mountain Lodge (139 rooms) ✆ 027 255 5217–26; f 027 255 5227/8; e Ngurdoto@thengurdotomountainlodge.com; www.thengurdotomountainlodge.com. Situated on a lush 70ha coffee plantation alongside the road between Usa River and Arusha National Park, this impressive new tourist village, affiliated to the Impala Hotel in Arusha, has some of the best facilities of any lodge or hotel in the Arusha area, including a 9-hole golf course, a gym, a 600-seat conference centre, a large swimming pool, 24-hour internet access, 2 restaurants and 2 bars. Given the hotel's vast size, the rooms – all en-suite with king-size bed, fireplace and balcony – possess a surprising amount of character, making use of wrought iron and wood to create a feel that is at once contemporary and ethnic. *Standard rooms US$90/130 sgl/dbl B&B; cottages US$120/150, additional meals US$15 pp.*

If you arrange your own climb, check hut availability at the National Parks office in Arusha before you head off to the gate. At present the huts are rarely full, but Meru is growing in popularity so this could change.

Day 1 The trail starts at Momela Gate (1,500m). From there it is a relatively gentle three-hour ascent to Miriakamba Hut (2,600m). On the way you pass through well-developed woodland where there is a good chance of seeing large animals such as giraffe. At an altitude of about 2,000m you enter the forest zone. If you leave Momela early, there will be ample time to explore Meru Crater in the afternoon. The 1,500m cliff rising to Meru Peak overlooks the crater. The 3,667m-high ash cone in the crater is an hour from Miriakamba Hut, and can be climbed.

Day 2 It is three hours to Saddle Hut (3,600m), a bit steeper than the previous day's walk. You initially pass through forest, where there is a good chance of seeing black-and-white colobus, then at about 3,000m you will enter a moorland zone similar to that on Kilimanjaro. It is not unusual to see Kilimanjaro peeking above the clouds from Saddle Hut. If you feel energetic, you can climb Little Meru (3,820m) in the afternoon. It takes about an hour each way from Saddle Hut.

Day 3 You will need to rise very early to ascend the 4,566m peak, probably at around 02.00. This ascent takes four to five hours. It is then an eight- to nine-hour walk back down the mountain to Momela Gate.

Note Some people prefer to climb from Miriakamba Hut to Saddle Hut and do the round trip from Saddle Hut to Meru Peak on the second day (eleven hours altogether), leaving only a five-hour walk to Momela on the third. Others climb all the way up to Saddle Hut on the first day (six hours), do the round trip to the peak on the second (eight hours), and return to Momela from the Saddle Hut on the third (five hours).

Momela Lodge (55 rooms) ↘ 057 255 3743/5; f 057 250 8264; e lions-safari@safaristal.com; www.safaristal.com. Set in the shadow of Mount Meru about 3km past Momela Gate, this cosy, low-key and little-used lodge is a world away from its slick, crowded counterparts elsewhere in the northern circuit. It is possessed of a rather Alpine atmosphere, reinforced by the log fires in the bar and lounge, while black-and-white movie posters – *Hatari!* of course – decorate the dining area and bar. Though undeniably a bit rundown, the en-suite chalets seem decent value. Facilities include a large swimming pool and satellite TV. *Non-residents' rate US$56/74 sgl/dbl B&B, or US$80/122 FB; residents pay about one-third of that rate.*

Moderate
Meru View Lodge (9 rooms) ↘ 027 255 3876; e meru.view.lodge@habari.co.tz; www.meru-view-lodge.com. This small German-owned lodge lies on the eastern side of the road from Usa River, about 1km south of where the road enters the national park. The comfortable en-suite rooms, dotted around flowering gardens and a large swimming pool, are superb value. *US$35/50 sgl/dbl B&B; other meals additional US$10 pp.*

National Park Resthouse Situated 2km from Momela Gate, this self-catering resthouse sleeps up to 5 people. You can book it in advance through the National Parks office outside Arusha. *US$20 pp per night.*

Budget and camping
Colobus Mountain Lodge ↘ 027 255 3632; www.colobusmountainlodge.com. Clearly signposted and only 200m from the public road between Usa River and Ngare Nanyuki, this relatively new lodge lies in the shadow of Mount Meru immediately outside the southern boundary of the park. The centrepiece of the rustic site is an open-sided bar and restaurant with a tall *makuti* roof, serving sensibly priced Western and local dishes. *Camping on the large, green lawn US$5 pp; spacious semi-detached chalet rooms US$35 pp inc breakfast and dinner.*

National Park campsites 3 sites lie at the foot of Tululusia Hill, 2km from Momela Gate, and one is situated in the forest near Ngurdoto Gate. All are scenically located close to a stream, have drop toilets and firewood. Note, however, that you may not walk between the campsites and the entrance gates without an armed ranger. *US$20 pp.*

THE MOSHI ROAD
With the exception of Lake Duluti, the Moshi road running eastward from Arusha boasts no tourist attractions of note. It's an attractive area, however, run through by numerous forest-fringe streams that rise on Mount Meru, and there is no shortage of midrange to upmarket accommodation between Arusha and the small town of Usa River near the turn-off for Arusha National Park.

Between Arusha and Lake Duluti
The road between Arusha and Lake Duluti gives access to one of the most popular lodges in the Arusha area, Moivaro, set on the coffee plantation of the same name, as well as the newer but equally commendable Kigongoni Lodge. More affordable options include Klub Afriko and the new Songota Falls Lodge.

Where to stay
Upmarket
Kigongoni Lodge (20 units) ↘ 027 250 2799; m 0748 763338; e info@kigongoni.net/info@asilialodges.com; www.kigongoni.net/www.asilialodges.com. Set on a forested hilltop in a 70ha coffee plantation about 10km from Arusha along the Moshi road, this superb new lodge consists of 20 large, airy and organic en-suite chalets, all

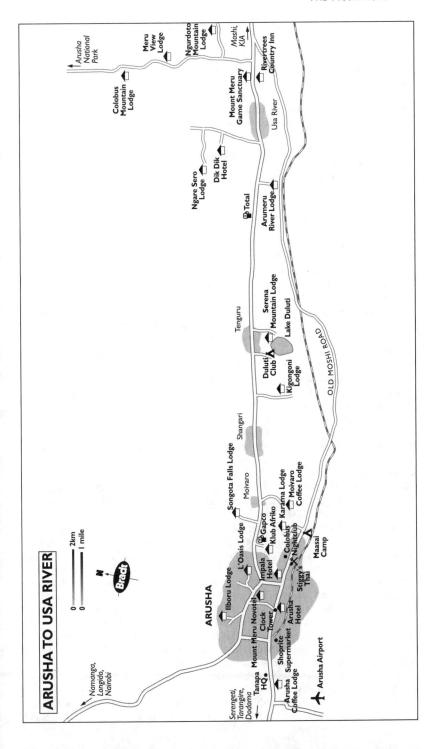

of which come with a private balcony, 2 dbl beds with netting, hot shower and bath, and log fire. The countrified atmosphere of the accommodation is complemented by superb food and a good wine list, while other attractions include a swimming pool and plenty of monkeys and birds in the grounds. A significant portion of the profits is used to support Sibusiso, a home for disabled Tanzanian children situated on the same coffee estate. *US$140/180 sgl/dbl B&B or US$170/240 FB; significant discount in low season of Apr and May.*
Moivaro Coffee Plantation Lodge (20 units) ✆ 027 255 3242/3326; m 0744 324193; f 027 255 3243; e moivaro@habari.co.tz or info@moivaro.com; www.moivaro.com. This elegantly rustic lodge, set on a 40-acre coffee estate 7km from central Arusha and 1.5km from the Moshi road, has received consistently good reports from travellers and tour operators since it opened in the late 1990s. The self-contained bungalows are set in a circular arrangement around a clean swimming pool and flowering lawns. The main dining and reception building has a large patio facing Mount Meru. Facilities include walking and jogging paths, internet and a massage room. *US$100/136 sgl/dbl B&B or US$135/206 FB, with substantial discount in Apr and May.*

Moderate

Klub Afriko Hotel (7 rooms) ✆ 027 250 9205; m 0744 369475; e info@klubafriko.com; www.klubafriko.com. The intimate and stylish Klub Afriko is a newly opened lodge set in compact, neat grounds on the Moshi road about 3km out of Arusha. The 6 self-contained chalets have a traditional African appearance with a bright and airy interior, while the spacious dining area is decorated in a more classical style. The accommodation is excellent value, while 3-course set lunches and dinners cost Tsh8,000 and 9,000 respectively. *US$30/50 sgl/dbl B&B; suites sleeping up to 4 people US$70.*
Songota Falls Lodge (5 rooms) ✆ 0744 095576/688806; e joice_kimaro@yahoo.com. Situated along a monumentally bad 1.5km dirt road that runs northward from the Moshi road 2km east of Club Afriko, Songota Lodge currently consists of a few unfussy but clean en-suite bungalows overlooking the large green valley below the Songota Waterfall – to which guided walks are offered when underfoot conditions are reasonably dry. It's a refreshingly unpretentious set-up, owned and managed by a friendly Tanzanian woman with years of experience in the hotel trade, and likely to expand its facilities in due course, but as things stand it feels slightly overpriced for what you get. *US$30/45 sgl/dbl B&B or US$48/70 FB.*

Lake Duluti

The small but attractive Lake Duluti lies roughly 10km east of Arusha and only 2km from the Moshi road near the busy little market town of Tenguru. Some 70ha in extent, 15m deep and fed by subterranean springs, the lake is nestled within an extinct volcanic crater whose formation was linked to that of Mount Meru. Although much of the surrounding area is cultivated and settled, the steep walls of the crater support a fringing gallery of riparian forest, while the lake itself is lined with beds of papyrus. The lake and its environs are of particular interest to birdwatchers. Forest birds that are resident or regular visitors include Hartlaub's turaco, crowned and silvery-cheeked hornbills, Narina trogon, brown-breasted and white-eared barbets, Africa broadbill, little greenbul, black-throated wattle-eye, paradise flycatcher, white-starred robin and black-breasted apalis. The lake supports numerous diving and shore birds, as well as seven kingfisher species and breeding colonies of various weavers. An added attraction is the good views of Mount Meru and Kilimanjaro from the lakeshore on clear days.

Getting there and away

Lake Duluti lies about 2km south of the Arusha–Moshi road, and the side roads to Mountain Village Lodge and the Duluti Club, both on the lakeshore, are signposted.

On public transport, any vehicle heading from Arusha towards Moshi can drop you at the junction – hop off when you see a large carved wooden giraffe to your left coming from Arusha. The turn-off to Duluti Club is signposted to the right opposite this statue, and the turn-off to Mountain Village Lodge is another 200m or so towards Moshi. It's about 20 minutes' walk from the main road to the campsite.

Where to stay
Upmarket
Serena Mountain Village Lodge ✆ 027 255 3313/4/5; f 027 255 3316; e mtvillage@serena.co.tz. With expansive green lawns verging on the northern shore of the gorgeous Lake Duluti, and fabulous views across to Mount Meru and Kilimanjaro, Mountain Village Lodge is easily one of the most attractive upmarket lodges in the greater Arusha area. The main building is a converted thatched farmhouse dating to the colonial era, and accommodation is in comfortable self-contained chalets. Subsequent to the lodge being taken over by the excellent Serena chain, the quality of service, meals and décor have all been upgraded to match the atmospheric setting. *US$160/200 sgl/dbl B&B or US$195/285 FB, with significant discount in low season of Apr–Jun.*

Camping
Duluti Club The lovely and surprisingly little-used campsite at the Duluti Club is slightly rundown, but the lakeshore setting more than compensates. Facilities include an ablution block and a cafeteria serving basic meals and cold drinks. *Camping Tsh2,000 pp.*

Usa River
The small and rather amorphous village of Usa River flanks the Moshi road about 20km east of Arusha near the turn-off to Arusha National Park. It is of interest to tourists primarily for a cluster of upmarket hotels, several of which rank as among the most attractive in the Arusha area, as well as being conveniently located for day safaris into the national park.

Where to stay
Upmarket
Dik Dik Hotel (21 rooms) ✆ 027 255 3498 or (Switzerland) 41 24 441 1078; f 027 255 3499; e dikdik@ATGE.automail.com; www.dikdik.ch. Owned and managed by the same Swiss family since it first opened back in 1990, this attractive small hotel with comfortable, well-equipped en-suite chalets, lies about 1km north of Kilala, a small village on the Arusha–Moshi road a few hundred metres west of Usa River. The thickly wooded 10ha grounds are bisected by an energetic stream, and contain a swimming pool, a small dam, a viewing tower offering clear views of Kilimanjaro, and a restaurant rated as one of the best in the Arusha area. Rooms 19 and 20 are particularly recommended for their view onto a riverine gallery forest inhabited by monkeys and numerous bird species. *US$140/180 sgl/dbl B&B, or US$165/230 FB.*
Ngare Sero Lodge (12 rooms) ✆ 057 250 3638; m 0741 512138; e Ngare-Sero-Lodge@habari.co.tz; www.Ngare-Sero-Lodge.com. One of the nicest places to stay in the Arusha area is this small, exclusive country-style lodge set on a forested 25ha estate dating to the German colonial era, and accessible along the same dirt road as the Dik Dik Hotel. As is implicit in the name Ngare Sero (Maasai for 'dappled water'), the owner-managed estate is fed by several streams flowing from the higher slopes of Mount Meru, and a crystal clear reservoir below the lodge is stocked with barbel and trout, while also driving the turbine that generates the lodge's electricity. The forest and lake support an incredibly varied selection of birds and butterflies, while blue monkey and black-and-white colobus are both resident on the grounds. A superb range of activities and facilities includes horseback excursions, coffee

farm tours, boat rides on the lake, cultural visits to a nearby village, a swimming pool, internet access after 17.00, yoga and meditation classes, and massages. The rooms, though attractively decorated, are set out in a rather cramped row opposite the main building, but overall this is an excellent option for those who enjoy outdoor pursuits. *US$120 pp FB.*

Mount Meru Game Sanctuary (17 rooms) ✆ 027 255 3643; f 027 255 3730; e reservations@intimate-places.com; www.mountmerugamelodge.com. Established in 1959, about 1km east of Usa River immediately before the turn-off to Arusha National Park, this long-serving lodge has something of an *Out of Africa* ambience, consisting of a main stone building and a few semi-detached wooden cabins surrounded by bougainvillaea-draped gardens. A large open enclosure in front of rooms 1 and 2 is stocked with various antelope, nicely setting the tone for your safari, and it is also the site of a papyrus heronry where hundreds of cattle egrets roost at dusk. Rooms are stylishly decorated in classic Edwardian safari style. *US$135/185 sgl/dbl B&B or US$166/250 FB, with huge discount in low season of Apr–Jun.*

Rivertrees Country Inn (12 rooms) ✆ 027 255 3894 or 0741 339873; f 027 255 3893; e rivertrees@habari.co.tz; www.rivertrees.com. Situated 300m from the main Moshi road facing the Mount Meru Game Sanctuary, this highly regarded owner-managed lodge is set in magnificently shady green gardens on an old family estate offering great views to Mount Meru and Kilimanjaro, and bounded by a forest-fringed stretch of the Usa River. Centred on a rambling old farmhouse, the inn offers comfortable accommodation in spacious en-suite rooms with large wooden 4-poster beds, as well as a more exclusive river cottage and a stunning river house with 2 dbl bedrooms (the latter used by the German head of state on a recent visit to Tanzania). Facilities include a TV room (with digital satellite TV), internet access, a swimming pool and a highly rated restaurant serving hearty country food, while activities on offer include horseback excursions, village tours and bird walks. *Standard rooms US$125/150 sgl/dbl B&B; river cottage US$240 dbl; river house US$1,000 for up to 4 people.*

Arumeru River Lodge (20 rooms) ✆ 027 255 3573; m 0748 459639; f 027 255 3574; e info@arumerulodge.com; www.arumerulodge.com. The newest lodge in the Usa River area, having opened in Apr 2005, German-owned Arumeru consists of 10 2-room thatch chalets set on a 6ha plot bounded by 2 rivers. A stunning open-sided thatch common area overlooks the heated swimming pool, and the restaurant, complete with French chef, serves top-notch continental cuisine. The gardens currently feel a little underdeveloped, but you won't notice this if you ask for one of the rooms facing the river and associated swampland – home to 3 monkey species and a wide variety of birds – and there is also talk of introducing some antelope into the undeveloped 'bush' part of the property. The en-suite semi-detached rooms have a pleasing airy organic feel, and seem good value. *US$102/144/189 sgl/dbl/triple B&B or US$138/216/2 97 FB; hefty discounts in Apr and May.*

Kilimanjaro International Airport (KIA)

The only international airport serving northern Tanzania lies in almost total isolation roughly midway between Arusha and Moshi, making it a reasonably convenient point of access for both towns but absolutely ideal for neither. All Air Tanzania flights in and out of KIA are connected to both Arusha and Moshi by a free shuttle service, and KLM flights are connected to Arusha by a shuttle run by the Impala Hotel (US$10 per person). Otherwise, arriving at normal hours, you can arrange for your safari operator or hotel to meet you, or catch a taxi. Another option for your first or last night in town is to book into KIA Lodge, 1km from the airport.

Where to stay

KIA Lodge (20 units) ✆ 027 255 3242/3326; m 0744 324193; f 027 255 3243; e kialodge@africaonline.co.tz; www.kialodge.com. Under the same management as

Moivaro Lodge, and similar in feel and quality, the recently opened KIA Lodge is recommended to visitors with unusual or inconvenient flight times, as it lies just 1km from the airport and the staff are used to monitoring flight arrivals and departures for guests. It's an attractive set-up, with a good restaurant and swimming pool and great views towards Kilimanjaro (the mountain, that is), but the noise from overhead flights makes it less than ideal for an extended stay. *Self-contained bungalows US$100/136 sgl/dbl B&B or US$135/206 FB, with substantial discount in Apr and May.*

CULTURAL TOURS AROUND ARUSHA

A number of widely praised and increasingly popular cultural tourism programmes have been implemented around Arusha in recent years with the assistance of the Dutch agency SNV. Any one of these programmes makes for an excellent half- or full-day trip out of Arusha, offering tourists the opportunity to experience something of rural Africa away from the slick lodges and main safari circuit. You can ask your safari company to tag a visit to one of the cultural programmes on to your main safari, or can arrange a stand-alone day trip once you arrive in Arusha. Several of the programmes also offer the opportunity to spend a night locally, though it should be stressed that accommodation is not up to accepted tourist-class standards. Of the various programmes, the one at Longido can easily be visited on public transport, but the rest are only realistically visited in a private vehicle. Details of recommended safari operators can be found on page 110. The TTB office on Boma Road stocks useful pamphlets about all the cultural programmes, and can advise you about current costs and accessibility.

Longido

The cultural tourism project run out of the overgrown village of Longido is one of the most accessible in the region for independent travellers, and it is an excellent place to visit for those who want to spend time among the Maasai. The original programme co-ordinator was a local Maasai who studied abroad as a sociologist before he was paralysed in a serious accident, and his successor can tell you anything you want to know about Maasai culture. Three different walking modules are on offer to tourists. On all modules, you can expect to see a variety of birds (including several colourful finches and barbets), and there is a fair amount of large game left in the area, notably gerenuk, lesser kudu, giraffe, Thomson's gazelle and black-backed jackal. It is worth trying to be in Longido on Wednesday, when a hectic cattle market is held on the outskirts of the village.

The first module is a half-day bird walk through the Maasai Plains, which also includes a visit to a rural Maasai *boma* (homestead), and a meal cooked by the local women's group. Then there is a full-day tour which follows the same route as the bird walk does, before climbing to the top of Longido Mountain, an ascent of roughly 400m, offering views to Mount Meru and Kilimanjaro on a clear day, as well as over the Maasai Plains to Kenya. The two-day module follows the same route as the one-day walk, but involves camping out overnight in the green Kimokouwa Valley, before visiting a dense rainforest that still harbours a number of buffaloes as well as the usual birds and monkeys.

Longido straddles the main Namanga road roughly 100km from Arusha, so any of the regular minibuses and taxis that run between Arusha and Namanga can drop you there – these usually leave Arusha from the north end of the bus station opposite the stadium. The tourist project maintains a neat and inexpensive guesthouse about 100m from the main road, or you can arrange to pitch a tent at a Maasai *boma* for a small fee. All visitors are charged a daily

ALL THAT GLISTERS...

In 1962, local legend goes, a Maasai cattle herder called Ali Juyawatu was walking through the Mererani Hills after a bush fire, and noticed some unusual blue crystals lying on the ground. Ali picked up the beautiful stones, and took them to the nearby town of Arusha, from where they somehow made their way to the New York gemstone dealer Tiffany & Co, which had never seen anything like them before. In 1967, Tiffany launched the newly discovered gem on the market, naming it tanzanite in honour of its country of origin.

Tanzanite is by any standards a remarkable stone. A copper brown variety of zoisite, it is rather dull in its natural condition, but responds to gentle heating, transforming into a richly saturated dark-blue gem, with purple and violet undertones that have been compared among other things to the, um, eyes of Elizabeth Taylor! The stone is known only from Tanzania's Mererani Hills – rumours of a second deposit in Usangi, 75km from Arusha, have yet to be confirmed – and it is in the order of being a thousand times rarer than diamonds. Despite its upstart status in the jewellery world, tanzanite has rocketed in popularity since its discovery. By 1997, 30 years after its launch, it had become the second most popular gemstone in the North American market, second to sapphires and ahead of rubies and emeralds, generating an annual trade worth US$300 million in the USA alone.

Remarkable, too, is the degree of controversy that the tanzanite trade has attracted in recent years. In the late 1990s, the Tanzanian government, comparing international tanzanite trade figures against their documented exports, realised that as much as 90% of the tanzanite sold in the USA was being smuggled out of Tanzania, resulting in a huge loss of potential government revenue in taxes and royalties. The ease with which the stones were being smuggled was clearly linked to the unregulated nature of the workings at Mererani, which consisted of more than 300 small claims operating in what has been described by more than one observer as a Wild West atmosphere. For the small claim holders, rather than distributing the stones they collected through legitimate sources, it was more profitable – and considerably more straightforward – to sell them for cash to illicit cross-border traders.

The lack of regulations at Mererani, or at least the lack of a body to enforce what regulations do exist, is also largely to blame for a series of tragedies that has dogged the workings in recent years. The greatest single catastrophe occurred during the El Niño rains of 1998, when one of the shafts at Block D flooded and at least 100 miners drowned. But it has been estimated that a similar number of miners died underground subsequent to this mass tragedy, as a result either of suffocation, or of inept dynamite blasting, or of periodic outbreaks of violent fighting over disputed claims. Aside from such accidents, it has long been rumoured that miners who are down on their luck will kidnap

development fee of US$7.50, which goes towards local community developments such as a cattle dip. In addition to this, visitors must pay a co-ordination fee of US$7.50 per group per visit, a daily guide fee of US$6 per group, and a 'present' of around US$3–6 to any *boma* visited. A limited selection of cheap Tanzanian fare is available from one or two small restaurants that lie along the main road, and a couple of local bars (with pool table) serve cold beers and soft drinks.

and sacrifice children from neighbouring villages, in the hope it will bring them good fortune and prosperity.

In 1999, the Tanzanian government put out to tender a lease on Block C, the largest of the four mining blocks, accounting for about 75% of the known tanzanite deposit. The rights were acquired by a South African company – with a 25% Tanzanian stake – called African Gem Resources (AFGEM), which reputedly pumped US$20 million into establishing the mine with the intention of going online in early 2000. This goal proved to be highly optimistic, as local miners and stakeholders, understandably hostile to the corporate intrusion on their turf, not to mention the threat it posed to the illicit tanzanite trade, attempted to disrupt the new project and persuade AFGEM to withdraw.

The long-simmering tensions erupted in April 2001, when a bomb was set off in the new mining plant, killing nobody, but causing large-scale material damage nonetheless. Later in the same month, AFGEM security guards opened fire on a group of 300 irate miners that had invaded the plant, killing one trespasser and causing serious injury to nine. When the Minister for Energy and Minerals visited the scene a few days later, the trespassers claimed to have been protesting against AFGEM's alleged complicity in the alleged death of 20 miners who were buried alive. AFGEM refuted the claims as pure fabrication, part of a smear campaign designed to discredit them and protect the illicit tanzanite trade. The result of the official investigation into the incident has yet to be released.

The tanzanite plot took a new and wholly unexpected twist in late December 2001, when press reports linked four of the men convicted on charges relating to the 1998 US embassy bombings in Nairobi and Dar es Salaam with the illicit tanzanite trade. Amid wild speculation that the underground tanzanite trade was funding Osama bin Laden and his Al-Qaeda organisation, three major US jewellery dealers announced a total boycott on the purchase or sale of the gem. Among them, ironically, was the retailer that had first placed it in the spotlight back in 1967. Tiffany & Co publicly conceded a lack of hard evidence supporting the bin Laden link, but announced that it 'troubled' them regardless. By the end of January 2002, the price of tanzanite had fallen from around US$300 per gram to below US$100.

The Tanzanian government elected to suspend operations at Mererani until the claims were fully investigated. At a Tucson trade fair in February 2002, the American Gem Trade Association and the Tanzanian Minister of Energy and Minerals signed a protocol that placed several significant new controls on local access to the tanzanite mines. After the protocol was signed, Mike O'Keefe of the US State Department made the following declaration: 'Tanzania... has done everything in its power to assist us in the war against terrorism.' The same office also announced that: 'We have seen no evidence that Al-Qaeda or any other terrorist group is currently using tanzanite sales to finance its efforts or launder money.' Sales of the gem have since returned to normal.

Ng'iresi Village

Set on the slopes of Mount Meru some 7km from Arusha town, this cultural tourism programme based in the traditional Wa-Arusha village of Ng'iresi offers many insights into the local culture and agricultural practices. There are also some lovely walks in the surrounding Mount Meru foothills, an area characterised by fast-flowing streams, waterfalls and remnant forest patches. From Ng'iresi, it is possible to walk to Lekimana Hill, from where there are good views over the

TANZANIA'S GREAT TREK

Among Germany's more improbable – and less successful – attempts to populate the Arusha area with Europeans was the sponsored settlement of 100 Boer families, mostly of German descent, in the aftermath of South Africa's divisive Anglo-Boer War. In 1904, the Germans arranged for the Boers to be taken by boat to Tanga, from where they travelled to Arusha by ox-wagon. When the oxen all succumbed to tsetse-borne disease, the Germans provided the Boers with teams of local Africans as a substitute. The families were granted large ranches, mainly around Ol Doinyo Sambu on the northern slopes of Mount Meru, but most of them fell out with their benefactors and eventually packed up their ox-wagons to head across the border into Kenya, where several settled in the Eldoret area. A neatly whitewashed stone monument to this latter-day Great Trek still stands in a field near Ol Doinyo Sambu, visible from the road between Arusha and Longido.

Maasai Steppes and on a clear day to Kilimanjaro. Another walk takes you to Kivesi Hill, an extinct volcano whose forested slopes support a variety of birds and small mammals.

Three different 'modules' are available at Ng'iresi. The half-day module costs US$16, the full-day module US$21, and the overnight module US$27. All prices include meals prepared by the Juhudu Women's Group and guided activities, while the overnight module also covers the fee for camping in the garden of Mzee Loti. For all modules, a sum of US$4 goes directly towards the improvement of the local primary school. There is no public transport to Ng'iresi, so you must either set up a visit through a safari company or make arrangements with a private vehicle.

Mulala Village

This is another cultural tourism programme situated in a village on the footslopes of Mount Meru. Mulala lies at an altitude of 1,450m, some 30km from Arusha, in a fertile agricultural area, which produces coffee, bananas and other fruit and vegetables. Several short walks can be undertaken in the surrounding hills, including one to the forested Marisha River, home to a variety of birds and primates, and to Mazungu Lake, where it is said that a *mazungu* was once lured to his death by a demon. Another local place of interest is Mama Anna's dairy, which supplies cheese to several upmarket hotels in Arusha. The tourist programme here is run in conjunction with the Agape Women's Group, which provides most of the guides as well as snacks and camping facilities.

All visitors must pay a village development fee of US$3, while a daily guide fee of US$4.50 is charged per group. Camping costs US$1.50 per person per night, and meals cost around US$4 each.

Mkuru Camel Safari

This cultural tourism programme is based at Mkuru, at the northern base of Mount Meru near a pyramid-shaped mountain known as Ol Doinyo Landaree. The main attraction here is organised camelback trips, which range in duration from a short half-day excursion to a week-long camel safari through the surrounding dry plains, which are rich in birds and still support small numbers of game animals. Other options include a bird walk on the plain, or a hike to the top of Ol Doinyo Landaree.

Camel trips cost roughly US$25 per person per night all-inclusive. Visitors must provide their own tent. If you only visit the camel camp, this costs US$5 per person. For walks and hikes, you will pay a village development fee of US$2.50 per person as well as a guide fee of US$6 per group. A cottage is available to tourists at a charge of US$15/18 single/double.

Monduli Juu

The settlement of Monduli Juu ('Upper Monduli') is situated some 50km west of Arusha in the Monduli Hills, a forested range that rises from the Rift Valley floor to an altitude of 2,660m, offering some superb views to other larger mountains such as Kilimanjaro, Meru and Ol Doinyo Lengai. Monduli Juu consists of a cluster of four Maasai villages, namely Emairete, Enguiki, Eluwai and Mfereji, the first of which is set alongside a spectacular crater that betrays the mountains' volcanic origins and is still held sacred by locals.

The cultural programme at Monduli Juu offers several programmes, ranging from a few hours to several days in duration. For nature lovers, a recommended option is the hike to Monduli Peak, passing through patches of montane forest that support a large variety of monkeys, antelope, birds and butterflies as well as relict populations of elephant and buffalo – an armed ranger is mandatory. Other attractions include visits to a traditional healer, Naramatu bead factory and general cultural programmes including a Maasai *boma* visit and a meat market.

A few local families in Monduli Juu offer camping sites, only one of which, Esserian Maasai Camp, has running water. Meals – traditional or Western, as you like – can be prepared with a bit of notice. A useful contact for setting up trips to this area is Tanzania Adventures (see Arusha safari company listing page 111).

West Kilimanjaro Conservation Area

Wedged between the northwestern base of Kilimanjaro and Kenya's Amboseli National Park some two to three hours' drive northeast of Arusha, West Kilimanjaro consists of six contiguous blocks of Maasai communal land that are currently in the process of amalgamating as a formal Wildlife Management Area. Effectively a southern extension of Amboseli, West Kilimanjaro supports a near-pristine cover of lightly wooded acacia savanna where Maasai herdsmen co-exist with a remarkable variety of wildlife, including wildebeest, zebra, eland, impala, Grant's gazelle, hartebeest and yellow baboon, as well as one of the few Tanzanian populations of the remarkable stretch-necked gerenuk.

Much of West Kilimanjaro is comprised of very flat land whose fine volcanic soil once formed the bed of Lake Amboseli – then twice as big as present-day Lake Manyara – before it started to dry up some 10,000-15,000 years ago. As the lake dried it left calcareous deposits that were later mined by the Germans in order to make the famous Meerschaum tobacco pipes. The abandoned pits left behind by the open-cast mines are now an important part of the ecosystem, since they trap rainwater to provide drinking for the Maasai cattle as well as the wildlife at the driest times of the year.

As with Amboseli, the main attractions of West Kilimanjaro are the superb close-up views of Kilimanjaro and a well-protected elephant population noted for the even temperament and immense tusks of its bulls. Unlike its cross-border neighbour, however, West Kilimanjaro attracts very few tourists – perhaps a couple of hundred annually – and retains a genuine wilderness feel. The main reason for this is that just one of the six land blocks is currently open to tourists, run as an exclusive concession by Hoopoe Adventure Tours, though there is some talk of two other concessions opening in the near future.

West Kilimanjaro effectively forms part of a migration corridor used by elephants to cross between Amboseli and the forested slopes of Kilimanjaro. Many impressive bulls are resident throughout the year, but numbers peak in June/July, after the rains, when the smaller family groups merge to form 100-strong herds. This also is when mating takes place, and irascible bulls follow the family herds accompanied by a fanfare of trumpeting.

At present, accommodation in West Kilimanjaro is limited to Hoopoe's West Kilimanjaro Tented Camp, which functions like an upmarket mobile camp but with a few extra frills. The camp consists of five double tents with solar lighting and en-suite showers set out in a stand of mature Acacia tortilis trees at the base of an extinct volcanic cone offering views to Kilimanjaro and Meru, as well as the more distant mountains at Longido and Namanga. In addition to standard game drives, which can offer superb opportunities to track and photograph giant tuskers in the shadow of Kilimanjaro, the camp can arrange night drives and bush walks led by local Maasai guides.

West Kilimanjaro Tented Camp is normally booked out to one party at a time, though more than one party can share it by arrangement, and a minimum booking of two nights is mandatory. Full-board rates are US$420/540 single/double daily, or US$620/840 inclusive of all activities. In addition, a conservancy fee of US$30 per person per night is levied. The camp closes in April/May and from 1 November to 15 December. For more details contact Hoopoe Adventure Tours (\ *027 250 7011 or (UK) 1923 255462;* f *027 254 8226 or (UK) 1923 255452;* e *hoopoeUK@aol.com or hoopoesafari@africaonline.co.tz; www.hoopoe.com).*

Moshi and Surrounds

Situated at the heart of a major coffee-growing region about 80km east of Arusha, the smaller but not insubstantial town of Moshi – population 250,000 – is a likeable if intrinsically unremarkable commercial centre salvaged from anonymity by its spectacular location. At dusk or dawn, when the great white-helmeted dome of Kilimanjaro is most likely to emerge from its customary blanket of cloud, Moshi can boast a backdrop as imposing and dramatic as any in Africa. And yet, the teasing proximity of that iconic snow-capped silhouette notwithstanding, Moshi is not the cool, breezy highland settlement you might expect it to be. Indeed, situated at an altitude of 810m, it is generally far hotter than Arusha, and not so drizzly, with a hint of stickiness in the air that recalls the coast.

Prior to the arrival of the Germans, Moshi was the capital of the area ruled by Rindi, who came into power in about 1860 and, largely through his diplomatic skills, became one of the most important chiefs in the area. By allying with the Maasai, Rindi extracted large taxes from passing caravans. He made a favourable impression on John Kirk, the British consul in Zanzibar, and signed a treaty with Carl Peters in 1885. When the first German colonial forces arrived at Kilimanjaro in 1891, Rindi assured them he ruled the whole area. At his insistence, they quelled his major rival, Sina of Kibosha.

Moshi is the Swahili word for smoke, but exactly when and why the town acquired that name is something of a mystery. Some sources suggest that it is because Moshi served as the terminus for the steam railway line from Tanga after 1911, but my understanding is that the name pre-dates the arrival of the railway by many years. Equally improbable is the suggestion that the reference to smoke is due to the town lying at the base of a volcano, since Kilimanjaro hadn't displayed any significant activity for thousands of years when its present-day Bantu-speaking inhabitants arrived there.

Stirring views of Kilimanjaro aside, there is little to do or see in Moshi that you couldn't do or see in pretty much any similarly sized African market town. But it's a pleasant enough place to explore on foot, with an interesting central market area, and it comes across as far less tourist-oriented than Arusha, despite the inevitable attention paid to any visiting *mazungu* by a coterie of (mostly very affable) flycatchers offering cheap 'n' dodgy Kilimanjaro climbs. In terms of facilities, Moshi boasts an immense selection of decent budget to midrange hotels, as well as several commendable and affordable restaurants, but tourists seeking something more upmarket are better catered for in the villages of Marangu and Machame, on the Kilimanjaro footslopes, or at one of the many lodges along the main road between Arusha and Usa River.

GETTING THERE AND AWAY

Note that passenger trains between Moshi, Tanga and Dar es Salaam were suspended indefinitely several years ago, and are unlikely to resume.

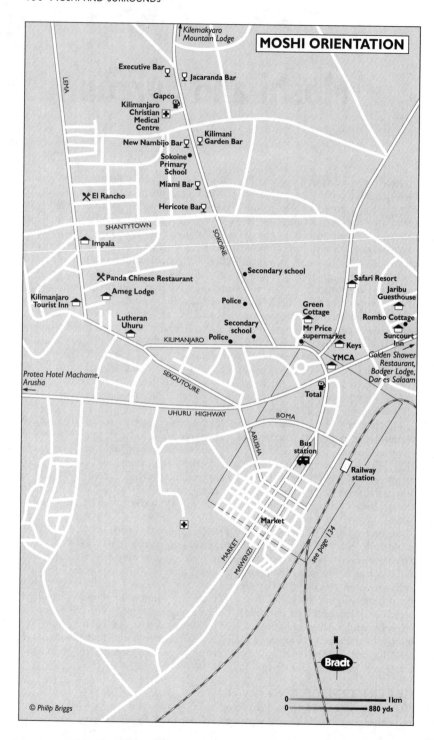

MOSHI ORIENTATION

Air

KIA lies about 40km from Moshi town centre off the Arusha road. The national carrier Air Tanzania flies directly to KIA from some international destinations, and KLM operates a daily direct flight there from Europe. For domestic flights, Air Tanzania and several private airlines fly daily between KIA and Dar es Salaam or Zanzibar, while regular Air Tanzania flights also connect KIA to Mwanza and other major urban centres. A potential source of confusion to travellers booking their own flights is that flights to the parks on the northern safari circuit don't leave from KIA, but from Arusha Airport on the outskirts of Arusha town.

If you fly to KIA with Air Tanzania, note that all their flights tie in with a free shuttle service to Moshi, easily located at the airport. When you leave Moshi for the airport, the correct shuttle departure time can be checked in advance at the Air Tanzania office near the Clock Tower. For flights operated by other airlines, you'll need to charter a taxi (around Tsh10–15,000) or to arrange to be met by a safari company.

Road

The town centre runs southward from the main surfaced road to Dar es Salaam some 80km east of Arusha. The driving time from Arusha in a private vehicle is about 60–90 minutes, and from Dar es Salaam at least seven hours. It is possible to drive from Nairobi (Kenya) to Moshi via Namanga and Arusha in about five hours.

Express coaches between Dar es Salaam and Moshi take roughly seven hours, with a 20-minute lunch break in Korogwe or Mombo. A recommended coach service is Freshi Ya Shamba, which leaves Moshi daily at 10.00 from a private terminal at the Caltex Garage on Market Street. Tickets, best booked a day in advance, cost around Tsh10,500. Also recommended, but slightly more expensive, are Akamba Bus (*next to the Buffalo Hotel,* \ *027 275 3108 or 0744 057779*), Royal Coach (\ *027 275 0940*) and Scandinavia Coach (\ *0744 295245*). Numerous cheaper bus services leave from the main bus station, mostly in the morning. There are also plenty of direct buses between Moshi and Tanga, which can drop you off at Same, Mombo, Muheza and other junction towns *en route*.

A steady flow of buses and *dalla-dallas* connects Arusha to Moshi, taking up to two hours, and to a lesser extent between Moshi and Marangu. There is no need to book ahead for these routes, as vehicles will leave when they fill up, but be warned that there is a high incidence of accidents, particularly with minibuses.

Most shuttle bus services between Nairobi and Arusha continue on to Moshi, or start there. The Impala Shuttle (\ *027 275 1786*), based in an office on Kibo Road next to Chrisburgers, runs two services daily, as does the Riverside Shuttle (\ *027 275 0093*) in the THB building on Boma Road. These coaches generally leave Moshi at 06.30 and 12.00 and Nairobi at 08.00 and 14.00 daily, and take about six hours in either direction, but timings may change to fit in with departure and arrival times for Arusha.

WHERE TO STAY
Upmarket

Protea Hotel Machame (30 rooms) \ 027 275 6941/8; f 027 275 6821; e proteaaishareservations@satconet.com; www.proteahotels.com. Situated along the surfaced Machame Road about 12km from Moshi and 27km from KIA, this smart rural hotel, managed by the South Africa Protea Hotels group, is easily the most upmarket option in the vicinity of Moshi. The recently refurbished motel-style en-suite rooms aren't exactly bursting with character, but the property itself is lovely, with a large thatched dining room and bar area facing a patch of indigenous forest on the footslopes of the great

A DESCENT INTO HELL...

Moshi Central Bus Station has a justified reputation as one of the most hellish in Africa, and it is certainly the most chaotic and daunting in Tanzania, thanks to gaggles of persistent hustlers who will say anything to get a punter on to any bus, provided they can secure a commission. In my experience, when you've half a dozen hustlers yelling at you, punching each other and trying to grab your bags, the instinct for self-preservation tends to prevail, and you're likely to get on to any bus heading in the right direction before things turn ugly. One traveller who spent several weeks in Moshi wrote of how she was pushed into 'a couple of nightmarish journeys, sitting on a stationary bus for two hours after it was scheduled to leave, then stopping for half an hour at practically every settlement it passed'. This isn't such a problem for short trips, for instance to Arusha or Marangu, but for long trips you should use your judgement in boarding the first 'express bus' that is pointed out to you, and be aware that overcharging *wazungu* is commonplace. Better still, go to the bus station the day before you want to travel and book a seat with a reputable company such as Hood, Royal or Tawfiq in advance – that way, you don't have to deflect the hustlers while also protecting your luggage at the same time.

mountain. The hotel specialises in Kilimanjaro climbs, and has good equipment, but it also offers a variety of excursions to more sedentary guests, ranging from local cultural tours and horseback trips to day visits to Lake Chala, Arusha National Park and a short walk to the 30m-high Makoa Waterfall and bat-infested Matangalima Cave. The swimming pool is solar heated. *US$91/120 sgl/dbl B&B.*

AMEG Lodge (20 rooms) ☎ 027 275 0175/0185; f 027 275 0196; e info@ameglodge.com; www.ameglodge.com. This modern new lodge, set in a 2ha plot in the leafy northern suburbs of Moshi, is probably now the smartest hotel within the city limits, and certainly the best value option in the mid to upper price range. The large, airy en-suite rooms are unusually stylish, combining an ethnic feel with a contemporary touch, and they all come with digital satellite TV, fan and private balcony. Other facilities include a swimming pool with views of Kilimanjaro, a gym, a business centre with 24-hour internet access, and a good restaurant serving Indian and continental cuisine. The only negative is that the gardens are still rather bare and undeveloped, but this is bound to change with time. *US$55 B&B for standard dbl, US$75 for larger dbl with walk-in dressing area, US$95 for suite with AC and unlimited internet use.*

Kilemakyaro Mountain Lodge (20 rooms) ☎ 027 275 4925/9; m 0744 264845/287616; e kyaro@habari.co.tz; www.kilimanjarosafari.com. Wonderfully sited, on a hilltop 9km north of the town centre, this smart new hotel was formerly part of the Kifumbu Tea Estate, and the gracious reception and dining areas are housed in the restored 1880s homestead of the estate owner. The attractive landscaped gardens offer wonderful views to the forested slopes and peak of Kilimanjaro, and a swimming pool was under construction in 2005. The accommodation, in newly built self-contained chalets with digital satellite TV, is nothing special and is a touch overpriced, but still a good choice for atmosphere and location. *US$55 pp B&B or US$85/150 sgl/dbl FB.*

Impala Hotel (18 rooms) ☎ 027 275 3443/4; f 027 275 3440; e impala@kilinet.co.tz; www.impalahotel.com. Related to the synonymous hotel in Arusha, but smaller and plusher, the recently opened Impala Hotel lies in the leafy suburbia of Lema Road about 2km from the town centre. The large wood-panelled rooms with fan, hot bath and satellite

TV are fair value Although the Impala Hotel lacks the fine location of the Kilemakyaro, the rooms are better and there are more facilities, notably a swimming pool, internet café and forex bureau, and a good restaurant specialising in Indian dishes. *US$72/83 sgl/dbl B&B, while vast suites with video cost US$100 dbl.*

Moderate

Keys Hotel (16 rooms) ☎ 027 275 2250/1875; f 027 275 0073; e keys-hotel@africaonline.co.tz; www.keys-hotels.com. Situated in attractive suburban grounds about 1km from the Clock Tower, the Keys Hotel has offered good value for several years, and it remains, with justification, the most popular hotel within its price range. Keys is also one of the more reliable places to organise climbs of Kilimanjaro, and while rates are a little higher than at some other places, they do include 1 night's HB accommodation at the hotel on either side of the climb. *Self-contained rooms US$30/50 sgl/dbl, discounted by roughly 50% for Tanzanian residents. Camping US$5 pp.*

Kilimanjaro Crane Hotel (40 rooms) ☎ 027 275 1114/3037; f 027 275 4876; e kilicrane@eoltz.com; www.kilimanjarocranehotels.com. The smartest place in the town centre is this modern high-rise hotel, with its en-suite rooms with large beds, digital satellite TV, private balcony, netting, fan and hot bath. The garden is compact but green, there's a welcome swimming pool, and the rooftop bar is a great spot for sundowners facing Kilimanjaro. A good restaurant serves pizzas for around Tsh3,000 and other meals – mostly Chinese and Indian – for around Tsh4,000. The ground-floor souvenir shop stocks probably the most comprehensive selection of books in Moshi. *US$40/45 sgl/dbl B&B.*

Bristol Cottages Kilimanjaro ☎ 027 275 5083/3745; f 027 275 2833; e bristol@daiichicorp.com or bristol@kilinet.co.tz; www.bristolkilimanjaro.com. Located behind the Standard Chartered Bank close to the bus station, this commendable lodge consists of 20 newly constructed self-contained cottages with AC and hot shower set in peaceful manicured gardens. Facilities include secure parking, internet, email, fax and secretarial services. *US$40/50 sgl/dbl B&B.*

Moshi Leopard Hotel (24 rooms) ☎ 027 275 0884/5134; f 027 275 1261; e leopardhotel@eoltz.com; www.leopardhotel.com. For some years the most commodious option in the town centre, the Leopard Hotel is clean, comfortable and thoroughly adequate without approaching the Kilimanjaro Crane Hotel in terms of quality or amenities. For an en-suite sgl/dbl with fan, netting and hot shower, it seems indifferent value, though the 50% discount for residents would make it a considerably more attractive option. *US$35/45 B&B.*

Kilimanjaro Tourist Inn (8 rooms) ☎ 027 275 3252; f 027 275 2748; e kkkmarealle@yahoo.com. This converted colonial house set in a large suburban garden has a friendly, homely atmosphere that will appeal to travellers who avoid more institutionalised hotels. *Resident rate Tsh12,000 for self-contained twin or dbl with large beds, net, fan and shower is good value, but not so non-resident rate US$25/30 sgl/dbl.*

Lutheran Uhuru Hostel ☎ 027 275 4084; f 027 275 3518; e uhuru@elct.com; www.uhuruhostel.org. Set in vast and pretty suburban gardens 1.5km from the town centre, this hostel used to be popular with tourists, but the recent boom in hotel construction in and around Moshi seems to have reduced its custom. It consists of 60 self-contained rooms, all with running hot water and private balconies. The attached Bamboo Restaurant serves decent meals, but smoking and drinking are strictly prohibited. The hostel is about 3km out of town on Sekou Toure Road. *From US$14–35 for a sgl to US$15–45 for a dbl (about 30% cheaper for residents).*

Budget

Honey Badger Lodge (5 rooms) ☎/f 027 275 4608/3365; e honeybadger@africamail.com; www.honeybadgerlodge.com. Situated 6km out of town along the Dar es Salaam road, this

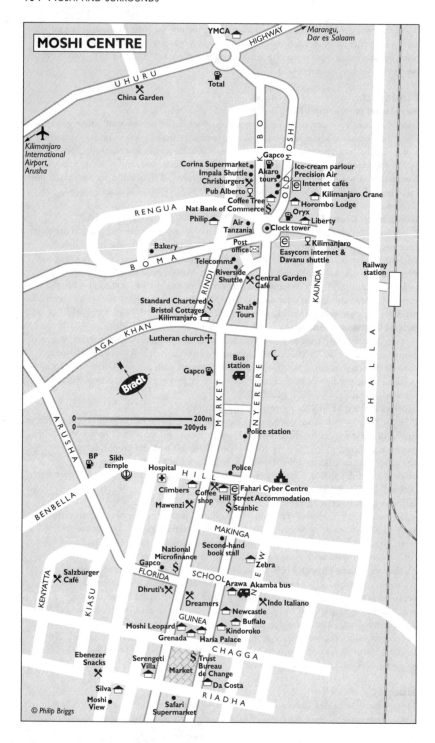

MOSHI CENTRE

YMCA
HIGHWAY
Marangu, Dar es Salaam

UHURU
Total
China Garden

K I B O
M O S H I

Kilimanjaro
International
Airport,
Arusha

Gapco
Corina Supermarket
Ice-cream parlour
Impala Shuttle
Akaro
Precision Air
Chrisburgers
tours
Internet cafés
Pub Alberto
Kilimanjaro Crane
Coffee Tree
Horombo Lodge
RENGUA
Nat Bank of Commerce
Oryx
Philip
Liberty
Air
Clock tower
Tanzania
Bakery
Post
Kilimanjaro
office
Easycom internet &
B O M A
Telecomms
Davanu shuttle
Riverside
Railway
Shuttle
Central Garden
station
R I N D I
Café
Standard Chartered
Shah
Bristol Cottages
Tours
Kilimanjaro
A G A   K H A N
Lutheran church
K A U N D A

Bradt
Bus
station
Gapco

ARUSHA
M A R K E T
N Y E R E R E
G H A L L A

0   200m
0   200yds

Police station

BP
Sikh
temple
Hospital
H I L L
Climbers
Coffee
Fahari Cyber Centre
shop
Hill Street Accommodation
Mawenzi
Stanbic

BENBELLA
Police

MAKINGA
Second-hand
book stall
National
V I E W
Microfinance
Zebra
Gapco
FLORIDA
SCHOOL
Salzburger
Arawa Akamba bus
Café
KENYATTA
KIASU
Dhruti's
Indo Italiano
Dreamers
Newcastle
GUINEA
Buffalo
Moshi Leopard
Kindoroko
Grenada
Haria Palace
CHAGGA
Ebenezer
Trust
Snacks
Serengeti
Bureau
Villa
Market
de Change
Silva
Da Costa
Moshi
View
RIADHA
Safari
Supermarket

© Philip Briggs

rustic, friendly lodge forms a refreshingly low-key alternative to the budget hotels in town. Basically a converted house set within a fenced green compound, the lodge consists of large dbl rooms with use of a common hot bath. Camping is also available in individual campsites (named, somewhat bizarrely, after various universities around the world) and a common hot shower. Meals are available by advance order only, but there is a self-catering kitchen and a *makuti* bar. Traditional drumming performances and lessons can be arranged. They also arrange performances of traditional Chagga *ngoma* (drums) with songs and acting depicting stories about marriage, harvesting time and initiation rites. Other cultural activities include traditional face painting, traditional fashion shows and culinary lessons. *US$10–20 pp, camping US$5 pp.*

Kindoroko Hotel (46 rooms) ❧ 027 275 4054; f 027 275 4062; e kindoroko@eoltz.com; www.africaonline.co.tz/kindorokohotel. Currently the smartest and priciest of several long-serving hotels situated on and around Mawenzi Road a couple of blocks south of the bus station, the 4-storey Kindoroko has maintained high standards and reasonable prices over several years. Following a complete refurbishment, the small but very clean rooms come with hot shower, fan, netting and digital satellite TV. Facilities include a lively courtyard bar, popular with travellers and locals alike, a restaurant serving good meals for around Tsh3,000, and an on-site internet café. *US$15/30 sgl/dbl B&B.*

Horombo Lodge (29 rooms) ❧ 027 275 0134; e horombolodge@kilionline.com. With a central location on Old Moshi Road immediately north of the Clock Tower, this neat new hotel is a good compromise between quality and cost, with compact but clean en-suite rooms with TV, fan, net, telephone and hot water. *From US$15/25 sgl/dbl.*

Zebra Hotel ❧ 027 275 0611; e zebra@yahoo.com or zebrahotels@kilinet.co.tz. Opened in June 2005, this smart new hotel around the corner from the Kindoroko looks like exceptional value for money. All rooms are spacious with en-suite hot shower. A ground-floor restaurant is attached. *US$25 sgl, US$30 dbl (king-size bed) or twin (2 ³/₄ beds).*

Buffalo Hotel ❧ 027 275 2775; e buffalocompany2000@yahoo.com. This clean, popular budget hotel situated behind the Kindoroko charges US$10/15/20 for an en-suite sgl/dbl/triple. Dbls using communal showers cost US$8. The attached restaurant serves tasty Indian and Chinese meals for around Tsh2,500 per main course.

Shoestring

Hill Street Accommodation (6 rooms with 6 more under construction) ❧ 027 275 3455. This new hotel, situated close to the bus station and right next to the Coffee Shop, looks to be about the best value in this range. *US$7/10 for very clean, tiled sgl/dbl room with en-suite hot shower, fan and net.*

Haria Palace Hotel (12 rooms) ❧ 027 285 1118; f 027 275 4062; e hariapalace@yahoo.com. This downmarket annexe to the Kindoroko Hotel is designed for backpackers for whom the refurbished main hotel – which it faces – is now too pricey. The clean rooms are good value. *US$5 for a sgl using common showers or US$10 en-suite dbl.*

Coffee Tree Hotel (57 rooms) ❧ 0741 683381. This long-standing cheapie really couldn't be more centrally located, and the spacious rooms, though admittedly a bit rundown, are very good value. The restaurant isn't up to much, but if affords good views towards Kilimanjaro. *Tsh3,500 sgl using common shower or Tsh4,000/6,000 self-contained sgl/dbl with net, fan and cold water.*

Hotel Newcastle (16 rooms) ❧ 0744 432405. A couple of doors down from the en-suite Kindoroko, this used to be similar in feel and standard but these days it's a lot more rundown – and considerably cheaper. The self-contained rooms are fair value with hot shower, fan and nets. The ground-floor restaurant/bar is sometimes very lively. *US$10 dbl.*

YMCA Hostel (42 rooms) ❧ 027 275 1754/4240; f 027 275 1734. On the opposite side of town to the above hotels, the YMCA is a perennial favourite with travellers, for reasons that escape me, though it is very secure, and the swimming pool actually held water on our most recent inspection. Overpriced. *US$13/15 for small sgl/dbl B&B using communal showers.*

Camping

The best place to camp close to Moshi is in the grounds of the **Golden Shower Restaurant**, which lies 1km from the town centre along the Marangu road and charges US$3 per person. Camping is also available at US$5 per person at the **Keys Hotel**. Further out of town, the campsite at the **Honey Badger Lodge** (see *Budget* accommodation above) is nicer than either of the above.

WHERE TO EAT

Many of the places listed under *Where to Stay* have restaurants. Of the costlier places, the one most likely to attract passing custom to its restaurant is the **Kilimanjaro Crane Hotel**, which has a central location, good Indian food at around Tsh4,000, pizzas for Tsh2,500, and a great view of Kilimanjaro from the rooftop bar. The restaurant at the **Kindoroko Hotel** is popular with budget travellers, and there's a lively bar attached.

El Rancho Top-notch Indian restaurant and bar in a converted old house and green garden close to the Impala Hotel. A broad selection of vegetarian meals is available at around Tsh3,000, while meat dishes are slightly more expensive. Highly recommended, though the distance from the town centre will enforce travellers starting more centrally to walk back (probably not a clever idea after dark) or to arrange to be collected by taxi. Closed Mon.

Golden Shower Restaurant Long-serving and highly regarded continental restaurant 1km out of town along the Dar es Salaam road. The menu includes everything from steaks and fried fish to curry, with most main dishes costing less than Tsh5,000. Walking out here at night would be dodgy, so arrange for a taxi to collect you.

Salzburger Café Owned by a Tanzanian formerly resident in Austria, this new restaurant is an unexpected gem, decorated with mementoes of the old European city to create an atmosphere of full-on kitsch. If the décor doesn't do it for you, then the food certainly should – Tsh2,000–3,000 for a variety of very good steak, chicken and spaghetti dishes, with the unusual (for Tanzania) accompaniment of mashed potato and salads in addition to the conventional chips and rice.

Indo Italiano Restaurant This new restaurant opposite the Buffalo Hotel serves excellent Indian food and decent pizzas in the Tsh2,500–3,500 range; meals are served indoors or on the veranda.

China Garden Excellent and well-established Chinese restaurant situated in the CCM building on the Arusha–Dar highway a few hundred metres from the YMCA. A main course with rice or noodles will set you back around Tsh6,000.

The Coffee Shop Tucked away on Hill St between the bus station and market, this is the place to head for when you're craving a fix of real coffee, and it also serves a selection of cakes, pies, snacks and light lunches at very reasonable prices. Irresistible!

Chrisburgers Cheap daytime snacks such as hamburgers, samosas and excellent fruit juice, opposite the Clock Tower. Open daily except Sun from 08.00 to 15.00.

Pub Alberto Not much food on offer at this brightly decorated nightclub next to Chrisburgers, but – open from 18.00 to 04.00 – it's a good place for an early morning last round. Closed Mon.

PRACTICALITIES

Tourist information There's no tourist information office as such in Moshi, but if you are spending some time there it's worth getting hold of the *Moshi Guide*, compiled and sold by the people who run the Coffee Shop on Hill St. Most of the tour operators in town can provide – not necessarily impartial – local travel information.

Books A good second-hand bookstall can be found on Mawenzi St, between the bus station and the Newcastle Hotel. For new books, particularly material relating specifically to Tanzania, the bookshop on the ground floor of the Kilimanjaro Crane Hotel is the best-stocked in town.

Foreign exchange The National Bank of Commerce opposite the Clock Tower changes cash and travellers' cheques at the usual rate and commission. Several forex bureaux are dotted around town, but while exchange rates are fairly good, you will generally get better in Arusha or Dar es Salaam. One exception is the Trust Bureau de Change, diagonally opposite the Kindoroko Hotel, which offers good rates on US dollar travellers' cheques or cash, charges no commission, and is open 09.00–18.00 Mon–Sat and 09.00–14.00 on Sun. There is an ATM at the Standard Chartered Bank, where up to Tsh200,000 in local currency can be drawn against a Visa or Master card.

Internet and email Numerous internet cafés are dotted around town, with a standard rate of Tsh500 per 15 minutes. We regularly used IBC Internet and Twiga Communications, which are set alongside each other near the Coffee Tree Hotel, and found the service speedy and helpful. The Kilimanjaro Computer Centre in the THB Building on Boma Rd, and Kilimanjaro Information Technology on Ghalla St, have both been recommended. Although some hotels have internet cafés, they are generally a lot pricier than average.

Supermarkets and shops Aleem's supermarket on Boma Rd (behind the post office) stocks a good range of imported goods and foods. The Carina supermarket next to Chrisburgers is also very well stocked. Opposite Aleem's, the Hot Bread Shop sells freshly baked bread as well as a selection of cakes and pies.

Swimming pool Use of the swimming pool at the YMCA is free to hostel residents, but visitors must pay a daily entrance fee of Tsh3,000 pp. The Keys Hotel charges a similar price to casual swimmers, but the pool is smaller and it is further out of town. You could also try the pool at the Kilimanjaro Crane Hotel.

Telephone Phone cards can be bought and used at the Tanzania Telecommunications Centre next to the post office near the Clock Tower. This is also the best place to make international phone calls, and to send and receive faxes.

AROUND MOSHI

The most popular tourist destination in the vicinity of Moshi is of course Mount Kilimanjaro, the upper slopes and ascent of which are detailed in the next chapter *Mount Kilimanjaro National Park*. Other lesser attractions in the region, such as the villages of Marangu and Machame on the Kilimanjaro foothills, or the spectacular lakes Chala and Jipe and remote Mkomazi Game Reserve are covered below, together with a selection of eco-tourist projects relating to Chagga culture.

Marangu

The village of Marangu, whose name derives from the local Chagga word meaning 'spring water', is situated on the lower slopes of Kilimanjaro about 40km from Moshi and 5km south of the main entrance gate to Mount Kilimanjaro National Park. Unlike lower-lying Moshi, Marangu has an appropriately Alpine feel, surrounded as it is by lush vegetation and bisected by a babbling mountain stream, and it remains a popular springboard for Kilimanjaro ascents using the Marangu Route. For those who lack the time, inclination or money to climb Kilimanjaro, Marangu is a pleasant place to spend a night or a few days exploring the lower slopes of the great mountain, with several attractive waterfalls situated within easy striking distance.

Getting there and away

The 40km drive from Moshi shouldn't take much longer than 30 minutes in a private vehicle. To get there, you must first head out along the Dar es Salaam road,

CULTURAL TOURS AROUND MOSHI

The type of cultural tourism project developed by the SNV in association with local communities around Arusha has more recently been introduced to the Kilimanjaro foothills. Two such projects have been implemented in the area, one near Machame, about 15km from Moshi, and the other at the popular trekking base of Marangu. In addition to offering insights into Chagga culture and the opportunity to limber up the limbs before a full-on ascent of Kilimanjaro, these cultural tours allow non-climbers to get a good look at the scenic Kilimanjaro foothills, with a chance of catching a glimpse of the snow-capped peak itself. In addition to the local telephone contacts given below, full details of the programmes can be obtained through the central website www.tourismtanzania.org (e info@tourismtanzania.org). One operator in Moshi that specialises in setting up budget-friendly day trips to the cultural programmes, as well as running its own day hike in the Kilimanjaro foothills, is Akaro Tours (see *Kilimanjaro recommended tour operators*, page 155, for contact details).

Machame Cultural Tourism Programme

This programme is based at the village of Kyalia, close to the Machame Gate of Kilimanjaro National Park. A good day tour for those with a strong interest in scenery is the five-hour Sieny-Ngira Trail, which passes through the lush montane forest to a group of large sacred caves, a natural rock bridge over the Marire and Namwi rivers, and a nearby waterfall. For those with a greater interest in culture, the five-hour Nronga Tour, which visits a milk purification and processing co-operative run by women, is best done on Monday, market day in Kyalia village. Of similar duration, the Nkuu Tour focuses instead on agriculture, in particular coffee production. Longer excursions include the two-day Ng'uni Hike and three-day Lyamungo Tour. In a private vehicle, Kyalia can be reached by following the Arusha road out of Moshi for 12km, then following the turn-off signposted for Machame Gate and driving for another 14km. The road to Kyalia is surfaced in its entirety, and regular minibuses run to Kyalia from the junction on the Moshi–Arusha road. ℡ 027 275 7033; f 027 275 1113.

bearing left after 23km as if heading towards Taveta, then after another 4km turning left again at Himo. Buses between Moshi and Marangu leave in either direction when they are full, which is normally every hour or so, and they generally take from 45 minutes up to one hour.

Where to stay and eat
Upmarket

Marangu Hotel (25 rooms) ℡ 027 275 6591; f 027 275 6594; e marangu@africaonline.co.ke; www.maranguhotel.com. This comfortable, family-run hotel, situated back along the Moshi road 5km before Marangu, has an unpretentiously rustic feel, all ivy-draped walls and neat hedges that might have been transported straight from the English countryside. It also has a long-standing reputation for organising reliable Kilimanjaro climbs, whether you're looking at the standard all-inclusive package or the 'hard way' package aimed at budget travellers. Accommodation is in self-contained rooms. The large green campsite behind the main hotel buildings has a hot shower and is probably the best value for campers in the Marangu area. *US$70/100 sgl/dbl B&B; camping US$3 pp.*

Capricorn Hotel (48 rooms) ℡ 027 275 1309; f 027 275 2442; e capricorn@africaonline.co.tz; www.capricornhotel.com. Straggling over a steep hillside some 2km from Marangu along the road towards Kilimanjaro National Park's Marangu entrance gate, this relatively new hotel has spacious, colourfully decorated and carpeted en-

Marangu Cultural Tourism Programme

Geared primarily towards travellers staying in Marangu prior to a Kilimanjaro climb, this programme offers a variety of half-day trips taking in various natural and cultural sites in the surrounding slopes. Popular goals include any of three waterfalls, as well as the first coffee tree planted in Tanzania more than a century ago, and a traditional conical Chagga homestead. Few prospective climbers will be unmoved by the grave of the legendary Yohanu Lauwo, who guided Hans Meyer to the summit of Kilimanjaro back in 1889, continued working as a guide into his seventies, and lived to the remarkable age of 124! Other walks lead to nearby Mamba and Makundi, known for their traditional Chagga blacksmiths and woodcarvers, and for the Laka Caves, where women and children were hidden during the frequent 19th-century clashes with the Maasai of the surrounding plains. Guided tours can be arranged through any of the hotels in and around Marangu.

Materuni and Kuringe Waterfall Tour

Operated exclusively by Akaro Tours, whose owner grew up in a nearby *shamba*, this rewarding half- or full-day tour starts at the village of Materuni on the foothills of Kilimanjaro some 14km from Moshi. The walk follows sloping roads and footpaths through the surrounding mountainside to the Kuringe Waterfall, a 70m-high 'bridal veil' fall set at the head of a steep wooded gorge. One of the loveliest waterfalls I've seen anywhere in Africa, Kuringe is genuinely worth making an effort to visit, something I don't say lightly after having regularly hiked for miles in the line of duty to check out what, it transpired, was yet another unmemorable small cataract. On the full day, you continue from the waterfall, climbing steep cultivated slopes, to a Chagga homestead, where lunch and home-grown coffee are provided. From here, you can continue on to the Rua Forest, which harbours black-and-white colobus monkeys as well as most of the montane forest birds associated with Kilimanjaro. The full-day version can also incorporate a visit to a typical Chagga coffee and banana subsistence farm.

suite rooms. The hotel is situated within the forest zone, and the lushly wooded grounds are teeming with birds. The restaurant has an excellent reputation, as do Kilimanjaro climbs arranged through the hotel. *US$60/80 B&B for sgl/dbl occupancy or US$70/100 FB.*
Nakara Hotel (17 rooms) ☎ 027 275 6571; f 027 275 6599; e nakara-hotels@iwayafrica.com; www.nakara-hotels.com. This smart but rather soulless high-rise hotel lies about 1km past the Capricorn Hotel and 2km before the park entrance gate. There's nothing wrong with the compact but comfortable self-contained twin rooms, though they hardly qualify as outstanding value, and the rather cramped grounds lack the greenery and character of other options in this price range. *US$70/100 sgl/dbl B&B or US$90/140 FB.*
Kilimanjaro Mountain Resort (11 rooms) ☎ 027 275 8950; f 027 275 8949; e kiliresort@africaonline.co.tz; www.kilimanjaromtresort.com. Situated about 2km further out of Marangu than the Kibo Hotel, this relatively new hotel – it opened in 2003 – has an attractive rural setting in cultivated footslopes dotted with relict forest patches, and the large en-suite rooms with balconies and digital satellite TV seem pretty good value, the rather bombastic décor notwithstanding. Worth a visit, even if you are staying elsewhere, is the small private cultural museum set in a traditional Chagga homestead within the hotel grounds – hotel residents can check it out for free, non-residents must pay a US$2 entrance fee. There is live drumming in the evenings every Wed and Sun. *US$45/50 sgl/dbl B&B.*

Moderate

Kibo Hotel (16 rooms) $\mathbb{V}$f 027 275 1308; e info@kibohotel.com or kibohotel@yahoo.com; www.kibohotel.com. The venerable Kibo Hotel stands in attractive flowering gardens roughly 1km from the village centre towards the park entrance gate. Formerly on a par with the Marangu Hotel, the Kibo has emphatically seen better days – incredibly, lest it escape your attention, former US President Jimmy Carter stayed here several years ago – but it has retained a winning air of faded dignity epitomised by the liberal wood-panelling and creaky old verandas. If nothing else, following a recent change of management and sensible cut in rates, the large, self-contained rooms are decent value. *US$32/52 sgl/dbl B&B or US$53/90 FB.*

Babylon Lodge (28 rooms) $\mathbb{V}$f 027 275 1315; e babylon@africaonline.co.tz. Situated 500m from Marangu Post Office along the Mwika road, this once popular budget hotel has undergone a recent facelift that nudges it right into the moderate category. En-suite rooms with hot water are immaculately clean but rather cramped. 4-course meals cost US$7 pp. Overall, it lacks the character of the similarly priced Kibo Hotel, but it's firmly in the lead when it comes to cleanliness and quality of service. *US$25/40 sgl/dbl B&B.*

Ashanti Lodge e ashantilodge@habari.co.tz. This low-key lodge lies about 2km out of town along the Mwika road, next door – appropriately – to the Ghana Bar. The grounds are very pretty, and the accommodation is in small circular self-contained chalets with banana-leaf roofing. It was very quiet and overhung with a gentle air of neglect when we last looked in, but the lodge lacks not for ambience, and it seems pretty decent value in its price range. *US$25/40 sgl/dbl B&B.*

Budget and camping

Coffee Tree Campsite $\mathbb{\hat{1}}$ 027 275 6604; m 0744 691433; e alpinetrekking@eoltz.com. Situated along the road to the park entrance gate, alongside the Nakara Hotel, this neatly laid out site is also a good place to arrange budget Kilimanjaro climbs. Accommodation in dbl chalets costs US$12 pp, while a bed in a rondavel costs US$10 pp – not exactly great value, but you won't find cheaper in Marangu. The camping seems a bit dear at US$8 pp, and even allowing for the above-average facilities – fridge, bar, barbecue, sauna and hot shower – the campsite at the Marangu Hotel (see *Upmarket* above) seems infinitely better value. Tents and gas stoves are available for hire, various cultural tours can be arranged, and there are on-site email and internet facilities. If you don't fancy self-catering, you could eat at the nearby Nakara Hotel.

Amin's Cottages $\mathbb{\hat{1}}$ 027 275 0667; m 0744 290447; e kiliclimber_2000@yahoo.com. Situated near the Moonjo Waterfall about 1km past the Kibo Hotel, this new campsite charges US$3 pp for camping, and should soon have en-suite rooms available for US$20 pp. It's a lovely rustic spot, but do note that the last 300m of track leading there requires a powerful 4x4 at the best of times and may well be impassable after heavy rain.

Gilman's Camping Site $\mathbb{\hat{1}}$ 027 275 6490; m 0744 299486; e gilmanscamp@yahoo.com. Situated on the opposite side of the road to Amin's Cottages, where it is reached by a rather less perilous 200m dirt track, this new campsite charges US$10 pp to pitch a tent, a rather hefty price only partially justified by its superior facilities, namely a clean ablution block with hot showers, and access to a kitchen and comfortable lounge. The tall, conical traditional Chagga house behind the campsite is one of the last in existence and well worth a look.

Excursions from Marangu

Kinukamori Waterfall

The most central tourist attraction in Marangu is the Kinukamori – 'Little Moon' – Waterfall. Situated about 20 minutes' walk from the town centre, from where it is signposted, this approximately 15m-high waterfall lies in a small park maintained by the district council (US$1 entrance) as an eco-tourism project in collaboration with two nearby villages. It's pretty enough without being an essential side trip, though the wooded banks of the Unna River above the waterfall harbour a variety of forest birds, and regularly attract troops of black-and-white colobus in the rainy season. A legend associated with Kinukamori relates to an unmarried girl called Makinuka, who discovered she was pregnant, a crime punishable by death in strict Chagga society, and decided to take her own life by jumping over the waterfall. When Makinuka arrived at the waterfall and looked over the edge, she changed her mind and turned to go home to plead for mercy. As she did so, however, she came face to face with a leopard and ran back screaming in fear, forgetting about the gorge behind her, to plunge to an accidental death. A statue of Makinuka and her nemesis stands above the waterfall. The waterfall can be visited independently, or by arrangement with your hotel as part of a longer sightseeing tour.

Kilasia Waterfall
Clearly signposted to the left of the dirt road connecting the Kibo Hotel and Kilimanjaro Mountain Resort lies the rather spectacular Kilasia Waterfall, the centrepiece of a new eco-tourist community that charges US$3 for a guided nature walk. Approximately 30m high, the waterfall tumbles into the base of a sheer-sided gorge before running through a set of violent rapids into a lovely pool that's said to be safe for swimming. The waterfall is at its most powerful during the rains, but it flows solidly throughout the year – the name Kilasia derives from a Chagga word meaning 'without end', reputedly a reference to its reliable flow. The path to the base of the falls, though no more than 500m long, is very steep and potentially dangerous when wet. The rocky gorge below the waterfall is lined with ferns and evergreen trees, and a troop of blue monkeys often passes through in the early morning and late afternoon. For further details, you can email the community project manager at kilasiawaterfalls@yahoo.com.

Lake Chala
Straddling the Kenyan border some 30km east of Moshi as the crow flies, this roughly circular crater lake, a full 3km wide yet invisible until you virtually topple over the rim, is one of northern Tanzania's true off-the-beaten-track scenic gems. The brilliant turquoise water, hemmed in by sheer cliffs draped in tropical greenery, is an arresting sight at any time, and utterly fantastic when Kilimanjaro emerges from the clouds to the immediate west. Not for the faint hearted, a very steep footpath leads from the rim to the edge of the lake, its translucent waters plunging near-vertically to an undetermined depth from the rocky shore. Abundant birdlife aside, wildlife is in short supply, though Chala, in common with many other African crater lakes, is said locally to harbour its due quota of mysterious and malignant Nessie-like beasties. A more demonstrable cause for concern should you be nurturing any thoughts of dipping a toe in the water, however, is the presence of crocodiles, one of which savaged and drowned a British volunteer off the Kenyan shore in March 2002.

Attempts to attract tourism to Chala, most notably a tourist lodge on the Kenyan rim (memorable for the bat colony in the toilet when we popped in a couple of years ago), could hardly be deemed an unqualified success. It remains to be seen whether the opening of the Kilimanjaro Chala Lodge and Campsite on the Tanzanian side will change that, but the signs are not good – the lodge, under construction when we dropped by in early 2002, has yet to open almost four years later. For the time being, the only practical way to reach Chala is as an organised day or overnight trip out of Moshi, or in a private 4x4 vehicle. If you're driving, follow the Dar es Salaam road out of Moshi for 25km until you reach the junction at Himo, where a left turn leads to the Kenyan border at Taveta. About 7km along the Taveta Road, turn left on to the rough road signposted for Kilimanjaro Mountain Lodge, which you must follow for about 40 minutes to reach the lake.

Lake Jipe

Shallow, narrow and enclosed by dense beds of tall papyrus, Lake Jipe runs for 10km along a natural sump on the Kenyan border between Kilimanjaro, the main source of its water, and the Mkomazi Game Reserve. It's an atmospheric body of water, with a fabulous setting: the Pare Mountains to the south, Chala crater rising from the flat plain to the east, and – when the clouds clear – Kilimanjaro hulking over the northeast skyline. Lake Jipe is seldom visited, and almost never from the Tanzanian side, but it is reasonably accessible, and there's quite a bit of wildlife around, since part of the northern shore is protected within Kenya's unfenced Tsavo National Park. Gazelle and other antelope are likely to be seen in the arid country approaching the lake, and cheetah and lion are occasionally observed darting across the road. The lake itself is teeming with hippopotami and crocodiles, and the papyrus beds harbour several localised birds, such as lesser jacana, African water rail, pygmy goose and black egret. Elephants regularly come to drink and bathe the northern shore, especially during the dry season. Look out, too, for the lovely impala lily – this shrub-sized succulent, known for its bright pink and white flowers, is common in the dry acacia plains approaching the lake.

Although the papyrus that encloses Lake Jipe gives the lake much of its character, the rapid expansion of the plant over some 50% of the water in the last few decades is possibly symptomatic of a dying lake. Certainly, local fishermen, who now have to reach the open water along shallow canals cut through the crocodile-infested reeds, claim that the fish yield decreases every year along with the amount of open water. The probable explanation for the recent proliferation of papyrus – which can only grow at depths where it can take root in soil – is that the lake has gradually become shallower, due to increased silt levels in the water that flows down from Kilimanjaro. In a chain of cause and effect, the infestation of papyrus on Jipe would thus appear to be a result of the extensive deforestation and a corresponding increase in erosion on Kilimanjaro's lower slopes over the last 50 years.

Whether or not this process will result in the lake drying up entirely is a matter of conjecture, but researchers have expressed serious concerns for its future. The loss of Jipe would be immense, not only to the thousands of villagers for whom the lake has traditionally formed a source of fresh water and protein, but also to the wildlife that is drawn to its water during the dry season. Measures that would contribute to the lake's future – and which are in any case ecologically sound – include an extensive reforestation programme on the Kilimanjaro footslopes, and an attempt to modernise traditional farming methods that tend to cause soil erosion as land pressure intensifies and the earth is worked harder.

The junction town for Lake Jipe, called Kifaru, straddles the B1 some 40km south of Moshi. At Kifaru, turn to the east along a reasonable dirt road towards Kiwakuku. After about 15km, turn on to a track running to the left, distinguished by a blue signpost reading 'Jipe' and, up ahead, a hill with a prominent bald boulder on top. Follow this track for about 2km, and you'll be in Makayuni on the lakeshore. In a private vehicle, the drive from Kifaru takes 30–45 minutes, depending on the condition of the road, so it would be feasible to visit Jipe as a day trip from Moshi. The only public transport from Kifaru is the daily bus to Kiwakuku. This generally leaves Kiwakuku at 04.00, passes the Makayuni junction at around 06.30 and arrives in Kifaru at 09.00 to start the return trip at around 14.00. One Moshi-based safari company that regularly arranges day or overnight trips to Lake Jipe is Akaro Tours.

Once at Makayuni, it's straightforward enough to arrange to be poled on to the lake in a local dugout canoe, whether you want to fish, watch birds or just enjoy the lovely scenery and hope for glimpses of big game on the nearby Kenyan shore. Expect to pay around Tsh3,000 for a short excursion or Tsh10,000 for a full day on the lake. The best time to head on to the lake is in the early morning or late afternoon, when it's not too hot, game is more active and Kilimanjaro is most likely to be visible. Getting out on to the open water first involves a long pole through shallow papyrus marsh, with brightly coloured kingfishers darting in front of the boat and hippos grunting invisibly in the nearby reeds. This stretch can be quite difficult with two passengers weighing down the dugout, so it's best to take one per person. There is no accommodation near Lake Jipe (along the Tanzanian shore, anyway) but it is permitted to pitch a tent in Makayuni for about Tsh1,000 per head. Aside from fish, no food is available locally, and you'll need to bring all drinking water with you too. Mosquitoes (and occasionally lake flies) are prolific on the shore, so do cover up at dusk. Away from the lake, a few basic guesthouses can be found in Kifaru.

Mkomazi Game Reserve

Mkomazi Game Reserve is the southern extension of Kenya's vast Tsavo National Park, covering an area of 3,701km^2 to the east of Kilimanjaro and immediately north of the Pare Mountains. The reserve is practically undeveloped for tourism, and it has been subject to considerable pressure over the last 20 years as the human population around its peripheries has grown in number. Together with Tsavo, Mkomazi forms part of one of east Africa's most important savanna ecosystems, characterised by the semi-arid climatic conditions of the Sahel arc.

In 1992, the Tanzanian government invited the Royal Geographical Society to undertake a detailed ecological study of Mkomazi. Although mammal populations are low, it was determined that most large mammal species present in Tsavo are either resident in Mkomazi or regularly migrate there from Kenya, including lion, cheetah, elephant, giraffe, buffalo, zebra, impala and Tanzania's most significant gerenuk population. African hunting dogs were recently re-introduced into Mkomazi, as was a herd of black rhinos from South Africa. The reserve is listed as an Important Bird Area, with more than 400 species recorded, several of which are northern dry-country endemics newly added to the Tanzania list by the RGS – for instance three-streaked tchagra, Shelley's starling, Somali long-billed crombec, yellow-vented eremomela and the extremely localised Friedmann's lark.

Mkomazi doesn't offer game viewing to compare to other reserves in northern Tanzania, and it is certainly not a conventional safari destination. However, this is compensated for by the wild scenery and near certainty of not seeing another tourist. So far as facilities go, there is a two-bedroom *banda* available at Ibaya Camp on a first-come, first-served basis. Otherwise, there is a basic campsite (little more than cleared areas) about 2km from Zange Gate and another about 20km from Zange overlooking Dindera Dam, a good place to see large mammals. The reserve is best avoided in the rainy season, due to the poor roads, and all visitors should be self-sufficient in water, food and fuel.

Because Mkomazi is not a national park, walking is permitted. The northeast of the reserve, near Zange Gate, is very hilly (tough walking but great scenery) and there is a very real chance of encountering large game animals such as lions and buffaloes on foot. The best way to go about organising a walking trip into

Mkomazi would be to walk or hitch the 5km from Same to Zange Gate, where you can make arrangements with the warden to hire an armed ranger/guide. To stand a chance of seeing a fair range of large mammals, you would need to spend a couple of days walking in the reserve, so you'd need camping gear and adequate provisions. The owner of the Sasa Kazi Hotel in Same can organise car hire into the reserve.

The dusty small town of Same, which straddles the B1 105km south of Moshi, is the gateway to the Mkomazi Game Reserve. The most notable feature of Same, aside from the mountainous backdrop, is a strong Maasai presence – otherwise it's not a terribly interesting place. You're only likely to stop here if you plan on visiting Mbaga or Mkomazi, in which case there is a fairly good chance you'll have to spend the night. The tourist centre at the Sasa Kazi Hotel is the best place to ask for current advice about lifts to Mbaga, or about anything else.

The drive from Moshi to Same, along a good surfaced road, shouldn't take longer than 90 minutes in a private vehicle. Any public transport heading from Moshi to places further south can drop you off at Same. The smartest accommodation is at the recently refurbished church-run **Elephant Motel** (*24 rooms; ☏ 027 275 8193 or 0744 839545;* e *dioceseofsame@kilionline.com*), which lies in large green grounds 1.5km south of the town centre along the B1 towards Dar es Salaam. It offers clean en-suite rooms with netting, TV and hot running water for US$15/20 single/double, and also serves good Indian, Tanzanian and Western meals for around US$3. In the town centre, 100m from the bus station, the **Kambeni Guesthouse** is an excellent local lodging, with standard rooms for less than US$3 and self-contained doubles for US$4. Also recommended in this range are the **Tumaine Guesthouse** and **Amani Lutheran Centre**. The **Sasa Kazi Hotel** doesn't have rooms but it serves reasonable local meals.

Entrance to Mkomazi costs US$20 per person per 24-hour period, but this might change as and when a mid-2005 announcement that it will be upgraded to national park status comes to fruition.

Mount Kilimanjaro National Park

Reaching an altitude of 5,895m (19,330ft), Kilimanjaro is the highest mountain in Africa, and on the rare occasions when it is not veiled in clouds, its distinctive silhouette and snow-capped peak form one of the most breathtaking sights on the continent. There are, of course, higher peaks on other continents, but Kilimanjaro is effectively the world's largest single mountain, a free-standing entity that towers an incredible 5km above the surrounding plains. It is also the highest mountain anywhere that can be ascended by somebody without specialised mountaineering experience or equipment.

In geological terms, Kilimanjaro is a relatively young mountain. Like most other large mountains near the Rift Valley, it was formed by volcanic activity, first erupting about one million years ago. The 3,962m-high Shira Peak collapsed around half a million years ago, but the 5,895m-high Uhuru Peak on Mount Kibo and 5,149m-high Mawenzi Peak continued to grow until more recently. Shira plateau formed 360,000 years ago, when the caldera was filled by lava from Kibo after a particularly violent eruption. Kibo is now dormant, and nobody knows when it last displayed any serious volcanic activity. The Kilimanjaro National Park, gazetted in 1977, protects the entire Tanzanian part of the mountain above the 2,700m contour, an area of 756km².

Kilimanjaro straddles the border with Kenya, but the peaks all fall within Tanzania and can only be climbed from within the country. There are several places on the lower slopes from where the mountain can be ascended, but most people use the Marangu Route (which begins at the eponymous village) because it is the cheapest option and has the best facilities. The less heavily trampled Machame Route, starting from the village of the same name, has grown in popularity in recent years. A number of more obscure routes can be used, though they are generally only available through specialist trekking companies. Most prospective climbers arrange their ascent of 'Kili' – as it is popularly called – well in advance, through an overseas tour operator or online with a local operator, but you can also shop around on the spot using specialist trekking companies based in Moshi, Marangu or even Arusha. Kilimanjaro can be climbed at any time of year, but the hike is more difficult in the rainy months, especially between March and May.

VEGETATION AND BIOLOGY

There are five vegetation zones on Kilimanjaro: the cultivated lower slopes, the forest, heath and moorland, Alpine, and the barren arctic summit zone. Vegetation is sparse higher up due to lower temperatures and rainfall.

The **lower slopes** of the mountain were probably once forested, but are now mainly covered in cultivation. The volcanic soils make them highly fertile and they support a dense human population. The most biologically interesting aspect of the lower slopes is the abundance of wild flowers, seen between Marangu and the park entrance gate.

HUMANS AND THE MOUNTAIN

Blessed by fertile volcanic soil and reliable rainfall, Kilimanjaro has probably always been a magnet for human settlement. Ancient stone tools of indeterminate age have been found on the lower slopes, as have the remains of pottery artefacts thought to be at least 2,000 years old. Archaeological evidence suggests that, between 1,000 and 1,500 years ago, Kilimanjaro was the centre of an Iron Age culture spreading out to the coastal belt between Pangani and Mombasa. Before that, it's anybody's guess really, but references in Ptolemy's *Geography* and the *Periplus of the Erythraean Sea* suggest that the mountain was known to the early coastal traders, and might even have served as the terminus of a trade route starting at modern-day Pangani and following the synonymous river inland. Kilimanjaro is also alluded to in an account written by a 12th-century Chinese trader, and by the 16th-century Spanish geographer, Fernandes de Encisco.

These ancient allusions fired the curiosity of 19th-century geographers, who outdid each other in publishing wild speculations about the African interior. In 1848, locals told Johan Rebmann, a German missionary working in the Taita Hills, about a very large silver-capped mountain known to the Maasai as Ol Doinyo Naibor – White Mountain – and reputedly protected by evil spirits that froze anybody who tried to ascend it. When Rebmann visited the mountain, he immediately recognised the spirit-infested silver cap to be snow, but this observation, first published in 1849, was derided by European experts, who thought it ludicrous to claim there was snow so near the Equator. Only in 1861, when an experienced geologist, Von der Decken, saw and surveyed Kilimanjaro, was its existence and that of its snow-capped peaks accepted internationally. Oral tradition suggests that no local person had successfully climbed Kilimanjaro – or at least returned to tell the tale – before Hans Meyer and Ludwig Purtscheller reached the summit in 1889.

Kilimanjaro is home to the Chagga people, a group of Bantu-speaking agriculturists whose ancestors are said to have arrived in the area in the 15th century. This dating is contradicted by an intriguing local legend relating to an eruption of Kilimanjaro, which doesn't tally with the geological evidence for the past 500 years, so it's probable that the story was handed down by earlier inhabitants. The Chagga have no tradition of central leadership, and an estimated 100 small chieftaincies existed in the region in the mid-19th century.

The **montane forest zone** of the southern slopes lies between the altitudes of 1,800m and 3,000m. Receiving up to 2,000mm of rainfall annually, this zone displays a high biological diversity, and still supports a fair amount of wildlife. The most frequently seen mammals are the black-and-white colobus and blue monkey, while typical forest antelope include three duiker species and the beautifully marked bushbuck. Leopard, bushpig and porcupine are fairly common but seldom encountered by hikers, while eland, buffalo and elephant are present in small numbers. The forest is home to many varieties of butterfly, including four endemic species. The forests of Kilimanjaro are less rich in birds (particularly endemics) than the more ancient forests of the Eastern Arc Mountains, but some 40 species peculiar to Afro-montane forest have been recorded. Most forest birds are quite difficult to observe, but trekkers should at least hear the raucous silvery-cheeked hornbill and beautiful Hartlaub's turaco.

The semi-Alpine **moorland zone**, which lies between 3,000m and 4,000m, is

Today, the Chagga have a reputation for industriousness, and are generally relatively well educated, for which reason you'll find that a high proportion of salaried workers and safari guides come from Kilimanjaro region.

An unsubstantiated legend holds that Emperor Menelik I of Ethiopia, the illegitimate son of King Solomon and the Queen of Sheba, visited Kilimanjaro about 3,000 years ago while returning from a successful military campaign in east Africa. The emperor camped on the saddle for a night, and then ascended Kibo, where he suddenly fell ill and died, possibly from exposure and/or altitude-related causes. Menelik's slaves buried the imperial corpse in the snowy crater, where it remains to this day, so the story goes, together with a royal cache of jewels, religious scrolls and other treasures. An extension of this legend prophesies that a descendant of Menelik I will one day ascend Kibo, find the frozen body, and claim the seal ring of Solomon worn by it, endowing him with the wisdom of Solomon and heroic spirit of Menelik. Pure apocrypha, so far as I can ascertain, is the story that the ancient Ethiopian emperor's 19th-century successor and namesake Menelik II once climbed Kilimanjaro in an unsuccessful bid to fulfil this centuries-old prophecy.

The names of Kilimanjaro's two main peaks, Kibo and Mawenzi, derive from local Chagga words respectively meaning 'cold' and 'jagged'. According to Chagga legend, the peaks are sisters, and both were once as smoothly shaped as the perfect dome of Kibo is today. But the younger sister Mawenzi was habitually too lazy to collect her own firewood and kept borrowing from Kibo until one day the elder sister instructed her to go out and gather her own. When Mawenzi refused, the enraged Kibo reached into her woodpile, grabbed the largest log there, and started beating her over the head, resulting in the jagged shape of the younger sister today.

Rather less clear is the origin of the name Kilimanjaro, or even whether it is Swahili, Maasai or Chagga in origin. That the term 'kilima' is Swahili for little mountain (a joke?) is not in doubt. But 'njaro' could derive from the Chagga word for caravan (the mountain was an important landmark on the northern caravan route), or from the Maasai word 'ngare' meaning water (it is the source of most of the region's rivers), or the name of a Swahili demon of cold. Another unrelated version of the name's origin is that it's a bastardisation of the phrase 'kilema kyaro' (impossible journey), the initial Chagga response to European queries about trekking to the peak!

characterised by heath-like vegetation and abundant wild flowers. As you climb into the moorland, two distinctive plants become common. These are *Lobelia deckenii*, which grows to 3m high, and the groundsel *Senecio kilimanjarin*, which grows up to 5m high and can be distinguished by a spike of yellow flowers. The moorland zone supports a low density of mammals, but pairs of klipspringer are quite common on rocky outcrops and several other species are recorded from time to time. Hill chat and scarlet-tufted malachite sunbird are two birds whose range is restricted to the moorland of large east African mountains. Other localised birds are lammergeyer and Alpine swift. Because it is so open, the views from the moorland are stunning.

The **Alpine zone** between 4,000 and 5,000m is classified as a semi-desert because it receives an annual rainfall of less than 250mm. The ground often freezes at night, but ground temperatures may soar to above 30°C by day. Few plants survive in these conditions; only 55 species are present, many of them lichens and grasses. Six species of moss are endemic to the higher reaches of

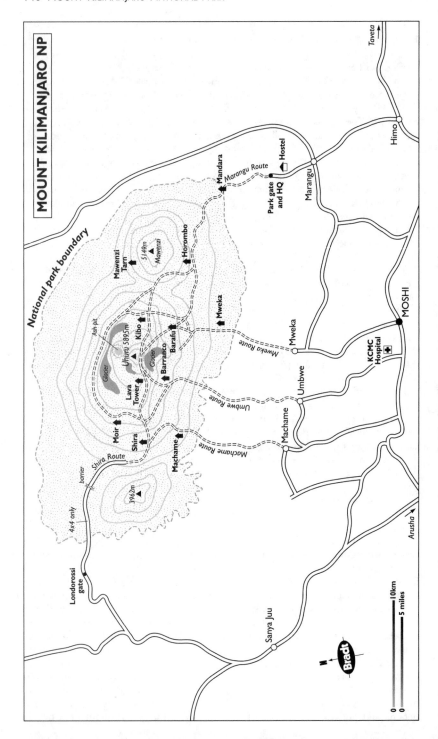

MOUNT KILIMANJARO NP

CHAGGA HOME GARDENS
Emma Thomson

For decades the Chagga have been making use of the fertile soil that lies at the foot of Kilimanjaro. Originally, the land was divided into family allotments or *shamba* (usually 0.68ha) and passed from father to son. Later on land was seized by the state, and re-allocated depending on the size of the family. These lush plots are used to grow coffee, plantain, bananas and medicinal herbs and were unique in their ability to allow the Chagga to be self-sufficient. This cropping system remained stable for at least a century, and only recently has it come under pressure from rapid population growth, diminishing land resources, changes in dietary habits and economic pressures for improved housing and schooling. These pressing needs have forced the younger generations to travel into the towns in search of paid work. However, this migration of youngsters to urban areas not only leads to labour shortages on the farms but also disrupts the traditional transmission from one generation to the next of the knowledge and experience required for the successful management of the farms.

Kilimanjaro. Large mammals have been recorded at this altitude, most commonly eland, but none is resident.

Approaching the summit, the **arctic zone** starts at an altitude of around 5,000m. This area receives virtually no rainfall, and supports little permanent life other than the odd lichen. Two remarkable records concern a frozen leopard discovered here in 1926, and a family of hunting dogs seen in 1962. The most notable natural features at the summit are the inner and outer craters of Kibo, surrounding a 120m-deep ash pit, and the Great Northern Glacier, which has retreated markedly since Hans Meyer first saw it in 1889.

CLIMBING KILIMANJARO

As Africa's highest peak and most identifiable landmark, Kilimanjaro offers an irresistible challenge to many tourists. Dozens of visitors to Tanzania set off for Uhuru Peak every day, ranging from teenagers to pensioners (a seven-year-old boy recently became the youngest person to the summit), and those who make it generally regard the achievement to be the highlight of their time in the country. A major part of Kilimanjaro's attraction is that any reasonably fit person stands a fair chance of reaching the top. The ascent requires no special climbing skills or experience; on the contrary, it basically amounts to a long uphill slog over four days, followed by a more rapid descent.

The relative ease of climbing Kilimanjaro should not lull travellers into thinking of the ascent as some sort of prolonged Sunday stroll. It is a seriously tough hike, with potentially fatal penalties for those who are inadequately prepared or who belittle the health risks attached to being at an altitude of above 4,000m. It should also be recognised that there is no such thing as a cheap Kilimanjaro climb. Indeed, following the increase in official entrance fees to the park for 2006 (where rates per visitor per day have been increased from US$40 to US$60 for climbers), it seems likely the minimum amount payable in park fees alone (entrance, camping, guide, porter and rescue) is in excess of US$500 per person for a standard five-day hike up the relatively cheap Marangu Route. Realistically, it would be difficult for any reputable local operator to put together a reasonably well-equipped package at much under US$750

PORTER TREATMENT GUIDELINES

These guidelines are produced by the Kilimanjaro Porters Assistance Project (KPAP), an initiative of the International Mountain Explorers Connection, a non-profit organisation based out of the United States. Visit the website www.kiliporters.org for further information, or drop into the office in Moshi to attend a 'Porter Briefing', obtain a free Swahili/English language card, purchase discounted maps, arrange for off-the-beaten-path trips and home-stays which directly support the local people, report any instances of porter abuse, or make a donation of clothing, money or volunteer help.

1 Ensure your porters are adequately clothed with suitable footwear, socks, waterproof jackets and trousers, gloves, hats, sunglasses, etc. Clothing for loan is available at the KPAP Office in Moshi.

2 Fair wages should be paid. Kilimanjaro National Park recommends US$6 daily on Marangu Route and US$8 on other routes. Ask your company how much your porters are paid (and whether it includes food) to encourage fair treatment from operators and guides.

3 Porters should eat at least two meals a day and have access to water.

4 Check the weights of the loads. The recommended maximum of 25kg includes the porter's personal gear (assumed to be 5kg), so the load for the company should not exceed 20kg. If additional porters need to be hired make sure that the tour company is paying each porter their full wage when you return.

5 Count the number of porters every day: you are paying and tipping for them. Porters should not be sent down early as they will not receive their tips, and the other porters are then overloaded.

6 Make sure your porters are provided with proper shelter. Where no shelter is available, porters need proper sleeping accommodation that include tents and sleeping bags. Sleeping in the mess tent means that the porters have to wait outside for climbers to finish their meals.

7 Ensure that each porter receives the intended tip. If you give tips to one individual you run the risk that they may not distribute the proper amount to the crew.

8 Take care of sick or injured porters. Porters deserve the same standard of treatment, care and rescue as their clients. Sick or injured porters need to be sent down with someone who speaks their language and understands the problem. If available, porters should also be provided insurance.

9 Get to know your porters. Some porters speak English and will appreciate any effort to speak with them. Free Swahili-language cards are available at the KPAP Office in Moshi. The word *pole* (which translates loosely as 'sorry') shows respect for porters after a long day carrying your bags. *Asante* means 'thank you'.

10 After your climb, report any instances of abuse or neglect by emailing info@kiliporters.org, and complete our Post Climb Survey at www.kiliporters.org (click on 'Climb Survey' to complete).

per person, and small groups and/or those using top-notch operators and/or those using the more obscure route should be prepared to pay considerably more!

Marangu Route

Starting at the Marangu Gate some 5km from the village of the same name, the so-called 'tourist route' is the most popular way to the top of Kilimanjaro, largely because it is less arduous than most of the alternatives, as well as having better facilities and being cheaper to climb. Marangu is also probably the safest route, due to the volume of other climbers and good rescue facilities relative to more obscure routes, and it offers a better chance of seeing some wildlife. It is the only route where you can sleep in proper huts throughout, with bathing water and bottled drinks normally available too. The main drawback of the Marangu route is that it is heavily trampled by comparison with other routes, for which reason many people complain that it can feel overcrowded.

Day 1: Marangu to Mandara Hut (12km, 4 hours) On an organised climb you will be dropped at the park entrance gate a few kilometres past Marangu. There is a high chance of rain in the afternoon, so it is wise to set off on this four-hour hike as early in the day as you can. Foot traffic is heavy along this stretch, which means that although you pass through thick forest, the shy animals that inhabit the forest are not likely to be seen. If your guide will go that way, use the parallel trail which meets the main trail halfway between the gate and the hut. Mandara Hut (2,700m) is an attractive collection of buildings with room for 200 people.

Day 2: Mandara Hut to Horombo Hut (15km, 6 hours) You continue through forest for a short time before reaching the heather and moorland zone, from where there are good views of the peaks and Moshi. The walk takes up to six hours. Horombo Hut (3,720m) sleeps up to 120 people. It is in a valley and surrounded by giant lobelia and groundsel. If you do a six-day hike, you will spend a day at Horombo to acclimatise.

Day 3: Horombo Hut to Kibo Hut (15km, 6–7 hours) The vegetation thins out as you enter the desert-like Alpine zone, and when you cross the saddle Kibo Peak comes into view. This six- to seven-hour walk should be done slowly: many people start to feel the effects of altitude. Kibo Hut (4,703m) is a stone construction that sleeps up to 120 people. Water must be carried there from a stream above Horombo. You may find it difficult to sleep at this altitude, and as you will have to rise at around 01.00 the next morning, many people feel it is better not to bother trying.

Days 4 and 5: Kibo Hut to the summit to Marangu The best time to climb is during the night, as it is marginally easier to climb the scree slope to Gillman's Point on the crater rim when it is frozen. This 5km ascent typically takes about six hours, so you need to get going between midnight and 01.00 to stand a chance of reaching the summit in time to catch the sunrise. From Gillman's Point it is a further two-hour round trip along the crater's edge to Uhuru Peak, the highest point in Africa. From the summit, it's a roughly seven-hour descent with a break at Kibo Hut to Horombo Hut, where you will spend your last night on the mountain. The final day's descent from Horombo to Marangu generally takes 7–8 hours, so you should arrive in Marangu in the mid-afternoon.

Other routes

Although the vast majority of trekkers stick to the Marangu Route, some prefer to ascend Kilimanjaro using one of five relatively off-the-beaten-track alternatives. While the merits and demerits of avoiding the Marangu Route are hotly debated, there is no doubt about two things: firstly that you'll see few other tourists on the more obscure routes, and secondly that you'll pay considerably more for this privilege. Aesthetic and financial considerations aside, two unambiguous logistical disadvantages of the less-used routes are that they are generally tougher going (though only the Umbwe is markedly so), and that the huts – where they exist – are virtually derelict, which enforces camping.

Machame Route

In recent years, the Machame Route has grown greatly in popularity. It is widely regarded to be the most scenic viable ascent route, with great views across to Mount Meru, and as a whole it is relatively gradual, requiring at least six days for the full ascent and descent. Short sections are steeper and slightly more difficult than any part of the Marangu Route, but this is compensated for by the longer period for acclimatisation.

The route is named after the village of Machame, from where it is a two-hour walk to the park gate (1,950m). Most companies will provide transport as far as the gate (at least when the road is passable), and then it's a six- to eight-hour trek through thick forest to Machame Hut, which lies on the edge of the moorland zone at 2,890m. The Machame Hut is now a ruin, so camping is necessary, but water is available. The second day of this trail consists of a 9km, four- to six-hour hike through the moorland zone of Shira Plateau to Shira Hut (3,840m), which is near a stream. Once again, this hut has fallen into disuse, so the options are camping or sleeping in a nearby cave.

From Shira, a number of options exist: you could spend your third night at Lava Tower Hut (4,630m), four hours from Shira, but the ascent to the summit from there is tricky and only advisable if you are experienced and have good equipment. A less arduous option is to spend your third night at Barranco

MOUNTAIN HEALTH

Do not attempt to climb Kilimanjaro unless you are reasonably fit, or if you have heart or lung problems (although asthma sufferers should be all right). Bear in mind, however, that very fit people are more prone to altitude sickness because they ascend too fast.

Above 3,000m you may not feel hungry, but you should try to eat. Carbohydrates and fruit are recommended, whereas rich or fatty foods are harder to digest. You should drink plenty of liquids, at least three litres of water daily, and will need enough water bottles to carry this. Dehydration is one of the most common reasons for failing to complete the climb. If you dress in layers, you can take off clothes before you sweat too much, thereby reducing water loss.

Few people climb Kilimanjaro without feeling some of the symptoms of altitude sickness: headaches, nausea, fatigue, breathlessness, sleeplessness and swelling of the hands and feet. You can reduce these by allowing yourself time to acclimatise by taking an extra day over the ascent, eating and drinking properly, and trying not to push yourself. If you walk slowly and steadily, you will tire less quickly than if you try to rush each day's walk. Acetazolamide (Diamox) helps speed acclimatisation and many people find it useful; take 250mg twice a day for five days, starting two or three days before reaching 3,500m. However, the side effects from this drug may resemble altitude sickness and therefore it is advisable to try the medication for a couple of days about two weeks before the trip to see if it suits you.

Campsite (3,950m), a tough 12km, six-hour hike from Shira, then to go on to Barafu Hut (4,600m) on the fourth day, a walk of approximately seven hours. From Barafu, it is normal to begin the steep seven- to eight-hour clamber to Stella Point (5,735m) at midnight, so that you arrive at sunrise, with the option of continuing on to Uhuru Peak, a two-hour round trip, before hiking back down to Mweka Hut via Barafu in the afternoon. This day can involve up to 16 hours of walking altogether. After spending your fifth night at Mweka Hut (3,100m), you will descend the mountain on the sixth day via the Mweka Route, a four- to six-hour walk.

Although the huts along this route are practically unusable, you still get to pay the US$40 'hut fee'. Any reliable operator will provide you with camping equipment and employ enough porters to carry the camp and set it up.

Mweka Route

This is the steepest and fastest route to the summit. There are two huts along it – Mweka (3,100m) and Barafu (4,600m), uniports that sleep up to 16 people – though neither is reputedly habitable at the time of writing. There is water at Mweka but not at Barafu. This route starts at the Mweka Wildlife College, 12km from Moshi. From there it takes about eight hours to get to Mweka Hut, then a further eight hours to Barafu, from where it replicates the Machame Route. The Mweka Route is not recommended for ascending the mountain, since it is too short for proper acclimatisation, but is often used as a descent route by people climbing the Machame or Shira routes.

Shira Route

Although this route could technically be covered in five days by driving to the high-altitude trailhead, this would allow one very little time to acclimatise, and

Should symptoms become severe, and especially if they are clearly getting worse, then descend immediately. Even going down 500m is enough to start recovery. Sleeping high with significant symptoms is dangerous; if in doubt descend to sleep low.

Pulmonary and cerebral oedema are altitude-related problems that can be rapidly fatal if you do not descend. Symptoms of the former include shortness of breath when at rest, coughing up frothy spit or even blood, and undue breathlessness compared with accompanying friends. Symptoms of high altitude cerebral oedema are headaches, poor co-ordination, staggering like a drunk, disorientation, poor judgement and even hallucinations. The danger is that the sufferer usually doesn't realise how sick he/she is and may argue against descending. The only treatment for altitude sickness is descent.

Hypothermia is a lowering of body temperature usually caused by a combination of cold and wet. Mild cases usually manifest themselves as uncontrollable shivering. Put on dry, warm clothes and get into a sleeping bag; this will normally raise your body temperature sufficiently. Severe hypothermia is potentially fatal: symptoms include disorientation, lethargy, mental confusion (including an inappropriate feeling of well-being and warmth!) and coma. In severe cases the rescue team should be summoned.

A US$20 rescue fee is paid by all climbers upon entering the national park. The rescue team ordinarily covers the Marangu Route only; if you use another route their services must be organised in advance.

CHAGGA FAMILIES
Emma Thomson

Clan identity is highly important to the Chagga – to the extent that when individuals address each other, they will mention their clan name before revealing their Christian or family name.

This sense of solidarity and membership is reinforced within the family unit, where every son is appointed a specific role. The first-born must protect and care for his grandmother, by visiting her at least once a month. The second son is raised to inherit the role of the father and must apply himself to his father's bidding. The third son must protect and cherish his mother.

Every year, between Christmas and the New Year, all family members must return to their home villages for at least three days, so they can be accounted for and to introduce new family members. If unable to attend, the absentee must provide a valid excuse, or from then on they are considered outsiders.

greatly decrease the odds of reaching the summit. A minimum of six days is recommended, but better seven so that you can spend a full day at Shira Hut to acclimatise. The route starts at Londorossi Gate on the western side of the mountain, from where a 19km track leads to the trailhead at around 3,500m. It is possible to motor to the trailhead in a 4x4, but for reasons already mentioned it would be advisable to walk, with an overnight stop to camp outside Simba Cave, which lies in an area of moorland where elephants and buffalo are regularly encountered. From the trailhead, it's a straightforward 4km to the campsite at the disused Shira Hut. If you opt to spend two nights at Shira in order to acclimatise, there are some worthwhile day walks in the vicinity. From Shira Hut, the route is identical to the Machame Route, and it is normal to return along the Mweka Route.

Rongai Route

The only route ascending Kilimanjaro from the northeast, the recently re-opened Rongai Route starts close to the Kenyan border and was closed for several years due to border sensitivity. In terms of gradients, it is probably less physically demanding than the Marangu Route, and the scenery, with views over the Tsavo Plains, is regarded to be as beautiful. The Rongai Route can be covered over five days, with equally good if not better conditions for acclimatisation than the Marangu Route, though as with Marangu the odds of reaching the summit improve if you opt for an additional day.

The route starts at the village of Nale Moru (2,000m) near the Kenyan border, from where a footpath leads through cultivated fields and plantation forest before entering the montane forest zone, where black-and-white colobus monkeys are frequently encountered. The first campsite is reached after between three and five hours, and lies at about 2,700m on the frontier of the forest and moorland zone. On the five-day hike, the second day involves a gentle five- to six-hour ascent, through an area of moorland where elephants are sometimes seen, to Third Cave campsite (3,500m). On the third day, it's a four- to five-hour walk to School Campsite (4,750m) at the base of Kibo, with the option of camping here or else continuing to the nearby Kibo Hut, which is more crowded but more commodious. The ascent from here is identical to the Marangu Route. A six-day

KILIMANJARO: RECOMMENDED TOUR OPERATORS

The most popular base for organising a Kilimanjaro climb on the spot is Moshi, but most of the hotels at Marangu arrange reliable climbs, and many tourists who pre-book a climb prefer to work through a company based in Arusha. The following companies are all recommended.

Moshi

Shah Tours ☎ 027 275 2370; f 027 275 1449; e kilimanjaro@eoltz.com. Situated on Mawenzi Road, between the bus station and Clock Tower, this long-standing operator has been arranging mid- to upper-range Kili climbs for as long as I can remember.

Keys Hotel ☎ 027 275 2250/1870; f 027 275 0073; e keys-hotel@africaonline.co.tz; www.keys-hotels.com. Excellent and experienced operator based out of one of the town's best hotels, and very reasonably priced.

Akaro Tours ☎ 027 275 2986; m 0744 272124; f 027 275 2249; e safaris@akarotours.com; www.akarotours.com. This relatively new company is owned and managed by a dynamic former Kilimanjaro guide with vast hands-on experience of the mountain. Good prices for Kili climbs, as well as a great range of cultural day tours out of Moshi.

Marangu

The family-run Marangu Hotel has been taking people up Kilimanjaro for decades, and they have an impeccable reputation. The standard packages aren't the cheapest available, but the standard of service and equipment is very high. The 'hard-way' climbs organised by the Marangu Hotel are probably the cheapest reliable deals you'll find, assuming that you are prepared to self-cater. Also regarded to be reliable are the Capricorn and Kibo hotels and Babylon Lodge. Contact details for these hotels are found under *Where to stay* in Marangu.

Arusha

Most safari companies in Arusha arrange Kilimanjaro climbs, but will generally work through a ground operator in Moshi or Marangu, which means that they have to charge slightly higher rates. Any of the Arusha-based safari companies listed in that section can be recommended, and short-stay visitors who are already going on safari with one of these companies will probably find that the ease and efficiency of arranging a Kilimanjaro climb through that company outweighs the minor additional expenditure.

There are a few companies that arrange their own Kili climbs out of Arusha. Hoopoe Adventure Tours has a long track record of organising ascents along the lesser-known routes, and is well worth contacting should you want to do that sort of thing and you're prepared to pay a premium for top guides and equipment. So too is Nature Discovery, a highly regarded company that specialises in the more obscure routes up the mountain, and routinely sets up camp in the crater of Kibo, allowing you to explore the peaks area and ash cone at relative leisure. Tropical Trails, based at Maasai Camp on the outskirts of Arusha, has an excellent reputation for Kili climbs. Roy Safaris also arranges its own trekking and climbing on Kilimanjaro, Mount Meru and elsewhere. Contact details of all these companies are on page 110.

variation on the above route involves spending the second night at Kikelewa Caves (3,600m, six- to seven-hour walk), a night at Mawenzi Tarn near the synonymous peak (4,330m, four-hour walk), then crossing the saddle between Mawenzi and Kibo to rejoin the five-day route at School Campsite.

Umbwe Route

This short, steep route, possibly the most scenic of the lot, is not recommended as an ascent route as it is very steep in parts and involves one short stretch of genuine rock climbing. It is occasionally used as a descent route, and can be tied in with almost any of the ascent routes, though many operators understandably prefer not to take the risk, or charge a premium for using it. Umbwe Route descends from Barranco Hut, and comes out at the village of Umbwe. It is possible to sleep in two caves on the lower slopes along this route.

Arranging a climb

The *only* sensible way to go about climbing Kilimanjaro is through a reliable operator that specialises in Kili climbs. Readers who pre-book a climb through a known tour operator in their own country can be confident that they will be going with a reputable ground operator in Tanzania. For readers who want to make their arrangements online or after they arrive in Tanzania, several trekking companies operate out of Moshi, Arusha and Marangu, and you should be able to negotiate a far better price by cutting out the middleman, but do be very circumspect about dealing with any company without a verifiable pedigree. A list of respected operators is included in the box on page 155, and while such a list can never be comprehensive, it is reasonable to assume that anybody who can offer you a significantly cheaper package than the more budget-friendly companies on this list is not to be trusted.

In 2005, five-day Marangu climbs with a reliable operator started at an all-inclusive price of around US$700–800 per head for two people, but this is certain to increase by another US$150 per person when park entrance fees double in January 2006. You may be able to negotiate the starting price down slightly, especially for a larger group, but when you are paying this sort of money, it strikes me as sensible to shop around for the best quality of service rather than a fractional saving. A reputable operator will provide good food, experienced guides and porters, and reliable equipment – all of which go a long way to ensuring not only that you reach the top, but also that you come back down alive. You can assume that the cost of any package with a reputable operator will include a registered guide, two porters per person, park fees, food, and transport to and from the gate. It is, however, advisable to check exactly what you are paying for, and (especially for larger parties) to ensure that one porter is also registered as a guide, so that if somebody has to turn back, the rest of the group can still continue their climb. It might also be worth pointing out the potential risk attached to forming an impromptu group with strangers merely to cut 5% or so off the price. If you hike on your own or with people you know well, you can dictate your own pace and there is less danger of personality clashes developing mid-climb.

The standard duration of a climb on the Marangu Route is five days. Many people with repeated experience of Kilimanjaro recommend adding a sixth day to acclimatise at Horombo Hut. It is often said that this will improve the odds of reaching the summit by as much as 20%. Others feel that the extra day makes little difference except that it adds a similar figure to the cost of the climb. One person who owns a climbing company in Arusha kept records for three years and noted only a slightly increased success rate in people who take the extra day, and which

ABBOTT'S DUIKER

An antelope occasionally encountered by hikers on Kilimanjaro is Abbott's duiker *Cephalophus spadix*, a montane forest species that was formerly quite widespread in suitable east African habitats, but is today endemic to eastern Tanzania due to environmental loss and poaching elsewhere in its natural range. After Ader's duiker, a lowland species of the east African coastal belt, Abbott's is the most threatened of African duikers, categorised as Vulnerable in the IUCN Red Data list for 2000, but based on present trends likely to decline to a status of Critically Endangered in the foreseeable future. Abbott's duiker is today confined to five forested montane 'islands' in eastern Tanzania, namely Kilimanjaro, Usambara, Udzungwa, Uluguru and Rungwe. The total population is unknown – a 1998 estimate of 2,500 based on limited data is not implausible – but Udzungwa probably harbours the most substantial and secure single population, followed by Kilimanjaro. Should you be lucky enough to stumble across this rare antelope, it has a glossy, unmarked off-black torso, a paler head and a distinctive red forehead tuft. Its size alone should, however, be diagnostic: the shoulder height of up to 75cm is the third-largest of any duiker species, and far exceeds that of other more diminutive duikers that occur in Tanzania.

he attributes to their extra determination to reach the top after having paid more money.

In this context, it is worth noting that the exhaustion felt by almost all hikers as they approach the peak is not merely a function of altitude. On the Marangu Route, for instance, most people hike for six to eight hours on day three, and then after a minimal dose of sleep (if any at all) rise at around midnight to start the final five- to six-hour ascent to the peak. In other words, when you reach the peak following the conventional five-day hike, you will have been walking for up to 14 of the last 20-odd hours, without any significant sleep – something that would tire out most people even if they weren't facing an altitudinal climb of around 2,000m. On that basis alone, an extra night along the way would have some value in pure recuperative terms. And certainly, my firm impression is that travellers who spend six days on the mountain enjoy the climb far more than those who take five days, whether or not they reach the peak. The choice is yours.

Of the less popular routes up Kilimanjaro, the one most frequently used by tourists is the Machame Route, which requires a minimum of six days. Most operators will charge at least 25% more for this route, because it requires far more outlay on their part. The huts along the Machame Route are in such poor condition that tents and camping equipment must be provided, along with a coterie of porters to carry and set up the makeshift camp. The same problem exists on all routes except Marangu, so that any off-the-beaten-track climb will be considerably more costly than the standard one. Should you decide to use a route other than Marangu, it is critical that you work through an operator with experience of that route.

The dubious alternative to using a reputable company is to take your chances with a small operator or private individual who approaches you in the street. These guys will offer climbs for around US$100 cheaper than an established operator, but the risks are greater and because they generally have no office, there is little accountability on their side. Many of these guides *are* genuine and reliable, but it's difficult to be certain unless you have a recommendation from somebody who has used the same person. A crucial point when comparing this situation with the similar one that surrounds arranging a safari out of Arusha is that you're not merely talking about losing a day through breakdown or something like that. With Kilimanjaro, you could literally die on the mountain. I've heard several stories of climbers being supplied with inadequate equipment and food, even of travellers being abandoned by their guide mid-climb. The very least you can do, if you make arrangements of this sort, is to verify that your guide is registered; he should have a small wallet-like document to prove it, though even this can be faked.

The reason why climbing Kilimanjaro is so expensive boils down to the high park fees. In 2006, there is a daily entrance fee of US$60 per person, plus a rescue fee of US$20 per person per climb, plus a hut fee of US$40 per person per night. In addition to this, a daily entrance fee of US$10 is charged for the guide, along with a rescue fee of US$20. In other words, the fixed costs attached to a five-day Marangu climb work out at more than US$500 per person, to which must be added the cost of transport, food and cooking fuel, and the guide's and porters' salaries. Hikers are expected to tip their guides and porters. The company you go with can give you an idea of the going rate, but around US$5 per day per guide/porter per climbing party is fair.

Other preparations

Two climatic factors must be considered when preparing to climb Kilimanjaro. The obvious one is the cold. Bring plenty of warm clothes, a windproof jacket, a pair of gloves, a balaclava, a warm sleeping bag and an insulation mat. During the rainy season, a waterproof jacket and trousers will come in useful. A less obvious factor is the sun, which is fierce at high altitudes. Bring sunglasses, sunscreen and a hat.

Other essentials are water bottles, and solid shoes or preferably boots that have already been worn in. Most of these items can be hired in Moshi or at the park gate, or from the company you arrange to climb with. I've heard varying reports about the condition of locally hired items, but standards seem to be far higher than they were only a few years back.

A good medical kit is essential, especially if you are climbing with a cheap company. You'll go through plenty of plasters if you acquire a few blisters (assume that you will), and can also expect to want headache tablets.

You might want to buy biscuits, chocolate, sweets, glucose powder and other energy-rich snacks to take with you up the mountain. No companies supply this sort of thing, and although they are sometimes available at the huts, you'll pay through your nose for them.

Maps and further reading

Trekkers are not permitted on the mountain without a registered guide, and all sensible trekkers will make arrangements through a reliable operator, which means that there is no real need for detailed route descriptions once you're on the mountain. Nevertheless, many trekkers will benefit from the detailed practical advice and overview of route possibilities provided in the highly regarded *Kilimanjaro and Mount Kenya Climbing and Trekking Guide* by Cameron Burns, published in 1998 by The Mountaineers, Seattle. This book is essential reading for anybody planning to do serious rock climbing or to hike away from the main routes.

More concerned with the overall geology and natural history of Kilimanjaro, making it a more useful companion to trekkers on organised hikes, *Kilimanjaro: Africa's Beacon* is one of a series of glossy and informative pocket-sized guides published by the Zimbabwe-based African Publishing Group in association with TANAPA. It is widely available in Arusha and Moshi for around US$8. Its predecessor, the 60-page national park handbook *Kilimanjaro National Park*, is arguably more informative but less attractively put together, and is still widely available in Arusha and Moshi for around US$5.

The Walker's Guide and Map to Kilimanjaro by Mark Savage (*African Mountain Guides, 32 Sea Mill Crescent, Worthing, UK*) is a popular and reliable map, with useful practical information printed on the back. It is difficult to locate in Arusha, and has to some extent been superseded by Giovanni Tombazzi's more current *New Map of Kilimanjaro National Park*, published in 1998 in conjunction with Hoopoe Adventure Tours and available all over Arusha and Moshi. Current climbing tips are printed on the back of this map, along with a close-scale map of the final ascent to Kibo, and day-by-day contour 'graphs' for the Machame and Marangu routes.

Before you leave home – or as a memento when you get back – try to get hold of *Kilimanjaro* by John Reader (*Elm Tree Books, London, 1982*). Although it is superficially a coffee-table book, it offers a well-written and absorbing overview of the mountain's history and various ecosystems. The photographs are good too.

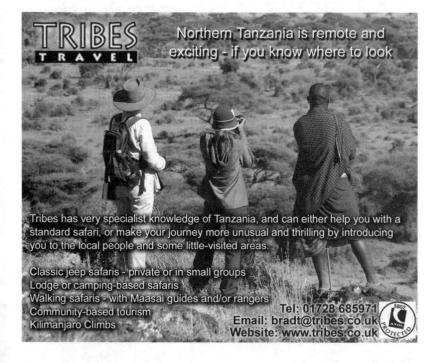

Tarangire and the Central Rift Valley

The least-celebrated of the quartet of wildlife sanctuaries that comprise northern Tanzania's established safari circuit, Tarangire National Park is nevertheless highly rewarding, especially during the latter half of the year, when it is a recommended inclusion on any safari itinerary of longer than a week in duration. The park is best known for its density of baobab trees and year-round proliferation of elephants, but predators are also well represented, the birdlife is excellent, and from July until November large herds of migrant grazers are drawn to the perennial water of the Tarangire River.

Tarangire lies in the floor of the Central Rift Valley, a semi-arid region that's still inhabited by various traditional pastoralists, most famously the Maasai, who live in the immediate vicinity of the national park, but also the Barabaig and other subgroups of the Datoga further southwest. And although most tourists confine their exploration of this area to the national park, there is plenty else to see in the area, ranging from the underrated rock art of the Maasai Escarpment to the pretty Lake Babati to the little-known Mount Hanang, an isolated volcanic relict that rises from the Rift Valley floor to the impressive altitude of 3,417m.

As with the other game reserves along the northern circuit, Tarangire is serviced by a range of lodges to suit most tastes, and is most easily explored as part of a road safari out of Arusha, though fly-in packages are available. At a push, the rock art of the Maasai Escarpment could be visited as a day trip out of Tarangire, but more sensible perhaps to make an overnight excursion of it, either camping at Kolo near the paintings or bedding down at one of the basic lodges in the small town of Kondoa further south. Babati and Mount Hanang are rather more accessible by public transport, and an excellent cultural tourism project in Babati can arrange mountain hikes as well as trips on the lake.

TARANGIRE NATIONAL PARK

The 2,600km^2 Tarangire National Park lies at the core of a much more expansive ecosystem, one that also comprises the 585km^2 Tarangire Conservation Area and some 5,000km^2 of unprotected land extending across the Maasai Steppes. As with the Serengeti, there is a great deal of migratory movement within this greater ecosystem. During the wet season, most of the wildlife disperses from the park onto the Maasai Steppes, while the wildebeest and zebra move northwest to the Rift Valley floor between lakes Natron and Manyara. In direct contrast to the Serengeti, Tarangire comes into its own during the dry season, between July and November, when the large herds of game attracted to the permanent waters of the Tarangire River make this reserve as alluring as any in Tanzania.

In general, Tarangire is more densely vegetated than the Serengeti, covered primarily in acacia and mixed woodland. Near the Tarangire River, however, there is a cover of dense elephant grass broken by the occasional palm tree, and baobab

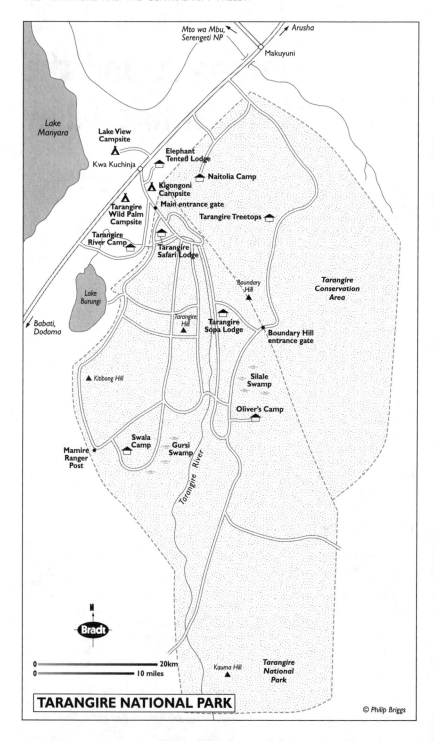

TARANGIRE NATIONAL PARK

© Philip Briggs

trees are abundant throughout. Tarangire supports a similar range of large mammals to the Serengeti. The full range of large predators is harboured within the park, but the dense vegetation can make it difficult to pick up the likes of lion and leopard, even though they are common on the main tourist road circuit. Tarangire is justifiably famous for the prolific elephant herds that congregate along the river during the dry season. It is no exaggeration to say that you might see 500 elephants over the course of a day in the park, though they are generally a little more skittish than their counterparts in Manyara and Ngorongoro. Two localised antelope found in Tarangire are the fringe-eared oryx and gerenuk. According to the 1980 census, the greater Tarangire ecosystem supported 25,000 wildebeest, 30,000 zebra, 6,000 buffalo, 3,000 elephant, 2,700 giraffe, 5,500 eland, 30,000 impala and 2,000 warthog, and there is no reason to think these numbers have altered dramatically in the interim, though the elephant population is definitely on a steady upward curve. Of the smaller mammals, the colonial dwarf mongoose is characteristic of the park, and often seen on the termite hills where it breeds.

Tarangire's reputation as the best of the northern reserves for birds is, in my experience, slightly overstated, since Lake Manyara has a far greater habitat and avian diversity. All the same, with around 500 species recorded in the park, you should see a good variety of birds over the course of a day. A wide range of resident raptors includes bateleur, fish eagle and palmnut vulture, while the river supports saddle-billed and yellow-billed storks and several other waterbirds. Characteristic acacia birds are yellow-necked spurfowl, orange-bellied parrot, barefaced go-away bird, red-fronted barbet, and silverbird. A personal favourite is the red-and-yellow barbet, with its quaintly comical clockwork duet, typically performed on termite mounds. Tarangire's location means it lies at the western limit of the normal range of several species associated with drier parts of the Somali-Maasai biome, for instance vulturine guineafowl, Donaldson-Smith's nightjar, pink-breasted lark, northern pied babbler and mouse-coloured penduline tit. It is also the easiest place to observe a pair of bird species endemic to the dry heartland of central Tanzania: the lovely yellow-collared lovebird, and the somewhat drabber ashy starling, both of which are common locally.

Most people spend only one day in Tarangire and thus concentrate on the roads of the well-developed northern circuit, which follows the river between the two main lodges within the park boundaries. And this is unambiguously the best game-viewing area, typically hosting large numbers of elephant as well as other grazers. For those who have more time, however, the Lake Burungi circuit offers the best chance of seeing bushbuck and lesser kudu, while the Kitibong Hill area is home to large herds of buffalo, and Lamarkau Swamp supports hippo and numerous waterbirds during the wet season. Further south, cheetahs favour the southern plains, while the Mkungero Pools is a good place to look for buffalo, waterbuck and gerenuk.

Abutting the northeastern border of the national park, the 585km² Tarangire Conservation Area consists of four contiguous tracts of land (Lolkisale Concession Area, Naitolia Concession Area, Makuyuni Elephant Dispersal Area and Lolkisale Livestock and Wildlife Zone) used for trophy hunting until ownership was restored to their traditional Maasai inhabitants in the late 1990s. The four blocks of communal land now function collectively as a buffer conservation area to the national park, generating revenue from levies raised by the tourist lodges that lie within them. Two tourist lodges, Tarangire Treetops and Boundary Hill Lodge (the latter not operational at the time of writing), lie within the 165km² Lolkisale Concession Area, which encompasses the main watershed for the Tarangire River, the wetlands around Gosuwa Swamp, and the migration routes used by wildebeest and zebra to reach their breeding grounds near Lolkisale Mountain. There is also an eponymous lodge set within Naitolia. An important difference between these lodges and their counterparts within the national park is that game walks and night drives are permitted.

A 56-page booklet, *Tarangire National Park*, is available from the National Parks office in Arusha. As of January 2006, the park entrance fee is US$35 per person per 24 hours.

Getting there and away

Tarangire lies about 7km off the main Arusha–Dodoma road. Coming from Arusha, this road is tarred as far as the turn-off to the park, which is clearly signposted about 100km south of Arusha and 20km past Makuyuni (the junction for Manyara and the Serengeti). Most people tag a visit to Tarangire on to a longer safari, but if your time or money is limited, a one- or two-day stand-alone safari would be a viable option.

Where to stay
Exclusive

Swala Camp (9 rooms) ☎ 027 250 9817; f 027 250 8273; e tanzania@sanctuarylodges.com; www.sanctuarylodges.com. Situated in the southern half of the park, this classic luxury tented camp stands in a grove of tall acacia trees overlooking the remote Gurusi Swamp, where it is wonderfully isolated from any other lodge or the more popular game-viewing circuits. The camp itself is something of a magnet for wildlife: the *swala* (antelope) for which it is named are much in evidence, especially a resident herd of impala, accompanied by a noisy entourage of vervet monkeys, guineafowl and various plovers, buffalo-weavers and starlings. The small waterhole in front of the camp attracts elephants in Jul and Aug, while a near-resident lion pride and the occasional leopard pass through with surprising regularity. The food is excellent, especially the bush dinners held in a grove of baobabs about 5 minutes' drive from camp, and the quality of tented accommodation is in line with the best lodges of this type in southern Africa. *US$405/610 FB inc drinks, or US$505/810 for a full game package; substantial discount Nov–mid-Dec; premium charged in peak season Jan–Mar. Closed Apr and May.*

Tarangire Treetops Lodge (20 rooms) ☎ 027 254 0630–9; f 027 254 8245; e info@elewana.com; www.elewana.com. Situated to the northeast of the national park within the Tarangire Conservation Area, this architecturally innovative lodge consists of 20 spacious and luxurious en-suite tree houses, each with a floor area of 65m², perched up in the branches of a stand of massive baobab trees – so atmospheric and comfortable it almost seems a shame to leave them to go on a game drive! Because the lodge lies on private land, activities such as game walks, birding walks along a nearby watercourse, night drives and mountain biking excursions supplement the usual diurnal game drives. The quality of game viewing in the immediate vicinity varies seasonally, but it's only 45 minutes by road to Boundary Hill Gate, the main road circuit in northern Tarangire. Ideal for honeymooners, this lodge is also a wonderful place to recover from jetlag at the start of a safari, or to stretch your legs at the end of one. A portion of the room rate funds community projects such as the construction of schools and bore holes. *Drive-in rates US$335 pp FB, inc most drinks, laundry, transfer to/from Kuro airstrip, and daytime game drives, rising to US$425 pp in Feb, Jul and Aug. Closed Apr and May.*

Oliver's Camp (5 rooms) ☎ 027 250 4118; m 0748 763338; e info@asilialodges.com; www.asilialodges.com. This excellent bush camp is located near the Silale Swamp within the park boundaries, but far away from the busy northern section of the park so that activities can usually be undertaken without seeing other tourists. It caters both for 2-night stays incorporated into more wide-ranging safaris as well as for extended stays of 3 days or more, in which visitors explore the area on foot (it is the only location where walking safaris can be undertaken inside Tarangire) and by vehicle, as well as spending one or more nights at a mobile fly-camp. The lodge itself is unpretentious and comfortable rather than opulently luxurious, the guides are unusually personable and knowledgeable, and a superb library of natural-history books underscores the emphasis on substance over style – strongly recommended to anybody seeking a genuinely holistic bush experience. *US$440/640 sgl/dbl FB, inc drinks, game walks, game drives in open vehicles, and any pre-arranged fly-camping excursions.*

Upmarket

Tarangire Safari Lodge (40 rooms) ↘ 027 253 1447; m 0748 202777; f 027 254 4752; e sss@habari.co.tz; www.tarangiresafarilodge.com. This owner-managed lodge is the oldest in the park, with a sublime location on a tall bluff overlooking the Tarangire River. Game viewing from the veranda can be excellent, with large herds of hippo, giraffe and other animals coming down to the river to drink. The grounds are also highly attractive to birders, not only for the remarkably habituated hornbills, buffalo-weavers and starlings that parade around the common areas, but also for the host of smaller birds that are resident in the acacia scrub. Facilities include a swimming pool. This comfortable, unpretentious and well-managed lodge ranks as one of my favourites anywhere on the northern circuit. The accommodation in standing tents with en-suite toilets is outstanding value. *US$78/98 sgl/dbl B&B; bungalows US$84/106/120 sgl/dbl/triple, with 50% reduction in low season. Lunch US$16, dinner US$20, limited selection of snacks is available at around US$4 each.*

Tarangire Sopa Lodge (75 rooms) ↘ 057 250 6886; f 057 250 8245; e info@sopalodges.com; www.sopalodges.com. Set in the heart of the national park, the Tarangire Sopa is the largest and most conventionally luxurious – and least 'bush' – of the lodges around Tarangire. The facilities and accommodation match the customary high standards of this chain, with smart self-contained suites and excellent food. My one, rather large, reservation is the indifferent location, alongside a small and normally dry watercourse below a baobab-studded slope – surely a more scenic site could have been chosen? *US$175/280 sgl/dbl FB in peak season, dropping to US$88/175 in low season.*

Naitolia Camp ↘ (UK) 01923 255462; f 01923 255452; e hoopoeUK@aol.com; www.kirurumu.com. Now managed by Hoopoe Adventure Tours, this excellent bush camp is set in 11,000 acres of Maasailand on the northern border of the park. The main camp consists of 3 attractively furnished canvas, stone and thatch huts, each of which has a king-size bed with walk-in netting and a private balcony, shower and a toilet with a view. Because the camp lies on communal land, guided game walks can be undertaken, with a good chance of spotting giraffe, elephant, zebra and a variety of antelope and birds, and it is possible to be taken to Maasai *bomas* that don't normally receive tourists. They also do overnight walking safaris within the community area, using fly-camps. There is a separate campsite close to the main camp where campers can pitch their own tents. *US$173/266 sgl/dbl FB, inc some activities.*

Tarangire River Camp (18 rooms) ↘ 0748 593008; f 027 250 8937; e mawenzisaf@habari.co.tz or twc-reservations@habari.co.tz; www.africawilderness.com. Situated just 3.5km outside the main gate as the crow flies (but more like 15km by road) this new tented camp lies within a 250km² concession, set aside for conservation by the Maasai community of Minjingu, along the northwest boundary of the national park. The camp is set below a massive old baobab on a cliff overlooking the (normally dry) Minjingu River, a tributary of the Tarangire, and wildlife can be quite prolific in the vicinity seasonally, even though it is not in the park. The lodge is centred on a vast stilted thatch and timber structure comprised of a main lounge, a small library, and a dining and cocktail area, offering sweeping views across the riverbed to the Maasai Steppes. The large en-suite tents with private balcony, 2 ¾ beds and 24-hour solar power are good value. *US$160/200 sgl/dbl FB.*

Moderate

Elephant Tented Lodge (12 rooms) ☏ 027 250 9536; f 027 250 9584;
e info@kilimanjarosafari.com; www.kilimanjarosafari.com. Situated just 9km from the
entrance gate and clearly signposted from the main road coming from Arusha, this new
lodge consists of just 12 standing tents facing a waterhole that regularly attracts elephants
and other wildlife, including nocturnal species such as the bouncy springhare.
Unfortunately, the lodge is laid out so that the tents are very close together, and the
balconies all face each other, meaning that you would have little privacy. The décor also
leaves something to be desired. Still it's not bad value. *US$70/110 sgl/dbl B&B; light meals
and snacks available for around US$3.*

Budget and camping

Kigongoni Campsite This small private camp, which lies a few kilometres outside the
park entrance gate, is firmly aimed at budget travellers and used by most budget camping
safaris to Tarangire. To get to Kigongoni, turn off from the main Arusha–Dodoma road as
if heading towards the entrance gate to Tarangire. After about 2km, you'll see the campsite
immediately to your left. There is also a small local guesthouse in the village on the
junction of the Arusha–Dodoma road and the turn-off to Tarangire. There is no reason
why you couldn't catch a Dodoma-bound bus to the turn-off and walk to the camp from
there; hitching into the park might not be easy, but at least you don't stand to lose anything
in terms of paying park fees while you wait. *Camping US$5 pp, rooms US$7 pp.*

For those on camping safaris, there are a couple of campsites within Tarangire.
These are strong on bush atmosphere, but short on facilities, and rather costly at
the customary US$20 per person.

MAASAI ESCARPMENT ROCK ART RESERVE

Soon to be accorded official protection within the 600km² Maasai Escarpment
Rock Art Reserve, the prodigious rock art around Kolo, a village situated about
20km north of Kondoa and 50km south of Babati on the Great North Road, is
among the most ancient and stylistically varied on the African continent. About
three hours' drive from Tarangire, the reserve also makes for a reasonably
straightforward addition to a safari, even though it has thus far received greater
attention from academics and archaeologists than from tourists.

At least 200 painted panels are documented in Kondoa region, the largest
concentration north of the Zambezi and south of the Sahel. The major rock art
sites around Kolo are situated within small caves or beneath solid overhangs
aligned to an east–west axis, a propensity that might reflect the preferences of the
artists, or might simply have provided conditions favourable to preservation from
the elements. The paintings are tentatively placed at between 200 and 4,000 years
old, and the identity and intent of the artists is a matter of speculation.

A proposal to enshrine this rock art as a UNESCO World Heritage Site states
that 'in terms of conservation, most of the sites are stable and relatively well
preserved although there are a variety of problems including salt encrustation,
erosion, water damage, and fading caused by sunlight'. The rock art has been left
undisturbed by locals in the past because it is regarded as sacred or taboo, but the
erosion of traditional beliefs in recent years places the art at greater threat, and a
few sites have already been partially defaced by graffiti or scratching. Unofficial
guides have also been recorded splashing the paintings with water to bring out the
colours for snap-happy visitors, and many tourists photograph the paintings using
a flash, which can cause great damage to sensitive organic pigments over repeated
exposure. More bizarrely, a local legend that the Germans buried a hoard of gold

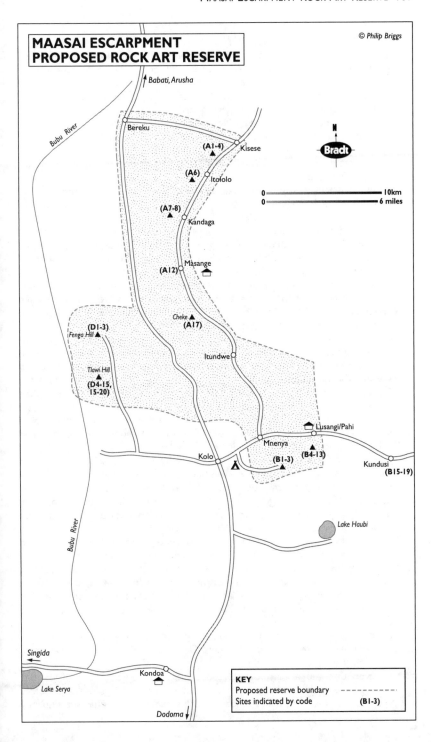

© Philip Briggs

**MAASAI ESCARPMENT
PROPOSED ROCK ART RESERVE**

↑ Babati, Arusha

Bubu River

Bereku

(A1-4) ▲ Kisese

(A6) ▲ Itololo

(A7-8) ▲ Kandaga

(A12) Masange 🏠

0 ─────── 10km
0 ─────── 6 miles

N
Bradt

Cheke ▲
(A17)

Itundwe

(D1-3)
Fenga Hill ▲

Tlawi Hill
▲
(D4-15,
15-20)

Lusangi/Pahi 🏠

Mnenya

Kolo ⛺ (B1-3) ▲ (B4-13) ▲

Kundusi
(B15-19)

Lake Haubi

Bubu River

Singida
←

Kondoa 🏠

Lake Serya

↓ Dodoma

KEY
Proposed reserve boundary ─ ─ ─ ─ ─
Sites indicated by code   (B1-3)

BUT WHAT DOES IT MEAN?

There is a strangely eerie sensation attached to emerging from a remote and nondescript tract of bush to be confronted by an isolated panel of primitive paintings executed by an artist or artists unknown, hundreds or maybe thousands of years before the time of Christ. Faded as many of the panels are, and lacking the perspective to which modern eyes are accustomed, one can still hardly fail to be impressed by the fine detail of many of the animal portraits, or to wonder at the surrealistic distortion of form that characterises the human figures. And, almost invariably, first exposure to these charismatic works of ancient art prompts three questions: how old are they, who were the artists, and what was their intent?

When, who and why? The simple answers are that nobody really knows. The broadest time frame, induced from the absence of any representations of extinct species in the rock galleries of Kondoa, places the paintings at less than 20,000 years old. The absence of a plausible tradition of attribution among the existing inhabitants of the area – a Gogo claim that the paintings were the work of the Portuguese can safely be discounted – makes it unlikely that even the most modern paintings are less than 200 years old. Furthermore, experts have noted a clear progression from the simplest early styles to more complex, expressive works of art, and a subsequent regression to the clumsy graffiti-like finger painting of the 'late white' phase, indicating that the paintings were created over a substantial period of time.

Early attempts at dating the Kondoa rock art concentrated on categorising it chronologically based on the sequence of superimposition of different styles on busy panels. The results were inconclusive, even contradictory, probably because the superimposition of images was an integral part of the art, so that a foreground image might be roughly contemporaneous with an image underneath it. It is also difficult to know the extent to which regional style, or even individual style, might be of greater significance than chronological variation. The most useful clue to the age of the paintings is the stratified organic debris deposited alongside red ochre 'pencils' at several sites. Carbon dating of a handful of sites where such deposits have been found suggests that the artists were most active about 3,000 years ago, though many individual paintings are undoubtedly much older. The crude 'late white' paintings, on the other hand, are widely agreed to be hundreds rather than thousands of years old, and there is evidence to suggest that some underwent ritual restoration by local people who held them sacred into historical times.

The identity of the artists is another imponderable. In the first half of the 20th century, the rock art of southern Africa was solely attributed to 'Bushmen' hunter-gatherers, a people whose click-based Khoisan tongue is unrelated to Bantu and who are of vastly different ethnic stock to any Bantu speakers. True, the Bushmen are the only people who practised the craft in historical times, but much of the rock art of southern Africa (like that of eastern Africa) dates back thousands of years. Coincidentally, two of east Africa's few remaining click-tongued hunter-gatherers, the Sandawe and the Hadzabe, both live in close proximity to the main concentration of Tanzanian rock art, but neither has a tradition relating to the paintings.

Given that the archaeological record indicates east-southern Africa was populated entirely by hunter-gatherers when the paintings were probably executed, furthermore that a succession of human migrations has subsequently passed through the region, postulating an ancestral link between the artists of Kondoa and modern hunter-gatherers would be tenuous in the extreme. If anything, the probable chronology of the rock art points in the opposite direction. Assuming that creative activity peaked some 3,000 years ago, it preceded the single most important known migration into east Africa, the mass invasion of the Bantu-speakers who today comprise the vast majority of Tanzania's population. Most probable, then, that a Bantu- or perhaps Nilotic-speaking group, or another group forced to migrate locally as a ripple effect of the Bantu invasion, moved into the Kondoa region and conquered or assimilated the culture responsible for the rock art, resulting in the gradual stylistic regression noted by archaeologists. All that can be said about the artists with reasonable certainty is they were hunter-gatherers whose culture, were it not for the painted testament left behind on the granite faces of Kondoa, would have vanished without trace.

The most haunting of the questions surrounding the rock art of Kondoa is the intent of its creators. In determining the answer to this, one obstacle is that nobody knows just how representative the surviving legacy might be. Most extant rock art in Kondoa is located in caves or overhangs, but the small number of faded paintings that survive on more open sites must be a random subset of similarly exposed panels that have been wiped clean by the elements. We have no record, either, of whether the artists dabbled on canvases less durable than rock, but unless one assumes that posterity was a conscious goal, it seems wholly presumptuous to think otherwise. The long and short of it, then, is that the extant galleries might indeed represent a sufficiently complete record to form a reliable basis for any hypothesis, but they might just as easily represent a fraction of a percentage of the art executed at the time. Furthermore, there is no way of telling whether rocks were only painted in specific circumstances – it is conceivable that the rock art would maker greater sense viewed in conjunction with other types of painting that have not survived.

Two broad schools of thought surround the interpretation of Africa's ancient rock art. The first has it that the paintings were essentially recreational, documentary, and/or expressive in intent – art for art's sake if you like – while the second regards them to be mystical works of ritual significance. It is quite possible that the truth of the matter lies between these poles of opinion. A striking feature of the rock art of Kondoa is the almost uniform discrepancy in the styles used to depict human and non-human subjects. Animals are sometimes painted in stencil form, sometimes filled with bold white or red paint, but – allowing for varying degrees of artistic competence – the presentation is always naturalistic. The people, by contrast, are almost invariably heavily stylised in form, with elongated stick-like bodies and disproportionately round heads topped by a forest of unkempt hair. Some such paintings are so downright bizarre that they might more reasonably described as humanoid than human (a phenomenon that has not gone unnoticed by UFO theorists searching for prehistoric evidence of extraterrestrial visits).

The discrepancy between the naturalistic style favoured for animals and highly stylised presentation of humans has attracted numerous theoretical explanations. Most crumble under detailed examination of the evidence, but all incline towards supporting the mystical or ritualistic school of interpretation. Ultimately, however, for every tentative answer we can provide, these enigmatic ancient works pose a dozen more questions. It is an integral part of their charisma that we can speculate to our heart's content, but will never know the whole truth!

near one of the rock art sites during World War I has resulted in fortune-seekers manually excavating and dynamiting close to several rock sites.

The pigments for the paintings were made with leaf extracts (yellow and green), powdered ochre and manganese (red and black), and possibly bird excrement (white), and were bound together by animal fat. The subjects and styles vary greatly. Most common are various animals, with giraffe and eland probably the most widely depicted creatures. A large number of panels also contain human figures, generally highly stylised and often apparently engaged in ritual dances or ceremonies. At some sites, identifiable subjects are vastly outnumbered by abstract or geometric figures, the significance of which can only be guessed at.

Getting there and away

Although few people do so, it is perfectly feasible to tag Kolo on to a standard northern circuit safari. Some safari companies will visit the rock art sites as a day trip from Tarangire National Park, a slightly pressured but by no means impossible foray. Equally, you could spend a night in the region, either pitching tent at the campsite at Kolo or sleeping in a guesthouse in the small town of Kondoa 20km further south. Whatever you choose to do, all visitors must report to the Department of Antiquities office at the main junction in Kolo, to pay the nominal entrance fee and collect a guide.

Where to stay

Accommodation options in the immediate vicinity of Kolo are restricted to an attractive campsite run by the Department of Antiquities in Kolo on the banks of the seasonal Kolo River about 3km east of town towards Mungomi wa Kolo and Mnenya. Water and toilet facilities are available at the campsite, but food and other drinks must be brought from Kolo. There is no accommodation in Kolo, but basic local guesthouses can be found in Pahi and Masange, both of which lie below the Maasai Escarpment within walking distance of several good sites. Far better, though not exactly luxurious, are the **New Planet Hotel** (✆ *Kondoa 180*) and **Sunset Beach Hotel** (✆ *Kondoa 152*) in the town of Kondoa, both of which charge around US$5 for a no-frills en-suite room with net, fan and running water.

Some key sites

The region's recognised showpiece is the cluster of three sites situated about 10km from Kolo on Ichoi Hill and prosaically labelled B1–3 but more evocatively known as Mungomi wa Kolo (*Dancers of Kolo*). This cluster of panels provides a good overview of the region's rock art, and – aside from the last, very steep, foot ascent to the actual panels – is easily reached in a 4x4 vehicle. Probably the most intriguing of the panels is B1, which includes several fine, but very faded, paintings of animals (giraffe, leopard, zebra and rhino), as well as some abstract designs and numerous humanoid forms. One striking scene, dubbed *The Abduction*, depicts five humanoid forms with stick bodies, spindly limbs and distended heads. The two figures on the right have elongated heads, while the two on the left have round heads, as does the central figure, which also appears to have breasts and whose arms are being held by the flanking figures. Leakey interpreted the painting as a depiction of an attempted abduction, but it could as easily depict a ritual dance or similar. And one website makes an oddly compelling case for this haunting scene providing evidence of extraterrestrial visits – according to this interpretation, a separate scene to the right shows another alien standing in a hot-air balloon!

Panels B4–13 all lie close to the base of the escarpment near the twin villages of Lusangi and Pahi, about 12km from Kolo. The art here is not as impressive as

B1–3, but it is a more suitable goal to those unwilling or unable to climb steep footpaths. Several figures here stand out, the most notable being a 70cm-high outlined giraffe superimposed on a very old painting of a rhino. Below this, a red-and-yellow figure of an eland with a disproportionately small head is regarded to be one of the oldest paintings in the region. From Pahi, it's possible to drive another 12km to Kinyasi, where sites B14–19 are situated in a valley below Kome Mountain. The most interesting of these sites is a 1m² panel of small, finely executed antelopes, which also includes one of the few known examples of a painting depicting a homestead.

Those with more time could explore the Bubu River sites, clustered to the west of the Great North Road about 12km from Kolo. Here you'll find several well-preserved panels in close proximity. Don't miss panel D3 on Fenga Hill, sometimes referred to as the *Trapped Elephants* after the central painting of two elephants surrounded by a stencilled oblong line. Some experts believe that this depicts an elephant trap, a theory supported by three fronds below the elephants that might well represent branches used to camouflage a pit. Others believe that it might have a more mystical purpose, placing the elephants in a kind of magic circle. A trickle of circles dripping from the left base of the picture could be blood, or the elephants' spoor.

About 3km south of Fenga Hill, the immediate vicinity around Tlawi Hill hosts at least ten panels, numbered D4–5 and D15–22. A dedicated enthusiast could easily devote half a day to this cluster of very different sites – D19 is notable for an almost life-size and unusually naturalistic attempt to paint a human figure in a crouched or seated position, D20 depicts several seated human figures, D22 is also known as the *Red Lion* for the striking painting of a lion that dominates the shelter, and D17 has a rare action painting of a hunter killing a large antelope with bow and arrow. Several other interesting human figures are found on these twin shelters.

BABATI AND HANANG

The small but bustling market town of Babati, which lies on the Great North Road some 70km north of Kondoa and 170km south of Arusha, is known for the eponymous lake on its outskirts, which supports a good selection of egrets, waders, pelicans, storks and other waterbirds, as well as several pods of hippo. Babati is also the springboard for a visit to Mount Hanang, an extinct volcano which towers to an altitude of 3,418m – the fourth-highest point in Kilimanjaro, Meru and Lolomalasin – above the surrounding plains and is visible from hundreds of kilometres away on a clear day.

Seldom visited by tourists, Hanang is nevertheless eminently climbable, and – because it lies outside the national park system – it forms a very affordable prospect by comparison with Kilimanjaro or Meru. The slopes support the usual range of montane forest and grassland habitats, and offer excellent views over a stretch of the Rift Valley studded with smaller volcanic cones and shallow lakes. The normal springboard for climbing Hanang is the dusty and rather amorphous small town of Katesh, which straddles the Singida road 75km west of Babati at the southern base of the mountain.

The attractions of the Hanang area are not restricted to the mountain. Several substantial lakes also lie in the vicinity of Katesh, including the shallow and highly saline Lake Balangida, which is set at the base of the Rift Valley scarp immediately north of Mount Hanang. Katesh also forms the starting point for an obscure but not unrewarding back route to Karatu and the Ngorongoro Crater Highlands via Basotu, Dongobesh and Mbulu. And one could scarcely spend time in the area without being conscious of the Barabaig, charismatic pastoralists who have consciously retained their traditional way of life.

THE BARABAIG

The Barabaig are the most populous of a dozen closely related tribes, collectively known as the Datoga or Tatoga. At around 100,000, the Datoga are one of Tanzania's smaller ethno-linguistic groupings, but their territory, centred on Mount Hanang, extends into large semi-arid tracts within Arusha, Dodoma and Singida.

Superficially similar to, and frequently confused with, their Maasai neighbours by outsiders, the Barabaig are dedicated cattle-herders, speaking a Nilotic tongue, who have steadfastly resisted external pressure to forsake their semi-nomadic pastoralist ways. Unlike the Maasai, however, the Barabaig are representatives of the earliest known Nilotic migration into east Africa from southwest Ethiopia. Their forebears probably settled in western Kenya during the middle of the first millennium AD, splitting into two groups. One – the Kalenjin – stayed put. The other, the proto-Datoga, migrated south of Lake Natron 500 to 1,000 years ago to the highlands of Ngorongoro and Mbulu, and Rift Valley plains south towards Dodoma.

Datoga territory was greatest before 1600, thereafter being eroded by migrations of various Bantu-speaking peoples into northern and central Tanzania. The most significant incursion came in the early 19th century, with the arrival of the Maasai. Oral traditions indicate that several fierce territorial battles were fought between the two pastoralist groups, resulting in the Maasai taking over the Crater Highlands and Serengeti Plains, and the Datoga retreating to their modern homeland near Mount Hanang. The Lerai Forest in Ngorongoro Crater is said to mark the grave of a Datoga leader who fell in battle in about 1840, and the site is still visited by Datoga elders from the Lake Eyasi area. The Maasai call the Barabaig the 'Mangati' (feared enemies), and the Barabaig territory around Mount Hanang is sometimes referred to as the Mangati Plains.

The Barabaig used to move around the plains according to the feeding and watering requirements of their herds. They tend a variety of livestock, including goats, donkeys and chickens, but their culture and economy revolves around cattle, which are perceived to be a measure of wealth and prestige, and every part and product of the animal, including the dung, is ingested, or worn, or used in rituals. In recent years, agriculture has played an increasingly significant support role in the subsistence of the Barabaig, which together with increased population pressures has more or less put paid to the nomadic lifestyle.

Barabaig territory receives an average annual rainfall of less than 500mm, which means that water is often in short supply. Although the area is dotted with numerous lakes, most are brackish and unsuitable to drink from. Barabaig women often walk miles every day to collect gourds of drinking water, much of which comes from boreholes dug with foreign aid. The cattle cannot drink from the lakes directly when water levels are low and salinity is high, but the Barabaig get around this by digging wells on the lakes' edges and allowing the water to filter through the soil. Even so, the herders won't let their cattle drink from these wells on successive days for fear that it will make them ill.

Barabaig social structure is not dissimilar to that of the Maasai, although it lacks the rigid division into hierarchical age-sets pivotal to Maasai and other east African pastoralist societies. The Barabaig do not recognise one centralised leader, but are divided into several hereditary clans, each answering to a chosen elder who sits on a tribal council. The central unit of society is the family homestead or *gheida*, dwelt in by one man, his wives, and their unwed offspring.

This consists of a tall outer protective wall, built of thorny acacia branches and shaped like a figure eight, with one outer gate entered through a narrow passage. Within this wall stand several small rectangular houses – low, thick-roofed constructions of wooden poles plastered with mud – and the all-important cattle stockade. Different huts are reserved for young men, young women, wives and elders. A number of *gheida* may be grouped together to create an informal community, and decisions are made communally rather than by a chief.

Patrilineal polygamy is actively encouraged. Elders accumulate four or more wives, up to three of which might share one hut, but marriage within any given clan is regarded to be incestuous. The concept of divorce is not recognised, but a woman may separate from her husband and return to her parents' home under some circumstances. The Barabaig openly regard extramarital sex to be normal, even desirable, although a great many taboos and conventions dictate just who may have intercourse with whom, and where they can perform the act. Traditionally, should a married woman bear a child whose biological father is other than her husband, the child remains the property of the husband – even when husband and wife are separated.

The appearance of the Barabaig is striking. The women wear heavy ochre-dyed goatskin or cowhide dresses, tasselled below the waist, and decorated with colourful yellow and orange beads. They adorn themselves with brass bracelets and neck-coils, tattoo circular patterns around their eyes, and some practise facial scarification. Men are less ornate, with a dyed cotton cloth draped over the shoulders and another around the waist. Traditionally, young men would prove themselves by killing a person (other than a Datoga) or an elephant, lion or buffalo, which might be used as the base of a ceremonial headdress along with the pelts of other animals they had killed.

The Barabaig are monotheists who believe in a universal creator whom they call Aseeta. The sun – which they give the same name – is the all-seeing eye of Aseeta, who lives far away and has little involvement in their lives. Barabaig legend has it that they are descended from Aseeta's brother Salohog, whose eldest son Gumbandaing was the first true Datoga. Traditionally, most Barabaig elders can trace their lineage back over tens of generations to this founding father, and ancestral worship plays a greater role in their spiritual life than direct worship of God. Oddly, given the arid nature of their homeland, the Barabaig have a reputation as powerful rainmakers. It is said that only 1% of the Barabaig have abandoned their traditional beliefs in favour of exotic religions – a scenario which, judging by the number of internet sites devoted to the state of the Barabaig's souls, has spun quite a few evangelical types into a giddy froth.

The above statistic is indicative of the Barabaig's stubborn adherence to a traditional way of life. In the colonial era, the Barabaig refused to be co-opted into the migrant labour system, on the not unreasonable basis that they could sell one good bullock for more than the typical labourer would earn in a year. Other Tanzanians tend to view the Barabaig as embarrassingly primitive and ignorant – when the Nyerere government outlawed the wearing of traditional togas in favour of Westernised clothing, the Barabaig resolutely ignored them. Even today, few have much formal education or speak a word of English – it would, for that matter, be pretty unusual to meet a Barabaig who could hold a sustained conversation in Swahili.

LEGEND OF THE CAT

Emma Thomson

To maintain the balance of power between the sexes the Rangi people have devised an ingenious plan. From sunrise to sunset the men are in charge, but come sunset the rule of power shifts to the women, allowing them to reign supreme until daybreak.

This female empowerment was established following the legend of the cat, told to me by a village member one starry night near Kelema:

The cat was looking for a hero. While walking through the jungle one day he befriended a cheetah. 'This cheetah is surely the strongest and fastest animal in the forest – he will be my hero,' exclaimed the cat.

The next day, while walking with the cat through the undergrowth, the cheetah encountered a lion. They fought until the cheetah fell to the ground dead. 'The lion then must be the strongest and fiercest animal in the forest – he will be my new hero,' decided the cat.

The following day the two felines encountered an elephant foraging in the trees. Startled, the elephant charged, killing the lion. Bemused, the cat approached the elephant; 'You truly are the king of the jungle – will you be my hero?'

One day the elephant and cat were surprised by a man hunting. In fear the man killed the elephant and after cutting the meat from the body he turned for home. The cat decided to follow this beast that could defeat an animal without even touching it.

On arriving home the man approached his wife who took the elephant meat from him and set to work in the kitchen. The cat gasped: 'This woman surely must be the queen of all beasts – an animal that can take from another without fighting! She will forever be my hero.' From that day on the cat can always be found in the kitchen admiring his heroine.

The best way to explore this region is with the Babati and Hanang Cultural Tourism Programme (also known as Kahembe's Trekking and Cultural Safaris), a commendable set-up that started life in the mid-1990s and is still managed by founder Jaos Kahembe. This is an excellent contact for anybody who wants to explore a little-known part of Tanzania in an organised manner, but without paying through the nose. A variety of local tours are offered, of which the most popular are the three-day and two-day Hanang climbs. Other trips range from a three-day walking safari in Barabaig country to a 16-day expedition that includes overnight stays with a number of different ethnic groups, as well as an ascent of Mount Hanang, and game walks around Lake Burungi (bordering Tarangire National Park). These overnight trips are not luxurious by any standard, but they are well organised and offer an unforgettable glimpse into an ancient way of life. They are also very reasonably priced, at US$40 all-inclusive per person per day for one or two people, or US$30 for larger groups. For further details check out the website www.authenticculture.org or contact ☏ 027 253 1088/1377; m 0748 397477; e kahembeculture@hotmail.com.

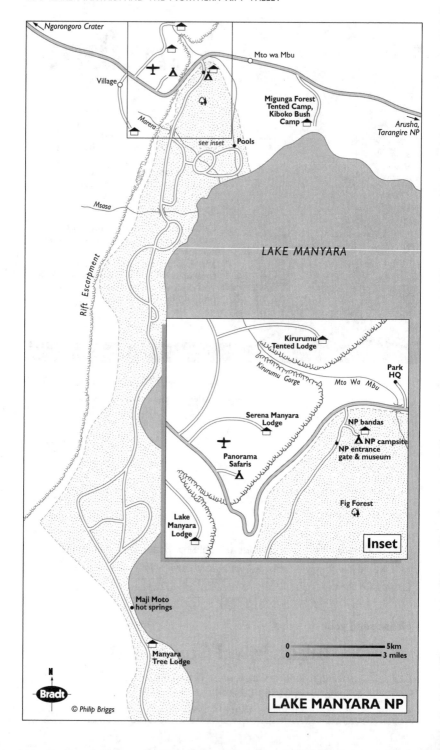

Ngorongoro Crater

Mto wa Mbu

Village

Migunga Forest Tented Camp, Kiboko Bush Camp

Arusha, Tarangire NP

Marera

see inset

Pools

Msasa

LAKE MANYARA

Rift Escarpment

Kirurumu Tented Lodge

Kirurumu Gorge

Mto Wa Mbu

Park HQ

Serena Manyara Lodge

NP bandas

NP campsite

Panorama Safaris

NP entrance gate & museum

Lake Manyara Lodge

Fig Forest

Inset

Maji Moto hot springs

0 ——————— 5km
0 ——————— 3 miles

Manyara Tree Lodge

N

Bradt

© Philip Briggs

LAKE MANYARA NP

Lake Manyara and the Northern Rift Valley

Before it ascends to the Ngorongoro Highlands and Serengeti, the main road heading westward from Arusha runs through a dramatic stretch of the Rift Valley whose semi-arid, acacia-studded floor, hemmed in by a sheer western escarpment, supports a chain of shallow mineral-rich lakes. The largest of these lakes, Eyasi, Manyara and Natron, are prone to substantial cyclic fluctuations in their water level, dependent to some extent on local rainfall patterns, but each one of them reaches a length of 50km or greater when full.

The most accessible and popular tourist attraction in this area is Lake Manyara, the northwestern shores of which are protected within an eponymous national park known for its dense elephant population, tree-climbing lions and prodigious birdlife. Only two hours' drive from Arusha on a good asphalt road, Lake Manyara makes for an obvious first port of call on any northern Tanzanian safari. It is serviced by several upmarket lodges, most of which run along the escarpment above the lake, while a selection of cheaper lodgings and campsites is centred on the village of Mto wa Mbu near the entrance gate.

Considerably more remote, Lake Natron is the site of a legendary but practically inaccessible flamingo breeding ground, as well as the majestic (and, if you're up to it, climbable) volcano known to the Maasai as Ol Doinyo Lengai (God's Mountain). Relatively few tourists pass through the Natron area, but it makes for a worthy off-the-beaten-track addition to any safari, especially as it can be used as an alternative route between the northern Serengeti and Mto Wa Mbu, meaning that you don't need to retrace your steps by driving through Ngorongoro Conservation Area in both directions. One midrange lodge and a few more basic campsites service Lake Natron.

More remote still, Eyasi is the largest of these Rift Valley lakes, and of interest primarily for the Hadzabe hunter-gatherers who inhabit its semi-arid hinterland. The lake is also something of a travel cul-de-sac, since it is connected to the outside world by just one rough road running southwest from the small town of Karatu. A basic campsite and one recently opened lodge can be found in the vicinity of Eyasi; both can arrange visits to Hadzabe encampments.

LAKE MANYARA NATIONAL PARK

Lake Manyara is a shallow, alkaline lake set at the base of a sheer stretch of the Western Rift Valley escarpment. The northwest of the lake and the land around it are protected in a scenic 330km^2 national park, which contains a remarkably wide diversity of terrestrial habitats given that some two-thirds of its surface area is comprised of water. These include the open grassy floodplain that follows the lakeshore, the rocky base of the escarpment, the belt of thick acacia woodland that divides them, as well as a lush and extensive patch of groundwater forest around the northern entrance gate. The park's varied fauna reflects this habitat diversity, with some of the more common and visible large mammal species being elephant, buffalo, wildebeest, giraffe and lion. I've read elsewhere that Lake Manyara is frequently a disappointment to visitors. It's difficult to see why, since Manyara is a valuable addition to a safari of several days' duration, offering the opportunity to see several species that are less common or shyer elsewhere on the northern circuit. Those on shorter safaris, however, might reasonably elect to forsake Manyara and its biodiversity for an additional day on the predator-rich plains of the Serengeti.

Lake Manyara National Park and its well-defined game-viewing circuit kick off a high proportion of safaris through northern Tanzania. For logistical reasons, most safari operators visit this national park in the afternoon, but if you have any say in things, I would strongly recommend a morning game drive, starting as soon as possible after the entrance gate opens at 06.30. The park is wonderfully and unexpectedly peaceful in the morning, and you'll probably see fewer other vehicles over two or three hours than you would in five minutes in the late afternoon. Less certainly, by being the first car through the gate, we have twice disturbed one of the park's profuse but skittish leopards before it vanished into the thickets for the day.

At whatever time of day you enter it, your game drive will start at the park's only entrance gate, which lies on the northern boundary near the village of Mto wa Mbu. From the entrance gate, the main road winds for several kilometres through a cool, lush, mature groundwater forest dominated by large ficus trees and a tangle of green epiphytes. With appropriate jungle noises supplied by outsized silvery-cheeked hornbills, this is the one part of the northern safari circuit that might conjure up images of Tarzan swinging into view. But, unless you're hoping for a rare glimpse of a leopard, the forest isn't really big game territory. The most notable residents of the forest are the olive baboons – the park supports a remarkable density of 2,500 baboons in 100km² of land – which are normally plonked down alongside the road, sometimes in the company of the

ACTIVITIES AROUND LAKE MANYARA

An exciting new development at Lake Manyara is the introduction of several mild adventure activities that allow safari-goers tired of bouncing around dusty roads within the confines of a vehicle the opportunity to stretch their legs or arms in natural surrounds. The activities are operated exclusively by Serena Active, which is based out of the Manyara Serena Lodge, but takes on guests staying at other lodges in the area. No experience is required for any of the activities, and all equipment is supplied at no extra cost. On-the-spot enquiries are welcomed, but bookings can be made through any safari operator or directly through Serena Active; ☎ 027 253 9160/1/2; f 027 253 9163; e serenaactive@serena.co.tz.

The most popular of these activities is mountain biking down the Rift Valley escarpment, with different itineraries ranging in price from US$30 to US$35 per person. Also offered are an afternoon walk through the groundwater forest in the Kirurumu Gorge outside the national park entrance for US$35 per person, and a village walk with a local guide through agricultural areas around Mto wa Mbu. For more hardcore adventurers, there is the option of abseiling down the rift escarpment above the lake with a qualified instructor, which costs US$55 per person. A more recent – and costly – addition to the programme is a microlight flight over the lake or (if you like) as far north as Natron.

smaller and more beautiful blue monkey. The shy bushbuck might also be encountered here, but otherwise the main point of faunal interest is the diversity of birds and butterflies.

Most safari vehicles emerge from the forest on to the northern floodplain, where currently a series of small pools on the Mto wa Mbu River supports a wide variety of birds, notably giant kingfisher and African and painted snipe. This is a lovely spot, too, with the Rift Valley escarpment rising to the west, and the sparsely vegetated floodplain of Lake Manyara stretching to the south. Giraffes are common in this area, many of them so dark in colour that they appear to be almost melanistic. The nearby hippo pool was submerged for several years following the El Niño floods of 1997/8, causing the hippos to relocate to the main lake, but it recently re-emerged after a few drier years and it now harbours several dozen soaking, yawning hippos, as well as an impressive selection of waterbirds. An ongoing relic of the El Niño floods is the ghost forest of dead tree stumps lining the floodplain between the fig forest and the lakeshore.

The best mammal viewing in this national park is generally along the road running inland of the lake towards Maji Moto Lodge and the hot springs in the south of the park. *En route*, you pass through tangled acacia woodland with views over the floodplain, where you should see large herds of zebra and wildebeest, and the occasional warthog, impala, Kirk's dik-dik and giraffe. The acacia woodland is the place to look out for the famous tree-climbing lions of Manyara (see box, pages 182–3) – though on an afternoon game drive, the safari driver grapevine is bound to ensure that you know about any arboreal lions long before you encounter them. The marshy area around the springs reliably harbours waterbuck and plenty of buffaloes, while several pairs of klipspringer are resident on the rocky escarpment base towards the southern end of the park.

A notable feature of Lake Manyara is its prolific elephants, as immortalised by Iain Douglas-Hamilton in his 1970s book *Amongst the Elephants*. Although the elephant population suffered a subsequent decline due to poaching, this was not as severe as in many larger parks in southern Tanzania and the numbers are today almost fully recovered. The elephants in Manyara are generally very relaxed around vehicles by comparison with their counterparts in Tarangire and the southern reserves, which makes for great elephant watching – especially as there are still some serious tuskers around.

Worth noting is that Manyara, despite its small size, is a *great* birding reserve, with almost 400 species recorded due to the great habitat diversity. As Duncan Butchart, writing in the CCA's *Ecological Journal*, noted, 'If a first-time birdwatcher to Africa had the time to visit only a single reserve in Tanzania, then Manyara must surely be it.' It's perfectly feasible for a casual birder to see 100 species here in a day, ranging from a variety of colourful bee-eaters, barbets, kingfishers and rollers to the gigantic ground hornbill and white-backed pelican. Prior to the El Niño floods, the flocks of flamingoes that gathered on the shallow lake rivalled those on Kenya's famous Lake Nakuru. The flamingoes vanished after the flooding, which diluted the lake's alkaline level, but small flocks started to return in 2001 and quite substantial numbers were present in 2005. A remarkable 51 diurnal raptor species are known from the park, of which 28 are resident or regular. In addition, six species of owl are regularly recorded.

The 44-page booklet *Lake Manyara National Park*, published by Tanzania National Parks, gives detailed coverage of the park's flora and fauna, as does the newer booklet *Lake Manyara* published by the African Publishing House in association with TANAPA. An entrance fee of US$35 per 24 hours is charged.

Getting there and away

The main – indeed only – entrance gate to Lake Manyara lies at the northern end of the park on the outskirts of the village of Mto wa Mbu. The 120km drive from Arusha currently takes less than two hours following the completion of the new surfaced road from Makuyuni.

Where to stay and eat

There is only one lodge sited within the park boundaries, the new Lake Manyara Tree Lodge. There is, however, plenty of accommodation bordering the park. Most of the tourist-class lodges are situated on the Rift Valley escarpment overlooking Lake Manyara, while the budget accommodation and campsites are dotted around the small village of Mto wa Mbu outside the main entrance gate.

Exclusive

Lake Manyara Tree Lodge (10 rooms) ☎ 027 254 8549/8038 or (South Africa) 11 809 4447; e res@ccafrica.co.tz or reservations@ccafrica.com; www.ccafrica.com . Opened in 2003 as a replacement for the defunct Maji Moto Lodge, Lake Manyara Tree Camp is a small luxurious CCAfrica tented camp set deep in a mahogany forest about 20 minutes' drive south of the hot springs at Maji Moto. Like other CCAfrica lodges, Lake Manyara Tree Lodge offers the ultimate in exclusive bush luxury, consisting of 10 stilted en-suite treehouses built with wood and makuti, and with private decks offering great views of the escarpment. Exciting walking routes run from the lodge to the lakeshore through the forest, while other facilities include a swimming pool and personal butler service. *The FB rates of US$490 pp in the mid-season (Oct to Jan except the Christmas and New Year period) and US$630 in the high season are inclusive of all meals, drinks and activities. The camp closes for April and May.*

Upmarket

Lake Manyara Serena Lodge (54 rooms) ☎ 027 250 4058; f 027 250 8282; e reservations@serena.co.tz; www.serenahotels.com. This smart and popular upmarket lodge is situated on the edge of the escarpment overlooking the lake and its environs. Like other lodges in the Serena chain, it is a very appealing set-up, run through by a small wooded stream that attracts a wide range of birds including chattering flocks of breeding weavers. Adventure activities such as abseiling and mountain biking, are offered by Serena Active, a company based in the lodge. Accommodation is in attractively furnished ethnic-looking rondawels with private balconies. The buffet food is generally very good. *US$285/420 sgl/dbl FB, dropping to US$170/255 Apr–Jun.*

Lake Manyara Lodge (100 rooms) ☎ 027 254 4595; f 027 254 8633; e sales@hotelsandlodges-tanzania.com; www.sales@hotelsandlodges-tanzania.com. This government property, though barely recognisable from its rundown state of a few years ago, remains somewhat Spartanly decorated and architecturally confrontational, though the rooms do have mosquito nets and en-suite bathrooms with running hot water. A definite attraction of the lodge is a large swimming pool, but its single best feature remains its peerless position right on the edge of the escarpment. The grounds offer a panoramic view over the forest and lake, with the Rift Valley hills fading to the horizon. With binoculars, you should be able to pick out elephants, giraffes and buffaloes on the Rift Valley floor; closer to home, there is good birding within the lodge grounds. *US$155/180 sgl/dbl FB.*

Kirurumu Tented Lodge (20 rooms) ☎ (UK) 1923 255462; f 1923 255452; e hoopoeUK@aol.com; www.kirurumu.com. Owned and managed by Hoopoe Adventure Tours, this popular tented lodge is perched on the rift escarpment to the north of the Serena, from where it offers a grand view across the plains of the Rift Valley to the north of Lake Manyara. The unpretentious rustic bush atmosphere that characterises Kirurumu contrasts strongly with that of the other more built-up lodges on the Rift escarpment, and it will be far more attractive to people who want to feel like they are sleeping in the bush rather than in a large hotel. There's plenty of small wildlife around too, ranging from bush squirrels to foot-long yellow-speckled plated lizards by day to hedgehogs and bushbabies by night – plus a wide variety of birds. The food is good and the service friendly and efficient. Accommodation is in comfortable and secluded en-suite dbl tents, each of which has a private veranda. *US$135/190 sgl/dbl B&B or US$173/266 FB in high season, dropping to US$106/162 FB in low season.*

Moderate

Migunga Forest Tented Camp (12 rooms) ☎ 027 255 3242/3326; m 0744 324193; f 027 255 3243; e moivaro@habari.co.tz or info@moivaro.com; www.moivaro.com. This well-established but little-known tented camp, recently taken over by Moivaro Lodge, shares many assets with Kirurumu, but it is considerably more downmarket in feel, and priced accordingly. Migunga has a winning location in a yellow fever forest about 2km by road from Mto wa Mbu. When the lake is high, the camp lies close to the northeast and can be reached by a short walking trail, but at the time of writing the distance to the lake is around 5km. Reedbuck, bushbuck and buffalo sometimes pass through, while a troop of vervet monkeys is more or less resident and the lesser bushbaby is often seen at night. Roughly 70 acacia-associated bird species have been recorded within the camp. Accommodation is in comfortable dbl standing tents with en-suite hot showers. Pricewise, it's an excellent compromise between the smarter but more expensive lodges and the relatively utilitarian accommodation in Mto wa Mbu. *US$65/110 sgl/dbl FB, with low-season discount in Apr and May; and premium over Christmas period.*

Kiboko Bush Camp (12 rooms) ☎ 027 253 9152; e kibokotz@yahoo.co.uk; www.equatorialsafaris.com. Situated a few hundred metres away from Migunga, and similar in price and standard, though with a more nondescript setting, this new camp

---

MTO WA MBU

This village, which lies close to the Lake Manyara entrance gate, sees a large volume of tourist traffic and is said locally to be the only place in Tanzania where representatives of 120 Tanzanian tribes are resident. Mto wa Mbu is the normal base for budget safaris visiting Lake Manyara, and even if you aren't staying in the village or visiting Lake Manyara, your safari driver will probably stop at the huge curio market in the hope of picking up a commission. Mto wa Mbu (pronounced as one word, mtowambu) means River of Mosquitoes, and if you do spend the night here, then you'll be in no doubt about how it got its name. By day, the curio dealers who will swarm around you the moment you leave your vehicle might draw an obvious analogy.

A clutch of walking tours out of Mto wa Mbu have been set up as part of a cultural tourism programme with the assistance of SNV. One of the most interesting of these walks is the papyrus lake tour, which takes you to the Miwaleni waterfall, as well as to a papyrus lake where Rangi people collect basket- and mat-weaving material, and to the homesteads of Sandawe hunter-gatherers. Other tours take you to Balaa Hill, which boasts excellent views over the village and lake, and to Chagga farms and Maasai *bomas*. The tourism programme is run out of the Red Banana Restaurant in the centre of the village, where you must pay your fees, arrange a guide and (if you like) rent a bicycle. The guide fee works out at US$7.50 per group per day, in addition to which you must pay a village development fee of US$1.50 per person. Bicycle hire costs US$2 per day.

THE TREE-CLIMBING LIONS OF MANYARA

Lake Manyara National Park is famous for its tree-climbing lions, which, unlike conventional lions, habitually rest up in the branches for most of the day, to the excitement of those lucky tourists who chance upon them. But while the tree-climbing phenomenon is well documented, the explanation behind it remains largely a matter of conjecture.

In the 1960s, Stephen Makacha undertook research into lion behaviour at Manyara to compare with similar studies being conducted by George Schaller in the Serengeti. In Schaller's book, *The Serengeti Lion: A Study of Predator–Prey Relations*, he noted that:

> The lions in the Lake Manyara National Park climbed trees far more often than those in the Serengeti. They were resting in trees on two-thirds of the occasions on which we encountered them during the day… The reason why Manyara lions rest in trees so often is unknown. Fosbrooke noted that lions in the Ngorongoro Crater ascended trees during an epidemic of biting flies, but this is an unusual situation… and the vegetation in the various parks is in many respects so similar that no correlation between it and tree climbing is evident. The Manyara lions sometimes escaped from buffalo and elephant by climbing trees, but there would seem to be no reason for lions to remain in them all day because of the remote chance that they might have to climb one. I think that the behaviour represents a habit, one that may have been initiated by for example, a prolonged fly epidemic, and has since been transmitted culturally.

Schaller's suggestion that the lions were climbing trees to avoid flies made the most sense to me, but I had also heard that the lions climbed to enjoy the cool breezes that came off the lake, and to keep a lookout for prey and threats. So I decided to make notes whenever I saw the lions in order to explore these theories. For every sighting I noted whether flies were present on the ground or in the trees; the temperature and breeze conditions; whether buffalo or elephant were in the vicinity; how high up the tree the lions were and the view it afforded; and the species of tree.

In the 1960s, Iain Douglas-Hamilton noted that on 80% of the occasions when tree-climbing lions were observed, they were in one of just 17 individual

provides comfortable accommodation in en-suite standing tents, each with 2 ¾ beds, and set on a stilted wooden platform with a small private veranda. Once again, it's good value. *US$60 pp B&B or US$75–80 FB. Camping US$5 pp.*

Budget and camping

National Park *Bandas* **& Campsite** Situated in a lovely forest glade immediately outside the national park entrance gate, this is easily the most inherently attractive place to stay in this price category, though unfortunately it feels a bit overpriced for what you get. Clean self-contained brick *bandas* have hot water but no net – the latter a serious omission in Mto wa Mbu. Facilities include a kitchen and dining area, and an elevated tree house looking into the forest canopy. *US$20 pp for non-residents or Tsh5,000 for residents for bandas or camping.*

Migunga Campsite (12 rooms) ↘ 027 255 3242/3326; m 0744 324193; f 027 255 3243; e moivaro@habari.co.tz or info@moivaro.com; www.moivaro.com. Situated alongside the

trees. These favoured trees were so well known to park guides at the time that they were given particular names and – to protect them from debarking and destruction by elephants – wrapped in coils of wire mesh. My observations indicated a similar pattern. Lions were found to be resting in trees on about half of the times they were sighted, and although six different tree species were used, three – *Acacia tortilis*, *Kigelia africana* and *Balanites aegyptiaca* – accounted for 90% of sightings. Specific trees were usually favoured, and the lions often moved a considerable distance to reach them.

In most cases the lions were seen to be resting during the heat of the day, and they would usually come down at dusk. Only 5% of sightings coincided with hot weather and breezy conditions, and at most sightings there was no significant breeze, so it seems unlikely that the lions climb to escape the heat. Although buffalo have been documented killing lions at Manyara, there was never any sign of the lions taking to trees to avoid harassment. Most of the time the lions were found to be resting approximately 5–6m above the ground, which afforded them a better view of their surroundings, but since the trees were normally in densely vegetated areas, it would have been difficult for them to observe any potential prey or threat.

My conclusions were similar to those of Makacha and Schaller. Although lions that I found resting on the ground were apparently not greatly concerned by biting flies, lions observed in trees were surrounded by flies in only 10% of cases, when flies were present on the ground below them about 60% of the time. Because the lions generally rested above 5m and flies were seldom encountered at this height, it seems likely that the behaviour was originally initiated during a fly epidemic, and it has since been passed on culturally. I observed the cubs of the Maji pride begin their attempts to climb up to the adults when they were about seven or eight months old. It seemed definitely to be a case of 'lion see lion do', as there was no apparent reason as to why they should have climbed. Once they had mastered climbing, they too spent a lot of time playing and climbing up and down the trees. More thorough research would be required to fully understand the reasons for this unusual and fascinating behaviour.

Edited from Notes on Tree-climbing Lions of Manyara *by Kevin Pretorius, a former manager of Maji Moto Lodge, as originally published in the CCA* Ecological Journal *volume 2:79–81 (2000). The journal can be ordered online at www.wildwatch.com.*

eponymous tented camp and under the same management, this campsite boasts a stunning setting amid the yellow fever trees, and facilities include hot showers – highly recommended. *US$5 pp.*

Panorama Safari Camp ✆ 0745 417838. Boasting a prime location on the escarpment overlooking the lake, this relatively new campsite set only 500m from the main asphalt road towards Karatu forms an attractively located alternative to the more mundane cheapies in town. Accommodation in a large standing tent with bedding and towel provided costs US$7 pp, while a small standing tent with a mattress and no bed costs US$5 pp, and camping in your own tent costs US$4 pp. There's a clean shower and toilet block with running hot water, and other facilities include a bar and restaurant, though the swimming pool that was due to be constructed a few years back has yet to materialise.

Twiga Campsite and Lodge ✆ 025 253 9101; m 0744 264828. Justifiably the most popular of the locally run lodges in Mto wa Mbu, Twiga charges US$10 pp to pitch a tent in the spacious, neatly cropped campsite. It also has a block of large self-contained dbl rooms with hot water and nets for US$35 dbl B&B. A 3-course meal at the restaurant costs US$6, while most dishes on the à la carte menu work out at around US$4. There is a 'wild video show' in the lounge every evening, and a recently constructed swimming pool to flop around in by day.

Wild Fig Camp ↘ 025 253 9102; m 0748 377945. This is one of the older campsites in Mto wa Mbu, and the somewhat cramped grounds are starting to look very rundown. The parking-lot ambience is only furthered by the conspicuous presence of a swimming pool that has been empty on every occasion that I've dropped by. *Camping US$5 pp; small self-contained dbl rooms with fan, net and hot water US$30.*

Jambo Campsite ↘ 0744 288732. Undergoing extensive renovations in mid-2005, this well-established site in Mto wa Mbu should boast a great swimming pool area and 16 smart en-suite rooms when it re-opens in 2006, as well as a shady campsite. Prices should be comparable to Twiga Campsite.

KARATU

This small, dusty town straddling the main road between Manyara and Ngorongoro may not look like much when you pass through coming from Arusha, but it is probably the most populous settlement anywhere along the 400km length of the B142 between Arusha and Mwanza. Most tourists who are on a lodge-based safari will pass through Karatu in the blink of an eye, but quite a number of camping safaris stay in the small town – nicknamed 'safari junction' – and use it as a base for day trips to the nearby Ngorongoro Crater, since camping is a lot cheaper than in the conservation area. A worthwhile overnight trip (or, at a push, day trip) out of Karatu is to Lake Eyasi and one of the Hadzabe settlements in the surrounding area (see box *The last hunter-gatherers,* pages 186–7). The National Bank of Commerce next to Ngorongoro Safari Lodge is the one place on the safari circuit where foreign travellers' cheques and cash can be exchanged at normal rates.

Getting there and away

Karatu is now connected to Mto wa Mbu and Arusha by a good asphalt road and the drive from Mto wa Mbu takes about one hour. Regular buses connect Karatu to Arusha via Mto wa Mbu, and the Ngorongoro Safari Resort in Karatu rents 4x4 vehicles for day safaris to Ngorongoro and Manyara at US$120 per day.

Where to stay
Upmarket

Ngorongoro Farmhouse (29 rooms) ↘ 0748 593008; f 027 250 8937; e mawenzisaf@habari.co.tz or twc-reservations@habari.co.tz; www.africawilderness.com. Situated on a large coffee farm about halfway between Karatu and the NCA, this stylish new lodge offers luxurious en-suite accommodation in large semi-detached thatched cottages with views across what will eventually be a 9-hole golf course to the forested slopes of Ngorongoro. There's a very pleasant swimming pool area and the restaurant serves good country-style cooking. In terms of location, it doesn't quite match up to the lodges on the crater rim, but it's much smaller and has a less packaged feel than any comparably priced option within the NCA. *US$185/280 sgl/dbl FB.*

Gibb's Farm (20 rooms) ↘ 027 250 8930 or 253 4040; f 027 250 8930; e reservations@gibbsfarm.net; www.gibbsfarm.net. This small and appealingly idiosyncratic hotel lies 4km from the main road near Karatu, on an active coffee farm bordering a patch of indigenous forest on the footslopes of Ngorongoro. Extensively renovated over recent years, Gibb's Farm possesses a rustic colonial ambience which is far removed from the relative uniformity that characterises many of the more upmarket lodges

above left **Adult male serval**
Felis serval (NG)
page 260

above right **Cheetah**
Acynonix jubatus (AZ)
page 260

centre right **Lioness**
Panthera leo (AZ)
page 259

below left **Young male leopard**
Panthera pardus (NG)
page 259

below right **Large spotted genet**
Genetta tigrina (AZ)
page 262

above left **Hippopotamus**
Hippopotamus amphibius (AZ)
page 269

above right **Warthog**
Phacochoerus africanus (AZ)
page 269

below left **Giraffe**
Giraffa camelopardis (AZ)
page 269

below right **Burchell's zebra**
Equus burchelli (AZ)
page 269

above left
Young black-backed jackal
Canis mesomelas (AZ)
page 261

above right **Spotted hyena**
Crocuta crocuta (AZ)
page 261

below left **Bat-eared fox**
Otocyon megalotis (AZ)
page 261

below right **African wild dog**
Lycaon pictus (AZ)
page 261

above left **Female impala**
Aepeceros melampus (AZ)
page 267

above centre **Male impala**
Aepeceros melampus (AZ)
page 267

above right **Oribi**
Ourebia ourebi (AZ)
page 268

below **Kirk's dik dik**
Madoqua kirki (AZ)
page 268

below left **Roan antelope**
Hippotragus equinus (AZ)
page 264

above left **Topi**
Damaliscus lunatus jimela (AZ)
page 265

above right **Defassa waterbuck**
Kobus ellipsiprymnus defassa (AZ)
page 265

centre **Common eland**
Taurotragus oryx (AZ)
page 265

below left **Sable antelope**
Hippotragus niger (AZ)
page 265

below right **Jackson's hartebeest**
Alcelaphus buselaphus (AZ)
page 256

above left **Kirk's red colobus**
Procolobus pennantii kirkii (AZ)
page 263

above centre **Chimpanzee**
Pan troglodytes (AZ)
page 262

above right **Yellow baboon**
Papio cynocephalus (AZ)
page 263

below **Greater galago (bushbaby)**
Galago crassicaudatus (AZ)
page 264

above left **Rock hyrax**
Procavia capensis (AZ)
page 272

above right **Nile crocodile**
Crocodylus niloticus (AZ)
page 33

centre **Dwarf mongoose**
Helogale parvula (AZ)
page 262

below left **Cape
ground squirrel**
Xerus inauris (AZ)
page 272

below right **Flat-headed
rock agama lizard**
Agama mwanzae (AZ)
page 37

clockwise from top left

Greater flamingoes
Phoenicopterus ruber (AZ)

Fischer's lovebird
Agapornis fischeri (AZ)

Pearl-spotted owlet
Glaucidium perlatum (AZ)

Lilac-breasted roller
Coracias caudata (AZ)

White-fronted bee-eater
Merops bullockoides (AZ)

Kori bustard
Ardeotis kori (AZ)

Crowned crane
Balearica pavonina (AZ)

D'Arnaud's barbet
Trachyphonus darnaudii (AZ)

in northern Tanzania. Many safari-goers rate it among their favourite hotels in Tanzania, and the home-style cooking with organic produce grown on the farm is excellent. It's a popular base for day trips into the Ngorongoro Crater, though it does have the disadvantage of lying away from the spectacular crater rim. Other activities include bird walks with the resident naturalist and a 2-hour hike to a waterfall and cave made by elephants on the forested slopes of the crater. *Self-contained bungalows US$128/156 sgl/dbl B&B or US$172/245 FB for non-residents; residents pay US$63/88 B&B or US$107/176 FB. Significant low season discounts.*

Plantation Lodge ╲ 027 253 4364/5; ╲ 027 254 4360; e plantation-lodge@habari.co.tz or info@plantation-lodge.com; www.plantation-lodge.com. This popular German-owned lodge is set in flowering grounds only 2km from the Ngorongoro road a few kilometres out of Karatu. It has a classic whitewash and thatch exterior, complemented by the stylish décor of the spacious self-contained rooms. As with Gibb's Farm, Plantation Lodge stands in refreshingly individualistic contrast to the chain lodges that characterise the northern circuit, while also forming a good base for day trips to Ngorongoro Crater. *US$155/215 sgl/dbl HB or US$190/270 FB.*

Moderate
Octagon Lodge (14 rooms) ╲ 027 243 4525; m 0744 650324; e rory@octagonlodge.com; www.octogonlodge.com. This comfortable new lodge, set in compact but pretty green grounds on the outskirts of Karatu, offers good-value accommodation in neat wooden chalets. An unusual feature of the lodge is an Irish pub reflecting the owner-manager's nationality. *US$70 pp FB.*

Budget and camping
Ngorongoro Safari Resort ╲ 025 253 4287/89/90; f 025 253 4288; e safariresort@yahoo.com. This smart and modern complex in Karatu offers accommodation in clean, comfortable self-contained rooms for US$65/80 sgl/dbl, as well as camping in a neat well-maintained site for US$5 pp. The attached supermarket, though not cheap, is the best in Karatu, and the restaurant serves a good range of tasty Indian and continental dishes at around US$5. Other facilities include an internet café, a filling station, a large bar with satellite TV, and 4x4 rental.

Kudu Lodge & Campsite ╲ 025 253 4055; f 025 453 4268. Currently about the best of a few campsites in the Karatu area catering primarily to budget camping safaris, Kudu Lodge lies just outside town in the direction of Ngorongoro. Camping on the neat lawn costs US$7 pp, and rooms are available in the US$25–60 range.

LAKE EYASI AND SURROUNDS
The vast Lake Eyasi verges on the remote southern border of the Ngorongoro Conservation Area, and lies at the base of the 800m Eyasi Escarpment, part of the Western Rift Valley wall. In years of plentiful rain, this shallow soda lake can extend for 80km from north to south, but in drier periods it sometimes dries out altogether to form an expansive white crust. Most of the time, it falls somewhere between the two extremes: an eerily bleak and windswept body of water surrounded by a white muddy crust and tangled dry acacia scrub. When we visited in the middle of the day, the lake had a rather desolate appearance, but I imagine that it might be very beautiful in the early morning or late afternoon. There is little resident wildlife in the area, aside from dik-dik and baboons, but depending on the water level, the lake is an important source of fish for Arusha and it often supports hundreds of thousands of flamingoes as well as a variety of other waterbirds.

Lake Eyasi is primarily of interest to tourists as the home of the Hadza (see box *The last hunter-gatherers,* overleaf), and it is now reasonably straightforward to visit a

THE LAST HUNTER-GATHERERS

The Hadza (or Hadzabe) of the Lake Eyasi hinterland, which lies to the east of Karatu, represent a unique – and increasingly fragile – link between modern east Africa and the most ancient of the region's human lifestyles and languages. Numbering at most 2,000 individuals, the Hadza are Tanzania's only remaining tribe of true hunter-gatherers, and their Hadzame language is one of only two in the country to be classified in the Khoisan family, a group of click-based tongues that also includes the San (Bushmen) of southern Africa.

The Hadza live in nomadic family bands, typically numbering about 20 adults and a coterie of children. Their rudimentary encampments of light grass shelters are erected in the space of a couple of hours, and might be used as a base for anything from ten days to one month before the inhabitants move on. These movements, though often rather whimsical, might be influenced by changes in the weather or local game distribution, and a band will also often relocate close to a fresh kill that is sufficiently large to sustain them for several days. The Hadza are fairly indiscriminate about what meat they eat – anything from mice to giraffe are fair game, and we once saw a family roasting a feral cat, fur and all, on their campfire – but baboons are regarded to be the ultimate delicacy and reptiles are generally avoided. Hunting with poisoned arrows and honey gathering are generally male activities, while women and children collect roots, seeds, tubers and fruit – vegetarian fodder actually accounts for about 80% of the food intake.

The Hadza have a reputation for living for the present and they care little for conserving food resources, probably because their lifestyle inherently places very little stress on the environment. This philosophy is epitomised in a popular game of chance, which Hadza men will often play – and gamble valuable possessions on – to while away a quiet afternoon. A large master disc is made from baobab bark, and each participant makes a smaller personal disc, with all discs possessing distinct rough and smooth faces. The discs are stacked and thrown in the air, an action that is repeated until only one of the small discs lands with the same face up as the large disc, deciding the winner.

Many Hadza people still dress in the traditional attire of animal skins – women favour impala hide, men the furry coat of a small predator or baboon – which are often decorated with shells and beads. Hadza social groupings are neither permanent nor strongly hierarchical: individuals and couples are free to move between bands, and there is no concept of territorial possession. In order to be eligible for marriage, a Hadza man must kill five baboons to prove his worth. Once married, a couple might stay together for several decades or a lifetime, but there is no taboo against separation and either partner can terminate the union at any time by physically abandoning the other partner.

Hadza encampment and go hunting with its male inhabitants. These visits must be arranged through one of three appointed guides based in the largest village in the region, which is called Mang'ola but sometimes referred to as Lake Eyasi (misleadingly, since it actually lies about 10km from the lakeshore). In addition to the entrance fee of US$2 per person charged by the Council of Mang'ola, fees of around US$10 and US$15 per party must be paid respectively to the guide and to the Hadza encampment visited.

We felt our visit to a Hadza encampment highly worthwhile. The people struck us as being very warm and unaffected, and going on an actual hunt was a primal

The Hadza might reasonably be regarded as a sociological and anthropological equivalent of a living fossil, since they are one of the very few remaining adherents to the hunter-gatherer lifestyle that sustained the entire human population of the planet for 98% of its history. In both the colonial and post-independence eras, the Hadza have resolutely refused to allow the government to coerce them into following a more settled agricultural or pastoral way of life. The last concerted attempt to modernise Hadza society took place in the 1960s, under the Nyerere government, when a settlement of brick houses with piped water, schools and a clinic was constructed for them alongside an agricultural scheme. Within ten years, the model settlement had been all but abandoned as the Hadza returned to their preferred lifestyle of hunting and gathering. The government, admirably, has since tacitly accepted the right of the Hadza to lead the life of their choice; a large tract of communal land fringing Lake Eyasi has been set aside for their use and they remain the only people in Tanzania automatically exempt from taxes!

The Khoisan language spoken by the Hadza is also something of a relic, belonging to a linguistic family that would almost certainly have dominated eastern and southern Africa until perhaps 3,000 years ago. As Bantu-speaking agriculturists and pastoralists swept into the region from the northwest, however, the Khoisan-speaking hunter-gatherer communities were either killed, or assimilated into Bantu-speaking communities, or forced to retreat into arid and montane territories ill-suited to herding and cultivation. This slow but steady marginalising process has continued into historical times: it has been estimated that of around 100 documented Khoisan languages only 30 are still in use today, and that the total Khoisan-speaking population of Africa now stands at less than 200,000.

That most Khoisan languages, if not already extinct, are headed that way, takes on an added poignancy if, as a minority of linguists have suggested throughout the 20th century, the unique click sounds are a preserved element of the very earliest human language. In order to investigate this possibility, the anthropological geneticists Alec Knight and Joanna Mountain recently analysed the chromosome content of samples taken from the geographically diverse San and Hadza, and concluded that they 'are as genetically distant from one another as two populations could be'. Discounting the somewhat improbable scenario that the clicking noises of the Hadza and San languages arose independently, this wide genetic gulf would imply a very ancient common linguistic root indeed. Several linguists dispute Knight and Mountain's conclusion, but if it is correct, then Hadzame, along with Africa's other dying Khoisan languages, might represent one last fading echo of the first human voices to have carried across the African savanna.

and exciting experience – even if the waiting wives were mildly disappointed when their men returned to camp with only two mice and one bird to show for their efforts. Other travellers we've spoken to were luckier, though do be warned that a temporary conversion to vegetarianism might be in order should you come back from the hunt with a baboon or another large mammal – as a guest, you'll be offered the greatest delicacy, which is the raw liver. It could be argued that regular exposure to tourists might erode the traditional lifestyle of certain Hadza bands, but I saw no sign of this, and it should be borne in mind that the Hadza have chosen their nomadic lifestyle despite repeated attempts to settle them by successive governments. So far as I can ascertain, the guides ensure that no one band is visited more than once or twice a week, and the fee paid to the community is used to buy metal for spears and beads for decoration, but not food. And, incidentally, if you're the sort of daft bugger who wanders around African villages armed with piles of sweets or pens or whatever to hand out, then either don't visit the Hadza, or if you do, please leave the bag of goodies in Karatu.

Getting there and away

Mang'ola lies about one hour's drive from Karatu, and can be reached by following the Ngorongoro road out of town for about 5km, then taking a left turn towards the lake. Once at Mang'ola, it's easy enough to locate the guides and arrange a visit to a Hadza encampment. The full excursion can be completed as a half-day trip out of Karatu with private transport, and can easily be appended to a standard northern circuit safari.

Where to stay
Upmarket
Kisima Ngeda (6 rooms) ⟍ 027 253 4128/254 8840; f 027 250 2283; e kisima@habari.co.tz. This new owner-managed tented camp is set in a shady grove of doum palms near the eastern shore of Lake Eyasi, with magnificent views across to the kilometre-tall western Rift Valley escarpment, the Ngorongoro Highlands and the Oldeani Mountains. It makes an excellent base for visiting a Hadzabe encampment or exploring the arid lake hinterland. The accommodation is comfortable but simple, rather than luxurious, and the structures around the en-suite tents are made entirely from organic local materials. The excellent food includes tilapia caught fresh from the lake. *US$170/270/370 sgl/dbl/triple, FB.*

Camping
Council Campsite Mang'ola Council operates a lovely but basic campsite, set about 4km from the town on the road towards the lake, in a glade of acacias surrounding a hot spring. There are no facilities to speak of.

NORTH OF MANYARA

The vast majority of Serengeti safaris head directly west from Manyara along the new asphalt road that climbs the Rift Valley escarpment into the Ngorongoro Highlands, and then return to Arusha exactly the same way. An offbeat alternative to this well-trodden route, one that will transform your safari itinerary into a genuine loop, is the spine-jarring 265km road that connects Mto wa Mbu to the northern Serengeti via the parched stretch of the Rift Valley abutting the border with Kenya. This is not, it should be stressed, a route that should instil any great enthusiasm in anybody who nurses a dodgy back or chronic agoraphobia, or who has limited tolerance for simple travel conditions. But equally this half-forgotten corner of northern Tanzania also possesses some genuinely alluring off-the-beaten-track landmarks in the form of the ruined city of Engaruka, the malevolent Lake Natron, and above all perhaps the fiery volcanic majesty of Ol Doinyo Lengai.

Most experienced safari operators can arrange trips to the northern Rift Valley, taking Lake Natron as their focal point, but many will also discourage you from visiting the area as it is rough on vehicles and has been prone to outbursts of banditry in the past. Technically, it is possible to travel between Mto wa Mbu and the northern Serengeti via Natron in nine to ten hours of flat driving, but it would make for a very long day and would rather defeat the point of the exercise. More realistic is to split the drive over two days, stopping for a night at the lakeshore village of Ngare Sero, or two nights if you intend to climb Ol Doinyo Lengai or undertake any other exploration of the region. It is common practice to tag this area on to the end of a safari, but there is a strong case for slotting it in between the Tarangire/Manyara and Ngorongoro/Serengeti legs of your itinerary, if for no other reason than it would break up the vehicle-bound regime of game drives with a decent leg-stretch – whether you opt for a gentle stroll around the Engaruka Ruins or the southern shore of Natron, the slightly more demanding hike to the Ngare Sero Waterfall in the escarpment west of Natron, or the decidedly challenging nocturnal ascent of Ol Doinyo Lengai.

If you visit this area in your own vehicle, treat it as you would any wilderness trip: carry adequate supplies of food, water and fuel. If you go with a safari company, avoid those at the lower end of the price scale, or you risk getting stuck in the middle of nowhere in a battered vehicle. Note that the scenic 160km road between Natron and Klein's Gate suffered a spate of unrest in 1998–99, instigated by Somali exiles from Kenya. The insurgents killed at least one police officer and several local Maasai, and a tourist vehicle was attacked near Loliondo, fortunately without any fatalities. The situation has been stable for a few years now, but still you are advised to make enquiries with a specialised operator.

Engaruka Ruins

Situated below the Rift Valley escarpment about 65km north of Manyara, Engaruka is the Maasai name for the extensive ruins of a mysterious terraced city and irrigation system constructed at least 500 years ago by a late Iron Age culture in the eastern foothills of Mount Empakaai. Nobody knows for sure who built the city: some say it was the Mbulu, who inhabited the area immediately before the Maasai arrived there; others that it was built by Datoga settlers from the north. Locally, the city is said to have been home to forebears of the Sukuma, whose greeting 'mwanga lukwa' was later bastardised to Engaruka by the Maasai – more likely, however, that the name of this well-watered spot has roots in the Maasai word 'ngare' (water).

The discovery of the ruins by outsiders is generally credited to Dr Fischer, who followed the base of the Rift Valley through Maasailand in 1883, and wrote how 'peculiar masses of stone became suddenly apparent, rising from the plain to heights up to ten feet. Partly they looked like mouldering tree trunks, partly like the tumbled down walls of ancient castles.' An older reference to Engaruka can be found on the so-called Slug Map drawn up by the missionaries Krapf and Erhardt in 1855. The first person to excavate the site was Hans Reck in the early 20th century, followed by the legendary Louis Leakey, who reckoned it consisted of seven large villages containing roughly 1,000 homes apiece and thought the total population must have exceeded 30,000.

The ruined villages overlook a complex stone-block irrigation system that extends over some 25km² and is fed by the perennial Engaruka River. This highly specialised and integrated agricultural community was abandoned in the 18th century, probably due to a combination of changes in the local hydrology and the immigration of more militaristic pastoralist tribes from the north. Yet Engaruka is unique only in scale, since a number of smaller deserted sites in the vicinity form part of the same cultural and agricultural complex, and recent radiocarbon dating suggests it might be older than has been assumed in the past – possibly as old as the 4th century AD, which would make it a likely precursor to the great centralised empires that thrived in pre-colonial Uganda and Rwanda.

Guided tours of the ruins can be arranged easily in Engaruka village – the Engaruka Ruins Campsite is as good a place to ask around as any. Without a

PHOTOGRAPHING THE MAASAI

A common cause of friction on safaris is the matter of photographing Maasai people, something that invariably involves a payment, leading many tourists to conclude that the Maasai are 'too commercialised'. This misguided allegation has become something of a personal bugbear, not least because it strikes me as reflecting Western misconceptions and prejudices far more than it does any aspect of modern Maasai culture.

To diverge slightly, I expect that many visitors find it difficult to come to terms with the cocktail of traditionalism and exotic Western influences that informs modern African culture. To give one clearly identifiable example, you'll find that most Africans today are devout Christians or Muslims, yet many also simultaneously adhere to an apparently conflicting traditional belief system. Then look around the streets of Arusha, where cellphone-bearing businessmen and trendy safari guides brush past traditional Maasai street hawkers, and it's clear modernity and traditionalism co-exist here in a manner that seems contradictory to outsiders but is unremarkable to the country's inhabitants. And less immediately apparent is that the slick businessmen or casually dressed safari guide, should he happen to be Maasai, will probably return home for special occasions dressed in traditional attire, to all outward purposes indistinguishable from relatives who might always dress that way.

The point being that, as outsiders, it is all too easy to perceive an absolute cultural division between those Tanzanians who are outwardly modern and those who are outwardly traditional in their appearance. Just as many modern Tanzanian professionals might still visit traditional healers on occasion, or return home for important tribal ceremonies, it is absurd to attribute any modern influence in a Maasai pastoralist to a lack of cultural integrity. The Maasai, like us, are living in the 21st century, and a variety of external factors – among them, population growth, the gazetting of traditional grazing land as national parks, exposure to other Tanzanian cultures and exotic religions, the creation of a cash economy – all ensure that Maasai culture is not a static museum piece, but a dynamic, modern entity.

For most visitors to Tanzania, direct exposure to Maasai culture will take place in one of a number of *bomas* (family enclosures) that operate as tourist 'cultural villages' in the vicinity of Tarangire, Lake Manyara and Ngorongoro. Visiting such *bomas* is straightforward enough – ask your driver to arrange it – and the standard practice is to agree a price for the whole group, which will allow you to wander around as you please and photograph whomever you like. While I see absolutely nothing wrong with these cultural villages, and much that is commendable about them, any visitor should approach them with realistic expectations. The village you visit is basically operating as a cottage industry, and its inhabitants probably derive a substantial part of their living from tourist visits, so it stands to reason that there will be an element of contrivance to the

local guide, it's debatable whether the ruins would convey anything much to the average passing tourist. The floor plan of the main village is still quite clear, and a few of the circular stone houses remain more or less intact to around waist level, their floors strewn with shards of broken earthenware. Substantial sections of the irrigation canal are still in place, as are some old burial mounds that might or might not be related to the war with the Maasai that caused the village to be abandoned.

experience they offer. And accept, too, that it is we, the tourists, who are the distorting factor in what is otherwise a genuine working Maasai settlement, one that probably existed long before we came along and whose inhabitants are absolutely traditional in all but this one respect. In my view, to conclude that the Maasai are 'too commercialised' on the basis of an isolated visit to what is an inherently commercial enterprise is as daft as walking into a London shop and concluding that the English are 'too commercialised' because the assistant expects you to pay for the items you select.

If you want to photograph the Maasai, the only realistic alternative to visiting a cultural village would be to snap one of the individuals who hang around strategic spots along the northern safari circuit for the express purpose of selling their beadwork or image to tourists. If you do this, a payment will be demanded, and quite rightly so because you will be photographing a person who derives their income from passing tourist traffic. But, make no mistake: were you to wander off into a Maasai *boma* that doesn't routinely deal with tourists, the odds are that its inhabitants will simply refuse to be photographed no matter what payment you offer. What's more, you might well find a spear dangling from the end of your lens if you don't respect their wishes!

There is a deeper irony to this whole debate. Here we have well-off visitors from media-obsessed, materialistic Europe or North America twiddling their video cameras, straightening their custom-bought safari outfits, and planning the diet they'll go on back home to compensate for the endless lodge buffets. They are confronted by a culture as resilient, non-materialistic and ascetic as that of the Maasai, and they accuse it with a straight face of being 'too commercialised'. This genuinely concerns me: are we so culture bound, so riddled with romantic expectations about how the Maasai should behave, that any slight deviation from these preconceptions prevents us from seeing things for what they are?

So let's start again. The Maasai are proud and dramatically attired pastoralists who adhere almost entirely to the traditions of their forefathers. They fascinate us, but being the bunch of gadget-obsessed *wazungu* we are, our response is not to absorb their presence or to try to communicate with them, but to run around thrusting cameras in their faces. And this, I would imagine, irritates the hell out of those Maasai who happen to live along main tourist circuits, so they decide not to let tourists photograph them except for a fee or in the context of an organised tourist village. In theory, everybody should be happy. In practice, we somehow construe this reasonable attempt by relatively poor people to make a bit of honest money as rampant commercialism. Okay, I recognise this is a bit simplistic, but we create the demand, the Maasai satisfy it, and if we pay to do so, that's just good capitalism, something the West has always been keen to encourage in Africa. If you don't like it, save your film and buy a postcard – in all honesty, you'll probably get a lot more from meeting these charismatic people if you leave your camera behind and enjoy the moment!

Getting there and away

The ruins can be reached by forking westward at the modern village of Engaruka, which is almost exactly halfway along the 120km road between Mto wa Mbu and Ngare Sero, and takes about 90 minutes to reach coming in either direction. From the junction, continue through the semi-urban sprawl of Engaruka for about 5km until you reach the Jerusalem Campsite, from where it is a ten-minute walk to the nearest ruined village. No entrance fee is charged, but the local guides will expect to be paid around US$5 per party to show you around. At least one bus daily connects Arusha to Engaruka, leaving Arusha from opposite the Shoprite at 10.00 and passing through Mto wa Mbu at around 14.00 before dropping passengers at the station next to the Engaruka Ruins Campsite at around 18.00.

Where to stay

Engaruka Ruins Campsite ☎ 027 253 9103; m 0455 507939; e engaruka@yahoo.com. Set in compact green grounds next to the bus station, this friendly campsite has the best facilities in town, including hot running water, electricity, flush toilets, a bar and a restaurant. The staff can arrange guided tours of the ruins for around US$5 per party, as well as visits to local Maasai *bomas* and traditional dancing displays. Guided ascents of Ol Doinyo Lengai arranged through the campsite work out at around US$50 pp, and the camp can also lay on 4x4 transport to/from the base of the mountain for US$110 one-way for up to 4 or 5 people. *US$7 pp.*

Jerusalem Campsite Set in a pretty grove close to the ruins, this site has no facilities other than toilets, making it more suitable for groups than for independent travellers. *US$5 pp.*

Lake Natron

There are but a handful of places where the Rift Valley evokes its geologically violent origins with graphic immediacy. Ethiopia's Danakil Desert is one such spot; the volcanic Virunga Range in the Albertine Rift is another. And so too is the most northerly landmark in the Tanzanian Rift Valley, the low-lying Lake Natron, a shallow sliver of exceptionally alkaline water that extends southward from the Kenya border near Mount Shompole for 58km. The Natron skyline is dominated by the textbook volcanic silhouette of Ol Doinyo Lengai, which rises more than 2,000m above the Rift Valley floor, its harsh black contours softened by an icing of white ash that glistens brightly below the sun, as if in parody of Kilimanjaro's snows. Then there is the lake itself, a thrillingly primordial phenomenon whose caustic waters are enclosed by a crust of sodden grey volcanic ash and desiccated salt, punctuated by isolated patches of steamy, reed-lined swamp where the hot springs that sustain the lake bubble to the surface.

Thought to be about 1.5 million years old, Natron is a product of the same tectonic activity that formed the Ngorongoro Highlands and Mount Gelai, the latter being an extinct volcano that rises from the eastern lakeshore. Nowhere more than 50cm deep, it has changed shape significantly since that time, largely as a result of volcanic activity associated with the creation of Ol Doinyo Lengai to its immediate south. It lies at an altitude of 610m in an unusually arid stretch of the rift floor, receiving an average of 400mm of rainfall annually, and it would have probably dried out centuries ago were it not also fed by the freshwater Ewaso Ngiro River, which has its catchment in the central Kenyan Highlands, and the hot springs that rise below its floor. The alkaline level has also increased drastically over the millennia, partially because of the high salinity of ash and lava deposits from Lengai, partially because the lake's only known outlet is evaporation. Today, depending on recent rainfall, the viscous water has an average pH of 9–11, making it almost as caustic as ammonia when the level is very low, and it can reach a temperature of up to 60°C in extreme circumstances.

Natron's hyper-salinity makes it incapable of sustaining any but the most specialised life forms. The only resident vertebrate is the endemic white-lipped tilapia *Oreochromis alcalica*, a 10cm-long fish that congregates near hot spring inlets where the water temperature is around 36–40°C. The microbiology of the lake is dominated by halophytic (salt-loving) organisms such as Spirulina, a form of blue-green algae whose red pigments make the salt-encrusted flats in the centre of the lake look bright red when seen from the air. Natron is also the only known breeding ground for east Africa's 2.5 million lesser flamingoes, which usually congregate there between August and October, feeding on the abundant algae (whose pigments are responsible for the birds' trademark pink hue). The breeding ground's inhospitality to potential predators makes it an ideal flamingo nursery, but it also makes it difficult of access to human visitors – situated in the centre of the lake, it was discovered as recently as the 1950s and it can only be seen from the air today. In addition to the flamingoes, Natron attracts up to 100,000 migrant waterbirds during the European winter, and its hinterland supports a thin population of large mammals typical of the Rift Valley, including wildebeest, zebra, fringe-eared oryx, Grant's and Thomson's gazelle, and even the odd lion and cheetah.

Getting there and away

The centre of tourist activity on Natron is the small lakeshore village of Ngare Sero, bisected by the wooded freshwater stream from which its Maasai name is derived ('black water', 'clear water', 'dappled water' or 'forest of water', depending on who's doing the translating). The village lies about 120km north of Mto wa Mbu along a very rough road – bank on a four-hour drive, though this might improve if and when bridges are built across the larger watercourses north of Engaruka. The village is about 160km from Klein's Gate in the northern Serengeti, a drive that takes five to six hours without stops, and involves a spectacular ascent (or descent) of the Rift escarpment to the west of the lake. There is no public transport to Ngare Sero, but buses do run twice daily as far as Engaruka, where you can hire a 4x4 to Natron and/or Lengai from the Engaruka Ruins Campsite.

Where to stay

Lake Natron Camp (9 rooms, with 5 more scheduled for construction) ⏴ 027 255 3242/3326; **m** 0744 324193; **f** 027 255 3243; **e** moivaro@habari.co.tz or info@moivaro.com; www.moivaro.com. Established in Ngare Sero in 1989, this low-key camp has a spectacular setting alongside a stream some 4km from the southern lakeshore, and offers great views across the floodplain to Mount Gerai, an extinct volcano less impressive in outline but actually marginally taller than nearby Lengai. Though it has a decidedly no-frills feel in keeping with the austere surrounds, the camp does have a welcoming swimming pool, and there's a pleasant restaurant and bar area. Accommodation is in en-suite tents with hot water. Inexpensive organised guided climbs of nearby Ol Doinyo Lengai are offered too. *US$85/150 sgl/dbl FB; low-season discount Apr and May, premium charged over Christmas period.*

Riverside Campsite (5 rooms) ⏴ 027 250 7145; **f** 027 250 8035; **e** info@sunnysafaris.com or sunny@arusha.com. This new campsite is run by a local Maasai elder and set alongside the river running through Ngare Sero. *US$45 pp FB for a bed in a basic en-suite twin standing tent with netting; US$10 pp to pitch a tent on the green lawn.*

Waterfall Campsite Situated a kilometre or two out of town close to the starting point for the walk to Ngare Sero Waterfall, this basic campsite has a great location but it seems very overpriced. *US$10 pp to pitch a tent.*

Activities

Southern Lakeshore

To reach the southern lakeshore from Ngare Sero, you need to drive for around 5km to an unofficial parking spot about 1km from the water's edge, then walk for about ten minutes across salt-encrusted flats to a series of pockmarked black volcanic protrusions that serve as vantage points over the water. It's a lovely spot, with Lengai looming in the background, and it hosts a profusion of waterbirds, most visibly large flocks of the pink-tinged lesser flamingo, but also various pelicans, egrets, herons and waders. Wildebeest and zebra are also often seen in the area. If your driver doesn't know the way to the lakeshore – it's a rather obscure track – then ask for a local guide at one of the campsites. Whatever else you do, don't let the driver take the vehicle beyond the tracks left behind by his predecessors, or you run a serious risk of getting stuck in the treacherously narrow saline crust that surrounds the lake.

Ngare Sero Waterfall

The Ngare Sero River forms a series of pretty waterfalls as it descends from the Nguruman Escarpment west of Lake Natron. The lowest two falls can be reached by driving out to Waterfall Campsite, then following the river upstream on foot for 45–60 minutes, through the gorge it has carved into the escarpment wall. If you are not already sufficiently doused by the time you reach the second waterfall, there's a chilly natural swimming pool below it. There is no clear footpath through the gorge: you will need to wade across the river several times (potentially dangerous after heavy rain) and can also expect to do a fair bit of clambering along ledges and rocks. This walk can only be recommended to reasonably fit and agile travellers, and it's advisable to take somebody who knows the way to help you navigate a couple of tricky stretches – a guide can be arranged at any of the camps listed above.

Ol Doinyo Lengai

Estimated to be around 350,000–400,000 years old, Ol Doinyo Lengai – the Maasai 'Mountain of God' – is one of the youngest volcanoes in east Africa and possibly the most active. Its crater is known to have experienced almost continuous low-key activity since 1883, when Dr Fischer, the first European to pass through this part of Maasailand, observed smoke rising from the summit and was told second-hand that the mountain regularly emitted rumbling noises. At least a dozen minor or major eruptions have occurred since then, the most recent having been in 2004, when plumes in the crater could be seen from as far away as Ngare Sero and the local Maasai herdsmen moved their livestock out of the area, and there is widespread consensus among volcanologists that another eruption is likely before the decade is out. An interesting feature of Lengai us that it is the only active volcano known to emit carbonate lava, a form of molten rock that contains almost no silicon, is about 50% cooler than other forms of lava at around 500°C, and is also exceptionally fluid, with a viscosity comparable to water.

An increasingly popular option with adventurous travellers is the ascent of Lengai, which passes through some magnificently arid scenery and offers spectacular views back towards the Rift Valley, before leading to the bleakly visceral lunar landscape of the crater, studded with ash cones, lava pools, steam vents and other evidence of volcanic activity. Suitable only for reasonably fit and agile travellers, the track to the top of Lengai is very steep, climbing in altitude from around 800m to over 2,878m, while the descent can be very tough on knees and ankles. The climb normally takes five to six hours along slopes practically bereft of shade, for which reason many locals recommend leaving at midnight to avoid the intense heat and to reach the crater rim in time for sunrise. If you ascend by day, a 05.00 start is advised, and precautions should be taken against dehydration and sunstroke. Either way, the descent takes about two hours.

Most adventure safari operators in Arusha offer guided Lengai climbs, but it is also possible to arrange a one-day climb locally for around US$50 per person. The best place to pick up a reliable guide is either at Engaruka Ruins Campsite or at one of the camps dotted around Ngare Sero. The mountain lies outside any

THE 1966 ERUPTION

The most impressive eruption of Ol Doinyo Lengai in recorded history occurred in the latter part of 1966, when ash fall was reported as far away as Seronera, more than 100km to the west, as well as at Loliondo and Shombole, both some 70km further north. It is believed that the otherwise inexplicable death of large numbers of game around Empakaai Crater in that year was a result of an ash fall that coated the grass up to 2cm deep, though it is unclear whether the animals starved to death or they succumbed to a toxin within the ash. The effect on Maasai livestock was also devastating, according to Tepilit Ole Saitoti, who recalled the incident as follows in his excellent book *Worlds of a Maasai Warrior*:

> In the year 1966, God, who my people believe dwells in this holy mountain, unleashed Her fury unsparingly. The mountain thunder shook the earth, and the volcanic flame, which came from deep down in the earth's crust, was like a continuous flash of lightning. During days when the eruption was most powerful, clouds of smoke and steam appeared. Many cattle died and still more would die. Poisonous volcanic ash spewed all over the land as far as a hundred miles away, completely covering the pastures and the leaves of trees. Cattle swallowed ash each time they tried to graze and were weakened. They could not wake up without human assistance. We had to carry long wooden staffs to put under the fallen animals to lift them up. There must have been more than enough reason for God to have unleashed Her anger on us, and all we could do was pray for mercy. My pastoral people stubbornly braved the gusting warm winds as they approached the flaming mountain to pray. Women and men dressed in their best walked in stately lines towards God, singing. The mountain was unappeased and cattle died in the thousands. Just before the people started dying too, my father decided to move; as he put it: 'We must move while we still have children, or else we will all lose them.'

conservation area, so no park fees are charged, but you may be required to pay a daily fee of around US$20 per person. If you are thinking of sleeping on the mountain, then it is strongly recommended that you set up camp in the inactive south crater rather than the active north crater – not only is it far more pleasant to camp in the south crater, but you also don't run the risk of your camp being engulfed by an unexpected lava flow or bombarded by eruptive rocks. All hikers should be aware that the cones on the crater floor can easily collapse under pressure and they often cover deadly lava lakes. Under no circumstances should you climb on a cone, or walk inside a partially collapsed cone.

For further information on the Ol Doinyo Lengai, check out the excellent websites www.mtsu.edu/~fbelton/lengai.html (good practical information) or http://it.stlawu.edu/~cnya/ (with detailed geological background).

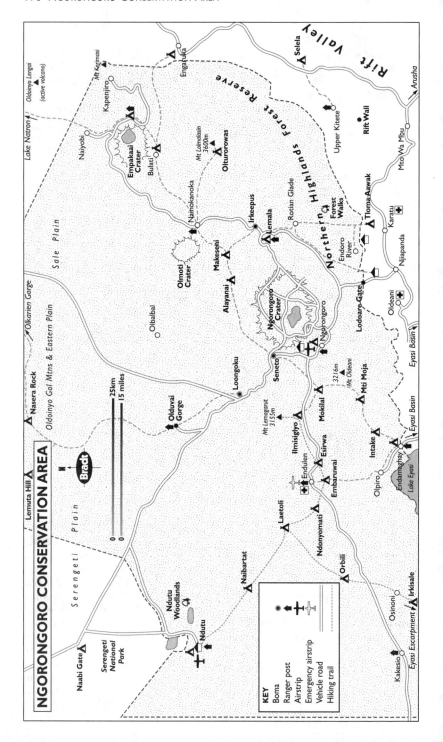

Ngorongoro Conservation Area

An eastern annexe to the Serengeti National Park, the 8,300km² Ngorongoro Conservation Area (NCA) can be divided into two broad ecological zones. The sparsely wooded western plains are essentially a continuation of the Serengeti ecosystem, supporting a cover of short grass that attracts immense concentrations of grazers during the rainy season. The east, by contrast, protects the Ngorongoro Highlands, an extinct volcanic range whose numerous peaks include the 3,648m-high Lolomalasin, the third-highest in Tanzania after Kilimanjaro and Meru. The centrepiece of the NCA is the legendary Ngorongoro Crater, the world's largest intact volcanic caldera, and a shoo-in contender for any global shortlist of natural wonders – not only for its inherent geological magnificence, but also because its verdant floor serves as a quite extraordinary natural sanctuary for some of Africa's densest large mammal populations.

The approach road from Karatu to the rim of Ngorongoro Crater is sensational, winding through the densely forested outer slopes to Heroes Point, where most visitors will catch their first breathtaking view over the 260km² crater floor lying 600m below. Even at this distance, it is possible to pick out ant-like formations chomping their way across the crater floor – in fact, thousand-strong herds of wildebeest, zebra and buffalo – and with binoculars you might even see a few of the elephants that haunt the fringes of Lerai Forest. The drive along the crater rim to your lodge will be equally riveting: patches of forest interspersed with sweeping views back across to the Rift Valley, and the possibility of encountering buffalo, zebra, bushbuck, elephant and even the occasional leopard.

The mountains of the NCA date from two periods. The Gol Range, which lies to the north of the main road to the Serengeti, consists of an exposed granite block that formed some 500 million years ago. Somewhat less antiquated, at least in geological terms, the Ngorongoro Highlands and associated free-standing mountains are volcanic in origin, their formation linked to the same fracturing process that created the Rift Valley 15 to 20 million years ago. Ngorongoro Crater itself is the relic of an immense volcanic mountain that attained a similar height to that of Kilimanjaro before it imploded violently some two to three million years ago. Two other smaller craters, Olmoti and Empakaai, are the product of similar eruptions. The Ngorongoro Highlands are now more or less volcanically extinct, but the free-standing Ol Doinyo Lengai immediately north of the main highland block last erupted most spectacularly in 1966 and is certain to do so again at some point in the next few decades.

Based on fossil evidence unearthed at Olduvai Gorge in the western NCA, it is known that various species of hominid have occupied this area for at least three million years. It was the domain of hunter-gatherers until a few thousand years ago, when pastoralists moved in. The fate of these early pastoralists is unknown, because a succession of immigrants replaced them: the ancestors of the Cushitic-speaking Mbulu some 2,000 years ago and those of the Nilotic-speaking Datoga about 300 years ago. A century later the militaristic Maasai drove both of these groups out of what is now the NCA: the Datoga to the Eyasi Basin and the Mbulu to the highlands near Manyara. Most place names in the area are Maasai, and although several explanations for the name Ngorongoro are floating around, the most credible is that it is named after a type of Maasai bowl.

Europeans settled in the NCA around the turn of the 20th century. Two German brothers farmed on the crater floor until the outbreak of World War I. One of their old farmhouses is still used by researchers, and a few sisal plants dating to this time can be seen in the northeast of the crater. Tourism began in the 1930s when the original Ngorongoro Crater Lodge was built on the crater rim. The NCA formed part of the original Serengeti National Park as gazetted in 1951, but Maasai protests at being denied access to such a huge tract of their grazing land led to it being split off from the national park and downgraded to a multi-use conservation area.

The Ngorongoro Crater, proclaimed a World Heritage Site in 1978, is the main focal point of tourist activity in the NCA. Those who have the time can explore any number of less publicised natural features further afield. Olduvai Gorge, for instance, is the site of some of Africa's most important hominid fossil finds, and can easily be visited *en route* from the crater rim to the Serengeti. An excellent 84-page booklet, *Ngorongoro Conservation Area*, similar in style to the national park booklets, is readily available in Arusha and has good information on the crater and Olduvai Gorge. It is especially worth buying if you plan to visit some of the off-the-beaten-track parts of the conservation area.

The Ngorongoro Conservation Authority charges an entrance fee of US$30 per person per 24 hours. This fee must be paid even if you just pass through the conservation area in transit between Arusha and the Serengeti National Park, and it is likely to rise significantly during the lifespan of this edition. An additional 'crater service fee' is levied on all visits to the crater floor; this increased from US$30 to US$100 per vehicle as of January 2006, and in order to curb congestion it is now valid for only half a day. Note that the crater rim gets very cold at night, and is often blanketed in mist in the early morning, so you will need a jumper or two, and possibly a windbreaker if you are camping.

GETTING THERE AND AWAY

The road from Arusha to the eastern entrance gate of the NCA via Makuyuni, Mto wa Mbu and Karatu is now surfaced in its entirely and it can be covered comfortably in less than three hours, with another 30–60 minutes required to get to any of the lodges on the crater rim. All roads within the NCA are unsurfaced, and a decent 4x4 is required to reach the crater floor. Most tourists visit Ngorongoro as part of a longer safari, but those with time or budgetary restrictions could think about visiting the crater as a self-contained one-night safari out of Arusha.

WHERE TO STAY AND EAT

No accommodation or camping facilities exist within Ngorongoro Crater, but four upmarket lodges are perched on the rim, all offering superb views to the crater floor, as does the public campsite there. The crater can be (and often is) visited as a day trip from one of the midrange to upmarket lodges that lie along the road between the NCA and Karatu, while budget-conscious travellers have a choice of more basic accommodation in Karatu itself (see page 184 for details of lodges in and around Karatu), though this does mean missing out on the views over the crater. The anomalous Ndutu Lodge, which lies just within the western border of the NCA, is not a realistic base from which to explore the Ngorongoro Highlands and ecologically it really feels like part of the Serengeti, so it is covered in that chapter.

Exclusive

Ngorongoro Crater Lodge (40 rooms) ☎ 027 254 8549/8038 or (South Africa) 27 11 809 4447; e res@ccafrica.co.tz or reservations@ccafrica.com; www.ccafrica.com. This top-of-the-range lodge was originally built in 1934 as a private hunting lodge with a commanding view over the crater, and was converted to a hotel shortly after independence in 1961. The property was bought by CCAfrica in 1995 and rebuilt from scratch with the stated aim of creating 'the finest safari lodge in Africa'. Architecturally, the lodge is literally fantastic. Each individual suite consists of 2 adjoining round structures, similar to African huts but distorted in an almost Dadaist style. The large interiors boast a décor as ostentatious as it is eclectic, combining elements of baroque, classical, African, colonial and much more besides in a manner the management describes as 'Maasai meets Versailles'. The entire lodge has been designed in such a way that the crater is almost constantly in sight (even the baths and the toilets have a view!), and the food, service and ambience are all world class. Whether or not CCAfrica has succeeded in creating Africa's finest safari lodge is a matter of taste and opinion – certainly, the decidedly non-'bush' atmosphere might offend some purists – but it is difficult to fault in terms of ambition and originality. The fact that it was commended in *Condé Nast Traveller*'s prestigious 1998 end-of-year listings says enough. *Low season US$320–490, high season US$730 pp inc all meals, most drinks and game drives.*

Upmarket

Ngorongoro Serena Lodge (75 rooms) ☎ 027 250 4058; f 027 250 8282; e reservations@serena.co.tz; www.serenahotels.com. Meeting the usual high Serena standards, this is arguably the pick of the more conventional lodges on the crater rim, receiving consistent praise from tourists and from within the safari industry. It lies on the western crater rim along the road towards Seronera, several kilometres past the park headquarters and Crater Lodge. It is the closest of the lodges to the main descent road into the crater, a decided advantage for those who want to get to the crater floor as early as possible. The setting is a secluded wooded valley rustling with birdlife and offering a good view over the crater. Serena Active, which operates out of the lodge, offers a good range of afternoon and full-day walks ranging from a gentle stroll through the grassy highlands to a rather more challenging ascent of Olmoti Crater. The facilities, food and service are all of a high standard, and rooms are centrally heated. *US$285/420 sgl/dbl FB, dropping to US$170/255 Apr–Jun.*

Ngorongoro Sopa Lodge (96 rooms) ☎ 057 250 6886; f 057 250 8245; e info@sopalodges.com; www.sopalodges.com. Situated on the forested eastern edge of the crater rim some 20km distant from the headquarters and main cluster of lodges, this attractive modern hotel is similar in standard to the Serena and arguably nudges ahead of it on the basis of location. Accommodation is in vast semi-detached suites, each with 2 dbl beds, a heater, a large bathroom, a fridge, and a wide bay window facing the crater and Ol Mokarot Mountain. There is a swimming pool in front of the bar, and the food and service are excellent. One thing that stands out about this lodge is the large, forested grounds, a good place to look for characteristic montane forest birds, with sunbirds (tacazze, golden-winged and eastern double-collared) well represented and a variety of weavers, seedeaters and robins present. Another is that it lies close to what, in effect, is a private road that can be used both to ascend from and descend into the crater, which greatly reduces the driving time either side of game drives – particularly useful for an early morning start. *US$175/280 sgl/dbl in peak season, FB, dropping to US$70/140 in low season.*

THE MAASAI

The northern safari circuit passes through the homeland of the Nilotic-speaking Maasai, whose reputation as fearsome warriors ensured that the 19th-century slave caravans studiously avoided their territory, which was also one of the last parts of east Africa ventured into by Europeans. The Maasai today remain the most familiar of African people to outsiders, even if their modern reputation rests as much on their continued adherence to a traditional lifestyle as on any of their past exploits. Instantly identifiable, Maasai men drape themselves in toga-like red blankets, carry long wooden poles, and often dye their hair with red ochre and style it in a manner that has been compared to a Roman helmet. And while the women dress similarly to many other Tanzanian women, their extensive use of beaded jewellery is highly distinctive, too.

Although the Maasai are often regarded to be the archetypal east African pastoralists, they are in fact relatively recent arrivals to the area. Their language, called Maa (Maasai literally means 'Maa-speakers'), is closely affiliated to those spoken by the Nuer of southwest Ethiopia and the Bari of southern Sudan, and oral traditions suggest that the proto-Maasai would have started to migrate southward from the lower Nile area in the 15th century. They arrived in their present territory in the 17th or 18th century, where they forcefully displaced earlier inhabitants such as the Datoga and Chagga, who respectively migrated south to the Hanang area and east to the Kilimanjaro foothills. The Maasai territory reached its greatest extent – covering virtually the entire Rift Valley and several neighbouring areas from Mount Marsabit in the north to Dodoma in the south – in the mid-19th century. Over the 1880s/90s, the Maasai were hit by a series of disasters linked to the arrival of Europeans – rinderpest and smallpox epidemics exacerbated by a severe drought and a bloody secession dispute – and much of their former territory was re-colonised by tribes whom they had displaced a century earlier. During the colonial era, a further 50% of their land was lost to game reserves and settler farms. These territorial incursions notwithstanding, the area occupied by the Maasai today is among the most extensive of any Tanzanian tribe, ranging across the vast Maasai Steppes of the northeast to large parts of the Ngorongoro Highlands and Serengeti Plains.

The Maasai are monotheists whose belief in a single deity with a dualistic nature – the benevolent Engai Narok (Black God) and vengeful Engai Nanyokie (Red God) – has some overtones of the Judaic faith. They believe that Engai, who resides in the volcano Ol Doinyo Lengai, made them the rightful owners of all the cattle in the world, a view that has occasionally made life difficult for neighbouring herders. Traditionally, this arrogance does not merely extend to cattle: agriculturist and fish-eating peoples are scorned, while Europeans' uptight style of clothing earned them the Maasai name *Iloredaa Enjekat* – Fart Smotherers! Today, the Maasai co-exist peacefully with their non-Maasai compatriots, but while their tolerance for their neighbours' idiosyncrasies has increased in recent decades, they show little interest in changing their own lifestyle.

The Maasai measure a man's wealth in terms of cattle and children rather than money – a herd of about 50 cattle is respectable, the more children the better, and a man who has plenty of one but not the other is regarded to be poor. Traditionally, the Maasai will not hunt or eat vegetable matter or fish, but feed almost exclusively off their cattle. The main diet is a blend of cow's milk and blood, the latter drained – it is said painlessly – from a strategic nick in the animal's jugular vein. Because the cows are more valuable to them alive than dead, they are generally slaughtered only on special occasions. Meat and milk are never eaten on the same day, because it is insulting to the cattle to feed off the living and the dead at the same time. Despite the apparent hardship of their chosen lifestyle, many Maasai are wealthy by any standards. On one safari, our driver pointed out a not unusually large herd of cattle that would fetch the market equivalent of three new Land Rovers!

The central unit of Maasai society is the age-set. Every 15 years or so, a new and individually named generation of warriors or *Ilmoran* will be initiated, consisting of all the young men who have reached puberty and are not part of a previous age-set – most boys aged between 12 and 25. Every boy must undergo the *Emorata* (circumcision ceremony) before he is accepted as a warrior. If he cries out during the five-minute operation, which is performed without any anaesthetic, the post-circumcision ceremony will be cancelled, the parents are spat on for raising a coward, and the initiate will be taunted by his peers for several years before he is forgiven. When a new generation of warriors is initiated, the existing *Ilmoran* will graduate to become junior elders, who are responsible for all political and legislative decisions until they in turn graduate to become senior elders. All political decisions are made democratically, and the role of the chief elder or *Laibon* is essentially that of a spiritual and moral leader.

Maasai girls are permitted to marry as soon as they have been initiated, but warriors must wait until their age-set has graduated to elder status, which will be 15 years later, when a fresh warrior age-set has been initiated. This arrangement ties in with the polygamous nature of Maasai society: in days past, most elders would typically have acquired between three and ten wives by the time they reached old age. Marriages are generally arranged, sometimes even before the female party is born, as a man may 'book' the next daughter produced by a friend to be his son's wife. Marriage is evidently viewed as a straightforward child-producing business arrangement: it is normal for married men and women to have sleeping partners other than their spouse, provided that those partners are of an appropriate age-set. Should a woman become pregnant by another lover, the prestige attached to having many children outweighs any minor concerns about infidelity, and the husband will still bring up the child as his own. By contrast, although sex before marriage is condoned, a girl who falls pregnant before she has been circumcised is regarded as having brought disgrace on her family, and in former times she would have been fed to the hyenas.

It is impossible to do full justice to the complexities of Maasai society and beliefs in this short space, and interested readers are urged to get hold of a copy of the coffee-table book *Maasai*, published by Harry N Abrams in New York in 1980 and reprinted in 1993. This visually sumptuous book is initially most impressive for the photography of Carol Beckwith, but the detailed and insightful text, written by the Maasai historian Tepilit Ole Saitoti, is exemplary – highly recommended!

For notes on photographing the Maasai, see box on pages 190–1.

NOT A BLOODY ZOO

A regular criticism of the Ngorongoro Crater, one that in my opinion is desperately misguided, is that it is 'like a zoo'. Aside from being yawningly unoriginal – I must have heard this phrase two dozen times in the course of researching this book – this allegation is as facile as it is nonsensical. The wildlife in the crater is not caged, nor is it artificially fed, surely the defining qualities of a zoo, but is instead free to come and go as it pleases. Yes, the crater's animals are generally very relaxed around vehicles, but that doesn't make them tame, merely habituated – no different, really, to the mountain gorillas of Rwanda or the chimps at Mahale.

The point that many visitors to Ngorongoro miss is that, for all the elitism attached to Africa's more remote game reserves, it is only in places where the wildlife is almost totally habituated that casual visitors can watch the animals behave much as they would were no human observers present. And, trust me, this is an infinitely more satisfying experience than travelling through a reserve where the wildlife is so skittish that most sightings amount to little more than a rump disappearing into the bush.

I suspect that the notion of Ngorongoro as a glorified zoo stems from something else entirely. This is the high volume of tourist traffic, which admittedly robs the crater floor of some of its atmosphere, and has some potential to cause environmental degradation, but is of questionable impact on the animals. On the contrary, the wildlife of Ngorongoro is apparently far less affected by the presence of vehicles than, say, the elephants and giraffes in the Selous, which regularly display clear signs of distress at the approach of a vehicle.

The problem, basically, is that the high volume of other tourists in the relatively small and open confines of the crater jars against our sense of aesthetics – especially when game spotting entails looking for a group of vehicles clustered together in the distance rather than looking for an actual animal! Personally, I feel that the scenery and abundance of animals more than makes up for the mild congestion, but if crowds put you off, then there are other places to visit in Tanzania. Instead of adding to the tourist traffic, then moaning about it, why not give the crater a miss? Or, better still, as suggested in the main body of the text, make the effort to be in the crater first thing in the morning, when, for a brief hour or two before the post-breakfast crowds descend, it really does live up to every expectation of untrammelled beauty.

Ngorongoro Wildlife Lodge (72 rooms) ☏ 027 254 4595; f 027 254 8633; e sales@hotelsandlodges-tanzania.com; www.sales@hotelsandlodges-tanzania.com. Situated roughly 2km away from Ngorongoro Crater Lodge, this former government hotel is one of the oldest on the crater rim and it shows its antiquity both in the architecture and the fittings. The once appalling service and food have improved since it was privatised a couple of years back, and the location – on the crater rim directly above the forest of yellow fever acacias – defies superlatives. But the rooms are no more than functionally comfortable, albeit with piping-hot baths (welcome at this chilly altitude) and windows facing the crater. You can pick out animals on the crater floor using a telescope fixed on the patio, and the grounds support a fair range of forest birds. It's acceptable value for money. *US$155/180 sgl/dbl FB.*

Budget and camping

Simba Campsite Situated about 2km from the park headquarters, this is the only place where you can pitch a tent on the crater rim, and it's hardly great value at US$20 pp, given that facilities are limited to a cold shower and rubbish pit. Still, the wonderful view makes it a preferable option to camping in Karatu, in my opinion at least. The village near the headquarters has a few basic bars and shops, and there is nothing preventing you from dropping into nearby Ngorongoro Wildlife Lodge for a drink or snack.

AROUND NGORONGORO CONSERVATION AREA
Ngorongoro Crater Floor

The opportunity of spending a day on the crater floor is simply not to be missed. There are few places where you can so reliably see such large concentrations of wildlife all year round, and your game viewing (and photography) will only be enhanced by the striking backdrop of the 600m-high crater wall. The crater is also excellent Big Five territory: lion, elephant and buffalo are all but guaranteed, rhino are regularly seen, and a leopard is chanced upon from time to time. The official road down to the crater descends from Malanja Depression to the western shore of Lake Magadi, while the official road up starts near Lerai Forest and reaches the rim on the stretch of road between Wildlife and Crater lodges. There is a third road into the crater, which starts near the Sopa Lodge, and this can be used either to ascend or to descend.

There are several notable physical features within the crater. Lerai Forest consists almost entirely of yellow fever trees, large acacias noted for their jaundiced bark (it was once thought that this tree, which is often associated with marsh and lake fringes, the breeding ground for mosquitoes, was the cause of

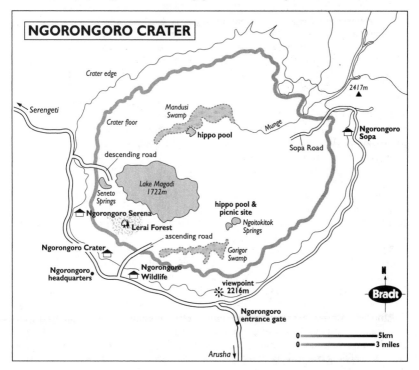

NGORONGORO CRATER

Crater edge

Serengeti

Crater floor

Mandusi Swamp

hippo pool

Munge

2417m

Ngorongoro Sopa

Sopa Road

descending road

Lake Magadi 1722m

Seneto Springs

Ngorongoro Serena

hippo pool & picnic site

Ngoitokitok Springs

Lerai Forest

ascending road

Ngorongoro Crater

Gorigor Swamp

Ngorongoro headquarters

Ngorongoro Wildlife

viewpoint 2216m

N

Bradt

Ngorongoro entrance gate

0 ———— 5km
0 ———— 3 miles

Arusha

THE RHINOS OF NGORONGORO

Ngorongoro Crater has always been noted for its density of black rhinos. Back in 1892, Dr Oscar Baumann, the first European to visit the area, remarked on the large numbers of rhino, particularly around Lerai Forest – and he shot seven of the unfortunate beasts to prove his point. More recently, the biologist John Goddard estimated the resident population at greater than 100 in 1964. By 1992, thanks to poachers, no more than 10 rhinos were left, although this number had increased to 18 by 1998, including a mother and calf relocated from South Africa's Addo National Park to boost the local genetic pool. Sadly, five of these rhinos have died since late 2000, one taken by a lion and the remainder thought to be victims of a tick-borne disease linked to the low rainfall of 2000/1.

Despite the decline in numbers, Ngorongoro is today the only accessible part of the northern safari circuit where these endangered animals haven't been poached to local extinction. For many visitors to the crater, therefore, seeing rhino is a very high priority, and fortunately the chances are pretty good. In the wet season, the rhinos are often seen in the vicinity of the Ngoitokitok Springs and the Sopa road. For most of the year, however, they range between the Lerai Forest by night and Lake Magadi by day. Early risers are very likely to encounter a pair on the road fringing the forest, since they tend to move towards the lake shortly after dawn.

The crater's rhinos display a couple of local quirks. The black rhino (unlike its 'white' cousin) is normally a diurnal browser, which makes it rather odd to see them spending most of the day in open grassland, but the story is that they mostly feed by night while they are in the forest. Baumann noted that the crater's rhinos were unusually pale in colour, a phenomenon that is still observed today, due to their predilection for bathing and rolling in the saline lake and fringing salt flats.

yellow fever and malaria). To the north of this forest, Lake Magadi is a shallow soda lake that varies greatly in extent depending on the season. Standing close to the lakeshore is a cluster of burial cairns that show some similarities with the tombs at the Engaruka Ruins further east, and are presumably a relic of the Datoga occupation of the crater prior to the arrival of the Maasai. To the south and east of this, the Gorigor Swamp also varies in extent seasonally, but it generally supports some water. There is a permanent hippo pool at the Ngoitokitok Springs at the eastern end of the swamp. The northern half of the crater is generally drier, though it is bisected by the Munge River, which is lined by thickets and forms a seasonally substantial area of swamp to the immediate north of Lake Magadi.

The open grassland that covers most of the crater floor supports large concentrations of wildebeest and zebra (the population of these species is estimated at 10,000 and 5,000 respectively), and smaller numbers of buffalo, tsessebe, and Thomson's and Grant's gazelle. The vicinity of Lerai Forest is the best area in which to see waterbuck, bushbuck and eland. The forest and adjoining Gorigor Swamp are the main haunt of the crater's elephant population, which typically stands at around 70. All the elephants resident in the crater are old males (though females and families sometimes pass through the area), and you stand a good chance of seeing big tuskers of the sort that have been poached away elsewhere in east Africa. Two curious absentees from the crater floor are impala and giraffe, both of which are common in the surrounding plains. Some researchers attribute the absence of giraffe to a lack of suitable browsing fodder, others to their presumed inability to descend the steep crater walls. Quite why there are no impala in the crater is a mystery.

The crater floor reputedly supports the densest concentration of predators in Africa. The resident lion population has fluctuated greatly ever since records were maintained, partly as a result of migration in and out of the crater, but primarily because of the vulnerability of the concentrated and rather closed population to epidemics. Over the course of 1962, the lion population dropped from an estimated 90 to about 15 due to an outbreak of disease spread by biting flies, but it had recovered to about 70 within a decade. In recent years, the pattern of fluctuation saw the population estimated at 80 in 1995, 35 in 1998, and 55 divided into four main prides and a few nomadic males in 2000. The crater's lions might be encountered just about anywhere, and are generally very relaxed around vehicles.

The most populous large predator is the spotted hyena, the population of which is estimated at around 400. You won't spend long in the crater without seeing a hyena: they often rest up on the eastern shore of Lake Magadi during the day, sometimes trying – and mostly failing – to sneak up on the flamingoes in the hope of a quick snack. Until recently, no cheetahs were resident within the crater, which might seem surprising given that the open grassland is textbook cheetah habitat, but is probably due to the high rate of competition from other predators. At least two female cheetahs recently colonised the crater floor – one of which had four cubs in late 2001 – and sightings are now fairly regular. Leopards are resident, particularly in swampy areas, but they are not often seen. Other common predators are the golden and black-backed jackals, with the former being more frequently encountered due to its relatively diurnal habits.

The crater floor offers some great birding. Lake Magadi normally harbours large flocks of flamingo, giving its edges a pinkish tinge when seen from a distance. The pools at the Mandusi Swamp can be excellent for waterbirds, with all manner of waders, storks, ducks and herons present. The grassland is a good place to see a number of striking ground birds. One very common resident is the kori bustard, reputedly the world's heaviest flying bird, and spectacular if you catch it during a mating dance. Ostrich are also common, along with the gorgeously garish crowned crane, and (in the rainy season) huge flocks of migrant storks. Less prominent, but common, and of great interest to more dedicated birders, is the lovely rosy-throated longclaw. Two of the most striking and visible birds of prey are the augur buzzard, sometimes seen here in its unusual melanistic form, and the foppish long-crested eagle. The localised Egyptian vulture – whose ability to crack open ostrich eggs by holding a stone in its beak makes it the only bird that arguably uses tools – is sometimes seen in the vicinity of Mungu Stream.

There are a few hippo pools in the crater, but the one most often visited is Ngoitokitok Springs, a popular picnic spot where lunch is enlivened by a flock of black kites which have become adept at swooping down on tourists and snatching the food from their hands.

The authorities rigidly forbid tourists from entering the crater before 07.00, and they must be out of the crater before 18.00. This is a frustrating ruling for photographers, since it means that you miss out on the best light of the day, and it has encouraged a situation where most safari drivers suggest that their clients take breakfast before going on a game drive, and carry a picnic lunch. This programme is difficult to avoid if you are on a group safari, but for those on a private safari, it is well worth getting down to the crater as early as permitted. Photography aside, this is the one time in the day when you might have the crater to yourself, the one time, in other words, when you can really experience the Ngorongoro Crater of television documentary land. Note that it is forbidden to descend to the base of the crater after 16.00, and that a 'crater service fee' of US$100 per vehicle is payable every time you enter the crater. A new ruling restricts the total duration of a visit to six hours (though you could presumably spend longer in the crater if you pay two sets of crater service fees).

Olduvai Gorge

Difficult to believe today perhaps, but for much of the past two million years the seasonally parched plains around Olduvai – or more correctly *ol-dupai*, the Maasai name for sisal – were submerged beneath a lake that formed an important watering hole for local animals and our hominid ancestors. This was a fluctuating body of water, at times expansive, at other times drying up altogether, creating a high level of stratification accentuated by sporadic deposits of fine ash from the volcanoes that surrounded it. Then, tens of thousands of years ago, volcanic activity associated with the rifting process caused the land to tilt, and a new lake formed to the east. The river that flowed out of this new lake gradually incised a gorge through the former lakebed, exposing layers of stratification up to 100m deep. Olduvai Gorge thus cuts through a chronological sequence of rock beds preserving a practically continuous archaeological and fossil record of life on the plains over the past two million years.

The significance of Olduvai Gorge was first recognised by the German entomologist Professor Katwinkle, who stumbled across it in 1911 while searching for insect specimens. Two years later, Katwinkle led an archaeological expedition to the gorge, and unearthed a number of animal fossils before the excavations were abandoned at the outbreak of World War I. In 1931, the palaeontologist Louis Leakey visited the long-abandoned diggings and realised that the site provided ideal conditions for following the hominid fossil record back to its beginnings. Leakey found ample evidence demonstrating that ancient hominids had occupied the site, but lacking for financial backing, his investigations went slowly and frustratingly refused to yield any truly ancient fossilised hominid remains.

The payoff for the long years of searching came in 1959 when Mary Leakey – Louis's wife, and a more than accomplished archaeologist in her own right – discovered a heavy fossilised jawbone that displayed unambiguous human affinities but was also clearly unlike any other hominid fossil documented at the time. Christened 'Nutcracker man' by the Leakeys in reference to its bulk, this jawbone proved to be that of an Australopithecine (now designated as *Australopithecus boisei*) that had lived and died on the ancient lakeshore some 1.75 million years ago. Subsequently superseded by more ancient fossils unearthed elsewhere in east Africa, this was nevertheless a critical landmark in the history of palaeontology: the first conclusive evidence that hominid evolution stretched back over more than a million years and had been enacted on the plains of east Africa.

This important breakthrough shot the Leakeys' work to international prominence, and with proper funding at their disposal, a series of exciting new discoveries followed, including the first fossilised remains of *Homo habilis*, a direct ancestor of modern man that would have dwelt on the lakeshore contemporaneously with *Australopithecus boisei*. After Louis's death in 1972, Mary Leakey continued working in the area until she retired in 1984. In 1976, at the nearby site of Laetoli, she discovered footprints created more than three million years ago by a party of early hominids which had walked through a bed of freshly

HIKING IN NGORONGORO CONSERVATION AREA

Because the NCA lies outside the national park system, it is permissible to walk and hike along a number of trails covering most main points of interest (but not the crater floor) in the company of an authorised guide. For those seeking a short morning or afternoon walk on the crater rim appended to a standard road safari, the best option is to take one of three short guided hikes offered by Serena Active, based in the Ngorongoro Serena Lodge. These walks can be pre-booked, but it's also fine just to pitch up at their booking desk spontaneously on the day, whether you're staying at the Serena (⟩ 027 253 9160/1/2; f 027 253 9163; e serenaactive@serena.co.tz) or at another lodge on the crater rim.

You could in theory spend a fortnight exploring the NCA along a network of longer trails that connects Lake Eyasi in the south to Lake Natron in the north, as well as running west across the plains towards Laetoli and Lake Ndutu and northwest to Olduvai Gorge. Other possible targets for hikers include the Olmoti and Empakaai craters, the 3,600m Mount Lolmalasin (the third-highest in Tanzania), and the remote Gol Mountains. In theory, any safari operator can advise you about routes and arrange hikes with the NCA authorities, but I would strongly advise the traveller thinking of doing this to work through an operator with specialist trekking experience (see the *Safari operators* listings in Arusha on pages 110–11).

It would also be possible to set up a trekking trip directly with the NCA, bussing to the crater rim from Arusha. Were you to attempt something like this, you would have to organise food yourself, to clarify arrangements for a tent, sleeping bag and other equipment, and to take warm clothes since parts of the NCA are very chilly at night. The best place to make initial enquiries and arrangements for a DIY trekking trip would be the NCA office on Boma Road in Arusha (e ncaa_hq@cybernet.co.za or ncaa_hq@habari.co.tz). At least five different one-day hiking trails from the crater rim can be arranged at very short notice. Some of the longer hikes and trekking routes require 30 days' notice to set up, so you will need to make advance contact.

deposited volcanic ash – still the most ancient hominid footprints ever found.

Olduvai Gorge lies within the conservation area about 3km north of the main road between Ngorongoro Crater and the Serengeti, and is a popular and worthwhile place to stop for a picnic lunch. The actual diggings may only be explored with a guide, and – since all fossils are immediately removed – they are probably of greater immediate interest for the geology than for the archaeology. Not so the excellent site museum, which displays replicas of some of the more interesting hominid fossils unearthed at the site as well as the Laetoli footprints. Also on display are genuine fossils of some of the extinct animals that used to roam the plains: pygmy and short-necked giraffes, giant swine, river elephant, various equines, and a bizarre antelope with long de-curved horns. Outside the museum, evolutionary diversity is represented by the variety of colourful – and very alive – dry-country birds that hop around the picnic area: red-and-yellow barbet, slaty- coloured boubou, rufous chatterer, speckle-fronted weaver and purple grenadier are practically guaranteed.

Lake Ndutu

This alkaline lake lies south of the B142 on the Ngorongoro–Serengeti border. When it is full, Maasai use it to water their cattle. In the rainy season it supports large numbers of animals, so Ndutu Lodge (see page 217) is a good base for game drives. The acacia woodland around the lake supports different birds to those in surrounding areas. The campsite on the lakeshore costs US$40 per person.

Olmoti and Empakaai Craters

Olmoti is a sunken caldera situated near to the village of Nainokanoka about 30km north of Ngorongoro Crater by road. A motorable track leads from the village to a ranger post further west, but the crater can only be reached on foot, so at the ranger post you will have to organise an armed ranger to guide you. From the ranger post it is a half-hour walk through montane forest to the rim. This is a shallow crater, covered in grass, and it offers good grazing for Maasai cattle and a variety of antelope. From the rim you can walk to a pretty waterfall where the Munge River leaves the crater.

With a diameter of almost 6km, the 300m-deep Empakaai Crater is considerably more substantial than Olmoti, and almost half of its floor consists of a deep soda lake. A road circles the forested rim and another leads to the crater floor. Bushbuck, buffalo and blue monkey are likely to be seen on the rim, which also boasts good views across to Ol Doinyo Lengai and, on clear days, Kilimanjaro and Lake Natron. The crater floor is home to a variety of antelope and waterbirds. With permission from park headquarters, you may camp wild on the crater rim or sleep in a cabin on the southern shore of the lake.

Serengeti National Park

There is little to say about the Serengeti that hasn't been said already. It is Africa's most famous wildlife sanctuary, renowned for its dense predator population and annual wildebeest migration, and the sort of place that's been hyped so heavily you might reasonably brace yourself for disappointment when you actually get to visit it. But the Serengeti is all it is cracked up to be. The sheer volume of wildlife that inhabits these vast plains is overwhelming, as is the liberating sense of space attached to exploring the area. The Serengeti is the best game reserve I have visited anywhere in Africa – no competition!

Serengeti National Park covers an area of almost 15,000km^2, but the Serengeti ecosystem – which includes a number of game reserves bordering the national park as well as Kenya's Maasai Mara National Reserve – is more than double that size. Most of the national park is open and grassy, broken by isolated granite hillocks or koppies (a Dutch or Afrikaans word literally meaning 'little heads') and patches of acacia woodland. There is little permanent water, so animal migration in the area is strongly linked to rainfall patterns.

The Maasai occupied the Serengeti Plains in the 17th century, displacing the Datoga pastoralists who had previously lived there. The name Serengeti derives from a Maasai word *Serengit*, meaning Endless Plain. The Maasai are no longer allowed to graze their cattle in the national park, but can still do so in the part of the Serengeti Plains protected within the NCA. Partly because it lay within Maasailand, the Serengeti area was little known to Europeans until after World War I, when hunters moved in. The national park was created in 1951 and became famous through the work of Professor Bernard Grzimek (pronounced *Jimek*) and his son Michael. At the age of 24, Michael died in an aeroplane crash over the Serengeti. He is buried at Heroes Point on the Ngorongoro Crater rim. Published in the late 1950s, Grzimek's book *Serengeti Shall Not Die* remains worthwhile reading.

The most recent census figures available for the Serengeti indicate that the most common large herbivore species are wildebeest (1,300,000), Thomson's gazelle (250,000), Burchell's zebra (200,000), impala (70,000), topi (50,000), Grant's gazelle (30,000), kongoni (15,000) and eland (10,000). Reliable anecdotal sources indicate that these figures are now on the low side. The current population of wildebeest may well be as high as two million, while the total number of zebra probably stands at around 500,000, with the two species often encountered together in immense mixed herds.

Other antelope species include Kirk's dik-dik, klipspringer, and small numbers of roan, oryx, oribi and waterbuck. There are significant numbers of buffalo, giraffe and warthog. Elephant are relatively scarce on the open plains, but more common in the north and west. The park's last resident black rhinoceros herd is restricted to the vicinity of the Moru Koppies in the far southeast, while another small population evidently range between Kenya's Maasai Mara National Reserve

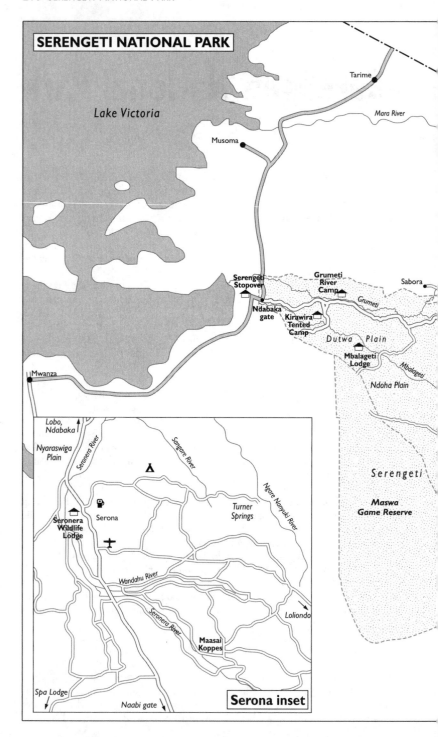

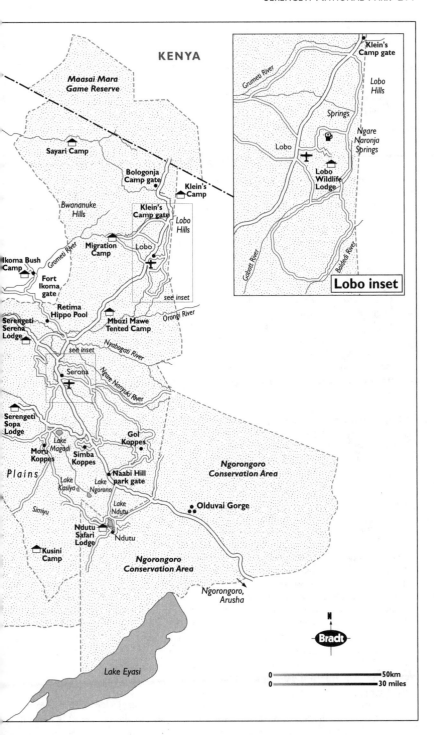

KENYA

Maasai Mara
Game Reserve

Sayari Camp

Bologonja
Camp gate

Klein's
Camp

Bwananuke
Hills

Klein's
Camp gate

Lobo
Hills

see inset

Migration
Camp

Lobo

Grumeti River

Ikoma Bush
Camp

Fort
Ikoma
gate

Retima
Hippo Pool

Mbuzi Mawe
Tented Camp

Orangi River

Serengeti
Serena
Lodge

see inset

Nyabogati River

Serona

Ngare Nanyuki River

Serengeti
Sopa
Lodge

Lake
Magadi

Morti
Koppes

Simba
Koppes

Gol
Koppes

Naabi Hill
park gate

Plains

Lake
Kisiya

Lake
Ngorono

Ngorongoro
Conservation Area

Olduvai Gorge

Simiyu

Lake
Ndutu

Ndutu
Safari
Lodge

Ndutu

Kusini
Camp

Ngorongoro
Conservation Area

Ngorongoro,
Arusha

Lake Eyasi

Lobo inset

Grumeti River

Klein's
Camp gate

Lobo
Hills

Springs

Ngare
Naronja
Springs

Lobo

Lobo
Wildlife
Lodge

Gabott River

Boldedi River

Bradt

| 0 | 50km |
| 0 | 30 miles |

THE GREAT MIGRATION

The annual migration of at least two million ungulates – predominantly wildebeest but also large concentrations of zebra and lesser numbers of Thomson's gazelle, Grant's gazelle and eland – through the greater Serengeti ecosystem is indubitably the greatest extant spectacle of its type in Africa. Dictated by local rainfall patterns, the Serengeti migration does follow a reasonably predictable annual cycle, though – as with the timing of the rainy seasons – there is a fair amount of variation from one year to the next.

The southeastern plains that stretch across into the Ngorongoro Conservaton Area form the main ungulate calving grounds of the Serengeti. The wildebeest typically disperse into the plains during the short rains, which fall in late November or early December, before calving in January, and staying put until the end of the long rains, generally in early May. Seronera being the most accessible part of the park, particularly for those on a budget safari, this is a fantastic time to be on safari in the Serengeti. True, you won't see the big herds on the move, but it's not uncommon to see herds of 10,000 animals, the scenery is lush and green, and predator concentrations around Seronera are at their peak.

Towards the end of April, the wildebeest and their entourage start to congregate on the southern plains in preparation for the 800km northward migration. The actual migration, regularly delayed in recent years due to late rain, might start any time from late April into early June, with a herd of more than a million migrating animals marching in a braying column of up to 40km long, one of the most impressive spectacles in the world. The major obstacle faced by the wildebeest on this migration is the crossing of the Grumeti River through the Western Corridor, which typically occurs from June into early July.

and the small wedge of the Serengeti that lies to the north of the Mara River. The most common and widespread diurnal primates are the olive baboon and vervet monkey, but an isolated and seldom seen population of patas monkey is resident in the north, and a few troops of black-and-white colobus haunt the riparian woodland along the Grumeti River through the Western Corridor.

Ultimately, the success of any safari lies in the number and quality of encounters with big cats. There is something infinitely compelling about these animals, a fascination that seems to affect even the most jaded of safari drivers – many of whom are leopard obsessive, content to drive up and down the Seronera Valley all day in the search for a telltale tail dangling from a tree. And when it comes to big cats, the Serengeti rarely disappoints. Lions are a practical certainty: some 250 to 300 of these animals stalk the plains around Seronera, with the main concentration around Simba Hills north of the Ngorongoro road. It's normal to see two or three prides in the course of one game drive. Sociable, languid and deceptively pussy-cat-like, lions are most often seen lying low in the grass or basking on rocks. The challenge is to see a lion exert itself beyond a half-interested movement of the head when a vehicle stops nearby. Cheetahs, too, are regularly sighted in the grasslands around Simba Hills, though in direct contrast to their more languid cousins, these streamlined, solitary creatures are most normally seen pacing the plains with the air of an agitated greyhound.

Of the other predators which can be seen in the Serengeti, spotted hyenas are very common, perhaps more numerous than lions. Golden jackals and bat-eared foxes appear to be the most abundant canine species on the plains around Seronera,

A great many animals die in the crossing, many of them taken by the Grumeti's ravenous and prolific population of outsized crocodiles, and the first herds to cross are generally at the greatest risk. For this reason, it can take up to two weeks from when the first wildebeest arrive at the southern bank of the river for the actual crossing to begin, by which time thousands upon thousands of wildebeest are congregated in the Western Corridor.

From July to October, the ungulates disperse again. About half of them cross the Mara River into Kenya's Maasai Mara National Reserve, and the remainder are spread out through the northern and western Serengeti. The best base at this time of year is the Lobo area in the northern Serengeti. By late October, the animals have generally started to plod back southward to the Seronera Plains, to arrive there in late November, when the cycle starts all over again.

Whether it is worth planning your safari dates around the migration is a matter of choice. With the best will in the world, it would be practically impossible to ensure that a few days in the Serengeti will coincide with the exact and unpredictable date of the spectacular river crossing. On the other hand, if you choose the right part of the Serengeti, large herds of grazers should be easy to locate at any time of the year, bar July to November. Furthermore, bearing in mind that most species other than zebra and wildebeest, and predators especially, are strongly territorial and do not stray far from their core territory over the course of any given year, there is a lot to be said for avoiding the migration. Most of the lodges now charge considerably lower rates over April and May, with a knock-on effect on the rates offered by safari companies that suddenly become hungry for business. Furthermore, the safari circuit as a whole is far less crowded outside of peak seasons, and in our experience the Serengeti, irrespective of season, will still offer game viewing to equal that of any game reserve in Africa.

while black-backed jackals are reasonably common in the thicker vegetation towards Lobo. Driving at dusk or dawn, you stand the best chance of seeing nocturnal predators such as civet, serval, genet and African wildcat. The real rarity among the larger predators is the African hunting dog, which was once common in the Serengeti but is now locally extinct, though occasional sightings elsewhere in northern Tanzania mean that recolonisation is not out of the question.

The entrance fee rose from US$30 to US$50 per 24 hours in January 2006 and there is speculation that this will rise to US$100 in the not too distant future. A 72-page booklet, *Serengeti National Park*, is sold at the National Parks office in Arusha for US$5. Like all the national park booklets, it contains good maps and is an excellent introduction to the local ecosystems. A newer booklet entitled *Serengeti*, similar in content but glossier in appearance, is published by African Publishing House in association with TANAPA.

SERONERA AND THE SOUTHERN PLAINS

The short grass plains stretching southeast from Seronera into the NCA might be termed the 'classic' Serengeti: a vast open expanse teeming with all manner of wild creatures ranging from the endearing bat-eared fox to the imperious lion, from flocks of habitually panicked ostrich to strutting pairs of secretary birds, and from the gigantic eland antelope to the diminutive mongooses. Densely populated with wildlife all year through, these southern plains are especially rewarding between December and May, when the rains act as a magnet to the migrant herds of wildebeest and zebra.

The southern plains form the most accessible part of the park coming from the direction of Arusha, and host several large lodges, a combination that ensures a relatively high volume of tourist traffic throughout the year. The main focal point of the region – indeed of the entire national park – is the park headquarters at Seronera, which is also the site of the oldest lodge in the Serengeti, as well as a campsite and staff village. The recently opened visitors' information centre at Seronera is well worth a visit: facilities include a small site museum, as well as a picnic area and coffee shop, while an elevated wooden walkway leads through an informative open-air display.

The southern plains are interspersed with several clusters of rocky koppies that stud the plains, each of which forms a microhabitat inhabited by non-plains wildlife such as klipspringer, rock hyrax, leopard, rock agama, rock thrushes, mocking chat and various cliff-nesting raptors. As their name suggests, the Simba Koppies, which straddle the main road between the NCA and Seronera, are particularly good for lions, while the grassland around the more easterly Gol Koppies is excellent for cheetah. About 25km south of Seronera, the Moru Koppies can also provide good lion and cheetah sightings, and are home to the park's last resident black rhino, a herd of seven that evidently migrated here from the NCA in the mid-1990s.

A striking feature of this part of the Serengeti is the paucity of trees, which flourish only at the sides of koppies and along the riparian belts that follow the Mbalageti and Seronera rivers. The most likely explanation for this quirk is that the soil, which consists of volcanic deposits from an ancient eruption of Ngorongoro, is too hard for most roots to penetrate, except where it has been eroded by flowing water. Slightly paradoxically, one consequence of this is that leopards are more easily seen along the Seronera Valley than they are practically anywhere else I've visited in Africa – the leopards here are fond of resting up in the canopy of sausage trees and tall acacias, and there are simply too few of these for them to be as elusive as they would be in denser woodland.

Aside from the two perennial rivers, both of which might be described as streams in another context, there is little permanent standing water in this part of the Serengeti. One exception is the small, saline Lake Magadi, which is fed by the Mbalageti River immediately northeast of Moru Koppies, and supports large numbers of aquatic birds, including thousands of flamingoes when the water level is suitable. A small hippo pool lies on the Seronera River about 5km south of Seronera along the road back towards the NCA. Far more impressive, however, is the Retima Hippo Pool, where up to a hundred of these aquatic animals can be seen basking near the confluence of the Seronera and Grumeti rivers about 15km north of the park headquarters.

An unusual relic of the Serengeti's former Maasai inhabitants is to be found at Moru Koppies in the form of some well-preserved rock paintings of animals, shields and other traditional military regalia near the base of a small koppie. This is one of the few such sites associated with the Maasai, and the paintings, which are mostly red, black and white, may well have been inspired by the more ancient and more accomplished rock art of the Kondoa area – though it's anybody's guess whether they possess some sort of ritual significance, or are purely decorative. On another koppie not far from the rock paintings is an ancient rock gong thought to have been used by the Datoga predecessors of the Maasai – a short but steep scramble up a large boulder leads to the rock gong, which also makes for a good picnic spot.

The most central base for exploring this region is Seronera Wildlife Lodge, or one of the nearby campsites at the park headquarters. Two of the other three large lodges in the Serengeti – respectively part of the Serena and Sopa chains – are also

SERENGETI BALLOON SAFARIS

Serengeti Balloon Safaris is – no prizes for guessing – the name of the company that runs balloon safaris from a launch site close to Seronera Lodge at 06.00 every morning. Although not cheap, a balloon safari is definitely worth the expense if you can afford it. Gliding serenely above the trees as the sun rises allows you to see the expansive plains from a new and quite thrilling angle. It also offers the chance to see secretive species such as bushbuck and reedbuck, and, because you leave so early in the morning, you are likely to spot a few nocturnal predators (we saw hyenas in abundance, civet twice and had a rare glimpse of an African wild cat). That said, any images you have of sweeping above innumerable wildebeest and zebra may prove a little removed from reality; you can only be confident of seeing large herds of ungulates if you're fortunate enough to be around during the exact week or two when animals concentrate immediately around Seronera.

The safari culminates with a champagne breakfast in the bush, set up at a different site every day, depending on which way the balloons are blown. The meal is presented with some flourish: the immaculately uniformed waiters in particular conjure up images of the safaris of old. Our particular mad-hatters' breakfast party was enlivened by the arrival of three male lions, who strolled less than 100m from the table apparently oblivious to the unusual apparition of 24 people eating scrambled eggs and sausages at a starched tablecloth in the bush. Presumably, this sort of thing doesn't happen every day, whether you're a lion or a human!

The package, which costs US$399 per person, includes the transfer to the balloon site, a balloon trip of roughly one hour's duration, and the champagne breakfast. There is a booking desk at the Seronera Wildlife Lodge, as well as at the Serengeti Sopa and Serena Lodges. The other Serengeti lodges are too far from the launching site to get there in time (as things stand the transfer from Seronera leaves at 05.30 and from the other lodges at around 04.30!). If you want to be certain of a place, however, it is advisable to book in advance, particularly during high season. Reservations can be made through your safari company, directly through Serengeti Balloon Safaris' Arusha office (✆ 027 250 8578 or 254 8967; e balloons@habari.co.tz) or through the UK office (✆ 01225 873756; e tpsafari@globalnet.co.uk).

well positioned for exploring the southern plains, and have far better facilities. Of the smaller lodges in the national park, the underrated Ndutu Safari Lodge (which actually lies within the NCA) and the wonderfully remote Kusini Camp are both well sited for exploring the southern plains.

Where to stay
Exclusive

Kusini Camp (9 rooms, soon to expand to 14) ✆ 027 250 9817; f 027 250 8273; e tanzania@sanctuarylodges.com; www.sanctuarylodges.com. With its fantastic location among a set of tall black boulders some 40km south of the Moru Koppies, this spaciously laid out camp is the most remote and exclusive place to stay in the southern Serengeti, especially in March when the area hosts immense herds of wildebeest and zebra. At other times of the year, elephant, giraffe and buffalo are quite common in the surrounding acacia

MEANINGS OF THE MAASAI BEADS
Emma Thomson

The colourful Maasai jewellery is comprised of nine main colours. Those who think these colours and their meanings are blended to create complex messages are wrong; the combinations are mainly for beauty. Tendons extracted from the meat consumed originally served as string to hold these intricate designs together. However, these have now been replaced by shredded plastic bags. The meanings for each colour vary from area to area but in general they mean the following:

black	God/rain
blue	water
dark blue	God in the sky
gold	ground water
green	life/spring (rainy season)
orange	rainbow
red	warrior/blood/bravery
white	milk/peace
yellow	sun

woodland – indeed, some impressively hefty buffalo bulls are resident in camp – and lion and leopard are seen with some frequency. The best goal for game drives out of Kusini is Moru Koppies, where lion are plentiful and rhino present but seldom seen, and there are plenty of birds around, including the striking secretary bird for which the camp is named. *US$385/585 sgl/dbl for large en-suite tent, inc superb meals and most drinks, or US$485/770 for full game package. Substantial discount Nov–mid-Dec; premium in peak season of Jan–Mar. Closed Apr and May.*

Olakira Camp (8 tents) ✆ 027 250 4118/9; m 0748 763338; e info@asilialodges.com; www.asilialodges.com. Opened in December 2005, this new mobile tented camp moves through the Serengeti, following the migration, a route designed to complement its sister camp, Sayari. The camp is based at Ndutu from mid-December through March for the calving season, before moving up to the central Serengeti for June and July, when the migration is in this area and a visit can be combined with a balloon flight from Seronera. From August to November, the camp lies outside Klein's Gate in Soit Sambu, an exclusive concession where game drives can be supplemented with night drives and guided walks. *US$425/640 sgl/dbl FB, inc drinks in spacious, en-suite standing tents in low season, or US$525/750 high season. Full game packages (inc game drives and walks) around US$50 pp higher.*

Upmarket

Seronera Wildlife Lodge (100 rooms) ✆ 027 254 4595; f 027 254 8633; e sales@hotelsandlodges-tanzania.com; www.sales@hotelsandlodges-tanzania.com. The most central lodge in the Serengeti, situated only a couple of kilometres from the park headquarters at Seronera, has an unbeatable location for game drives. It was built around a granite koppie in the early 1970s, and utilises the natural features to create an individual and unmistakably African character. The bar, frequented by bats and rock hyraxes, is reached through a narrow corridor between 2 boulders, while the natural rock walls of the cavernous restaurant are decorated with traditionally styled paintings. Unfortunately, the service, food and facilities leave something to be desired, certainly by comparison with all other lodges in the Serengeti, and the outmoded fittings just feel rather tacky after 3 decades of service. Rooms are small but comfortable, with en-suite bathrooms and large windows facing the surrounding bush. The best reason to select this lodge is simply its brilliant location for game drives, right on the fringe of the wonderful Seronera circuit. *US$155/180 sgl/dbl FB.*

Serengeti Serena Lodge (66 rooms) ⬥ 027 250 4058; f 027 250 8282; e reservations@serena.co.tz; www.serenahotels.com. Situated on a hilltop roughly 20km west of Seronera, this is probably the most comfortable of the larger lodges in this part of the Serengeti. Accommodation is in a village-like cluster of Maasai-style double-storey rondavels, built with slate, wood and thatch to create a pleasing organic feel. The spacious self-contained rooms each have 1 sgl and 1 king-size bed, nets and fans, and hot showers. There is a swimming pool, and the buffet meals are far superior to those in most east African safari lodges. The one negative is that game viewing in the thick scrub around the lodge is poor except for when the migration passes through, and it's a good half-hour drive before you reach the main game-viewing circuit east of Seronera Lodge. *US$285/420 sgl/dbl FB, dropping to US$170/255 Apr–Jun.*

Serengeti Sopa Lodge (73 rooms) ⬥ 057 250 6886; f 057 250 8245; e info@sopalodges.com; www.sopalodges.com. This large ostentatious lodge lies about 30 minutes' drive south of Seronera, on the side of a hill near the Moru Koppies. The rooms here are practically suites: each has 2 dbl beds, a small sitting room, a large bathroom complete with bidet, a private balcony and a large window giving a grandstand view over the plains below, perfectly appointed to catch the sunset. The building itself used to be a faintly preposterous construction with the rather misplaced appearance of an unfinished Greek villa, but once ongoing renovations are complete the interior should possess a more distinctively African character. The food is excellent and facilities include a swimming pool. Game viewing in the surrounding area is generally very good, and there's much less traffic in the immediate vicinity than there is closer to Seronera. *US$175/280 sgl/dbl FB in peak season, dropping to US$88/175 in low season.*

Ndutu Safari Lodge (35 rooms) ⬥ 027 250 2829/6702; f 027 250 8310; e bookings@ndutu.com; www.ndutu.com. Although it is actually situated just within the Ngorongoro Conservation Area on the southeast border with the Serengeti, Ndutu is most logically bracketed with the Seronera lodges, since the western plains of the conservation area essentially belong to the same seasonal ecosystem. A low-key and underrated retreat, Ndutu Safari Lodge is set in thick acacia woodland overlooking the seasonal Lake Ndutu, and it has a distinct 'bush' atmosphere lacking from other comparably priced lodges in the Serengeti ecosystem. The rooms are in small, unfussy stone chalets and have netting and hot water. The bar and restaurant are open-sided stone and thatch structures frequented by a legion of genets by night. This is an excellent place to stay if you want to avoid the crowds, and the surrounding plains offer good general game viewing, particularly during the wet season when they are teeming with wildebeest. Despite lying within the NCA, Ndutu isn't well positioned for visiting Ngorongoro Crater. It should also be noted that crossing into the Serengeti while staying at Ndutu would attract a separate national park entrance fee. *Accommodation in self-contained bungalows US$75/249 sgl/dbl FB in high season; slight premium mid-Jan to mid-Mar, significant discount Apr–Nov.*

Budget and camping

There is a simple resthouse at the Seronera park headquarters charging US$30 per person per night B&B, as well as a hostel with bunk accommodation at US$20 per person per night B&B. A cluster of seven campsites lies about 5km from Seronera Lodge. Camping costs the usual US$20 per person. Facilities are limited to long-drop toilets and a rubbish pit. You may be able to organise a shower and fill up water containers for a small fee at the lodge. There is a good chance of seeing nocturnal scavengers such as hyena and genet – even, rather disconcertingly, the occasional lion pride – pass through the campsites after dark.

MODERN–DAY MAASAI
Emma Thomson

The future of the Maasai seems an uncertain one. The Tanzanian government regards them as primitive and criticises them for 'holding the country back'. They are banned from wearing their distinctive *rubega/shuka* (robes) on public transport and in order to attend primary or secondary school the children are forced to remove their elaborate bead jewellery, and dress in Western-style clothes, while boys must shave off their long hair. All this follows a scheme launched by the government in the 1960s named the 'official national ideology of development', whose unspoken aims were to integrate the Maasai forcibly into mainstream society and settle them so the government could implement taxation.

Originally transhumant pastoralists, alternating the movement of their cattle between established wet and dry season pastures, the Maasai have now lost these latter areas to commercial farmers and wildlife conservation. Increasingly unpredictable rains leave grass and cattle dehydrated, and freak outbreaks of rinderpest and east coast fever (brought by explorers in the early 19th century) combine to often wipe out herds all together.

Squeezed into this bottleneck of depleted herds and land, the Maasai have had to overcome one of their greatest taboos – the ban on 'breaking the ground' and destroying grass, believed to have been sent by the Creator as sacred food for the cattle – in order to grow crops. Skills were acquired from nearby neighbours, the Chagga and Meru, and the latest studies show that now 40–45% of Maasai in east Africa trade meat for beans and maize, with only 50% living purely on the traditional diet of milk, blood and meat.

Unfortunately, when farming fails as a result of nutrient-poor soil, members of the family come back into the towns in search of paid work to supplement the unavoidable financial needs of providing for their families in the modern world. Men often find employment as night-watchmen, while the women may have to resort to petty trading, beer brewing and, increasingly, prostitution.

However, the Maasai are both resourceful and resilient and the developing tourist industry brings new opportunities. Gemma EnoLengila, co-founder of the NGO Serian UK, stresses that 'the real challenge lies in creating sustainable projects that are developed in partnership with (traditional) communities, in a way that empowers rather than oppresses them.'

LOBO AND THE NORTHERN SERENGETI

Wildly beautiful, and refreshingly untrammelled coming after Seronera, the northern third of the Serengeti is characterised by green, rolling hills that undulate gently towards the Kenya border, capped by some spectacular granite outcrops, particularly in the vicinity of Lobo. A cover of dense acacia woodland is interspersed with tracts of more open grassland, bisected by the ribbons of lush riparian woodland that enclose the Grumeti and Mara rivers and their various tributaries. Partially due to the relatively dense foliage, the northern Serengeti doesn't generally match up to the south in terms of game viewing, but then nor is it anything like as overrun with tourist traffic as the road circuits around Seronera

– I've often gone an entire game drive without seeing another vehicle in this part of the Serengeti.

If it is sheer volumes of wildlife you're after, Lobo and other relatively accessible parts of the northern Serengeti generally come into their own during September and October, when the wildebeest pass through on the southward migration from Kenya to the Serengeti Plains. But even at other times of year, there is plenty to hold your interest. The area supports most of the park's elephant population, and the base of the Lobo Hills in particular is noted for large prides of lions, as well as providing refuge to cheetah, leopard, spotted hyena, bat-eared fox and several pairs of the exquisite serval, a small spotted cat most often seen darting through open grassland shortly after sunrise.

The one part of the northern Serengeti to match the southern plains for general game viewing is the wedge of sloping grassland that divides the Mara River from the Kenya border. Sometimes referred to as the Mara Triangle, this southern extension of the legendary Maasai Mara National Reserve supports some of the most prodigious game I have seen in 20 years of African travel – vast herds of eland, topi, gazelle, zebra, wildebeest, buffalo et al – and it must be little short of mind-boggling when the migration moves in over July to September. Bizarrely, the Mara Triangle was effectively closed to casual tourism for years, partly due to its remoteness from any lodge, and partly due to problems with banditry and poaching. As of mid-2005, however, the area is readily accessed from the seasonal Sayari Camp, which lies to the south of the Mara River about 5km west of the Kogatende Rangers Post and a concrete causeway across the river – even so, you are likely to have the area practically to yourself.

Where to stay
Exclusive
Sayari Camp (8 rooms) ☏ 027 250 2799; m 0748 763338; e info@asilialodges.com; www.asilialodges.com. Opened in Jun 2005, this new camp is unique in that it more or less follows the annual wildebeest migration using 3 different locations within the national park over a 10-month cycle starting in the far north, near the Mara River, from mid-Jun to mid-Oct, relocating to the Lobo area for the rest of the year, then moving further south in Jan for the calving. The most northerly of these locations is the most interesting, since it offers unique access to what is arguably the best-kept game-viewing secret in all of northern Tanzania: the superb Mara Triangle. This untrammelled wedge of open grassland supports some of the densest grazer populations in east Africa, as well as all the Big Five (rhino sometimes cross from Kenya's Maasai Mara) and a great many birds. The lodge itself is as upmarket as a semi-permanent camp can be, but its main attraction is the genuine wilderness atmosphere and remoteness from other lodges. *FB rates inc drinks US$425/640 sgl/dbl in low season, or US$525/750 in high season; full game packages (inc game drives and walks) around US$50 pp higher.*

Migration Camp (20 rooms) ☏ 027 254 0630–9; f 027 254 8245; e info@elewana.com; www.elewana.com. Set in the Ndasiata Hills about 20km from Lobo, this formerly rather rundown camp has undergone two major makeovers in recent years, first in the late 1990s when it was taken over by the now defunct Halcyon Group, and then more recently after it was acquired by Elewana. Re-opened in September 2004, it now ranks as one of the most exclusive lodges within the Serengeti National Park. Accommodation is in spacious en-suite luxury 'tents' made of canvas and wood, complemented by stylish wooden décor evoking the Edwardian era, and with large balconies facing the perennial Grumeti River. The lushly wooded grounds are rustling with birds and lizards, and there is a hippo pool on the river, with larger mammals often passing through camp. The surrounding area supports resident populations of lion, leopard, elephant and buffalo, and is fantastic when the migration passes through. Facilities include a swimming pool, jacuzzi, cocktail bar, library and lounge. An unusual feature of the camp is that short, guided game walks can be undertaken along several trails leading out from it. *Room rates US$335 pp FB, inc most drinks, laundry, transfer to/from Lobo airstrip, and daytime game drives, rising to US$425 pp in Feb, Jul and Aug.*

Klein's Camp ℡ 027 254 8549/8038 or (South Africa) 11 809 4447; e res@ccafrica.co.tz or reservations@ccafrica.com; www.ccafrica.com. This excellent CCAfrica lodge lies just outside the eastern border of the national park, on a private conservancy leased from the local Maasai, and it effectively functions as an exclusive private game reserve, since camp residents have sole use of the concession. Because Klein's Camp lies outside the national park, there are no restrictions prohibiting night drives and guided game walks, both of which add an extra dimension to a safari. The camp has a stunning location on the side of a hill offering panoramic views in all directions, and game viewing in the region is generally good, particularly along the Grumeti River, with a similar range of species as found in the Lobo area. The camp consists of 10 self-contained *bandas*, all with hot shower, nets, and a private balcony with a view. *FB rates US$490 pp in mid-season (Oct–Jan except Christmas and New Year period) and US$630 in high season, inc all meals, drinks, game drives, game walks and a visit to a Maasai boma. Closed Apr and May.*

Loliondo Tented Camp (5 rooms) ℡ 027 250 7011 or (UK) 1923 255462; f 027 254 8226 or 1923 255452; e hoopoeUK@aol.com or info@kirurumu.com; www.kirurumu.com.

SERENGETI BIRDS

The Serengeti National Park, though popularly associated with grassland and open savanna, is in fact a reasonably ecologically varied entity. The western part of the national park consists of broken savanna, interspersed with impenetrable stands of whistling thorns and other acacias, and run through by the perennial Grumeti River and an attendant ribbon of riparian forest. The north, abutting Kenya's Maasai Mara National Reserve, is unexpectedly hilly, particularly around Lobo, and it supports a variety of more-or-less wooded savanna habitats. So, while the actual Serengeti Plains in the southeast of the park do support the relatively limited avifauna one tends to associate with open grassland, the national park ranks with the best of them in terms of avian variety. A working Serengeti checklist compiled by Schmidt in the 1980s tallied 505 species, and a further 30 species have been added since 1990.

The Serengeti-Mara ecosystem is one of Africa's Endemic Bird Areas, hosting five bird species found nowhere else, some of which are confined to the Tanzanian portion of the ecosystem. These 'Serengeti specials' are easy to locate and identify within their restricted range. The grey-throated spurfowl, a common roadside bird around the park headquarters at Seronera, is easily distinguished from the similar red-throated spurfowl by the white stripe below its red mask. In areas of woodland, parties of exquisite Fischer's lovebird draw attention to themselves by their incessant screeching and squawking as they flap energetically between trees. If the endemic spurfowl and lovebird are essentially local variations on a more widespread generic type, not so the rufous-tailed weaver, a fascinating bird placed in its own genus, but with nesting habits that indicate an affiliation to the sparrow-weavers. The rufous-tailed weaver is significantly larger and more sturdily built than most African ploceids, and its scaly feathering, pale eyes and habit of bouncing around boisterously in small flocks could lead to it being mistaken for a type of babbler – albeit one with an unusually large bill!

Bounded by the Serengeti National Park to the west, Lake Natron to the east and the Ngorongoro Conservation Area to the south, the vast Loliondo Game Controlled Area has been developed over recent years as an award-winning eco-tourism project run by Hoopoe Adventure Tours in collaboration with local Maasai communities. A good base for visits to Lake Natron and ascents of Ol Doinyo Lengai, Loliondo also supports a similar range of species to the neighbouring national park, with the advantage that game viewing can be undertaken on foot – with a local Maasai guide – as well as by vehicle. *FB rates US$420/540 sgl/dbl, all-inclusive package with game-viewing activities US$620/840, plus conservancy fee of US$30 pp per night.*

Upmarket

Lobo Wildlife Lodge (75 rooms) ✆ 027 254 4595; f 027 254 8633; e sales@hotelsandlodges-tanzania.com; www.sales@hotelsandlodges-tanzania.com. As with the other former government hotels in this chain, Lobo boasts an inalienable asset in the form of a stunning location, but this is not matched by the standard of service and maintenance. The lodge was built between 1968 and 1970, at which time the majority of tourism to the Serengeti came directly from Kenya, and it has waned in popularity now that visitors to the Serengeti come through Arusha. This is a shame, because it is an amazing construction. Like Seronera, it's built around a koppie, but the design is even more impressive and imaginative than that of the more southerly lodge, spanning 4 floors and

Of the two other Serengeti-Mara EBA endemics, the most visible and widespread is the Usambiro barbet, a close relative of the slightly smaller D'Arnaud's barbet, with which it is sometimes considered conspecific. Altogether more elusive is the grey-crested helmet-shrike, which strongly resembles the white helmet-shrike but is larger, has a more upright grey crest, and lacks an eye wattle. Although this striking bird indulges in typically conspicuous helmet-shrike behaviour, with small parties streaming noisily from one tree to the next, it is absent from the southern Serengeti, and thinly distributed in the north, where it is often associated with stands of whistling thorns.

Endemic chasing will be a priority of any serious birding visit to the Serengeti, but the mixed woodland and grassland of the north and west produce consistently good birdwatching, including many species that will delight non-birders. The massive ostrich is common, as are other primarily terrestrial giants such as the kori bustard, secretary bird and southern ground hornbill. Perhaps the most distinctive of the smaller birds is the lilac-breasted roller, an exquisitely coloured gem often seen perched on trees alongside the road. Highlights are inevitably subjective, but recent memorable sightings included a breeding colony of Jackson's golden-backed weaver at Grumeti River Camp, a magnificent black eagle soaring above the cliffs at Lobo, and six different vulture species squabbling over a kill in the Western Corridor. And there is always the chance of an exciting 'first'. Recent additions to the Tanzanian bird list from Serengeti include European turtledove (1997), short-eared owl (1998), long-tailed nightjar, black-backed cisticola and swallow-tailed kite (2000). In 2001, close to Grumeti River Camp, we were fortunate enough to see (and photograph) the first golden pipit ever recorded in the national park.

Adapted from an article by the author that originally appeared in the April/May 2002 issue of Africa Birds & Birding.

with a fantastic view over the surrounding plains. Once again, however, the tacky 1970s fittings detract from the architecture, and the rooms and food are perfectly acceptable without inviting any superlatives. The surrounding hills can offer some wonderful game viewing (a pride of 20 lions is resident in the immediate vicinity of the lodge), and the grounds are crawling with hyraxes and colourful agama lizards. Lobo is relatively good value. *US$155/180 sgl/dbl FB.*

Mbuzi Mawe Tented Camp (16 rooms, to be extended to 25) ❧ 027 250 4058; f 027 250 8282; e reservations@serena.co.tz; www.serenahotels.com. This new tented camp is set among a group of ancient granite koppies overlooking the Tagora Plains roughly 45km northeast of Seronera and 30km southwest of Lobo. The lodge's central location makes it a useful base from which to explore most of the key game-viewing areas in the Serengeti, and there is quite a bit of wildlife resident in the immediate vicinity (including the rock-dwelling klipspringer for which it is named), supplemented by the migration as it heads southwards in Nov or Dec. Accommodation is in large, earthily decorated en-suite standing tents, each of which contains 2 dbl beds and has a private stone patio with a view towards the rocks. *Current rates of US$230/340 sgl/dbl FB are likely to increase significantly once the lodge is better known and the swimming pool and other facilities currently under construction are completed.*

Camping

The campsite immediately outside of the Lobo Wildlife Lodge is little used by comparison with those at Seronera. It also costs US$20 per person. Facilities are limited to a toilet and rubbish pit. You can pop into the neighbouring lodge for a drink or meal if you like.

THE WESTERN CORRIDOR

The relatively narrow arm of the Serengeti that stretches westward from Seronera almost as far as the shore of Lake Victoria is generally flatter than the more northerly parts of the park, but moister and more densely vegetated than the southern plains. Aside from a few small isolated mountain ranges, the dominant geographic feature of the Western Corridor is a pair of rivers, the Grumeti and Mbalageti, whose near-parallel west-flowing courses, which run less than 20km apart, support tall ribbons of riparian forest before eventually they exit the national park to empty into Lake Victoria. The characteristic vegetation of the Western Corridor is park-like woodland, interspersed with areas of open grassland and dense stands of the ghostly grey 'whistling thorn' *Acacia drepanolobrium.*

Tourist traffic in this part of the park is relatively low: few camping safaris make it this far south, and accommodation is limited to a handful of smallish camps. Game viewing is pretty good throughout the year: the broken savanna to the south of the Grumeti River supports substantial resident populations of lion, giraffe, wildebeest, zebra and most other typical plains animals, while the riverine forest harbours a few troops of the exquisite black-and-white colobus monkey, and the little-visited vistas of open grassland north of the river are especially good for cheetah. Between May and July, the migration usually passes through the Western Corridor, though it may stick further east in years of heavy rain. The crossing of the Grumeti, usually in June or July, is one of the most dramatic sequences in the annual wildebeest migration, and a positive bonanza for a dense population of gargantuan crocodiles.

Where to stay
Exclusive

Grumeti River Camp (10 rooms) ❧ 027 254 8549/8038 or (South Africa) 11 809 4447; e res@ccafrica.co.tz or reservations@ccafrica.com; www.ccafrica.com. Overlooking a small pool near the Grumeti River, this archetypal bush camp easily ranks as our favourite lodge anywhere in the Serengeti. The mood here is pure in-your-face Africa: the pool in front of the bar supports a resident pod of hippos and attracts a steady stream of other large mammals coming to drink, while birdlife is prolific both at the water's edge and in the surrounding thickets. At night, the place comes alive with a steady chorus of insects and frogs, and hippos and buffaloes grazing noisily around the tents. This place isn't for the faint-hearted, and you shouldn't even think about walking around at night without an armed escort, as the buffaloes have been known to charge. Facilities include an outdoor *boma*, where evening meals are served (except when it rains), and a small circular swimming pool from where you can watch hippos bathing while you do the same thing. Accommodation consists of 10 stylish tents, each of which has a netted king-size bed and en-suite toilet and showers. The atmosphere is very informal, and the service is excellent without ever becoming impersonal. *FB rates US$490 pp in mid-season (Oct–Jan except Christmas and New Year period) and US$630 in high season, inc all meals, drinks and activities. Closed Apr and May.*

Kirawira Tented Camp (25 rooms) ❚ 027 250 4058; f 027 250 8282; e reservations@serena.co.tz; www.serenahotels.com. Part of the Serena chain, this is another very upmarket tented camp, set on a small acacia-covered hill offering sweeping views over the Western Corridor. The Edwardian décor of the communal areas creates something of an *Out of Africa* feel, and while the atmosphere is neither as intimate nor as 'bush' as at Grumeti, Kirawira does have a definite charm – and it will probably appeal more to safari-goers who don't find the thought of having hippo and buffalo chomping around their tent a major draw. Accommodation consists of 25 standing tents, each of which is set on its own raised platform, and is comfortably decorated with a netted king-size bed and en-suite shower and toilet. There is a large swimming pool, the service is immaculate, and the food is probably the best in the Serengeti. *US$870/1,340 sgl/dbl, inc all meals, drinks and game drives and walks.*

Upmarket

Mbalageti Serengeti (35 rooms) ❚ 0748 982211; e mbalageti@bol.co.tz. www.mbalageti.com. The newest and most isolated lodge in the Western Corridor, Mbalageti is perched on the northwestern slopes of Mwamnevi Hill, which lies 16km south of the main road through the Western Corridor, crossing the game-rich seasonal Dutwa floodplain and the Mbalageti River *en route*. Accommodation is in stunning thatch, wood, stone and canvas cottages, all of which are secluded in the evergreen woodland running along the ridge of the hill, and come with large wooden decks offering a superb view over the river to the Dutwa Plains from the outdoor bath. The dining area and bar are centred on a swimming pool, also offering panoramic views, and the food – different theme buffets every night – is excellent. Overall, it's a very comfortable and relatively affordable alternative to the more established lodges in the Western Corridor. *US$195/300 for a standard sgl/dbl, US$256/472 for a tented chalet. Sgl/dbl inc all meals and most drinks.*

Moderate

Ikoma Bush Camp (17 rooms) ❚ 027 255 3242/3326; m 0744 324193; f 027 255 3243; e moivaro@habari.co.tz or info@moivaro.com; www.moivaro.com. Recently taken over by Moivaro Lodges, this refreshingly unpretentious camp is situated on a concession immediately outside of the national park, roughly 3km from Ikoma Gate by road, and about 40km northwest of Seronera. The concession has been granted to the lodge by the nearby village of Robanda, which is paid a fee (used to fund the local school, water pump and clinic) in exchange for use of the land and assistance with anti-poaching patrols. Set in a glade of acacias, accommodation is in old-style no-frills dbl and twin tents with en-suite showers and small verandas facing out towards the bush. Because it lies outside the park,

OLOIBONI
Emma Thomson

The *oloiboni* acts as a spiritual psychiatrist within Maasai communities, using stones to divine past, present and future events. Members of the homestead are able to consult him about family or mental and physical health problems, the answers to which come to the *oloiboni* in dreams. A reading involves the patient sitting cross-legged before him, spitting on the stones to infuse them with his/her spirit, and waiting for the results.

The skills are only passed on through the patrilineal line, and even then sons are not permitted to practise their powers of mediation until their 20th birthday.

Intriguingly, two *oloibonis* are forbidden to meet each other, so if a neighbouring spiritual leader appears to be stealing business or enjoying good trade, villagers will claim that their *oloiboni* will send lions to attack the offending culprit.

guided game walks are on offer (US$10 pp), while night drives (US$20 pp) come with a chance of encountering the likes of leopard, genet and more occasionally the secretive aardvark. It's a great base at any time of year, but especially in Jun when the migration passes through, and very reasonably priced. *US$90/170 sgl/dbl FB, with significant discount in Apr and May and slight premium charged over Christmas holiday period.*

Kijireshi Tented Camp ☎ 028 2500517/617; f 018 2500141; e tilapia@mwanza.com. Under the same ownership as the Tilapia Hotel in Mwanza, this little-known camp lies close to Bunda on the western border of the Serengeti. It offers comfortable accommodation in furnished tents, and has a bar and restaurant. *US$75 self-contained dbl.*

Budget and camping

Serengeti Stopover (10 rooms) ☎ 0748 406996/422359; f 028 250 0388; e info@serengetistopover.com; www.serengetistopover.com. This budget lodge stands outside the national park, about 1km south of Ndaraka Gate, on the eastern side of the main Mwanza–Musoma road some 18km south of Bunda. The lodge consists of a row of simple but comfortable en-suite *bandas*, a campsite with hot showers and cooking shades, and an affordable restaurant and bar. A great advantage of staying here for motorised travellers coming from Kenya or Mwanza is that park fees are only payable once you enter the park. The lodge can arrange day and overnight safaris to Serengeti National Park, which will work out more cheaply than a safari out of Arusha (see pages 52–3). Other activities offered include a walking safari to Lake Victoria, traditional and game fishing trips, a visit to the Nyerere Museum, and dancing and other cultural activities. *Camping US$5 pp, bandas US$20–30 pp B&B.*

Lake Victoria and Rubondo Island

The world's second-largest freshwater body (after Lake Superior in North America), Lake Victoria extends over almost 70,000km^2 – an area comparable to Ireland – of which some 51% falls within Tanzania, with the remainder being spilt between Kenya and Uganda. The lake, which fills an elevated depression situated between the two major forks of the Great Rift Valley, is nowhere more than 75m deep and it contains numerous islands, of which four (including Ukerewe and Rubondo in Tanzania) rank among the 20 largest freshwater islands in the world. The level of Lake Victoria has remained more or less unchanged in historical times, but it probably dried up entirely as recently as 10,000–15,000 years ago. The lake's major affluent is the Kagera River, whose sources in the highlands of Burundi and Rwanda are also the most remote sources of the Nile River, which flows out of Lake Victoria near Jinja in Uganda.

Lake Victoria has never featured prominently on Tanzania's tourist circuit, even though it practically borders the Serengeti National Park and its eastern shore is easy enough to visit from any of the lodges in the Western Corridor. A more rewarding extension to a standard safari, however, is the lake's one nascent upmarket tourist attraction, the underrated and pedestrian-friendly Rubondo Island National Park, whose profile has been boosted in recent years by the opening of a proper lodge and introduction of scheduled daily flights from Arusha via the Serengeti and Mwanza.

MWANZA AND THE EASTERN LAKESHORE

An increasingly popular add-on to a visit to the Western Corridor is a short foray to the eastern shore of Lake Victoria. In most cases, this amounts to a lakeshore lunch at the likeable Speke Bay Resort, but it would also be possible to spend a night there, or even to undertake an overnight excursion to the port of Mwanza or its smaller northern counterpart, Musoma. Worthwhile attractions in the region include the Sukuma Museum and Saa Nane Island, both of which lie close to Mwanza.

The second-largest city in Tanzania, with a population approaching the 500,000 mark, Mwanza sprawls across the undulating and rocky southeastern shore of Lake Victoria, below the small hill where Speke reputedly first arrived at the lake back in 1858. The town (whose name is a European bastardisation of the Sukuma word *nyanza*, meaning lake) was founded as a German administrative outpost in 1890, and rose to local prominence in the 1920s following the discovery of gold in the region and the completion of the northern extension of the Central Railway from Dar es Salaam. Today, the city centre is likeably decrepit, lined with the usual mildly decaying colonial-era buildings, but it boasts few tourist attractions. The best-known local landmark is Bismarck Rock, a precariously balanced granite formation that lies within the main harbour, but several similarly impressive outcrops can be seen by wandering along Station Road on the peninsula to the south of the city centre.

Situated within Mwanza Bay, the rocky Saa Nane Island makes for a worthwhile, affordable and straightforward excursion from Mwanza, despite its

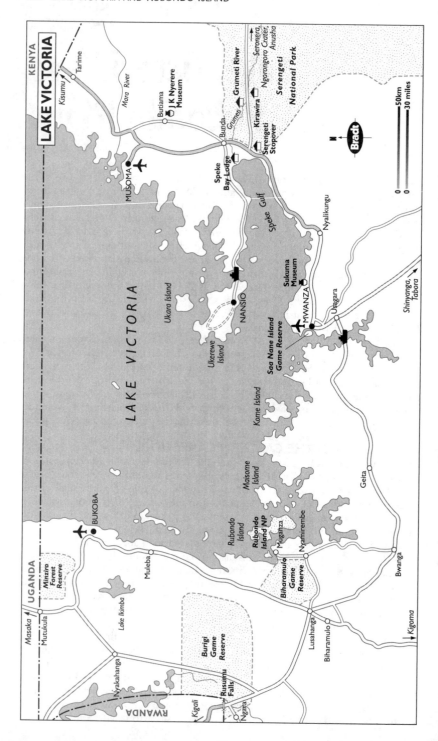

glaring failure to live up to its nominal billing as a game sanctuary. Founded in the 1960s as a halfway home for captive large mammals prior to their release on to Rubondo Island, Saa Nane is basically a glorified zoo, and not a very good one at that. But the caged animals cannot detract from the island's more persuasive attractions, which are the small animals that inhabit it naturally. Gaudily coloured agama lizards bask on the rocks, while water monitors (the largest African lizard) crash gracelessly through the undergrowth. Birdlife is profuse, with fish eagle, pied kingfisher and white-bellied cormorant common near the shore, and more localised species such as swamp flycatcher, yellow-throated leaflove, grey kestrel and slender-billed weaver present in the forest. A boat departs for the island from a jetty next to the Tilapia Hotel every two hours between 11.00 and 17.00 and does the return trip every two hours from 12.00 to 18.00.

Altogether different but even more worthwhile is the Sukuma Museum, situated within the Bujora parish grounds near Kissesa about 20km from Mwanza on the road back to the Serengeti. Dedicated to the culture and history of the Sukuma, Tanzania's most populous tribe, the museum was established in the 1950s by Father David Clement in collaboration with a Sukuma committee with the primary intent of preserving this culture for local visitors. It consists of five discrete pavilions or buildings, each of which is devoted to a particular aspect of Sukuma culture. Most impressive is the Royal Pavilion, a two-storey building housing a vast collection of royal Sukuma thrones and crowns. The colourful Bujora Church, on a hilltop overlooking the museum, is also worth a look around, since it incorporates large elements of Sukuma royal symbolism into its design, for instance an altar shaped like a traditional throne. The best day to visit is Saturday, when the Sukuma snake dance is sometimes performed with a live python.

The other main port of the eastern shore of Lake Victoria is Musoma, the administrative centre of Mara District, with a population estimated at around 150,000. Musoma's compact town centre shares with Mwanza a likeable combination of rundown colonial architecture and friendly African bustle, and its setting, on a narrow rocky peninsula that bounds the all but disused harbour, is the equal of any port on Lake Victoria, terminating in an impressive granite outcrop covered in clucking cormorants and offering an almost 360° vantage point for sunsets over the lake. Two possible water-based excursions from Musoma are to Lukuba Island, known for its impressive breeding bird colonies, and to the crocodile-infested Mara River mouth – the Peninsula Hotel can arrange these trips in its 13-seater boat for Tsh40,000 per hour. The Nyerere Museum in Butiama also makes for an easy day trip out of Musoma.

Getting there and away

Daily flights connect Mwanza to Arusha (via the Serengeti) and Rubondo Island. Mwanza Airport is situated on the lakeshore about 12km north of the city centre. If you are driving, Mwanza should take about two hours to reach from the Serengeti, and Musoma about 90 minutes – all on a surfaced road.

Where to stay
Upmarket
Speke Bay Lodge ✆ 028 262 1236; f 028 262 1237; e spekebay@raha.com. Situated about 1km from the main Musoma road, 15km south of the Ndaraka Gate to Serengeti National Park and 125km from Mwanza, this attractive and reasonably priced lakeshore lodge consists of 8 self-contained thatched bungalows and 10 standing safari tents using common showers and toilets. Activities include birdwatching on the lake and game fishing by boat. *Bungalows US$80/100 sgl/dbl B&B or US$102/145 FB, standing tents US$31/44 B&B or US$54/89 FB.*

A DYING LAKE

The risk of sodium cyanide from the gold mines finding its way into Lake Victoria is potentially the latest in a series of manmade ecological disasters to have afflicted the lake over the last century. The degradation started in the early colonial era, with the clearing of large tracts of indigenous vegetation and drainage of natural swamps to make way for plantations of tea, coffee and sugar. One result of this was an increase in the amount of topsoil washed into the lake, so that the water became progressively muddier and murkier during the 20th century. More serious was the wash-off of toxic pesticides and other agricultural chemicals, which in addition to polluting the water contain nutrients that promote algae growth, in turn tending to decrease oxygenation levels. The foundation of several large lakeshore cities and plantations attracted migrant labourers from around the region, many of whom settled at the lake, leading to a disproportionate population increase and – exacerbated by more sophisticated trapping tools introduced by the colonials – heavy overfishing.

By the early 1950s, the above factors had conspired to create a noticeable drop in yields of popular indigenous fish, in particular the Lake Victoria tilapia (ngege), which had been fished close to extinction. The colonial authorities introduced the similar Nile tilapia, which restored the diminishing yield without seriously affecting the ecological balance of the lake. More disastrous, however, was the gradual infiltration of the Nile perch, a voracious predator that feeds almost exclusively on smaller fish, and frequently reaches a length of 2m and a weight exceeding 100kg. How the perch initially ended up in Lake Victoria is a matter of conjecture – game fishermen might have introduced some perch, while others possibly swam downriver from Uganda's Lake Kyoga, where they had been introduced in the mid-1950s. But, however they first arrived in Lake Victoria, Nile perch regularly turned up in fishermen's nets from the late 1950s. The authorities, who favoured large eating fish over the smaller tilapia and cichlids, decided to ensure the survival of the alien predators with an active programme of introductions in the early 1960s.

It would be 20 years before the full impact of this misguided policy hit home. In a UN survey undertaken in 1971, the indigenous haplochromine cichlids still constituted their traditional 80% of the lake's fish biomass, while the introduced perch and tilapia had effectively displaced the indigenous tilapia without otherwise altering the ecology of the lake. A similar survey undertaken ten years later revealed that the perch population had exploded to constitute 80% of the lake's fish biomass, while the haplochromine cichlids – the favoured prey of the perch – now accounted for a mere 1%. Lake Victoria's estimated 150–300 endemic cichlid species, all of which have evolved from a mere five ancestral species since the lake dried out 10,000–15,000 years ago, are regarded to represent the most recent comparable explosion of vertebrate adaptive radiation in the world. Ironically, these fish also are currently undergoing what Boston University's Les Kauffman has described as 'the greatest vertebrate mass extinction in recorded history'.

For all this, the introduction of perch could be considered a superficial success within its own terms. The perch now form the basis of the lake's thriving fishing industry, with up to 500 metric tonnes of fish meat being exported from the lake annually, at a value of more than US$300 million, by commercial fishing concerns in the three lakeshore countries. The tanned perch hide is used as a substitute for leather to make shoes, belts and purses, and the dried swim bladders, used to filter beer and make fish stock, are exported at a rate of around US$10 per kg. The flip side of this is that as fish exports increase, local fishing communities are forced to compete against large commercial companies with better equipment and more economic clout. Furthermore, since the perch is too large to roast on a fire and too fatty to dry in the sun, it does not really meet local needs.

The introduction of perch is not the only damaging factor to have affected Lake Victoria's ecology. It is estimated that the amount of agricultural chemicals being washed into the lake has more than doubled since the 1950s. Tanzania alone is currently pumping two million litres of untreated sewage and industrial waste into the lake daily, and while legal controls on industrial dumping are tighter in Kenya and Uganda, they are not effectively enforced. The agricultural wash-off and industrial dumping has led to a further increase in the volume of chemical nutrients in the lake, promoting the growth of plankton and algae. At the same time, the cichlids that once fed on these microscopic organisms have been severely depleted in number by the predatorial perch.

The lake's algae levels have increased fivefold in the last four decades, with a corresponding decrease in oxygen levels. The lower level of the lake now consists of dead water – lacking any oxygenation or fish activity below about 30m – and the quality of the water closer to the surface has deteriorated markedly since the 1960s. Long-term residents of the Mwanza area say that the water was once so clear that you could see the lake floor from the surface to depths of 6m or more; today visibility near the surface is more like 1m.

A clear indicator of this deterioration has been the rapid spread of water hyacinth, which thrives in polluted conditions leading to high phosphate and nitrogen levels, and then tends to further deplete oxygen levels by forming an impenetrable mat over the water's surface. An exotic South American species, the water hyacinth was introduced to east Africa by expatriates in Rwanda, and made its way down to Lake Victoria via the Kagera River. Unknown on the lake prior to 1989, it has subsequently colonised vast tracts of the lake surface, and clogged up several harbours, where it is barely kept under control by constant harvesting. To complete this grim vicious circle, Nile perch, arguably the main cause of the problem, are known to be vulnerable to the conditions created by hyacinth matting, high algae levels and decreased oxygenation in the water.

As is so often the case with ecological issues, what might at first be dismissed by some as an esoteric concern of bunny-huggers in fact has wider implications for the estimated 20–30 million people resident in the Lake Victoria basin. The infestation of hyacinth and rapid decrease in indigenous snail-eating fish has led to a rapid growth in the number of bilharzia-carrying snails. The deterioration in water quality, exacerbated by the pumping of sewage, has increased the risk of sanitary-related diseases such as cholera spreading around the lake. The change in the fish biomass has encouraged commercial fishing for export outside of the region, in the process depressing the local semi-subsistence fishing economy, leading to an increase in unemployment and protein deficiency. And there is an ever-growing risk that Africa's largest lake will eventually be reduced to a vast expanse of dead water, with no fish in it at all – and ecological, economic and humanitarian ramifications that scarcely bear thinking about.

Hotel Tilapia (Mwanza) ↘ 028 250 0517/617; f 018 250 0141; e tilapia@mwanza.com. This comfortable hotel, situated about 1km from the town centre along Station Road, has an attractive lakeshore position adjacent to the jetty for Saa Nane Island. Facilities include a swimming pool, car hire, business centre, Thai and Indian restaurants, and an attractive wooden bar and patio overlooking the lake. *Large dbl chalets with satellite TV US$70 with fan or US$80 with AC, all B&B.*

New Mwanza Hotel (Mwanza) ↘ 028 250 1070/1; f 028 250 3202; e nmh@raha.com or nmh@mwanza-online.com. Recently privatised and renovated, this former government hotel on Post Road is now similar in standard to the Hotel Tilapia, with the advantages of a more central location and cheaper rates for non-residents, and disadvantages of a blander atmosphere and the absence of a lake view. A business centre, coffee shop, restaurant, casino and shopping arcade are all located within the hotel building. *Standard dbls with AC and satellite TV US$50 B&B, suites US$80, ostentatious presidential suite a hefty US$250.*

Moderate

Peninsula Hotel (Musoma) ↘ 028 264 2546. Musoma's best lodging is the former government Lake Hotel, a well-maintained and atmospheric wood and whitewash set-up situated on a somewhat sterile stretch of lakeshore about 500m west of the town centre. Coming from elsewhere in Tanzania, it's very good value. The open-sided restaurant on the ground floor serves a variety of inexpensive Western and Indian dishes. *US$25/30 for standard self-contained sgl/dbl with satellite TV, AC, fridge and hot bath, or US$45 upwards for various suites.*

Iko Hotel (Mwanza) ↘ 028 254 0900. A pleasant and friendly lodge on a rocky hill overlooking the lake behind the golf course and Hotel Tilapia. The rooms show some signs of wear, but they are fair value. The restaurant serves meals for around Tsh3,000, and the surrounding suburban lanes make for attractive rambling and birding. *US$15 for comfortable self-contained dbl, US$30 for a suite.*

Budget

Lake Hotel (Mwanza) ↘ 028 254 2030. The long-serving Lake Hotel is conveniently situated off Kenyatta Road between the railway station and town centre, and despite looking a bit rundown of late it remains a reliable fallback in the budget range. Large self-contained rooms with hot water, nets and fan cost Tsh7,000/8,400 sgl/dbl, inclusive of a derisory breakfast. Aside from slicing up stale bread in the morning, the restaurant has been closed for some years, but the outdoor bar remains one of the better drinking holes in Mwanza.

Where to eat and drink

Rock Beach Garden Hotel About 5 minutes' walk from the town centre, this slick new outdoor bar and restaurant is pretty much unique for Mwanza in that it actually has a view over the lake and Bismarck Rock. It's primarily a drinking hole – great sundowners spot! – but the restaurant serves decent Italian food and grills for around Tsh4,000.

Szechwan Mahal Restaurant This world-class restaurant, situated roughly opposite the New Mwanza Hotel, serves a huge variety of Indian and Chinese dishes for around Tsh4,000–5,000 with rice or naan bread. You won't find a better Indian restaurant anywhere in Tanzania, and it's definitely the first choice in Mwanza if price isn't an issue.

Practicalities

Tourist information There is no tourist information office in Mwanza. A website devoted to the town, www.mwanza.com, is currently under construction.

Foreign exchange All the main banks are represented, and have foreign exchange facilities. The banks are mostly clustered close to the roundabout at the junction of Makongoro and Nyerere Roads, or in the vicinity of the Clock Tower at the other end of Nyerere Road. The only private forex facilities are at the Pamba bureau de change on Kenyatta Road.

Internet There's no shortage of internet cafés dotted around Mwanza city centre. One of the best and most central is the Cyber Hot Café next to Golden Pizza on Kenyatta Road.

Tour operators The best is generally regarded to be **Fourways Travel** (↘ *028 250 2273 or 250 2630;* e *fourways.mza@raha.com*) on the main roundabout on Station Road. For budget travellers, a day or overnight safari to the Serengeti National Park from the Mwanza side will be far cheaper than a full northern circuit safari out of Arusha. A good contact for affordable Serengeti excursions is **Serengeti Stopover** near the national park's Ndaraka Gate (see page 224). You could also try a new company in Mwanza called **Masumin Tours and Safaris**, which deals with car hire and Serengeti safaris (↘ *028 241391 or 241628;* f *028 250 0192;* e *masumins@mbio.net).*

RUBONDO ISLAND NATIONAL PARK

The only bona fide tourist attraction on Lake Victoria is the underrated Rubondo Island National Park, which lies in the southwest corner of the lake, some 200km west of the Serengeti as the crow flies, where it forms a potentially very different extension to a standard northern Tanzania safari package. That so few tourists do actually make it to Rubondo is in some part because the island's attractions are more low-key and esoteric than those of Tanzania's high-profile savanna reserves. But a greater factor in Rubondo's obscurity is quite simply that the park long lacked for the sort of tourist infrastructure and ease of access that would have made it a realistic goal for any but the most intrepid or wealthy of travellers.

All this has changed, at least in theory, following the construction of Flycatcher Safaris' indisputably lovely Rubondo Island Camp, and the more recent introduction of scheduled flights to Rubondo from the Serengeti and Mwanza. In practice, however, Rubondo remains probably the most underpublicised and least visited of all Tanzania's national parks. This is a real shame, because it is a lovely retreat, offering the combination of a near-perfect climate, atmospheric jungle-fringed beaches, some unusual wildlife viewing, and the opportunity to explore it all on foot or by boat. Rubondo may not be to everybody's taste, but the island can be recommended without reservation to anybody with a strong interest in birds, walking or game fishing – or simply a yen to escape to an uncrowded and blissfully peaceful tropical paradise!

Gazetted in 1977, the 457km² national park is dominated by the green and undulating 240km² island for which it is named, but it does protect another 11 islets, none much larger than 2km², and there is talk of extending the boundary eastward to incorporate the forested west of Maisome Island. Rubondo Island itself essentially consists of a partially submerged rift of four volcanically formed hills, linked by three flatter isthmuses, and it measures 28km from north to south but is nowhere more than 10km wide. The highest point on Rubondo is the Msasa Hills in the far south, which reaches an elevation of 1,486m (350m above the level of the lake). The park headquarters, airstrip and various accommodation facilities lie within 2km of each other at Kageye, on the central isthmus, about 10km from the northern tip at the narrowest part of the island.

The dominant vegetation type is closed canopy lowland forest, which covers about 80% of the island's surface area. This is interspersed with patches of open grassland and, all but restricted to the Lukaya area, acacia woodland. The eastern lakeshore is characterised by rocky areas and sandy beaches (such as those in front of the lodge and camp), while the western shore supports extensive papyrus swamps, often lined with wild date palms. Between December and March, an estimated 40 terrestrial and epiphytic orchid species come into bloom, as do gloriosa and fireball lilies. The red coral tree, which flowers almost all year round, is also a spectacular sight. The fauna of Rubondo doesn't offer the easy thrills of many savanna reserves, but an unusual range of large mammals is present, notably

LAKE VICTORIA AND THE RIDDLE OF THE NILE

The first European to see Lake Victoria was John Hanning Speke, who marched from Tabora to the site of present-day Mwanza in 1858 following his joint 'discovery' of Lake Tanganyika with Richard Burton the previous year. Speke named the lake for Queen Victoria, but prior to that Arab slave traders called it Ukerewe (still the name of its largest island). It is unclear what name was in local use, since the only one used by Speke is Nyanza, which simply means lake.

A major goal of the Burton–Speke expedition had been to solve the great geographical enigma of the age, the source of the White Nile. Speke, based on his brief glimpse of the southeast corner of Lake Victoria, somewhat whimsically proclaimed his 'discovery' to be the answer to that riddle. Burton, with a comparable lack of compelling evidence, was convinced that the great river flowed out of Lake Tanganyika. The dispute between the former travelling companions erupted bitterly on their return to Britain, where Burton – the more persuasive writer and respected traveller – gained the backing of the scientific establishment.

Over 1862–63, Speke and Captain James Grant returned to Lake Victoria, hoping to prove Speke's theory correct. They looped inland around the western shore of the lake, arriving at the court of King Mutesa of Buganda, then continued east to the site of present-day Jinja, where a substantial river flowed out of the lake after tumbling over the cataract that Speke named Ripon Falls. From here, the two explorers headed north, sporadically crossing paths with the river throughout what is today Uganda, before following the Nile to Khartoum and Cairo.

Speke's declaration that 'The Nile is settled' met with mixed support back home. Burton and other sceptics pointed out that Speke had bypassed the entire western shore of his purported great lake, had visited only a couple of points on the northern shore, and had not attempted to explore the east. Nor, for that matter, had he followed the course of the Nile in its entirety. Speke, claimed his detractors, had seen several different lakes and different stretches of river, connected only in Speke's deluded mind. The sceptics had a point, but Speke had nevertheless gathered sufficient geographical evidence to render his claim highly plausible, and his notion of one great lake, far from being mere whimsy, was backed by anecdotal information gathered from local sources along the way.

Matters were scheduled to reach a head on 16 September 1864, when an eagerly awaited debate between Burton and Speke – in the words of the former, 'what silly tongues called the "Nile Duel"' – was due to take place at the Royal Geographical Society (RGS). And reach a head they did, but in circumstances more tragic than anybody could have anticipated. On the afternoon of the debate, Speke went out shooting with a cousin, only to stumble while crossing a wall, in the process discharging a barrel of his shotgun into his heart. The subsequent inquest recorded a verdict of accidental death, but it has often been suggested – purely on the basis of the curious timing – that Speke deliberately took his life rather than face up to Burton in public. Burton, who had seen Speke less than three hours earlier, was by all accounts deeply troubled by Speke's death, and years later he was quoted as stating 'the uncharitable [say] that I shot him' – an accusation that seems to have been aired only in Burton's imagination.

Speke was dead, but the Nile debate would keep kicking for several years. In 1864, Sir Stanley and Lady Baker were the first Europeans to reach Lake

Albert and nearby Murchison Falls in present-day Uganda. The Bakers, much to the delight of the anti-Speke lobby, were convinced that this newly named lake was a source of the Nile, though they openly admitted it might not be the only one. Following the Bakers' announcement, Burton put forward a revised theory, namely that the most remote source of the Nile was the Rusizi River, which he believed flowed out of the northern head of Lake Tanganyika and emptied into Lake Albert.

In 1865, the RGS followed up on Burton's theory by sending Dr David Livingstone to Lake Tanganyika. Livingstone, however, was of the opinion that the Nile's source lay further south than Burton supposed, and so he struck out towards the lake along a previously unexplored route. Leaving from Mikindani in the far south of present-day Tanzania, Livingstone followed the Rovuma River inland, continuing westward to the southern tip of Lake Tanganyika. From there, he ranged southward into present-day Zambia, where he came across a new candidate for the source of the Nile, the swampy Lake Bangweulu and its major outlet the Lualaba River. It was only after his famous meeting with Henry Stanley at Ujiji, in November 1871, that Livingstone (in the company of Stanley) visited the north of Lake Tanganyika and Burton's cherished Rusizi River, which, it transpired, flowed into the lake. Burton, nevertheless, still regarded Lake Tanganyika to be the most likely source of the Nile, while Livingstone was convinced that the answer lay with the Lualaba River. In August 1872, Livingstone headed back to the Lake Bangweulu region, where he fell ill and died six months later, the great question still unanswered.

In August 1874, ten years after Speke's death, Stanley embarked on a three-year expedition every bit as remarkable and arduous as those undertaken by his predecessors, yet one whose significance is often overlooked. Partly, this is because Stanley cuts such an unsympathetic figure, the grim caricature of the murderous pre-colonial White Man blasting and blustering his way through territories where Burton, Speke and Livingstone had relied largely on diplomacy. It is also the case, however, that Stanley set out with no intention of seeking out headline-making fresh discoveries. Instead, he determined to test out the various theories that had been advocated by Speke, Burton and Livingstone about the Nile's source. First, Stanley sailed around the circumference of Lake Victoria, establishing that it was indeed as vast as Speke had claimed. Stanley's next step was to circumnavigate Lake Tanganyika, which, contrary to Burton's long-held theories, clearly boasted no outlet sufficiently large to be the source of the Nile. Finally, and most remarkably, Stanley took a boat along Livingstone's Lualaba River to its confluence with an even larger river, which he followed for months with no idea as to where he might end up.

When, exactly 999 days after he left Zanzibar, Stanley emerged at the Congo mouth, the shortlist of plausible theories relating to the source of the Nile had been reduced to one. Clearly, the Nile did flow out of Lake Victoria at Ripon Falls, before entering and exiting Lake Albert at its northern tip to start its long course through the sands of the Sahara. Stanley's achievement in putting to rest decades of speculation about how the main rivers and lakes of east Africa linked together is estimable indeed. He was nevertheless generous enough to concede that: 'Speke now has the full glory of having discovered the largest inland sea on the continent of Africa, also its principal affluent as well as its outlet. I must also give him credit for having understood the geography of the countries we travelled through far better than any of us who so persistently opposed his hypothesis.'

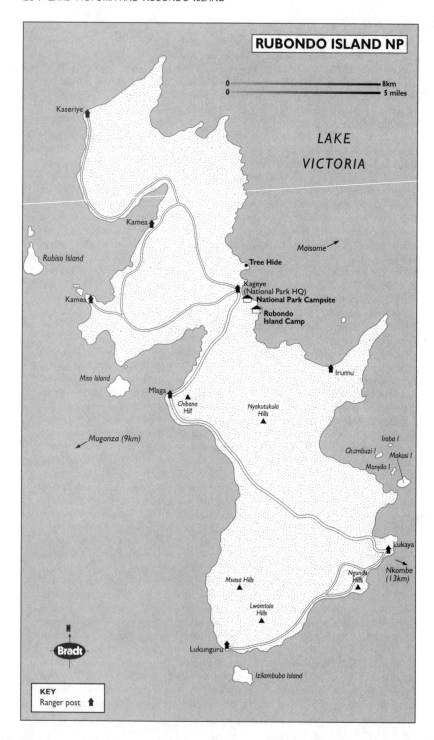

chimpanzee, elephant and sitatunga, as well as a profusion of birds and butterflies (see boxes *Rubondo's Wildlife* on pages 236–7 and *Birding in Rubondo* below).

A wide variety of activities can be arranged either through Rubondo Island Camp or through the National Park headquarters. A good, inexpensive introduction to the park, taking two to four hours depending on how often you stop, is the guided trail to Pongo Viewpoint and Nhoze Hide, the latter a good place to see sitatunga, a variety of birds and – very occasionally – elephant. Another popular activity is chimpanzee tracking from either Kamea or Irumu ranger posts (ask at headquarters which of the two currently offers the better chance). This generally takes about six hours, with a 50–60% chance of encountering chimps at present, and it costs US$25 per person inclusive of a guide and transport to the ranger post. Other options include boat trips to the swampy Mlaga Bay or Bird Island, fishing expeditions (the record catch is a 108kg Nile perch), and walks on more remote parts of the island to look for colobus monkeys or giraffes.

As for unguided activities, quite a bit of wildlife and lots of birds can be seen in the grounds of Rubondo Island Camp and the national park campsite, while the roughly 1km footpath and road between the two can be walked unaccompanied as a loop. Swimming is reputedly safe, at least at the beaches in front of the lodge and

BIRDING IN RUBONDO

With its combination of aquatic and forested habitats, Rubondo Island makes for an alluring destination for birdwatchers, especially as it can so easily be explored on foot. Oddly, the park's avifauna has never been properly studied, with the result that the only checklist, compiled from reported sightings by the Frankfurt Zoological Society and available at the Rubondo Island Camp, tallies up at a relatively low 225 species. It is likely that a substantial number of forest species that are resident on the island, or regular visitors, have thus far gone unrecorded.

The main avian attraction for casual visitors will be the concentrations of large waterbirds that occur along the island's swampy shores. Rubondo hosts Lake Victoria's densest fish eagle population – 638 individuals were recorded in a 1995 census – as well as large numbers of open-billed and yellow-billed storks. An excellent spot for varied waterbirds (as well as aquatic mammals and reptiles) is Mlaga Bay on the western side of the island, where some of the more prominent species are Goliath, purple and squacco heron, long-toed plover, blue-headed coucal, swamp flycatcher and various weavers. Of interest less for their variety than for their volume of birds are the so-called Bird Islands, a pair of tiny rocky islets that lie about 1km off the southeast shore of Rubondo, and support breeding colonies of various cormorants, egrets and ibises.

Dedicated birders are likely to be more interested in the forest and other terrestrial species. Two common birds on the island – Viellot's black weaver and black-and-white casqued hornbill – are Guinea-Congo biome species with a very limited range in Tanzania. The lodge grounds and adjacent road and forest loop – where it is permitted to walk unguided – is as good a place as any to seek out other forest birds. Among the more interesting species recorded in this area are the blue-breasted kingfisher, grey-winged akalat, snowy-headed robin-chat, paradise flycatcher, common wattle-eye and green twinspot. The area around the lodge is also the main stomping – and screeching – ground for the recently introduced flock of African grey parrots.

RUBONDO'S WILDLIFE

Rubondo Island is unique among Tanzania's national parks not only in its aquatic location, but also in that it was conceived less as a game reserve than as a sort of 'floating zoo'. Proclaimed a forest reserve in German times, the island was upgraded to a game reserve in 1966, at the behest of Professor Bernhard Grzimek of the Frankfurt Zoological Society. Grzimek, best known for his tireless efforts to protect the Serengeti, believed that the forested island would make an ideal sanctuary for the breeding and protection of introduced populations of endangered Congolese rainforest species such as golden cat, okapi, bongo and lowland gorilla. This plan never quite attained fruition, even though several chimpanzees were introduced to the island along with small numbers of elephant, giraffe, roan antelope, suni, black-and-white colobus monkey and black rhinoceros – most of which would not normally be regarded as forest-specific species. This arbitrary introduction programme was abandoned in 1973, only to be resurrected briefly in July 2000, when a flock of 37 grey parrots – captured in Cameroon for sale in Asia and confiscated in transit at Nairobi – were released on to the island.

Not all of the mammal re-introductions were a success. The 16 black rhinoceros that were relocated from the Serengeti in 1965 were poached in the 1970s, while the five roan antelope introduced in 1967 evidently died of natural causes before producing any offspring. By contrast, the six sub-adult elephants that were released on to the island over 1972–73 have bred up to a population of 30–40, with the larger herds concentrated in the south, and the lone bulls ranging all over the island – they are quite regularly seen around the park headquarters and lodge. Some concern has been expressed that an overpopulation of elephants could lead to the destruction of the natural forest, but the herd would probably need to grow to 200 before this became a real threat, and contraception can be used to keep numbers in check.

The introduced black-and-white colobus also occasionally roam close to the lodge, but the main population of about 30 is concentrated in the far south of the island, and their normal territory can be reached by boat or car, followed by a ten-minute walk. The giraffe herd is most likely to be encountered in the restricted area of acacia woodland around Lukaya, some distance south of the lodge and park headquarters. The suni are the most elusive of the introduced species, because they are so small, and secretive by nature.

Between 1966 and 1969, eight male and nine female chimpanzees were released on to the island, all of them born wild in the Guinean rainforest belt but captured when young to be taken to European zoos and circuses. Some had been held in good zoos where they had the company of other chimpanzees, while others were caged inadequately or in solitary confinement. Several individuals were regarded to be troublesome and had regularly attacked or bitten their keepers, and two of the males were shot after their release because they had attacked people living on the island. The others appeared to settle down quickly. Two newborn chimps were observed in 1968, and it is now estimated that the total community numbers at least 30, most of them second or third generation, but it is possible that a couple of the original individuals survive. The chimps are

camp. The lake water is regularly tested for bilharzia, thus far always with a negative result, and – bearing in mind that human beings form an integral part of the bacteria's life cycle – all residents of the island take the bilharzia cure as a precautionary routine every six months. Do be aware that crocs occasionally swim

normally resident in the central and northern parts of the island, near the Kamea and Irumu ranger posts, which respectively lie about 5km northwest and a similar distance southeast of the park headquarters at Kageye.

In 1996, the Frankfurt Zoological Society and Tanzania National Parks initiated a joint project with the dual purpose of monitoring chimpanzee numbers and behaviour, and habituating a community for tourist visits. Chimpanzee tracking is now offered to visitors, but with so few chimps ranging over such a large area, the odds of an encounter are far smaller than in the parks of Lake Tanganyika. At this stage, it is most sensible to view the excursion as a forest walk with a chance of seeing chimpanzees. However, a new research project recently implemented may hasten the habituation process as well as improving the day-to-day information regarding the exact whereabouts of the chimps.

The presence of glamorous introduced animals such as elephant and chimpanzee should not shift focus away from an interesting assemblage of naturally occurring residents, including the aquatic hippopotamus, crocodile and water monitor. There is no better place anywhere in Africa to observe the spot-necked otter, a widespread but elusive diurnal predator that feeds mainly on fish and frogs. A few pairs of otter are resident in the rocky bay around the lodge and camp – we regularly saw them swimming past on our recent visit, and were told that during the breeding season the den can sometimes be seen through binoculars. The only terrestrial predators that occur on the island are the marsh mongoose and large-spotted genet, the latter regularly coming to feed around the lodge at dinnertime. Vervet monkeys are numerous and easily seen all over Rubondo, but no other primate species occurs there naturally. This is difficult to explain given the variety of primates that are present in similar island habitats on the Ugandan part of the lake, and that the lake dried up fully in the biologically recent past, which would have allowed a free flow of species between the island and mainland forests.

Two closely related antelope species occur naturally on the island, the swamp-dwelling sitatunga and forest-dwelling bushbuck. The sitatunga is a widespread but localised species, with uniquely splayed hooves that allow it to manoeuvre through swampy habitats, and Rubondo is one of only two east African parks where it is easily observed. The males of both these antelopes are very handsome, with large spiralled horns, but the sitatunga is larger, shaggier in appearance, and grey where the bushbuck is chestnut brown. The females of both species are smaller and less striking, but easily distinguished from each other, since the bushbuck is striped on its sides, whereas the sitatunga is unmarked. Rubondo's sitatunga population probably exceeds ten individuals per km^2, and is not so habitat specific as elsewhere, apparently – and unexpectedly – outnumbering bushbuck even in the forest. Researchers have noted that the sitatunga of Rubondo's forests are more diurnal than is normally the case, and have less-splayed feet and darker coats than those resident in the swamps – whether this is genetically influenced, or a function of wear and sun bleaching, is difficult to say. A possible explanation for this anomalous situation is that sitatunga colonised the island and expanded into forested habitats before there were any bushbuck around.

past the beaches, so far without incident – still, you might want to look before you leap in!

Rubondo has a remarkably pleasant climate all year through, with temperatures rarely falling outside a range of 20–25°C by day or by night. The average annual rainfall is around 1,200m, with the driest months being June to September and January and February. These dry months are the perfect time to visit Rubondo, but the park and lodge are open all year round, and there is no serious obstacle to visiting during the rains. The entrance fee of US$15 per 24 hours must be paid in hard currency. A national park fishing licence valid for three days costs US$50.

Getting there and away

The only simple way to get to Rubondo is by air. Coastal Travel has recently implemented a daily scheduled service connecting Rubondo to Geita (US$40 one-way), Mwanza (US$70) and Grumeti in the Western Corridor of Serengeti National Park (US$110). For travellers appending a visit to Rubondo to a standard northern circuit safari, the easiest option would be to fly direct from Grumeti. For those trying to keep costs to a minimum, the best bet would be to bus from Mwanza to Geita and pick up the flight in Geita. For travellers coming from elsewhere in the country, it is easiest to fly to Mwanza (direct flights from Dar es Salaam and Kilimanjaro International Airport, connecting to Zanzibar) and hop on a Rubondo-bound flight there. At the time of writing, daily departures are guaranteed, with the provision that a minimum of three passengers is booked on to the flight.

Where to stay
Upmarket

Rubondo Island Camp ✆ 027 6983 or 027 254 4109; f 027 254 8261; e flycat@habari.co.tz; www.flycat.com. Flycatcher's Swiss head office can be contracted at ✆ 0041 32 392 54 50; f 0041 32 392 54 51 e flycat@swissonline.ch. Small emails without attachments can be sent directly to Rubondo Island Camp at rubondo@hf.habari.co.tz. This attractive and immensely tranquil tented lodge, owned and managed by Flycatcher Safaris, consists of 10 luxury self-contained *bandas*, each with a private veranda. It has a truly fabulous location, with a tall forest gallery rising high behind the tents, and a sandy palm-lined beach fringed by rocky outcrops directly in front of them. The open-sided communal areas stand on one of the rocky outcrops, offering a pretty view over the lake. This leads down to a secluded beachfront platform where a variety of large waterbirds have taken up more-or-less permanent residence. Pied and malachite kingfishers hawk for food, paradise flycatchers flutter in the trees – and the occasional pair of otters swims past. The swimming pool is built in a natural rock outcrop. A good selection of boat and foot excursions can be arranged at the camp, ranging in price from US$15 to US$35 pp, as can fishing trips for US$50 per boat plus US$20 rod hire. A stay of at least 3 nights' duration is recommended to make the most of Rubondo, and Flycatcher offers a variety of attractively priced fly-in packages ranging from 3 to 7 nights long. *FB US$160/280 sgl/dbl, all-inclusive rates (inc park fees, drinks, laundry, and all activities except for fishing) US$250/460.*

Budget

National Park Campsite and *bandas* The national park *banda* and camping site lies on a lovely forest-fringed beach about 1km north of Rubondo Island Camp and a similar distance from the park headquarters. Camping or accommodation in rather grotty chalets using common showers costs US$20 pp, while the much smarter new self-contained chalets cost US$50 pp. No meals are available, and it's advisable to bring most of what you will need with you, but a shop in the park headquarters does sell a few basic foodstuffs (essentially what the national park staff would eat), as well as warm beers and sodas. A cook can be arranged on request. Travellers staying at the *bandas* are welcome to visit Rubondo Island Camp for a chilled drink or a meal – it's fine to walk along the footpath or road between the *banda* site and camp unaccompanied, but the camp would need a bit of advance warning to prepare meals. They charge US$8 for breakfast, US$12 for lunch and US$15 for dinner.

Zanzibar

Zanzibar is one of those magical travel names, richly evocative even to the many Westerners who would have no idea where to start looking for it on a global map. Steeped in history, and blessed with a sultry tropical climate and a multitude of idyllic beaches, Zanzibar is also that rare travel destination which genuinely does live up to every expectation. Whether it's a quick cultural fix you're after, or scintillating diving, or just a palm-lined beach where you can laze away the day, a few days on Zanzibar is the perfect way to round off a dusty safari on the Tanzanian mainland.

A separate state within Tanzania, Zanzibar consists of two large islands, Unguja (Zanzibar Island) and Pemba, plus several smaller islets. Zanzibar Island is about 85km long and between 20km and 30km wide; Pemba is about 67km long and between 15km and 20km wide. Both are flat and low lying, surrounded by coasts of rocky inlets or sandy beaches, with lagoons and mangrove swamps, and coral reefs beyond the shoreline. Farming and fishing are the main occupations, and most people live in small villages. Cloves are a major export, along with coconut products and other spices. The capital, and by far the largest settlement, is Zanzibar Town on the west coast.

For many, the highlight of a stay on Zanzibar is the old Stone Town, with its traditional Swahili atmosphere and wealth of fascinating buildings. For others, it is the sea and the coral reefs, which offer diving, snorkelling and game fishing to compare with anywhere in east Africa. And then there are the clove and coconut plantations that cover the interior of the 'Spice Island'; the dolphins of Kizimkazi; the colobus monkeys of Jozani; and the giant sea turtles of Nungwi ... and above all, some will say, those seemingly endless tropical beaches.

This short chapter on Zanzibar, aimed at safari-goers rounding off their trip with a short stay on the island, is based on the more comprehensive companion guidebook *Zanzibar: The Bradt Travel Guide*, the sixth edition of which is published in 2006.

GETTING THERE AND AWAY
By air
An ever-increasing number of airlines offer direct flights between Zanzibar and Dar es Salaam, a 30-minute trip that costs around US$50–60. There are also regular flights to Zanzibar from Kilimanjaro International Airport (between Moshi and Arusha), some of which are direct, taking roughly one hour, while others require a change of plane at Dar and might take three to four hours depending on your connection. The main established airlines covering these routes are Air Tanzania, Precision Air, Zanair and Coastal Aviation, all of which offer a range of other domestic flights (as well as flights to Kenya), so the best choice will depend largely on your other travel plans. Any reliable tour operator will be able to advise you about this.

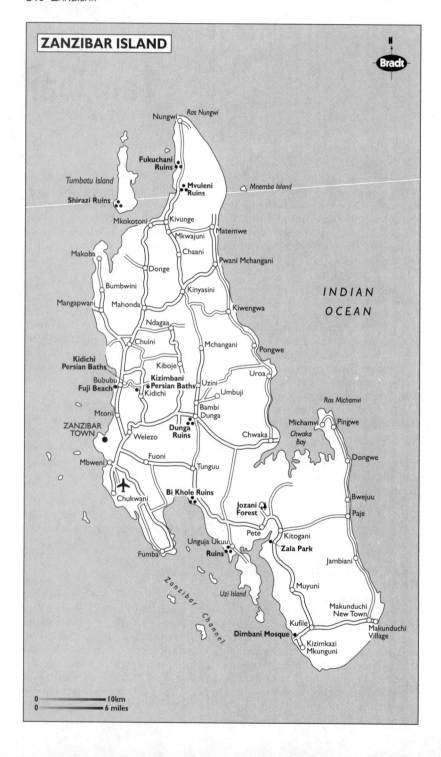

ZANZIBAR ISLAND

Bradt

Nungwi
Ras Nungwi

Fukuchani Ruins

Tumbatu Island

Mvuleni Ruins

Mnemba Island

Shirazi Ruins

Mkokotoni
Kivunge
Matemwe

Mkwajuni

Chaani

Makoba
Pwani Mchangani

Donge

Bumbwini
Kinyasini

Mangapwani
Mahonda
Kiwengwa

Ndagaa

INDIAN
OCEAN

Chuini
Mchangani
Pongwe

Kidichi Persian Baths
Kiboje
Uroa

Bububu
Kizimbani Persian Baths
Uzini

Fuji Beach
Kidichi
Umbuji

Mtoni
Bambi
Dunga

Ras Michamvi

ZANZIBAR
TOWN
Welezo
Dunga Ruins
Chwaka

Michamvi
Pingwe

Chwaka Bay

Mbweni
Fuoni
Tunguu

Dongwe

Bi Khole Ruins

Jozani Forest
Bwejuu

Chukwani
Paje

Unguja Ukuu
Pete
Kitogani

Ruins
Zala Park

Fumba
Jambiani

Uzi Island
Muyuni

Makunduchi
New Town

Zanzibar Channel
Kufile
Makunduchi
Village

Dimbani Mosque
Kizimkazi
Mkunguni

0 ———— 10km
0 ———— 6 miles

A BRIEF HISTORY

Zanzibar has been trading with ships from Persia, Arabia and India for about 2,000 years. From about the 10th century AD, groups of immigrants from Shiraz (Persia) settled in Zanzibar and mingled with the local Swahili. The Portuguese established a trading station on the site of Zanzibar Town in the early 16th century. At the end of the 17th century, the Sultan of Oman's navy ousted the Portuguese from the island.

In 1840, Sultan Said of Oman relocated his capital in Muscat to Zanzibar. Many Omani Arabs settled on Zanzibar as rulers and landowners, forming an elite group, while Indian settlers formed a merchant class. The island became an Arab state, an important centre of regional politics, and the focus of a booming slave trade. Britain had interests in Zanzibar throughout the 19th century; explorers such as Livingstone, Speke and Burton began their expeditions into the African interior from there. In 1890 Zanzibar became a British protectorate.

Zanzibar gained independence from Britain in December 1963. In 1964, the Sultan was overthrown in a revolution, and nearly all Arabs and Indians were expelled. Later the same year, Zanzibar and Tanganyika combined to form the United Republic of Tanzania.

Today, the distinctions between Shirazi and Swahili are often blurred. The islanders fall into three groups: the Hadimu of southern and central Zanzibar, the Tumbatu of Tumbatu Island and northern Zanzibar, and the Pemba of Pemba Island. Many people of mainland origin live on Zanzibar, some the descendants of freed slaves, others more recent immigrants. Many of the Arab, Asian and Goan people expelled in 1964 have since returned.

By boat

A number of hydrofoil and catamaran services run between Dar es Salaam and Zanzibar daily, and the booking kiosks for all these boats are clustered together at the ports on Zanzibar and in Dar. Among the more established services are Flying Horse, Sea Express, Sea Star and Sea Bus. New companies seem to come and go with remarkable speed, so there's a lot to be said for asking around before you make any firm arrangements, or for using a tour operator to make your booking (this won't cost much more and saves a lot of hassle). Do be wary of the hustlers who hang around both ports – many are con artists and some are thieves. Tickets cost between US$20 and US$35 and must be paid for in hard currency, as must the port tax of US$5.

Arrival and departure

Although Zanzibar is a separate state within Tanzania, visitors are no longer required to complete an immigration card or to show their passport and visa upon arrival from the mainland. Travellers flying into Zanzibar from outside of Tanzania can now buy a visa on arrival at the airport. The airport tax of US$20 for international flights out of Zanzibar will probably be included in your ticket cost, but if not it *must* be paid in US dollars cash. Domestic flights attract a US$3–5 airport tax, payable in local currency.

If you lose your passport while on Zanzibar, you will need to have an Emergency Travel Document issued at the Ministry of the Interior. This will allow you to travel back to the mainland (where nationals of most countries will find diplomatic representation in Dar es Salaam) or directly to your home country.

ZANZIBAR TOWN

Zanzibar's old quarter, usually called the Stone Town, is a fascinating maze of narrow streets and alleyways which lead the visitor past numerous old houses and mosques, ornate palaces, and shops and bazaars. Many buildings in the Stone Town date from the 19th-century slave boom. Houses reflect their builder's wealth: Arab houses have plain outer walls and large front doors leading to an inner courtyard; Indian houses have a more open façade and large balconies decorated with railings and balustrades. A striking feature of many houses is the brass-studded doors with their elaborately carved frames. The size of a door and intricacy of its design was an indication of the owner's wealth and status. The use of studs probably originated in Persia or India, where they helped prevent doors being knocked down by war-elephants. In Zanzibar, studs were purely decorative.

The area outside the Stone Town used to be called Ng'ambo (The Other Side), and is now called Michenzani (New City).

Where to stay

Recent years have seen a positive mushrooming of new hotels on Zanzibar, ranging from basic guesthouses to smart upmarket resorts, and the selective listings below include some of the most popular and well-established options. As a rule, room rates are quoted in US dollars and include breakfast. Smarter hotels may insist that you pay in hard currency, but cheaper places generally accept local currency. The rates quoted in this guide are high season only; most upmarket hotels will offer a discount out of season. At the lower end of the price range, rates may be negotiable depending on how busy the hotel is and the intended duration of your stay. It is advisable to make an advance reservation for any upmarket or mid-range hotel, particularly during peak seasons, but this shouldn't be necessary for cheaper lodgings.

Travellers who arrive on Zanzibar by boat can expect to be met by a group of hotel touts. Some are quite aggressive and likely to take you to whichever hotel gives them the largest commission, while others are friendly and will find you a suitable hotel if you tell them what you want. Either way, the service shouldn't cost you anything, since the tout will get a commission from the hotel, and it may save a lot of walking in the confusing alleys of the Stone Town. However you arrive, many hotels in the Stone Town cannot be reached by taxi – the drivers will be prepared to walk you to the hotel of your choice, but will expect a decent tip.

Upmarket

Zanzibar Serena Inn (51 rooms) ☎ 024 223 2306; f 024 223 3019; e zserena@zanzinet.com; www.serenahotels.com. This is the smartest hotel in Stone Town, combining international-class accommodation and service with atmospheric Zanzibari décor. The hotel spans 2 restored buildings on the beachfront, the early 20th-century Extelcommunications House and the 19th-century 'Chinese Doctor's residence' where Livingstone once slept. Facilities include a swimming pool, bar, restaurant, coffee shop, curio shop and business centre. Standard air-conditioned rooms have a sea-facing balcony, mosquito nets, TV and en-suite bathroom. *US$210/230 sgl/dbl B&B, cheaper rates available Apr–Jun.*

Emerson's & Green (16 rooms) ☎ 024 223 0171; f 024 223 1038; m 0747 423266; e emerson&green@zitec.com; www.emerson-green.com. This fabulously idiosyncratic hotel consists of 2 adjoining 19th-century buildings, one of which was the residence of Tharia Topan, principal financial advisor to Sultan Barghash, now faithfully restored and lavishly decorated in period style. The rooms are large and elaborately furnished, with high ceilings, fans, good ventilation through traditional shutters, amazing en-suite bathrooms and netted Arabic 4-poster beds. The rooftop restaurant offers excellent views over some of the major landmarks in the Stone Town and down to the harbour, as well as serving some of the best food in town. *US$165–200 dbl.*

Africa House Hotel (15 rooms) \ 0747 432340; f 0747 439340; theafricahouse@zanlink.com; www.theafricahouse-zanzibar.com. Under restoration for years prior to re-opening in 2003, this sea-facing hotel, which served as the English Club from 1888 until the end of the colonial era, is best known perhaps for its balcony bar, a wonderful place for a sundowner. But the AC en-suite rooms also rank with the finest on offer in the Stone Town. *US$125–200 for a dbl; substantial low season discounts Apr–Jun.*

Mbweni Ruins Hotel (13 rooms) \ 024 223 4578/9; f 024 223 0536; e hotel@mbweni.com; www.adventurecamps.co.tz. Situated a few kilometres south of town, off the airport road, this exclusive hotel lies in the lush beachfront grounds of a ruined mission school built for freed slaves in the 1870s. Accommodation is in air-conditioned en-suite rooms. Facilities include a private beach, swimming pool, nature trail, botanical garden, natural heath centre, airport and town shuttle service, top-class restaurant, and boat trips to the nearby islands. *US$100/180 sgl/dbl B&B.*

Moderate

Tembo Hotel (36 rooms) \ 024 223 3005/2069; f 024 223 3777; e tembo@zitec.org; www.tembohotel.com. Around the corner from the Serena, this smart hotel, centred on a restored Omani residence, combines an excellent beachfront position with ready access to the Stone Town. Facilities include a good restaurant and swimming pool. The swimming pool is open to non-residents at Tsh3,000 pp. *US$85/95 sgl/dbl.*

Mazson's Hotel \ 024 223 3694; f 024 223 3695; e mazsons@zanlink.net; www.mazsonshotel.com. Constructed in the early 1800s by one of the first Omani Arabs to settle on Zanzibar, Mazson's served as a hotel in the early 20th century before becoming a private residence. Now fully restored, the communal areas are decorated in period style, though the air-conditioned self-contained rooms are rather florid and soulless. Facilities include satellite TV and a business centre. *US$60/80 sgl/dbl B&B, with low-season discounts.*

Dhow Palace Hotel (28 rooms) \ 024 223 3012; f 024 223 3008; e dhowpalace@zanlink.net; www.tembohotel.com. Another hotel set in the heart of the Stone Town in a renovated old house, enclosing a cool central courtyard, the Dhow Palace is tastefully decorated in period style. The rooms come complete with Persian baths and the rooftop restaurant is recommended. *US$60/90 sgl/dbl B&B.*

Budget

Even the cheapest lodgings in Zanzibar are rather pricey, for which reason all hotels charging US$50 or below for a double room are listed in the budget category and the cut-off price for the shoestring category is around US$20 per double. There is not one hotel listed in either category that wouldn't be laughably overpriced were it situated anywhere on the Tanzanian mainland.

Hotel Kiponda (14 rooms) \ 024 223 3052; f 024 223 3020; e hotelkiponda@email.com. This small quiet hotel, formerly a sultan's harem and renovated in period style, is consistently popular with travellers. It has plenty of character, a welcoming atmosphere, and a convenient location in the Stone Town close to the seafront. *Rooms using common showers US$18/35/45 sgl/dbl/triple; en-suite dbl/triple US$45/55.*

Safari Lodge (28 rooms) \ 024 223 6523 or 0748 606177; f 022 2124507; e asc@raha.com; www.safarilodgetz.com. This new hotel in the Malindi quarter, though somewhat soulless, represents good value for money. *US$20/30 for a neat and spacious en-suite sgl/dbl with large beds and cable TV, US$35/40 for a suite.*

Island View Hotel (20 rooms) \ 054 223 4605; e islandview@africamail.com. This very reasonable family-run out-of-town hotel is on the road to the airport . There is no restaurant but the owners are helpful about lifts into town during the day and in the evening. It's exceptional value, and would be a useful option should you fly into Zanzibar late in the day. *US$20/30/40 for clean and spacious self-contained sgl/dbl/triple rooms with fan and netting. AC extra Tsh3,000 per room.*

Clove Inn (8 rooms) ℡ 0747 484567; e clovehotel@zanlink.com; www.zanzibar.nl. Re-opened in 2004 under new Dutch management, this renovated hotel on Harumzi St has small but stylish rooms with fans and nets. The hotel has a residents' only rooftop bar with a great view over the town, and it offers quick access to the waterfront. *US$35/50 sgl/dbl.*

Coco de Mer Hotel (13 rooms) ℡ 024 223 0852 or 0747 433550; e cocodemer_znz@yahoo.com. Clean and airy, the Coco de Mer charges US$35/50/60 for a small en-suite sgl/dbl/triple. The ground-floor rooms aren't as nice as those upstairs. One of the few bespoke bars in the Stone Town is attached.

Shoestring
Haven Hotel (9 rooms) ℡ 024 223 5677; f 024 223 8426; e havenhouse@hotmail.com. The rooms at this friendly and popular guesthouse are nothing special at US$10 pp using a common shower, but it's very clean, with extras such as free tea and coffee, hot water, a generator for power cuts, a travel information board and a self-catering kitchen. Recommended.

Manch Lodge ℡ 024 223 1918; f 024 223 7925; e kashamunch@axcitl.com. Just around the corner from the Haven Hotel, this adequate hotel charges US$10 pp for a spacious self-contained room.

Flamingo Guesthouse ℡ 024 223 2850; f 024 223 3144; e flamingoguesthouse@hotmail.com. This basic but pleasant hotel has a rather noisy location on Mkunazani St, but it's clean enough, and reasonably good value at US$8 pp for a room using common showers, or US$10 pp for a self-contained room. Facilities include satellite TV and a book exchange service.

Where to eat and drink
There are now dozens of restaurants catering specifically to tourists, and the following serves as an introduction only.

At the top end of the range, the rooftop restaurant at **Emerson's & Green** is generally regarded to live up to its billing as the 'best on the island'. The fixed-menu dinner is a languid affair stretched over the whole evening, and the emphasis is on seafood. Dinner normally costs US$25 per person, though the price rises to US$30 on weekends when the meal is accompanied by traditional dancing. Space is limited and booking is essential – though the spill over is now catered for in their adjacent **Kidude Restaurant**.

A more affordable experience is offered at the **Old Arab Fort** on the seafront, which puts on displays of traditional dancing at least three times a week, more often in peak season, accompanied by a reasonable buffet barbecue. Entrance costs US$10 per person, assuming that you want to eat, or US$5 per person to see the dancing only.

There are a few good places to eat on the Stone Town seafront. The trendiest spot in this area is **Mercury's Bar & Restaurant**, dedicated to (exploiting?) the memory of Zanzibar-born Queen vocalist Freddie Mercury, who has evidently managed to communicate his food preferences to the proprietor from the great opera house in the sky – 'Freddie's Favourite Salad' et al. The rooftop bar at the **Africa House Hotel** is popular at sunset.

Other recommended restaurants and hotels serving main courses in the US$5–10 range include the **Hotel Kiponda** (Zanzibari dishes and seafood), **Serena Zanzibar Inn** (continental and seafood), the **Fisherman Restaurant** on Shangani Road (seafood and grills), **Chit-Chat Restaurant** on Kenyatta Street (Zanzibari and Goan dishes), **Pagoda Chinese Restaurant** at the north end of the Stone Town (authentic Chinese food), **Luna Mare Restaurant** on Gizenga Street (European, Indian and Chinese), **Barracuda Restaurant** on Kenyatta Road (sandwiches, crayfish and other seafood), **Sweet Easy Restaurant** on the beachfront (Thai, Japanese and – soon to come – dishes from all over Africa) and **La Fenice** near the Zanzibar Serena Inn (top-notch continental and seafood). There are plenty more to choose from, and the level of competition for custom means that standards are generally reflected by prices.

The cheapest place to eat in the Stone Town is at **Forodhani Gardens**, opposite the fort, where dozens of vendors serve freshly grilled meat, chicken, fish, calamari and prawns with salad and chips or naan bread. This is far and away the best street food we've come across anywhere in Africa, and you'd have to be seriously hungry or prawn-obsessed not to come back with change from US$3. The stalls in the gardens cater primarily to locals, but plenty of travellers eat here, and many return night after night.

Books and newspapers

The best bookshop is the Zanzibar Gallery on Kenyatta Road. Newspapers from the mainland and Kenya can be bought at Masumo Bookshop behind the market, along with a limited selection of international magazines and paperback novels. Most of the upmarket hotels have curio shops selling guidebooks, field guides and glossier publications about Zanzibar and east Africa.

Communications

The main **post office**, which lies outside the Stone Town towards the stadium, is the place to collect poste restante mail addressed to Zanzibar. Other postal transactions can be conducted more conveniently at the old post office on Kenyatta Road. The old post office is also a good place from which to make international phone calls and send faxes, though the private services offered by Zanzibar Global Communications (near the Flamingo Guesthouse) and Next Step Services on Gizenga Street aren't a great deal more expensive and are generally more efficient. Numerous **internet cafés** have sprung up in Zanzibar Town over the past few years, charging a fairly uniform Tsh500 per 30 minutes.

Foreign exchange

A number of banks and forex bureaux are dotted around the Stone Town, offering similar exchange rates against cash to their mainland counterparts. The only place that exchanges travellers' cheques is the first-floor 'Foreign Trade Dept' at the National Bank of Commerce on Kenyatta Road. You can draw cash against Visa cards at the ATM outside the same bank, but the only place where you can draw against Master cards is the Barclays ATM a couple of kilometres out of town along the road towards the north coast. Most upmarket hotels will accept major credit cards.

Maps

The most accurate and attractive map of the Stone Town is Giovanni Tombazzi's *Map of Zanzibar Stone Town*, which also has a good map of the island on the flip side. Survey maps of the island are sold for around US$2 each at the map office in the Commission of Land and Surveys in the Ministry of Environment building near the old fort and People's Bank of Zanzibar.

Medical facilities

The Zanzibar Medical and Diagnostic Centre (↘ *024 223 3313; after hours: 024 233 3113 or 0747 413714*), which lies off Vuga Road near the Majestic Cinema, is regarded as having the best doctors on the island, and is run to Western standards. For cheap malaria tests, the Fahaud Health Centre near St Joseph's Cathedral has been recommended, and it normally sells various malarial cures.

The main public hospital on Zanzibar Island is at Mnazi Moja, on the south side of the Stone Town. Other private medical centres include Island Private Hospital on Soko Muhogo Street (↘ *024 233 1837*), Afya Medical Hospital near the Zanzibar Hotel (↘ *024 233 1228*) and Mkunazini Hospital near the market (↘ *024 233 0076*).

Spice tours and other excursions

The one organised trip that practically all visitors to Zanzibar undertake is a 'spice tour', something that would be logistically difficult to set up independently, and which relies heavily on the local knowledge of a guide. In addition to visiting a few spice plantations, most spice tours include a walk around a cultivated rural homestead, as well as a visit to one of the island's ruins. A traditional Swahili lunch is normally included in the price, which can range from US$10 to US$35 per person.

Several other short excursions can be undertaken out of Zanzibar Town, and while most visitors seem to prefer to do their exploring in the form of an organised day tour, most places of interest on the island can be visited independently. Popular excursions from the Stone Town include a boat trip to one or more of the nearby islands, a visit to the dolphins at Kizimkazi, and a trip to Jozani Forest to see the endemic Kirk's red colobus. Also easily explored from Zanzibar is the 10km of coastline stretching northwards to the small seaside settlement of Bububu, which boasts a number of interesting ruins, while Fuji Beach at Bububu is the closest public swimming beach to the Stone Town. In fact, the only parts of Zanzibar which are more often visited for a few nights than as a day trip are Nungwi and Mnemba Island in the north, and the several beach resorts that line the east coast of the island.

A number of tour companies operate out of Zanzibar Town, offering the tours mentioned above as well as transfers to the east coast and Nungwi. The better companies can set up bespoke trips to anywhere on the island, as well as make hotel reservations and other travel arrangements. For straightforward day trips and transfers, there is no real need to make bookings before you arrive in Zanzibar, as they can easily be set up at the last minute. If, however, you want to have all your travel arrangements fixed in advance through one company, or you have severe time restrictions, then it would be sensible to make advance contact with one of the companies with good international connections.

While prices vary greatly depending on standard of service, season and group size, the typical costs per person for the most popular outings are US$20 for a Stone Town tour, US$15 for a Prison Island tour, US$35 for a spice tour, US$35 for a trip to Jozani Forest and US$45 for a Kizimkazi dolphin tour. Prices are negotiable, particularly out of season when a group of ten people might be able to fix up a spice tour with a reputable company for as little as US$10 per head, but do be wary of unregistered companies offering sub-standard trips at very low rates.

It's possible to arrange many of the standard tours more cheaply through taxi drivers or independent guides (nicknamed *papaasi* after a type of insect). With spice tours, this may often turn out to be a false economy, in that the guide will lack botanical knowledge and may cut the excursion short, rendering the whole exercise somewhat pointless. One taxi driver who has been consistently recommended by travellers over many years is Mr Mitu (↘ 024 223 4636). His spice tours leave every morning from in front of the Ciné Afrique, though these days they are so popular that you might find yourself joining a fleet of minibuses rather than hopping into Mr Mitu's own vehicle! It makes little difference if you use *papaasi* to set up trips to the islands, because specialist knowledge isn't required, and you can agree in advance how long you want to spend on any given island.

You can assume that any tour operator working through one of the upmarket hotels will be reliable and accountable, bearing in mind that they will deal primarily with a captive, big-spending clientele, though their costs may be somewhat inflated. A list of a few recommended and well-established tour companies follows. Most of them offer a pretty similar selection of trips at reasonably uniform prices, and can also make flight, ferry and hotel bookings.

Eco & Culture Tours ` 024 223 6808; **e** ecoculture@gmx.net; www.ecoculture-zanzibar.org. Non-profit operator with office opposite Emerson's & Green Hotel offering slightly more expensive day trips for those who want to avoid the more established circuits.
Easy Travel & Tours ` 024 223 5372; **e** easytravel@zitec.org. Clued-up operator affiliated to a major Arusha-based safari company; runs a good variety of tours.
Sama Tours `/f 054 223 3543; **e** next@zanzinet.com. Office on Gizenga St behind House of Wonders. Spice tours guided by a knowledgeable local naturalist, who knows plant names in several languages. Offer all-inclusive tailor-made tours around the island with guides speaking English, French, German or Italian.
Sun 'n' Fun Tours ` 024 223 7381; **e** zanzibarsun@hotmail.com. Office in Sea View Indian Restaurant. Good range of trips (including Kizimkazi dolphins) at very reasonable prices. Can arrange car and bicycle hire.
Tropical Tours & Safaris ` 0747 413454; **e** tropicalts@hotmail.com. Small, efficient operator on Kenyatta Rd, opposite Mazson's Hotel, offering the usual tours, hotel and transport bookings and transfers, as well as Suzuki jeeps at US$45 per day, motorbikes at US$35 per day, and mountain-bike hire.
Zan Tours ` 024 223 3116; **f** 024 223 3042; **e** zantours@zitec.com; www.zantours.com. Large, professional organisation catering to international market, and able to arrange anything from accommodation (all budgets) and flights to day tours for walk-in clients. Recommended.

Stone Town walking tour

You can spend many idle hours getting lost in the fascinating labyrinth of narrow streets and alleys of the old Stone Town, and will almost inevitably hit most of the main landmarks within a couple of days of arriving. However, the following roughly circular walking tour through the Stone Town will allow those with limited time to do their sightseeing in a reasonably organised manner (though they are still bound to get lost), and should help those with more time to orientate themselves before they head out to explore the Stone Town without a map or guidebook in hand.

The obvious starting point for any exploration of Zanzibar Town is **Forodhani Gardens**, a small patch of greenery lying between Mizingani Road and the main sea wall. Laid out in 1936 to mark the silver jubilee of Sultan Khalifa, the gardens are a popular eating and meeting point in the evening, and the staircase rising from the gardens to the arched bridge to the south offers a good view over the old town.

Three significant buildings lie alongside each other behind the Forodhani Gardens. The **Palace Museum** (entrance US$3 per person, open 09.00–18.00 weekdays, 09.00–15.00 weekends) is the most northerly of these, a large white building with castellated battlements dating from the late 1890s. The palace was the official residence of the Sultan of Zanzibar from 1911 until the 1964 revolution, and it now houses an excellent museum. The graves of all the early sultans of Zanzibar are in the palace garden.

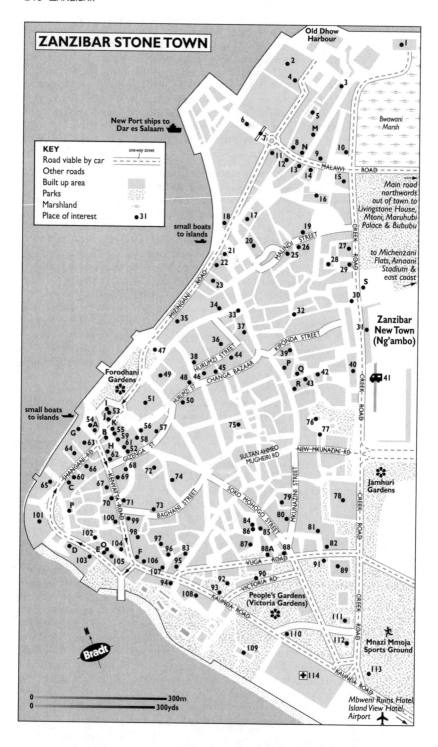

ZANZIBAR STONE TOWN

Old Dhow Harbour

New Port ships to Dar es Salaam

KEY
one-way street
Road viable by car
Other roads
Built up area
Parks
Marshland
Place of interest ●31

small boats to islands

small boats to islands

Bwawani Marsh

MALAWI ROAD

Main road northwards out of town to Livingstone House, Mtoni, Maruhubi Palace & Bububu

to Michenzani Flats, Amaani Stadium & east coast

CREEK ROAD

Zanzibar New Town (Ng'ambo)

Forodhani Gardens

MIZINGANI ROAD

MALINDI STREET

KIPONDA STREET

HURUMZI STREET

CHANGA BAZAAR

HURUMZI ST

GIZENGA ST

SHANGANI RD

KENYATTA ROAD

SULTAN AHMED MUGHEIRI RD

NEW MKUNAZINI RD

Jamhuri Gardens

BAGHANI STREET

SOKO MOHOGO STREET

MKUNAZINI STREET

VUGA ROAD

VICTORIA RD

People's Gardens (Victoria Gardens)

KAUNDA ROAD

CREEK ROAD

Mnazi Mmoja Sports Ground

KAUNDA ROAD

Bradt

N

0 ———— 300m
0 ———— 300yds

Mbweni Ruins Hotel Island View Hotel, Airport

Numerical key to Zanzibar Stone Town map opposite

1 Bwawani Hotel	68 Namaste Indian Restaurant
2 Clove Distillery	69 Post office & telephone office
3 Malindi Guesthouse	70 Memories of Zanzibar
4 Fish market	71 Barracuda Restaurant & Fanny's Green
5 Warere House	Restaurant
6 Shipping company ticket offices	72 St Joseph's Catholic Cathedral
7 Port gates	73 Chavda Hotel
8 Ciné Afrique	74 Chit-Chat Restaurant
9 Mzuri Guesthouse	75 Hamamni Baths
10 Petrol station Gapco	76 Anglican Cathedral
11 Hotel Marine	77 St Monica's Hostel
12 Malindi Bureau de Change	78 Haile Selassie School
13 Star Bureau de Change	79 Jambo Guesthouse
14 Passing Show Restaurant	80 Flamingo Guesthouse
15 Police station (main)	81 Zanzibar Medical & Diagnostic Centre
16 Zan Tours & Zan Air	82 Kiswahili Language Institute
17 Old Dispensary (Stone Town Cultural	83 Mauwani Inn
Centre)	84 Manch Lodge (guesthouse)
18 Mercury's Restaurant	85 Nyumbani Restaurant
19 Safari Lodge	86 Haven Hotel
20 Ijumaa Mosque	87 Florida Guesthouse
21 The Big Tree	88 Fisherman Tours, Fernandes Tours
22 Sea View Indian Restaurant, Seafront	88A Maha Travel & Tours
Internet, Sun N'Fun Tours	89 Ben Bella School
23 Old Customs House	90 Victoria House (guesthouse)
25 Pyramid Hotel	91 State University of Zanzibar
26 Narrow Street Hotel	92 Two Tables Restaurant
27 Zanzibar Tourism Corporation	93 Garden Lodge
28 Kokoni Hotel	94 Zanzibar Medical Group
29 BP petrol station	95 Dr Mehta's Hospital
30 Taxi rank	96 Afya Medical Hospital
31 Container shops	97 Zanzibar Hotel (closed for renovation 2005)
32 Narrow Street Annexe Hotel	98 Dhow Palace Hotel, Baghani House Hotel
33 Palace Restaurant (closed 2005)	99 Sunrise Restaurant & Pub
34 Hotel Kiponda	100 Mazsons Hotel, Precision Air, Kenya
35 Palace Museum	Airline, Cross Road Internet
36 Hindu Temple	101 Serena Inn
37 Aga Khan Mosque	102 Tippu Tip's House
38 Mandogo Café (shady, open air)	103 Amore Mio Restaurant
39 Hotel International, Bureau de change	104 Pagoda Chinese Restaurant
40 Market	105 Africa House Hotel
41 Bus & dala-dala station	106 Camlur's Restaurant
42 Masumo Bookshop	107 Rendezvous Les Spices Restaurant
43 Shamshuddin Cash & Carry Supermarket	108 High Court
44 Emerson's & Green Hotel	109 State House
45 Bottoms Up Guesthouse	110 Zanzibar Milestone
46 Clove Inn	111 Museum Annexe
47 Taxi rank	112 Peace Memorial Museum
48 Microwaves Internet	113 Old Cricket Pavilion
49 House of Wonders	114 Mnazi Moja Hospital
50 Sama Tours, Nassor curio shop	A Zanzibar Dive Centre
51 Old Arab Fort	B National Bank of Commerce
52 Supermarket	C Wings Fast Food, Abuso Inn, Air Tanzania
53 Orphanage	D Jojoba Tours
54 Sweet Easy Restaurant	E La Fenice
55 Radha Food House	F Casablanca Restaurant
56 People's Bank of Zanzibar	G Livingstone Beach Restaurant
57 The Zanzibar Gallery	H Dolly's Patisserie
58 People's Bank of Zanzibar (Foreign Exchange)	I Monsoon Restaurant
59 Karibu Inn	J Buni Café
60 Garage Club	K Bahari Dive Centre
61 Coco de Mer Hotel	L Bamdari Lodge, Nalindi Lodge Annexe
62 The Zanzibar Gallery	M Mitu Tours
63 Old British Embassy, Archipelago	N Malindi Lodge
Restaurant, Too Short Internet Café	O New Happy Club 2000
64 Tembo Hotel	P Zanzibar Coffee House, Beyt Al Char Hotel
65 Starehe Club	Q CD shop
66 Fisherman Restaurant	R Kaya Tea Room
67 Shangani Hotel & Shangani Internet Café	S Vodacom shop

Next to the Palace Museum, the **House of Wonders** is a square, multi-storey building surrounded by tiers of impressive balconies and topped by a clock tower. It was built as a ceremonial palace in 1883, and was the first building on Zanzibar to have electric lights. Local people called it Beit el Ajaib, meaning the House of Wonders. It also houses a worthwhile museum.

Directly facing Forodhani Gardens, the **Old Arab Fort** is probably the oldest extant building in the Stone Town, built by Omani Arabs between 1698 and 1701 over the site of a Portuguese church constructed a century before that, remnants of which can still be seen in the inner wall. A large, squarish, brown building with castellated battlements, the fort ceased to serve any meaningful military role in the 19th century, since when it has served variously as prison, railway depot and women's tennis club. The interior of the fort is open to visitors, who can climb to the top of the battlements and enter some of the towers. There is a restaurant in the fort, serving cold drinks, and traditional dancing shows take place there at least three evenings every week.

Heading southwest from the fort, under an arched bridge, the fork to your right is Shangani Road, the site of some important buildings. As you follow Shangani Road around a curve, you'll come out to a leafy green square, where the **Zanzibar Shipping Corporation Building**, dating to around 1850, stands to your left and the **Zanzibar Serena Inn**, formerly Extelcomms House, to your right. Perhaps 100m past the Serena Inn, to your left, you'll see the rear of **Tippu Tip's House**, a tall brown building which once served as the residence of Tippu Tip, the influential 19th-century slave trader who helped explorers such as Livingstone and Stanley with supplies and route planning. From here, wander up another 50m past the New Happy Bar, and you'll pass the **Africa House Hotel**, a good place to punctuate your walk with a cold drink on the attractively positioned balcony.

From the Africa House Hotel a small alley leads to Kenyatta Road, an important thoroughfare dotted with hotels, shops and restaurants, as well as a number of old buildings with traditional Zanzibari doors. Follow Kenyatta Road eastwards for about 300m, passing the somewhat unkempt **People's Gardens**, originally laid out under Sultan Barghash for the use of his harem, until you reach the **Zanzibar Milestone**. This octagonal marble pillar shows the distance from Zanzibar Town to various settlements on the island and further afield.

Cross the gardens in front of the milestone to the distinctive **Beit el Amani (House of Peace) Memorial Museum**, which houses interesting (though rather poorly organised and labelled) displays relating to the island's archaeology, the slave era, and various palaces, sultans, explorers, missionaries, traditional crafts and coins. In the annexe on the opposite side of the road there is a library and a natural history collection where dodo bones are exhibited. The Zanzibari door at the back of the building is reputedly the oldest in existence. The museum is open from 08.30 to 19.00 Monday to Friday and 08.30 to 15.00 Saturday and Sunday. There is a small entrance charge.

From the museum, follow Creek Road northwards for about 400m, and to your left you'll easily pick out the imposing **Anglican Cathedral** built by the Universities' Mission in Central Africa (UMCA) over the former slave market between 1873 and 1880. Tradition has it that the altar stands on the site of the market's whipping block, and the cellar of the nearby St Monica's Guesthouse is reputed to be the remains of a pit where slaves were kept before being sold. Sultan Barghash, who closed the slave market, is reputed to have asked Bishop Steere, leader of the mission, not to build the cathedral tower higher than the House of Wonders. The cathedral is open to visitors for a nominal fee, which also covers entrance to the dungeon below the guesthouse.

A short distance further along Creek Road lies the **covered market**, built at around the turn of the 20th century, and worth a visit even if you don't want to buy anything. It's a vibrant place where you can buy anything from fish and bread to sewing machines and second-hand car spares. Once you've taken a look around the market, follow Creek Road back southwards for 100m or so, passing the cathedral, then turn into the first wide road to your right. This is New Mkunazini Road, and if you follow it until its end, then turn right into Kajificheni Street and right again into Hammani Street, you'll come out at the **Hammani Baths**. This is one of the most elaborate Persian baths on Zanzibar, built for Sultan Barghash, and the caretaker will show you around for a small fee.

Barely 200m from the baths, on Cathedral Street, **St Joseph's Catholic Cathedral** is notable for its prominent twin spires, and was built between 1896 and 1898 by French missionaries and local converts. From the cathedral, continue northwards along Cathedral Street for perhaps 50m, then turn right into Gizenga Street, a good place to check out the work of local Tingatinga artists. If you follow Gizenga Street until you see the old Arab Fort to your left, you can conclude your walk by wandering back out to Forodhani Gardens.

Alternatively, if you want to keep going, turn right opposite the fort into Harumzi Street and, after continuing straight for about 300m, you'll come to an open square. A left turn as you enter this square takes you past the Jamat Khan Mosque and on to Jamatini Road, which after about 200m will bring you out at the seafront opposite the **Big Tree**. Known locally as Mtini, this well-known landmark was planted in 1911 by Sultan Khalifa and now provides shade for traditional dhow builders. On Mizingani Road, next to the Big Tree, the **Old Customs House**, a large, relatively plain building dating to the late 19th century, is where Sultan Hamoud was proclaimed sultan in 1896.

From the open area next to the Big Tree, a left turn along Mizingani Road will take you back to the Arab Fort, passing the above-mentioned buildings. Turn right into Mizingani Road, however, and after about 100m you'll pass the **Old Dispensary**, an ornate three-storey building built in the 1890s. Restored to its former glory by the Aga Khan, the dispensary now also contains a small exhibition hall of old monochrome photographs of the Stone Town. You can continue for a few hundred metres further, past the port gates, to the **traditional dhow harbour**, though based on our experience you are unlikely to be allowed inside.

If the above directions seem too complicated, or you want further insight into the historical buildings of the Stone Town, most tour operators can arrange a guided city tour for around US$20 (see pages 247 for tour-operator listings).

AROUND ZANZIBAR TOWN
Chumbe Island
The coral island of Chumbe, in near-pristine condition because it served as a military base for many years and visitors were not permitted, has been gazetted as a nature reserve along with several surrounding reefs. Snorkelling here is as good as anywhere around Zanzibar, with more than 350 reef fishes recorded, as well as dolphins and turtles. A walking trail circumnavigates the island, passing rock pools haunted by starfish, and beaches marched upon by legions of hermit crabs. Look out, too, for the giant coconut crab, an endangered nocturnal creature that weighs up to 4kg. Some 60 species of bird have been recorded on the island, including breeding pairs of the rare roseate tern, and the localised Ader's duiker, hunted out in the 1950s, has been re-introduced. Of historical interest are an ancient Swahili mosque and a British lighthouse built in 1904.

Day trips to the island cost US$70 per person, inclusive of transfers, guides, snorkelling equipment and lunch, and can only be arranged through reputable tour operators or from the Mbweni Ruins Hotel. Overnight stays are encouraged at a superb eco-lodge, all profits from which are pumped into conservation and education. The seven self-contained bungalows are very rustic and attractive, and have solar electricity, compost toilets, and funnelled roofs designed to collect rainwater. An ingenious main *boma* houses the dining room (good seafood), education centre, snorkelling equipment room and lounge/bar. Chumbe makes no pretension to be a chill-out beach resort, but it is highly recommended to those with a strong interest in wildlife and conservation and has won numerous global awards for eco-tourism. Full board accommodation costs US$200 per person. For further information and reservations, contact Chumbe Island Coral Park. \/f 024 223 1040; m 0747 413582; f info@chumbeisland.com; www.chumbeisland.com.

Changuu (Prison) Island

Changuu was originally owned by a wealthy Arab, who used it as a detention centre for disobedient slaves. A prison was built there in 1893, but never used. A path circles the island (about an hour's easy stroll). There is a small beach and a restaurant, and masks and flippers can be hired for snorkelling. The island is home to several giant tortoises, probably brought from the Seychelles in the 18th century, which spend much of their time mating, a long and noisy process which is apparently successful as the tortoise population is said to be growing. An entrance fee of US$5 per person must be paid in hard currency.

MNEMBA ISLAND LODGE

Private Bag X27, Benmore, South Africa; \ 024 223 3110; f 024 223 3117; e ccafricazanzibar@zanzinet.com

If you've ever fancied owning your own private tropical island, then a stay at the Mnemba Island Lodge may be the closest you ever get to realising that dream, if only for a few days. The tiny island of Mnemba, which lies a kilometre or so off the northeastern shore of Zanzibar, forms part of the much larger submerged Mnemba Atoll. The island itself boasts wide beaches of white coral sand, fine and cool underfoot, backed by patches of tangled coastal bush and a small forest of casuarina trees. The small reefs immediately offshore offer a great introduction to the fishes of the reef for snorkellers, while diving excursions further afield allow you to explore the 40m-deep coral cliffs, a good place to see larger fish including the whale shark, the world's largest fish. The bird checklist for the island, though short, includes several unusual waders and other marine birds.

Accommodation consists of ten large, airy beach chalets, constructed using organic materials. The chalets are very private, separated from the beach and other chalets by thick bush, and each one has a private balcony as well as netting, a fan and an en-suite bathroom. The food is good, and (weather permitting) evening meals are taken at a table on the beach. Accommodation costs US$500 per person per night, inclusive of all meals and drinks, transfers from Zanzibar Town, use of watersport and snorkelling equipment, and dives (including diving courses) with the resident diving instructor.

Chapwani (Grave) Island

This long, narrow and very pretty island has been the site of a Christian cemetery since 1879, and it also has a small swimming beach – good at low and high tide – and faces Snake Island, where thousands of egrets roost overnight. Most of the graves belong to British sailors who were killed fighting Arab slave ships, while others date from World War I, when the British ship *Pegasus* was sunk in Zanzibar harbour. The indigenous forest supports about a hundred duikers, large numbers of fruit bats, and various coastal scrub birds. The giant coconut crab is often seen along the shore.

Maharubi Palace

This is probably the most impressive ruin on this part of the coast, built in 1882 for the concubines of Sultan Barghash. At one time he kept around a hundred women here. It was destroyed by fire in 1899, and all that remains are the great pillars which supported the upper storey, the Persian-style bathhouse, and the original water tanks, now overgrown with lilies. The palace is signposted along the Bububu road roughly 3km from the Stone Town, and a nominal entrance fee is charged. Traditional dhow builders can be seen at work on the beach in front of the palace.

Mtoni Palace

The ruins of Mtoni Palace lie a short way north of Maharubi, and can be reached along the beach. Mtoni is the oldest palace on Zanzibar, built for Sultan Said in the 1840s. A book written by his daughter Salme describes the palace in the 1850s. At one end of the house was a large bathhouse, at the other the quarters where Said lived with his principal wife. Gazelles and peacocks wandered around the large courtyard. Mtoni was abandoned before 1885, and only the main walls and roof now remain.

Kidichi and Kizimbani Persian Baths

The Kidichi baths were built in 1850 for Said's wife, Binte Irich Mirza, the granddaughter of the Shah of Persia, and are decorated with Persian-style stucco. You can enter the bathhouse and see the bathing pool and toilets, but there is mould growing on much of the stucco. The baths lie about 3km east of Bububu; from the main crossroads follow the road heading inland (ie: turn right coming from Zanzibar Town) and you'll see the baths to your right after a walk of around 30 minutes.

Mangapwani Slave Cave

Near the epnonymous village, 20km north of Zanzibar Town, this large natural cavern and manmade slave cave can easily be visited using a no 2 *dalla-dalla*. The natural coral cavern has a narrow entrance and a pool of fresh water at its lowest point. The Slave Cave, a square cell cut into the coral, was used to hold slaves after the trade was abolished in 1873. The natural cavern may also have been used to hide slaves, but this is not certain. Coming by *dalla-dalla*, you'll have to disembark at Mangapwani, where a road forks left towards the coast. About 2km past the village this road ends and a small track branches off to the right. Follow this for 1km to reach the Slave Cave. About halfway between Mangapwani and the track to the Slave Cave, a narrow track to the left leads to the natural cavern.

NUNGWI AND THE FAR NORTH

The large fishing village of Nungwi, situated on the northern end of the island, is the centre of Zanzibar's traditional dhow-building industry. It has also emerged as probably the most popular tourist retreat on Zanzibar, thanks to a lovely beach lined with palm and casuarina trees, and the good snorkelling and

SAADANI NATIONAL PARK

Protected as a game reserve since 1969, Saadani – due to be gazetted as a national park in 2006 – is the only wildlife sanctuary in east Africa with an Indian Ocean beachfront. Situated on the mainland opposite the northern tip of Zanzibar, the original 200km² game reserve was centred on the small but ancient fishing village of Saadani. It was expanded to cover 500km² in 1996, and has subsequently doubled in area thanks to the incorporation of a tract of former ranchland.

As recently as ten years ago, Saadani – despite its proximity to Dar es Salaam – was among east Africa's most obscure conservation areas, subject to heavy poaching and lacking tourist facilities in any form. In recent years, however, it has received renewed attention from conservationists and tourists alike. One factor in this revival has been the establishment of two top-notch private tented camps within the proposed national park. Another has been the clampdown on poaching and integration of local villages into the conservation effort initiated with assistance from Germany's GTZ agency in 1998.

Viewed purely as a wildlife destination, Saadani cannot yet bear comparison to Tanzania's finest – though if present trends continue, it way well be up with them ten years hence. But even as things stand, Saadani is a thoroughly worthwhile and enjoyable retreat, allowing visitors to combine the hedonistic pleasures of a perfect sandy beach with guided bush walks, game drives, and a boat trip up the Wami River. The latter is a highlight of Saadani – close encounters with hippo are guaranteed, there's a good chance of seeing crocs, and a spectacular array of marine and woodland birds includes Pel's fishing owl, mangrove, pied and malachite kingfishers, broad-billed roller and various waders, herons and egrets.

Inland, Saadani supports a park-like cover of open grassland interspersed with stands of acacia trees and knotted coastal thicket, home to a wide range of ungulates, with game densities generally highest in January, February, June, July and August. At all times of year, however, you can be reasonably confident of encountering elephant, giraffe, buffalo, warthog, common waterbuck, reedbuck, hartebeest and wildebeest, along with troops of yellow baboon and vervet monkey. Something of a Saadani special is the red duiker, a diminutive, beautiful and normally very shy antelope of coastal scrub and forest. Saadani also harbours small populations of greater kudu, eland and the endangered Roosevelt's sable. Lions are also making something of a comeback, and leopard, spotted hyena and black-backed jackal are seen from time to time. The beaches in and around Saadani form one of the last major breeding sites for green turtles on mainland Tanzania.

In addition to a rather basic guesthouse run by Tanapa, two exclusive beachfront camps offer upmarket tented accommodation on a full-board basis, as well as a full selection of activities including boat trips, game walks and game drives:

Saadani Safari Camp \ 022 277 3294; m 0748 585401;
e info@saadanilodge.com; www.saadanilodge.com
Tent With A View \ 022 2151106; e tentview@cats-net.com; www.saadani.com

Both companies can also provide details of charter flights and/or road transfers and shuttles to/from Arusha, Zanzibar and Dar es Salaam.

diving in the surrounding waters. A few reasonably isolated upmarket hotels stand on the north end of the beach, while the southern end hosts a dense cluster of low-key and rather overpriced guesthouses and restaurants. A short walk along the beach east of Nungwi brings you to the headland of Ras Nungwi, where there is an old lighthouse (photography forbidden). Next to this, the Mnarani Turtle Sanctuary (entrance US$1) consists of a fenced-off saline natural pool, in which lives a community of perhaps 15 greenback and hawksbill turtles.

Getting there and away
An erratic handful of *dalla-dalla*s daily connect Zanzibar Town to Nungwi, but the vast majority of travellers prefer to be transferred by private minibus, which can cost up to US$10 per person depending on group size and your negotiating skills.

Where to stay and eat
Upmarket
Ras Nungwi Beach Hotel \ 024 223 3767; f 024 223 3098; e info@rasnungwi.com; www.rasnungwi.com. This widely praised hotel, built almost entirely with local materials such as fossilised coral limestone, has an organic feel, a lovely beach setting, and an atmosphere that is far less 'packaged' than at most equivalently priced places on the east coast. A dive centre is attached, and the emphasis is very much on this and other non-motorised watersports, although many visitors are content merely to laze on the idyllic beach. The superb restaurant specialises in seafood and Swahili dishes. All accommodation is en-suite with a ceiling fan, private balcony and netted 4-poster bed in the traditional Swahili style. *FB rates range upward from US$135 pp.*

Moderate
Mnarani Beach Cottages \ 024 224 0494; e mnarani@zanlink.com; www.lighthousezanzibar.com. Situated between the village and the lighthouse on Ras Nungwi, this small cluster of cottages, built in local style, is one of the more peaceful and attractively located retreats in the Nungwi area. The self-contained rooms are good value, too. *US$60/84 sgl/dbl B&B.*

Budget
Amaan Bungalows \ 024 224 0026; e amaanbungalow@yahoo.com; www.amaanbungalow.com. One of the oldest budget lodges in Nungwi, Amaan Bungalows is now also the largest, a sprawling complex of 35 self-contained bungalows with nets costing US$25 dbl B&B, with a few larger and pricier rooms also available. With good diving facilities on site, and a busy beach, it's a justifiably popular spot with sociable budget travellers, but not the place to head for if you're seeking a peaceful beach retreat.

JOZANI FOREST RESERVE
The Jozani Forest Reserve protects the last substantial remnant of the indigenous forest that once covered much of central Zanzibar. The main attraction is Kirk's red colobus, a beautiful and cryptically coloured monkey with an outrageous pale tufted crown. Unique to Zanzibar, Kirk's red colobus had been reduced to a population of around 1,500 individuals a few years back, but recent estimates now place it at around 2,500. A good network of forest trails runs through the forest, and the habituated troops are easily seen by tourists.

Jozani used to be the main haunt of the Zanzibar leopard, a race that is found nowhere else, but which recent research suggests may well be extinct. The forest is also home to Ader's duiker, a small antelope that effectively may now be a Zanzibar endemic, as it is probably extinct and certainly very rare in Kenya's Sokoke Forest, the only other place where it has ever been recorded. Several other mammal species live in Jozani, and the forest is one of the best birding sites on the island, hosting a good range of coastal forest birds, including an endemic race of the lovely Fischer's turaco.

The entrance and reception at Jozani Forest lie a short distance from the main road connecting Zanzibar Town to the east coast. Most tour operators can organise day trips to the forest, though it is perfectly possible to visit independently using a no 9 or 10 bus or *dalla-dalla*. A new development in the area, based in the village of Pete 1km from the entrance to the forest, is a mangrove boardwalk, allowing visitors a rare view into the unique mangrove habitat.

THE EAST COAST

The east coast of Zanzibar is where you will find the idyllic tropical beaches so beloved of travel brochures: clean white sand lined with palms, and lapped by the warm blue water of the Indian Ocean. The east coast is divided into two discrete stretches by Chwaka Bay, which lies at the same latitude as Zanzibar Town on the west coast. Traditionally, the most popular stretch of coast is to the south of this bay, between Bwejuu and Makunduchi, but recent years have seen an increasing number of developments further north, between Matemwe and Chwaka.

Getting there and away

The east coast can easily be reached by bus or *dalla-dalla* from Zanzibar Town. North of Chwaka Bay, no 6 buses go to Chwaka (directly east of Zanzibar Town), no 14 to Uroa via Chwaka, no 17 to Kiwengwa and no 18 to Matemwe. South of the bay, no 9 goes to Paje (sometimes continuing to Bwejuu or Jambiani) and no 10 to Makunduchi. Chwaka Bay can be crossed by lake-taxis between Chwaka and Michamvi.

Most travellers prefer to use private transport to the east coast: several tour companies and some independent guides arrange minibuses which cost between US$3 and US$5 per person each way. Unless you specify where you want to stay, minibus drivers prefer to take you to a hotel that gives them commission.

Where to stay
Upmarket

Matemwe Bungalows ◦ 024 223 6535 or 0747 425788; e matemwe-znz@twiga.com; www.matemwe.com. This small, simple but comfortable hotel to the north of Chwaka Bay lies near the pretty Matemwe village, on a low coral cliff above a palm-lined beach. It is a good base for diving and snorkelling, and is close to the exceptional Mnemba Atoll. *En-suite dbl chalets US$140.*

Shooting Star Inn ◦ 024 223 2926 or 0747 413294; e star@zanzibar.org; www.zanzibar.org/star. Situated on Kiwenga Beach, about 8km south of Matemwe, this small, friendly hotel is regarded as having one of the best restaurants on the island, and is visited by many people for the food alone, which costs from US$10 upwards. *Luxurious en-suite bungalows US$110 dbl B&B.*

Breezes Beach Club ◦ 0741 326595; e breezes@africaonline.co.tz. One of the best hotels to the south of Chwaka Bay, Breezes Beach Club is – despite its name and large size – a relatively unpackaged family-run set-up sprawling around a well-maintained sea-facing garden. A dive school is attached. *Around US$100 for a self-contained dbl.*

Moderate

Matemwe Beach Village ◦ 024 223 8374; e matemwebeachvillage@zitec.org; www.zanzibaroneocean.com. This comfortable small lodge situated about 1km from

Matemwe Bungalows has very spacious and attractively decorated dbl rooms with fan, netting and hot showers. There's a good dive centre on site. *US$60/100 sgl.*
Blue Oyster Hotel ⟍ 024 224 0163; e blueoysterhotel@gmx.de. The pick of perhaps a dozen hotels in Jambiani, south of Chwaka Bay, the Blue Oyster is an attractively laid out German-owned lodge with an open-air feel and a good restaurant. Bright, comfortable rooms with nets and fans. *US$25/30 sgl/dbl using common showers, US$40/50 self-contained.*

Budget
Shehe Bungalows ⟍ 024 224 0149; e shehebungalows@hotmail.com; www.shehebungalows.com. The long-serving Shehe in Jambiani remains decent value at US$20–35 for a self-contained sgl/dbl bungalow. The restaurant has an extensive menu, with most dishes in the Tsh5,000–6,000 range.
Red Monkey Bungalows ⟍ 024 224 0207; e standard@zitec.org. Above the beach at the south end of Jambiani, Red Monkey Bungalows is an atmospheric new set-up, charging US$20/30 sgl/dbl for a small but comfortable en-suite room. The restaurant serves inexpensive seafood and the endemic Kirk's red colobus is regularly seen in the nearby bush.

KIZIMKAZI
The small town of Kizimkazi lies on the southwestern end of the island, and is best known to tourists as *the* place to see humpback and bottlenose dolphins, both of which are resident in the area. Most tourists visit Kizimkazi on an organised day tour out of Zanzibar Town, which costs between US$25 and US$100 all-inclusive per person, depending on group size, season and quality. Sightings cannot be guaranteed, but the chances of seeing dolphins here are very good. It may also be possible sometimes to swim with the dolphins, though you should never encourage your pilot to chase them or try to approach them too closely yourself. With up to a hundred people visiting Kizimkazi daily in the high season, there is genuine cause to fear that tourism may be detrimental to the animals. If you do get close enough and you want to try your luck swimming with the dolphins, slip (rather than dive) into the water next to the boat, and try to excite the dolphins' interest by diving frequently and holding your arms along your body to imitate their streamlined shape!

If you stay overnight at Kizimkazi, it's worth heading out to the Kizimkazi Mosque at the nearby settlement of Dimbani. Kizimkazi is one of the oldest known mosques in east Africa, dated by Kufic inscriptions to AD1107, when it was part of a large walled city. The Kufic inscriptions, on the niche at the eastern end of the mosque, are in a decorative floriated style similar to some old inscriptions found in Persia. The silver pillars on either side of the niche are decorated with pounded shells from Mafia Island. Two clocks, which show Swahili time, were presented by local dignitaries. To see inside the mosque, now protected by a corrugated-iron roof, you must find the caretaker who lives nearby. It is respectful to cover any bare limbs and take off your shoes when you enter.

Getting there and away
Although most people visit Kizimkazi on an organised day trip, it can be reached independently in a hired car, or with a no 3 bus or *dalla-dalla* from Zanzibar Town.

Where to stay and eat
Kizidi Bungalows ⟍ 0747 417053; e kizidi@hotmail.com. Popular with tour groups for its excellent restaurant, Kizidi also offers accommodation in 14 comfortable bungalows at US$25/40 sgl/dbl. It has its own boats and arranges dolphin trips at good rates.

Appendix 1

WILDLIFE
Mammals

In the listings below, an animal's scientific name is given in parentheses after its English name, followed by the Swahili (Sw) name. The Swahili for animal is *nyama* (plural *wanyama*); to find out what animal you are seeing, ask '*Nyama gani?*'

Cats, dogs and hyenas

Lion (*Panthera leo*) Sw: *simba*. Shoulder height: 100–120cm; weight: 150–220kg. Africa's largest predator, the lion is the one animal that everybody hopes to see on safari. It is a sociable creature, living in prides of five to ten animals and defending a territory of between 20 and 200km². Lions hunt at night, and their favoured prey is large or medium antelope such as wildebeest and impala. Most of the hunting is done by females, but dominant males normally feed first after a kill. Rivalry between males is intense, and battles to take over a pride are frequently fought to the death, for which reason two or more males often form a coalition. Young males are forced out of their home pride at three years of age, and male cubs are usually killed after a successful takeover. When not feeding or fighting, lions are remarkably indolent – they spend up to 23 hours of any given day at rest – so the anticipation of a lion sighting is often more exciting than the real thing. Lions naturally occur in any habitat but desert and rainforest, and once ranged across much of the Old World, but these days they are all but restricted to the larger conservation areas in sub-Saharan Africa (one remnant population exists in India). The Serengeti and Ngorongoro Crater are arguably the best places in Africa for regular lion sightings.

Leopard (*Panthera pardus*) Sw: *chui*. Shoulder height: 70cm; weight: 60–80kg. The powerful leopard is the most solitary and secretive of Africa's large cat species. It hunts using stealth and power, often getting to within 5m of its intended prey before pouncing, and it habitually stores its kill in a tree to keep it from hyenas and lions. The leopard can be distinguished from the superficially similar cheetah by its rosette-like spots, lack of black 'tear marks' and more compact, powerful build. Leopards occur in all habitats, favouring areas with plenty of cover such as riverine woodland and rocky slopes. There are many records of individuals living in close proximity to humans for years without being detected. The leopard is the most common of Africa's large felines, found throughout Tanzania, yet a good sighting must be considered a stroke of fortune. One relatively reliable spot for leopard sightings is the Seronera Valley in the Serengeti. An endemic race of leopard occurs on Zanzibar, though recent research suggests that it is probably extinct on the island, and that the handful of local reports of leopard sightings were probably the result of confusion with the African civet and introduced Java civet.

Cheetah (*Acynonix jubatus*) Sw: *duma*. Shoulder height: 70–80cm; weight: 50–60kg. This remarkable spotted cat has a greyhound-like build, and is capable of running at 70km/h in bursts, making it the world's fastest land animal. It is often seen pacing the plains restlessly, either on its own or in a small family group comprised of a mother and her offspring. A diurnal hunter, favouring the cooler hours of the day, the cheetah's habits have been adversely affected in areas where there are high tourist concentrations and off-road driving is permitted. Males are territorial, and generally solitary, though in the Serengeti they commonly defend their territory in pairs or trios. Despite superficial similarities, you can easily tell a cheetah from a leopard by its simple spots, disproportionately small head, streamlined build, diagnostic black tear marks, and preference for relatively open habitats. Widespread, but thinly distributed and increasingly rare outside of conservation areas, the cheetah is most likely to be seen in savanna and arid habitats such as the Serengeti Plains (where sightings are regular on the road to Seronera) and the floor of the Ngorongoro Crater.

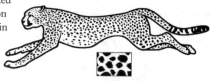

Similar species The **serval** (*Felis serval*) is smaller than a cheetah (shoulder height: 55cm) but has a similar build and black-on-gold spots giving way to streaking near the head. Seldom seen, it is widespread and quite common in moist grassland, reed beds and riverine habitats.

Caracal (*Felis caracal*) Sw: *simbamangu*. Shoulder height: 40cm; weight: 15–20kg. The caracal resembles the European lynx with its uniform tan coat and tufted ears. It is a solitary hunter, feeding on birds, small antelope and livestock, and ranges throughout the country favouring relatively arid savanna habitats. It is nocturnal and rarely seen.

Similar species The smaller **African wild cat** (*Felis sylvestris*) ranges from the Mediterranean to the Cape of Good Hope, and is similar in appearance to the domestic tabby cat. Like the caracal, it is common, but nocturnal, and infrequently seen.

African wild dog (*Lycaon pictus*) Sw: *mbwa mwitu*. Shoulder height: 70cm; weight: 25kg. Also known as the African hunting dog or painted dog, the wild dog is distinguished from other African canids by its large size and cryptic black, brown and cream coat. Highly sociable, living in packs of up to 20 animals, the hunting dog is a ferocious hunter that literally tears apart its prey on the run. Threatened with extinction as a result of its susceptibility to diseases spread by domestic dogs, it is indeed extinct in several areas where it was formerly abundant, for instance in the Serengeti and most other reserves in northern Tanzania. The global population of around 4,000 wild dogs is spread across much of eastern and southern Africa, but the Selous Game Reserve is the most important stronghold (estimated population 1,300) and Ruaha National Park also hosts a viable population. The only place in northern Tanzania where hunting dogs can reliably be observed is the Mkomazi Game Reserve, where a recently re-introduced population is reportedly thriving. A few recent scattered sightings in Tarangire and Lake Manyara national parks, and most notably a record of a pack denning with pups on the adjacent Manyara Ranch in 2002, provide some hope that this endangered creature might yet recolonise this area.

Black-backed jackal (*Canis mesomelas*) Sw: *mbweha*. Shoulder height: 35–45cm; weight: 8–12kg. The black-backed (or silver-backed) jackal is an opportunistic feeder capable of adapting to most habitats. Most often seen singly or in pairs at dusk or dawn, it is ochre in colour with a prominent black saddle flecked by a varying amount of white or gold. It is probably the most frequently observed small predator in Africa south of the Zambezi, and its eerie call is a characteristic sound of the bush at night. It is the commonest jackal in most Tanzanian reserves.

Similar species The **side-striped jackal** (*Canis adustus*) is more cryptic in colour, and has an indistinct pale vertical stripe on each flank and a white-tipped tail. Nowhere very common, it is distributed throughout Tanzania, and most likely to be seen in the southern reserves. The **common jackal** (*Canis aureus*), also known as the Eurasian or golden jackal, is a cryptically coloured North African jackal, relatively pale and with a black tail tip. Its range extends as far south as the Serengeti and Ngorongoro Crater, and it is probably more readily seen than the black-backed jackal on the crater floor, since it is more diurnal in its habits.

Bat-eared fox (*Otocyon megalotis*) Shoulder height: 30–35cm; weight: 35kg. This small, silver-grey insectivore, unmistakable with its huge ears and black eye-mask, is most often seen in pairs or small family groups during the cooler hours of the day. Associated with dry open country, the bat-eared fox is quite common in the Serengeti and likely to be encountered at least once in the course of a few days' safari, particularly during the denning season (November and December).

Spotted hyena (*Crocuta crocuta*) Sw: *fisi*. Shoulder height: 85cm; weight: 70kg. Hyenas are characterised by their bulky build, sloping back, brownish coat, powerful jaws and dog-like

expression. Despite looking superficially canine, they are more closely related to mongooses and bears than to cats or dogs. Contrary to popular myth, hyenas are not exclusively scavengers: the spotted hyena in particular is an adept hunter capable of killing an animal as large as a wildebeest. Nor are they hermaphroditic, an ancient belief that stems from the false scrotum and penis covering the female hyena's vagina. Sociable animals, and fascinating to observe, hyenas live in loosely structured clans of about ten animals, led by females who are stronger and larger than males. The spotted hyena is the largest hyena, distinguished by its blotchily spotted coat, and it is probably the most common large predator in eastern and southern Africa. It is most frequently seen at dusk and dawn in the vicinity of game reserve lodges, campsites and refuse dumps, and is likely to be encountered on a daily basis in the Serengeti and Ngorongoro Crater.

Similar species The north African **striped hyena** (*Hyaena hyaena*) is pale brown with several dark vertical streaks and an off-black mane. It occurs alongside the spotted hyena in dry parts of Tanzania, but is scarce and secretive. The equally secretive **aardwolf** (*Proteles cristatus*) is an insectivorous striped hyena, not much bigger than a jackal, occurring in low numbers in northern Tanzania.

African civet (*Civettictus civetta*) Sw: *fungo*. Shoulder height: 40cm; weight: 10–15kg. This bulky, long-haired, rather feline creature of the African night is primarily carnivorous, feeding on small animals and carrion, but will also eat fruit. It has a similarly coloured coat to a leopard or cheetah, and this is densely blotched with large black spots becoming stripes towards the head. Civets are widespread and common in many habitats, but very rarely seen.

Similar species The smaller, more slender **tree civet** (*Nandinia binotata*) is an arboreal forest animal with a dark-brown coat marked with black spots. The **small-spotted genet** (*Genetta genetta*) and **large-spotted genet** (*Genetta tigrina*) are the most widespread members of a group of similar small predators, all of which are very slender and rather feline in appearance, with a grey to golden-brown coat marked with black spots and an exceptionally long ringed tail. Most likely to be seen on nocturnal game drives or scavenging around game reserve lodges, the large-spotted genet is golden brown with very large spots and a black-tipped tail, whereas the small-spotted genet is greyer with rather small spots and a pale tip to the tail.

Banded mongoose (*Mungos mungo*) Shoulder height: 20cm; weight: around 1kg. The banded mongoose is probably the most commonly observed member of a group of small, slender, terrestrial carnivores. Uniform dark brown except for a dozen black stripes across its back, it is a diurnal mongoose occurring in family groups in most wooded habitats and savanna.

Similar species Several other mongoose species occur in Tanzania, though several are too scarce and nocturnal to be seen by casual visitors. The **marsh mongoose** (*Atilax paludinosus*) is large, normally solitary and has a very scruffy brown coat. It's widespread in the eastern side of Africa where it is often seen in the vicinity of water. The **white-tailed ichneumon** (*Ichneumia albicauda*) is another widespread, solitary, large brown mongoose, easily identified by its bushy white tail. The **slender mongoose** (*Galerella sanguinea*) is as widespread and also solitary, but it is very much smaller (shoulder height: 10cm) and has a uniform brown coat and black tail tip. The **dwarf mongoose** (*Helogate parvula*) is a diminutive (shoulder height: 7cm) and highly sociable light-brown mongoose often seen in the vicinity of termite mounds, particularly in Tarangire National Park.

Ratel (*Mellivora capensis*) Sw: *nyegere*. Shoulder height: 30cm; weight: 12kg. Also known as the honey badger, the ratel is black with a puppyish face and grey-to-white back. It is an opportunistic feeder best known for its symbiotic relationship with a bird called the honeyguide which leads it to a bee hive, waits for it to tear the nest open, then feeds on the scraps. The ratel is among the most widespread of African carnivores, but it is thinly distributed and rarely seen.

Similar species Several other mustelids (a mamal of the weasel family) occur in the region, including the **striped polecat** (*Ictonyx striatus*), a common but rarely seen nocturnal creature with black underparts and bushy white back, and the similar but much more scarce **striped weasel** (*Poecilogale albincha*). The **Cape clawless otter** (Aonyx capensis) is a brown freshwater mustelid with a white collar, while the smaller **spotted-necked otter** (*Lutra maculicollis*) is darker with white spots on its throat.

Primates

Chimpanzee (*Pan troglodytes*) Sw: *sokwe-mtu*. Standing height: 100cm; weight: up to 55kg. This distinctive black-coated ape, along with the bonobo (*Pan paniscus*) of the southern

Congo, is more closely related to man than to any other living creature. The chimpanzee lives in large troops based around a core of related males dominated by an alpha male. Females aren't firmly bonded to their core group, so emigration between communities is normal. Primarily frugivorous (fruit-eating), chimpanzees eat meat on occasion, and though most kills are opportunistic, stalking of prey is not unusual. The first recorded instance of a chimp using a tool was at Gombe Stream in Tanzania, where modified sticks were used to 'fish' in termite mounds. In west Africa, chimps have been observed cracking open nuts with a stone and anvil. In the USA, captive chimps have successfully been taught Sign Language and have created compound words such as 'rock-berry' to describe a nut. A

widespread and common rainforest resident, the chimpanzee is thought to number 200,000 in the wild. In east Africa, chimps occur in western Uganda and on the Tanzanian shore of Lake Tanganyika, where they can be seen at the research centre founded by primatologist Jane Goodall in Tanzania's Gombe Stream, as well as at Mahale Mountains. The only chimpanzee population to fall within the scope of this book is the introduced (but to all intents and purposes wild) community that can be visited on Rubondo Island.

Common baboon (*Papio cynocaphalus*) Sw: *nyani*. Shoulder height: 50–75cm; weight: 25–45kg. This powerful terrestrial primate, distinguished from any other monkey by its much larger size, inverted U-shaped tail and distinctive dog-like head, is fascinating to watch from a behavioural perspective. It lives in large troops that boast a complex, rigid social structure characterised by matriarchal lineages and plenty of intertroop movement by males seeking social dominance. Omnivorous and at home in almost any habitat, the baboon is the most widespread primate in Africa, frequently seen in most Tanzanian game reserves. There are several races of baboon in Africa, regarded by some authorities to be full species. Two taxa are present in northern Tanzania: you're most likely to see the olive or anubis baboon (*P. c. anubis*), which is the darker and hairier green-brown baboon found in the west, but in areas such as West Kilimanjaro you might encounter the yellow baboon (*P. c. cynocephalus*), a more lightly built and paler yellow-brown race whose range lies to the east of the Rift Valley.

Vervet monkey (*Cercopithecus aethiops*) Sw: *tumbili*. Length (excluding tail): 40–55cm; weight: 4–6kg. Also known as the green or grivet monkey, the vervet is probably the world's most numerous monkey and certainly the most common and widespread representative of the *Cercopithecus* guenons, a taxonomically controversial genus associated with African forests. An atypical guenon in that it inhabits savanna and woodland rather than true forest, the vervet spends a high proportion of its time on the ground and in most of its range could be confused only with the much larger and heavier baboon. However, the vervet's light-grey coat, black face and white forehead band should be diagnostic – as should the male's garish blue genitals. The vervet is abundant in Tanzania, and might be seen just about anywhere, not only in reserves.

Similar species The terrestrial **patas monkey** (*Erythrocebus patas*), larger and more spindly than the vervet, has an orange-tinged coat and black forehead stripe. Essentially a monkey of the dry northwestern savanna, the patas occurs in low numbers in the northern Serengeti.

Blue monkey (*Cercopithecus mitis*) Sw: *kima*. Length (excluding tail): 50–60cm; weight: 5–8kg. This most variable of African monkeys is also known as the samango, golden, silver and Sykes' monkey, or the diademed or white-throated guenon. Several dozen races are recognised, divided by some authorities into more than one species. Taxonomic confusion notwithstanding, *C. mitis* is the most common forest guenon in eastern Africa, with one or other race occurring in just about any suitable habitat. Unlikely to be confused with another species in Tanzania, the blue monkey has a uniformly dark blue-grey coat broken by a white throat, which in some races extends all down the chest and in others around the collar. It lives in troops of up to ten animals and associates with other primates where their ranges overlap. It is common in Arusha and Lake Manyara national parks and in many forest reserves.

Black-and-white colobus (*Colobus guereza*) Sw: *mbega mweupe*. Length (excluding tail): 65cm; weight: 12kg. This beautiful jet-black monkey has bold white facial markings, a long white tail and in some races white sides and shoulders. Almost exclusively arboreal, it is capable of jumping up to 30m, a spectacular sight with white tail streaming behind. Several races have been described, and most authorities recognise more than one species. The black-and-white colobus is a common resident of forests in Tanzania, often seen in the forest zone of Kilimanjaro and in Arusha National Park.

Lesser bushbaby (*Galago senegalensis*) Sw: *komba*. Length (excluding tail): 17cm; weight: 150g. The lesser bushbaby is the most widespread and common member of a group of small and generally indistinguishable nocturnal primates, distantly related to the lemurs of Madagascar. More often heard than seen, the lesser bushbaby can sometimes be picked out by tracing a cry to a tree and shining a torch into its eyes.

Similar species The most easily identified bushbaby due to its size, the **greater bushbaby** (*Galago crassicaudatus*) occurs throughout the eastern side of Africa as far south as East London. It produces a terrifying scream, which you'd think was emitted by a chimpanzee or gorilla. Recent studies in Tanzania have determined that the smaller bushbabies are far more specifically diverse than was previously realised; see box *Galago diversity in Tanzania*, page 30).

Large antelope

Roan antelope (*Hippotragus equinus*) Sw: *korongo*. Shoulder height: 120–150cm; weight: 250–300kg. This handsome equine antelope is uniform fawn-grey with a pale belly, short de-curved horns and a light mane. It could be mistaken for the female sable antelope, but this has a well-defined white belly, and lacks the roan's distinctive black-and-white facial markings. The roan is widespread but thinly distributed in southern Tanzania, though rare in the north, with one small population known to occur (yet seldom seen) in the Serengeti.

Sable antelope (*Hippotragus niger*) Sw: *pala hala*. Shoulder height: 135cm; weight: 230kg. The striking male sable is jet black with a distinct white face, underbelly and rump, and long de-curved horns. The female is chestnut brown and has shorter horns. The main stronghold for Africa's sable population is the *miombo* woodland of southern Tanzania; it is virtually absent from northern Tanzania.

Oryx (*Oryx gazella*) Sw: *choroa*. Shoulder height: 120cm; weight: 230kg. This regal, dry-country antelope is unmistakable with its ash-grey coat, bold black facial marks and flank strip, and unique long, straight horns. The fringe-eared oryx is the only race found in Tanzania, where it is most common (though still scarce) in Tarangire National Park and Mkomazi Game Reserve.

Waterbuck (*Kobus ellipsiprymnus*) Sw: *kuro*. Shoulder height: 130cm; weight: 250–270kg. The waterbuck is easily recognised by its shaggy brown coat and the male's large lyre-shaped horns. The Defassa race of the Rift Valley and areas further west has a full white rump, while the eastern race has a white U on its rump. The waterbuck is frequently seen in small family groups grazing near water in all but the most arid of game reserves in Tanzania.

Blue wildebeest (*Connochaetes taurinus*) Sw: *nyumbu*. Shoulder height: 130–150cm; weight: 180–250kg. This rather ungainly antelope, also called the brindled gnu, is easily recognised by its dark coat and bovine appearance. The superficially similar buffalo is far more heavily built. Immense herds of blue wildebeest occur on the Serengeti Plains, where the annual migration of more than a million heading into Kenya's Maasai Mara forms one of Africa's great natural spectacles. There are also significant wildebeest populations in the Ngorongoro Crater and Tarangire.

Hartebeest (*Alcelaphus buselaphus*) Shoulder height: 125cm; weight: 120–150kg. Hartebeests are ungainly antelopes, readily identified by the combination of large shoulders, a sloping back, red-brown or yellow-brown coat and smallish horns in both sexes. Numerous races are recognised, all of which are generally seen in small family groups in reasonably open country. The race found in northern Tanzania, Coke's hartebeest or kongoni, is common in open parts of the Serengeti and Ngorongoro.

Similar species The **topi** or **tsessebe** (*Damaliscus lunatus*) is basically a darker version of the hartebeest with striking yellow lower legs. Widespread but thinly and patchily distributed, the topi occurs alongside the much paler kongoni in the Serengeti National Park, where it is common.

Common eland (*Taurotragus oryx*) Sw: *pofu*. Shoulder height: 150–175cm; weight: 450–900kg. Africa's largest antelope, the common eland is light-brown in colour, sometimes with a few faint white vertical stripes. It has a somewhat bovine appearance, accentuated by the relatively short horns and large dewlap. It is widely distributed in east and southern Africa, and small herds may be seen almost anywhere in grassland or light woodland. The eland is fairly common in Serengeti National Park, but difficult to approach closely.

Greater kudu (*Tragelaphus strepsericos*) Sw: *tandala*. Shoulder height: 140–155cm; weight: 180–250kg. In many parts of Africa, the greater kudu is the most readily observed member of the genus *tragelaphus*, a group of medium to large antelopes characterised by the male's large spiralling horns and a dark coat generally marked with several vertical white stripes. The greater kudu is very large, with a grey-brown coat and up to ten stripes on each side, and the male has magnificent double-spiralled horns. A widespread animal occurring in most wooded habitats except for true forest, the greater kudu is rare in northern Tanzania, but small numbers persist in Tarangire.

Similar species The thinly distributed and skittish **lesser kudu** (*Tragelaphus imberbis*) is an east African species largely restricted to arid woodland. In Tanzania, it often occurs alongside the greater kudu, from which it can be distinguished by its smaller size (shoulder height: 100cm), two white throat patches and greater number of stripes (at least 11). Nowhere common, it is most likely to be encountered in Tarangire and Ruaha national parks. The semi-aquatic **sitatunga** (*Tragelaphus spekei*) is a widespread but infrequently observed inhabitant of west and central African swamps from the Okovango in Botswana to the Sudd in Sudan. Tanzania's Rubondo Island is one of the few places where it is readily observed. The male, with a shoulder height of up to 125cm and a shaggy fawn coat, is unmistakable in its habitat. The smaller female might be mistaken for a bushbuck (see below) but is much drabber.

Medium and small antelope

Bushbuck (*Tragelaphus scriptus*) Sw: *pongo*. Shoulder height: 70–80cm; weight: 30–45kg. This attractive antelope, a member of the same genus as the kudu and sitatunga, shows great regional variation in colouring. The male is dark brown, chestnut or in parts of Ethiopia black, while the much smaller female is generally pale red-brown. The male has relatively small, straight horns for a *tragelaphus* antelope. Both sexes have similar throat patches to the lesser kudu, and are marked with white spots and sometimes stripes. One of the most widespread antelope species in Africa, the bushbuck occurs in forest and riverine woodland throughout Tanzania, where it is normally seen singly or in pairs. It tends to be secretive and skittish except where it is used to people, so it is not as easily seen as you might expect of a common antelope.

Thomson's gazelle (*Gazella thomsoni*) Shoulder height: 60cm; weight: 20–25kg. Gazelles are graceful, relatively small antelopes that generally occur in large herds in open country, and have fawn-brown upper parts and a white belly. Thomson's gazelle is characteristic of the east African plains, where it is the only gazelle to have a black horizontal stripe. It is common to abundant in the Serengeti and surrounds.

Similar species Occurring alongside Thomson's gazelle in many parts of east Africa, the larger **Grant's gazelle** (*Gazella granti*) lacks a black side stripe and has comparatively large horns. An uncharacteristic gazelle, the **gerenuk** (*Litocranius walleri*) is a solitary, arid country species of Ethiopia, Kenya and northern Tanzania, similar in general colour to an impala but readily identified by its very long neck and singular habit of feeding from trees standing on its hind legs. Nowhere common in Tanzania, the gerenuk is present in small numbers in Mkomazi, Tarangire, West Kilimanjaro and the Loliondo area.

Impala (*Aepeceros melampus*) Sw: *swala pala*. Shoulder height: 90cm; weight: 45kg. This slender, handsome antelope is superficially similar to some gazelles, but in fact belongs to a separate family. Chestnut in colour, the impala has diagnostic black and white stripes running down its rump and tail, and the male has large lyre-shaped horns. One of the most widespread antelope species in sub-equatorial Africa, the impala is normally seen in large herds in wooded savanna habitats, and it is one of the most common antelope in many Tanzanian reserves.

Reedbuck (*Redunca spp*) Sw: *tohe*. Shoulder height: 65–90cm; weight: 30–65kg. The three species of reedbuck are all rather nondescript fawn-grey antelopes generally seen in open grassland near water. The mountain reedbuck (*Redunca fulvorufula*) is the smallest and most distinctive, with a clear white belly, tiny horns and an overall grey appearance. It has a broken distribution, occurring in mountainous parts of eastern South Africa, northern Tanzania, Kenya and southern Ethiopia. The Bohor reedbuck is found in northern Tanzania, whereas the southern reedbuck occurs in southern Tanzania.

Klipspringer (*Oreotragus oreotragus*) Sw: *mbuze mawe*. Shoulder height: 60cm; weight: 13kg. The klipspringer is a goat-like antelope, normally seen in pairs, and easily identified by its dark, bristly grey-yellow coat, slightly speckled appearance and unique habitat preference. Klipspringer means 'rockjumper' in Afrikaans, an apt name for an antelope that occurs exclusively in mountainous areas and rocky outcrops. It is found throughout Tanzania, and is often seen around the Lobo Hills in the Serengeti and the Maji Moto area in Lake Manyara.

Steenbok (*Raphicerus cempestris*) Sw: *tondoro*. Shoulder height: 50cm; weight: 11kg. This rather nondescript small antelope has red-brown upper parts and clear white underparts, and the male has short straight horns. It is probably the most commonly observed small antelope in Africa, though it has a broken range, and is absent from southern Tanzania despite being common in the north of the country and in areas further south. Like most other antelopes of its size, the steenbok is normally encountered singly or in pairs and tends to 'freeze' when disturbed.

Similar species The **oribi** (*Ourebia ourebi*) is a widespread but uncommon grassland antelope which looks much like a steenbok but stands about 10cm higher at the shoulder and has an altogether more upright bearing. **Kirk's dik-dik** (*Madoqua kirki*), smaller than the steenbok and easily identified by its large white eye-circle, is restricted primarily to Tanzania and Kenya, and it is particularly common in Arusha National Park.

Red duiker (*Cephalophus natalensis*) Sw: *pofu*. Shoulder height: 45cm; weight: 14kg. This is the most likely of Africa's 12 to 20 'forest duikers' to be seen by tourists. It is deep chestnut in colour with a white tail and, in the case of the east African race *C. n. harveyi* (sometimes considered to be a separate species), a black face. The red duiker occurs in most substantial forest patches along the eastern side of Africa, though it is less often seen than it is heard crashing through the undergrowth.

Similar species The **blue duiker** (*Cephalophus monticola*) is widespread in Africa and the only other forest duiker to occur in countries south of Tanzania, and it can easily be told from the red duiker by its greyer colouring and much smaller size (it is the smallest forest duiker, about the same size as a suni – dwarf antelope). **Abbott's duiker** (*Cephalophus spadix*) is a large duiker, as tall as a klipspringer, restricted to a handful of montane forests in Tanzania, including those on Kilimanjaro and the Usambara, Udzungwa and Poroto mountains. The endangered **Ader's duiker** (*Cephalophus adersi*) is presumably restricted to forested habitats on Zanzibar Island, where as few as 1,000 animals may survive, most of them in the Jozani Forest. Recent reports suggest that this duiker is extinct in the only other locality where it has been recorded, the Sokoke Forest in Kenya.

Common duiker (*Sylvicapra grimmia*) Sw: *nysa*. Shoulder height: 50cm; weight: 20kg. This anomalous duiker holds itself more like a steenbok and is the only member of its family to occur outside of forests. Generally grey in colour, the common duiker can most easily be separated from other small antelopes by the black tuft of hair that sticks up between its horns. It occurs throughout Tanzania, and tolerates most habitats except for true forest and very open country.

Other large herbivores

African elephant (*Loxodonta africana*) Sw: *tembe*. Shoulder height: 2.3–3.4m; weight: up to 6,000kg. The world's largest land animal, the African elephant is intelligent, social and often very entertaining to watch. Female elephants live in close-knit clans in which the eldest female plays matriarch over her sisters, daughters and granddaughters. Mother–daughter bonds are strong and may last for up to 50 years. Males generally leave the family group at around 12 years to roam singly or form bachelor herds. Under normal circumstances, elephants will range widely in search of food and water, but when concentrated populations are forced to live in conservation areas, their habit of uprooting trees can cause serious environmental damage. Elephants are widespread and common in habitats ranging from desert to rainforest and, despite heavy poaching, they are likely to be seen on a daily basis in most of Tanzania's larger national parks, the exception being the Serengeti where they are common only in the Lobo region.

Black rhinoceros (*Diceros bicornis*) Sw: *faru*. Shoulder height: 160cm; weight: 1,000kg. This is the more widespread of Africa's two rhino species, an imposing, sometimes rather aggressive creature that has been poached to extinction in most of its former range. It occurs in many southern African reserves, but is now very localised in east Africa, where it is most likely to be seen in Tanzania's Ngorongoro Crater.

Hippopotamus (*Hippopotamus amphibius*) Sw: *kiboko*. Shoulder height: 150cm; weight: 2,000kg. Characteristic of Africa's large rivers and lakes, this large, lumbering animal spends most of the day submerged, but emerges at night to graze. Strongly territorial, herds of ten or more animals are presided over by a dominant male who will readily defend his patriarchy to the death. Hippos are abundant in most protected rivers and water bodies, and they are still quite common outside of reserves, where they kill more people than any other African mammal.

African buffalo (*Syncerus caffer*) Sw: *nyati*. Shoulder height: 140cm; weight: 700kg. Frequently and erroneously referred to as a water buffalo (an Asian species), the African buffalo is a distinctive ox-like animal that lives in large herds on the savanna and occurs in smaller herds in forested areas. Common and widespread in sub-Saharan Africa, herds of buffalo are likely to be encountered in most Tanzanian reserves and national parks. The best place to see large buffalo herds is on the Ngorongoro Crater floor.

Giraffe (*Giraffa camelopardis*) Sw: *twiga*. Shoulder height: 250–350cm; weight: 1,000–1,400kg. The world's tallest and longest-necked land animal, a fully grown giraffe can measure up to 5.5m high. Quite unmistakable, the giraffe lives in loosely structured herds of up to 15, though herd members often disperse and are seen singly or in smaller groups. Formerly distributed throughout east and southern Africa, the giraffe is now more or less restricted to conservation areas, where it is generally common and easily seen.

Common zebra (*Equus burchelli*) Sw. *punda milia*. Shoulder height: 130cm; weight: 300–340kg. This attractive striped horse is common and widespread throughout most of East and southern Africa, where it is often seen in large herds alongside wildebeest. The common zebra is the only wild equine to occur in Tanzania, and is common in most conservation areas, especially the Serengeti, whose population may stand as high as half a million.

Warthog (*Phacochoreus africanus*) Sw: *ngiri*. Shoulder height: 60–70cm; weight: up to 100kg. This widespread and often conspicuously abundant resident of the African savanna is grey in colour with a thin covering of hairs, wartlike bumps on its face, and rather large upward-curving tusks. Africa's only diurnal swine, the warthog is often seen in family groups, trotting off briskly with its tail raised stiffly (a diagnostic trait) and a determinedly nonchalant air.

Similar species Bulkier, hairier and browner, the **bushpig** (*Potomochoerus larvatus*) is as widespread as the warthog, but infrequently seen due to its nocturnal habits and preference for dense vegetation. Larger still, weighing up to 250kg, the **giant forest hog** (*Hylochoerus meinertzhageni*) is primarily a species of the west African rainforest. It does occur in certain highland forests in northern Tanzania, but the chance of a sighting is practically non-existent.

TRACKS

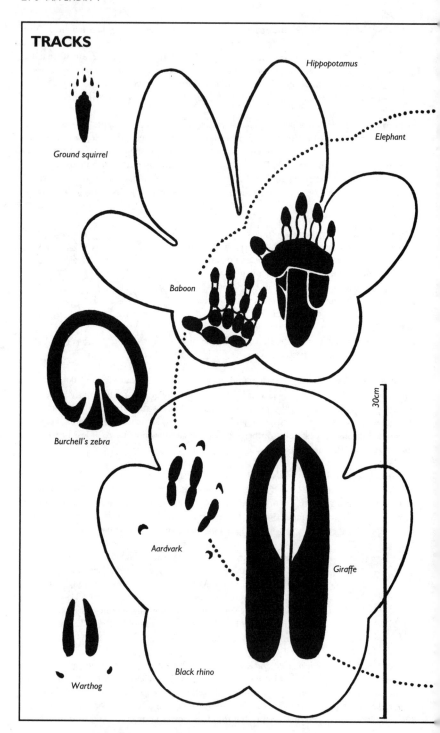

Ground squirrel

Hippopotamus

Elephant

Baboon

Burchell's zebra

Aardvark

Giraffe

Warthog

Black rhino

30cm

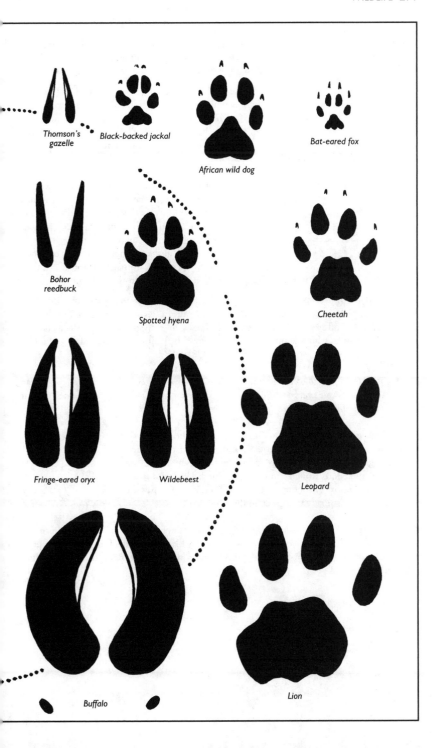

Thomson's gazelle

Black-backed jackal

African wild dog

Bat-eared fox

Bohor reedbuck

Spotted hyena

Cheetah

Fringe-eared oryx

Wildebeest

Leopard

Buffalo

Lion

Small mammals

Aardvark (*Orycteropus afer*) Shoulder height: 60cm; weight: up to 70kg. This singularly bizarre nocturnal insectivore is unmistakable with its long snout and huge ears. It occurs practically throughout the region, but sightings are extremely rare, even on night drives.

Similar species Not so much similar to an aardvark as equally dissimilar to anything else, **pangolins** are rare nocturnal insectivores with distinctive armour plating and a tendency to roll up in a ball when disturbed. Most likely to be seen in Tanzania is Temminck's pangolin (*Manis temmincki*). Also nocturnal, but spiky rather than armoured, several **hedgehog** and **porcupine** species occur in the region, the former generally no larger than a guinea pig, the latter generally 60–100cm long.

Rock hyrax (*Procavia capensis*) Sw: *pimbi*. Shoulder height: 35–30cm; weight: 4kg. Rodent-like in appearance, hyraxes are more closely related to elephants. The rock hyrax and similar bush hyrax (*Heterohyrax brucei*) are often seen sunning in rocky habitats and become tame when used to people, for instance at Seronera and Lobo lodges in the Serengeti. The less common tree hyrax (*Dendrohyrax arboreus*) is a nocturnal forest creature, often announcing its presence with an unforgettable shrieking call.

Similar species The **elephant shrews** (Sw: *sange*) are rodents that look like miniature kangaroos with absurdly elongated noses. A number of species are recognised, but they are mostly secretive and nocturnal, so rarely seen. The smaller species are generally associated with savanna habitats, but the much larger chequered elephant shrew is a resident of Eastern Arc forests – I've only ever seen it in Amani and Udzungwa.

Scrub hare (*Lepus saxatilis*) Weight: 2.7–4.5Kg. This is the largest and commonest African hare or rabbit. In some areas a short walk at dusk or after nightfall might reveal three or four scrub hares. They tend to freeze when disturbed.

Unstriped ground squirrel (*Xerus rutilus*) Weight: 1.4Kg. An endearing terrestrial animal of arid savanna, the unstriped ground squirrel is grey to grey-brown with a prominent white eye ring and silvery black tail. It spends much time on its hind legs, and has the characteristic squirrel mannerism of holding food in its forepaws. In Tanzania, it is most likely to be seen in the Serengeti.

Bush squirrel (*Paraxerus cepapi*) Weight: 1Kg. This is the typical squirrel of the eastern and southern savanna, rusty brown in colour with a silvery black back and white eye rings. A great many other arboreal or semi-arboreal squirrels occur in the region, but most are difficult to tell apart in the field.

Appendix 2

LANGUAGE
Swahili

Swahili, the official language of Tanzania, is a Bantu language that developed on the east African coast about 1,000 years ago and has since adopted several words from Arabic, Portuguese, Indian, German and English. It spread into the Tanzanian interior along with the 19th-century slave caravans and is now the lingua franca in Tanzania and Kenya, and is also spoken in parts of Uganda, Malawi, Rwanda, Burundi, Congo, Zambia and Mozambique.

In Dar es Salaam, Zanzibar, Arusha, Moshi and the northern game reserves, you can get by with English well enough. If you travel in other parts of the country, you will need to understand some Swahili. And even if you are sticking to tourist areas, it is polite and can be useful to know a bit of Swahili.

There are numerous Swahili–English dictionaries on the market, as well as phrasebooks and grammars. A useful dictionary for travellers is Baba Malaika's *Friendly Modern Swahili–English Dictionary* (MSO Training Centre for Development Co-operation, PO Box 254, Arusha, second edition, 1994), which costs around US$25. Better still, though probably too heavyweight for most travellers, is the *TUKI English–Swahili Dictionary* (University of Dar es Salaam, 1996), which costs around US$16. Peter Wilson's *Simplified Swahili* (Longman) used to be regarded as the best book for teaching yourself Swahili, but it has probably been superseded by Joan Russell's *Teach Yourself Swahili* (Hodder and Stoughton, 1996), which comes complete with a cassette and costs around US$15. Of the phrasebooks, Lonely Planet's or Rough Guide's *Swahili* are both good. It is best to buy a Swahili book before your trip, as they are difficult to get hold of once you are in Tanzania.

For short-stay visitors, all these books have practical limitations. Wading through a phrasebook to find the expression you want can take ages, while trying to piece together a sentence from a dictionary is virtually impossible. In addition, most books available are in Kenyan Swahili, which often differs greatly from the purer version spoken in Tanzania.

The following introduction is not a substitute for a dictionary or phrasebook. It is not so much an introduction to Swahili as an introduction to communicating with Swahili-speakers. Before researching this guide, my east African travels had mainly been in Kenya, Uganda and parts of Tanzania where English is relatively widely spoken. We learnt the hard way how little English is spoken in most of Tanzania. I hope this section will help anyone in a similar position to get around a great deal more easily than we did at first.

Pronunciation

Vowel sounds are pronounced as follows:

a	like the a in *father*
e	like the e in *wet*
i	like the ee in *free*, but less drawn-out
o	somewhere between the o in *no* and the word *awe*
u	similar to the oo in *food*

The double vowel in words like *choo* or *saa* is pronounced like the single vowel, but drawn out for longer. Consonants are in general pronounced as they are in English. *L* and *r* are often interchangeable, so that *Kalema* is just as often spelt or pronounced *Karema*. The same is true of *b* and *v*.

You will be better understood if you speak slowly and thus avoid the common English-speaking habit of clipping vowel sounds – listen to how Swahili-speakers pronounce their vowels. In most Swahili words there is a slight emphasis on the second last syllable.

Basic grammar

Swahili is a simple language in so far as most words are built from a root word using prefixes. To go into all of the prefixes here would probably confuse people new to Swahili – and it would certainly stretch my knowledge of the language. They are covered in depth in most Swahili grammars and dictionaries. The following are some of the most important:

Pronouns

ni	me	*wa*	they
u	you	*a*	he or she
tu	us		

Tenses

na	present
ta	future
li	past
ku	infinitive

Tenses (negative)

si	present
sita	future
siku	past
haku	negative, infinitive

From a root word such as *taka* (want) you might build the following phrases:

Unataka soda	You want a soda
Tutataka soda	We will want a soda
Alitaka soda	He/she wanted a soda

In practice, *ni* and *tu* are often dropped from simple statements. It would be more normal to say *nataka soda* than *ninataka soda*.

In many situations there is no interrogative mode in Swahili; the difference between a question and a statement lies in the intonation.

Greetings

There are several common greetings in Swahili. Although allowances are made for tourists, it is rude to start talking to someone without first using one or other formal greeting. The first greeting you will hear is *Jambo*. This is reserved for tourists, and a perfectly adequate greeting, but it is never used between Tanzanians (the more correct *Hujambo*, to which the reply is *Sijambo*, is used in some areas).

The most widely used greeting is *Habari?*, which more-or-less means *What news?* The normal reply is *Nzuri* (good). *Habari* is rarely used by Tanzanians on its own; you might well be asked *Habari ya safari?*, *Habari yako?* or *Habari gani?* (very loosely, *How is your journey?*, *How are you?* and *How are things?* respectively). *Nzuri* is the polite reply to any such request.

A more fashionable greeting among younger people is *Mambo*, especially on the coast and in large towns. Few tourists recognise this greeting; reply *Safi* or *Poa* and you've made a friend.

In Tanzanian society it is polite to greet elders with the expression *Shikamu*. To the best of my knowledge this means *I hold your feet*. In many parts of rural Tanzania, children will greet you in this way, often with their heads bowed and so quietly it sounds like *Sh..oo*. Don't misinterpret this by European standards (or other parts of Africa where *Mzungu give me shilling* is the phrase most likely to be offered up by children); most Tanzanian children are far too polite to swear at you. The polite answer is *Marahaba* (I'm delighted).

Another word often used in greeting is *Salama*, which means peace. When you enter a shop or hotel reception, you will often be greeted by a friendly *Karibu*, which means *Welcome*. *Asante sana* (thank you very much) seems an appropriate response.

If you want to enter someone's house, shout *Hodi!* It basically means *Can I come in?* but would be used in the same situation as *Anyone home?* would in English. The normal response will be *Karibu* or *Hodi*.

It is respectful to address an old man as *Mzee*. *Bwana*, which means *Mister*, might be used as a polite form of address to a male who is equal or senior to you in age or rank, but who is not a *Mzee*. Older women can be addressed as *Mama*.

The following phrases will come in handy for small talk:

Where have you just come from?	*(U)natoka wapi?*
I have come from Moshi	*(Ni)natoka Moshi*
Where are you going?	*(U)nakwenda wapi?*
We are going to Arusha	*(Tu)nakwenda Arusha*
What is your name?	*Jina lako nani?*
My name is Philip	*Jina langu ni Philip*
Do you speak English?	*Unasema KiIngereze?*
I speak a little Swahili	*Ninasema KiSwahili kidigo*
Sleep peacefully	*Lala salama*
Bye for now	*Kwaheri sasa*
Have a safe journey	*Safari njema*
Come again (welcome again)	*Karibu tena*
I don't understand	*Sielewi*
Say that again	*Sema tena*

Numbers

1	*moja*	30	*thelathini*
2	*mbili*	40	*arobaini*
3	*tatu*	50	*hamsini*
4	*nne*	60	*sitini*
5	*tano*	70	*sabini*
6	*sita*	80	*themanini*
7	*saba*	90	*tisini*
8	*nane*	100	*mia (moja)*
9	*tisa*	150	*mia moja na hamsini*
10	*kumi*	155	*mia moja hamsini na tano*
11	*kumi na moja*	200	*mia mbili*
20	*ishirini*	1,000	*elfu (moja)* or *mia kumi*

Swahili time

Many travellers to Tanzania fail to come to grips with Swahili time. It is essential to be aware of it, especially if you are catching buses in remote areas. The Swahili clock starts at the equivalent of 06.00, so that *saa moja asubuhi* (hour one in the morning) is 07.00, *saa mbili jioni* (hour two in the evening) is 20.00, etc. To ask the time in Swahili, say *Saa ngapi?*

Always check whether times are standard or Swahili. If you are told a bus leaves at nine, ask whether the person means *saa tatu* or *saa tisa*. Some English-speakers will convert to standard time, others won't. This does not apply so much where people are used to tourists, but it's advisable to get in the habit of checking.

Day-to-day queries

The following covers such activities as shopping, finding a room, etc. It's worth remembering that most Swahili words for modern objects, or things for which there would not have been a pre-colonial word, are often similar to the English. Examples are *resiti* (receipt), *gari* (car), *polisi* (police), *posta* (post office) and – my favourite – *stesheni masta* (station master). In desperation, it's always worth trying the English word with an *ee* sound on the end.

Shopping

The normal way of asking for something is *Ipo* or *Zipo?*, which roughly means *Is there?*, so if you want a cold drink you would ask *Soda baridi zipo?* The response will normally be *Ipo* or *Kuna* (there is) or *Hamna* or *Hakuna* (there isn't). Once you've established the shop has what you want, you might say *Nataka koka mbili* (I want two cokes). To check the price, ask *Shillingi ngape?* It may be simpler to ask for a brand name: Omo (washing powder) or Blue Band (margarine), for instance.

Accommodation

The Swahili for guesthouse is *nyumba ya wageni*. In my experience *gesti* works as well, if not better. If you are looking for something a bit more upmarket, bear in mind *hoteli* means restaurant. We found self-contained (*self-contendi*) to be a good keyword in communicating this need. To find out whether there is a vacant room, ask *Nafasi zipo?*

Getting around

The following expressions are useful for getting around:

Where is there a guesthouse?	*Ipo wapi gesti?*
Is there a bus to Moshi?	*Ipo basi kwenda Moshi?*
When does the bus depart?	*Basi itaondoka saa ngapi?*
When will the vehicle arrive?	*Gari litafika saa ngapi?*
How far is it?	*Bale gani?*
I want to pay now	*Ninataka kulipa sasa*

Foodstuffs

avocado	*parachichi*	food	*chakula*
bananas	*ndizi*	fruit(s)	*(ma)tunda*
bananas (cooked)	*matoke/batoke*	goat	*(nyama ya) mbuzi*
beef	*(nyama ya) ngombe*	mango(es)	*(ma)embe*
bread (loaf)	*mkate*	maize porridge	
bread (slice)	*tosti*	(thin, eaten at	
coconuts	*nazi*	breakfast)	*uji*
coffee	*kahawa*	maize porridge	
chicken	*kuku*	(thick, eaten as	
egg(s)	*(ma)yai*	staple with	
fish	*samaki*	relish)	*ugali*
meat	*nyama*	rice	*pilau*
milk	*maziwa*	salt	*chumvi*
onions	*vitungu*	sauce	*mchuzi/supu*
orange(s)	*(ma)chungwa*	sugar	*sukari*
pawpaw	*papai*	tea	*chai*
pineapple	*nanasi*	(black/milky)	*(ya rangi/maziwa)*
potatoes	*viazi*	vegetable	*mboga*
rice (cooked plain)	*wali*	water	*maji*
rice (uncooked)	*mchele*		

Days of the week

Monday	*Jumatatu*	Friday	*Ijumaa*
Tuesday	*Jumanne*	Saturday	*Jumamosi*
Wednesday	*Jumatano*	Sunday	*Jumapili*
Thursday	*Alhamisi*		

Useful words and phrases

afternoon	*alasiri*	night	*usiku*
again	*tena*	no	*hapana*
and	*na*	no problem	*hakuna matata*
ask (I am		now	*sasa*
asking for…)	*omba (ninaomba…)*	only	*tu*
big	*kubwa*	OK or fine	*sawa*
boat	*meli*	passenger	*abiria*
brother	*kaka*	pay	*kulipa*
bus	*basi*	person (people)	*mtu (watu)*
car (or any		please	*tafadhali*
vehicle)	*gari*	road/street	*barabara/mtaa*
child (children)	*mtoto (watoto)*	shop	*duka*
cold	*baridi*	sister	*dada*
come here	*njoo*	sleep	*kulala*
excuse me	*samahani*	slowly	*polepole*
European(s)	*mzungu (wazungu)*	small	*kidogo*
evening	*jioni*	soon	*bado kidogo*
far away	*mbale kubwa*	sorry	*polepole*
father	*baba*	station	*stesheni*
friend	*rafiki*	stop	*simama*
good	*mzuri*	straight or direct	*moja kwa moja*
(very good)	*(mzuri sana)*	thank you	*asante*
goodbye	*kwaheri*	(very much)	*(sana)*
here	*hapa*	there is	*iko/kuna*
hot	*moto*	there is not	*hamna/hakuna*
later	*bado*	thief (thieves)	*mwizi (wawizi)*
like	*penda*	time	*saa*
(I would like…)	*(ninapenda…)*	today	*leo*
many	*sana*	toilet	*choo*
me	*mimi*	tomorrow	*kesho*
money	*pesa/shillingi*	want	*taka*
more	*ingine/tena*	(I want…)	*(ninataka…)*
morning	*asubuhi*	where	*(iko) wapi*
mother	*mama*	yes	*ndiyo*
nearby	*karibu/mbale*	yesterday	*jana*
	kidogo	you	*wewe*

Useful conjunctions include *ya* (of) and *kwa* (to or by). Many expressions are created using these; for instance *stesheni ya basi* is a bus station and *barabara kwa Mbale* is the road to Mbale.

Health

flu	*mafua*	recover	*pona*
fever	*homa*	treatment	*tiba*
malaria	*malaria*	cure	*ponyesha*
cough	*kikohozi*	injection	*sindano*

vomit	*kutapika*	bone	*mfupa*
swollen	*uvimbe*	death	*mauti*
injure	*jeraha*	to examine	*vipimo*
weak	*dhaifu*	to fall down	*kuanguka*
pain	*maumizu*	to bleed	*kutokwa na damu*

Maa

Maa is the dialect of the Maasai. It does not exist in written form, so the spellings below are approximate.

Greetings

Father/Elderly man, I greet you	*Papa … supai*
Warrior/middle-aged man, I greet you	*Apaayia … supai*
Young woman, I greet you	*Siangiki … supai*
Boy, I greet you	*Ero … supai*
Girl, I greet you	*Nairo … supai*
Mother/middle-aged woman, I greet you	*Yeyio … takwenya*
Grandmother/elder woman, I greet you	*Koko … takwenya*
How are you?	*Koree indae?*
Are you fine/healthy?	*Kira sedan/kira biot?*
My name is…	*Aji …*
What is your name?	*Kekijaa enkarna?*
I come from…	*Aingwaa …*
Where do you come from?	*Kaingwaa?*
Goodbye	*Serae*

Numbers

1	*nabo*	13	*tomon ok ooni*
2	*are*	14	*tomon o ongwan*
3	*ooni*	15	*tomon o imiet*
4	*ongwan*	16	*tomon o ille*
5	*imiet*	17	*tomon o opishana*
6	*ille*	18	*tomon o isiet*
7	*naapishana*	19	*tomon o odo*
8	*isiet*	20	*tikitam*
9	*naudo*	100	*iip nabo*
10	*tomon*	1,000	*enchata nabo*
11	*tomon o obo*	2,000	*inkeek are*
12	*tomon o are*	3,000	*inkeek ooni*

Shopping

How much does it cost?	*Empesai aja?*
I want/need it	*Ayieu*
I don't want/need it today	*Mayieu taata*
I will buy this one	*Ainyang ena*
I will buy these	*Ainyang kuna*
I won't buy anything today	*Mainyang onyo taata*
I haven't got any money	*Maata empesai*

Useful words and phrases

Thank you	*Ashe*
Thank you very much	*Ashe naleng*

Take it (used when giving a gift)	*Ngo*
I receive it (used when accepting a gift)	*Au*
Leave me/it alone (to children)	*Tapala*
Go outside (to children)	*Shomo boo*
Expression of sympathy (like 'pole' in Swahili)	*Kwa adei*
May I take a picture?	*Aosh empicha?*
Yes	*Ee*
OK	*Ayia*
No, I don't want you to	*A-a, mayieu*
Stop it	*Tapala*

African English

Although many Tanzanians speak a little English, not all speak it fluently. Africans who speak English tend to structure their sentences in a similar way to how they would in their own language: they speak English with Bantu grammar.

For a traveller, knowing how to communicate in African English is as important as speaking a bit of Swahili, if not more so. It is noticeable that travellers who speak English as a second language often communicate with Africans more easily than first language English-speakers.

The following ground rules should prove useful when you speak English to Africans:

- *Unasema KiEngereze?* (Do you speak English?). This small but important question may seem obvious. It isn't.
- Greet in Swahili then ask in English. It is advisable to go through the Swahili greetings (even *Jambo* will do) before you plough ahead and ask a question. Firstly, it is rude to do otherwise; secondly, most Westerners feel uncomfortable asking a stranger a straight question. If you have already greeted the person, you'll feel less need to preface a question with phrases like 'I'm terribly sorry' and 'Would you mind telling me' which will confuse someone who speaks limited English.
- Speak slowly and clearly. There is no need, as some travellers do, to speak as if you are talking to a three-year-old, just speak naturally.
- Phrase questions simply and with Swahili inflections. This bus goes to Dodoma? is better than Could you tell me whether this bus is going to Dodoma?; You have a room? is better than Is there a vacant room? If you are not understood, don't keep repeating the same question; find a different way of phrasing it.
- Listen to how people talk to you, and not only for their inflections. Some English words are in wide use; others are not. For instance, lodging is more likely to be understood than accommodation.
- Make sure the person you are talking to understands you. Try to avoid asking questions that can be answered with a yes or no. People may well agree with you simply to be polite.
- Keep calm. No-one is at their best when they arrive at a crowded bus station after an all-day bus ride; it is easy to be short-tempered when someone cannot understand you. Be patient and polite; it's you who doesn't speak the language.

Glossary

Acacia woodland	type of woodland dominated by thorny, thin-leafed trees of the genus *Acacia*
AICC	Arusha International Conference Centre
banda	a hut, often used to refer to hutted accommodation at hotels and lodges
boma	traditional enclosure or homestead; administration building of the colonial era

bui-bui	black cloth worn veil-like by women, mainly in Islamic parts of the coast
bwana	mister (polite term of address to an adult man)
Brachystegia woodland	type of woodland dominated by broad-leaved trees of the genus *Brachystegia*
Chama Cha Mapinduzi (CCM)	ruling party of Tanzania since independence
cichlid	family of colourful fish found in the Rift Valley lakes
closed canopy forest	true forest in which the trees have an interlocking canopy
dalla-dalla	light vehicle, especially minibus, serving as public transport
dhow	traditional wooden seafaring vessel
duka	kiosk
endemic	unique to a specific country or biome
exotic	not indigenous, for instance plantation trees such as pines and eucalyptus
forex bureau	bureau de change
fly-camping	temporary private camp set up remotely from a permanent lodge
guesthouse	cheap local hotel
hoteli	local restaurant
indigenous	naturally occurring
kanga	colourful printed cloth worn by most Tanzanian women
KIA	Kilimanjaro International Airport
kitenge (plural *vitenge*)	similar to *kanga*
koppie (or *kopje*)	Afrikaans word used to refer to a small hill such as those on the Serengeti
mandazi	deep-fried doughball, essentially the local variant on a doughnut
mishkaki	meat (usually beef) kebab
mzungu (pl *wazungu*)	white person
NCA	Ngorongoro Conservation Area
ngoma	Swahili dance
Omani era	period when the coast was ruled by the Sultan of Oman, especially 19th century
self-contained room	room with en-suite shower and toilet
savanna	grassland studded with trees
Shirazi era	medieval period during which settlers from Shiraz (Iran) dominated coastal trade
taarab	Swahili music and dance form associated particularly with Zanzibar
TANAPA	Tanzania National Parks
ugali	stodgy porridge-like staple made with ground maize meal
woodland	area of trees lacking a closed canopy

Appendix 3

FURTHER INFORMATION
History and biography

A limited number of single-volume histories covering east Africa and/or Tanzania are in print, but most are rather textbook-like in tone, and I've yet to come across one that is likely to hold much appeal to the casual reader. About the best bet is Iliffe's *Modern History of Tanganyika* (Cambridge, 1979). For a more general perspective, Oliver and Fage's *Short History of Africa* (Penguin, sixth edition, 1988) is rated as providing the best concise overview of African history, but it's too curt, dry, wide-ranging and dated to make for a satisfying read.

If I were to recommend one historical volume to a visitor to Tanzania, it would have to be Richard Hall's *Empires of the Monsoon: A History of the Indian Ocean and its Invaders* (Harper Collins, 1996). This highly focused and reasonably concise book will convey a strong historical perspective to the general reader, as a result of the author's storytelling touch and his largely successful attempt to place the last 1,000 years of east and southern African history in an international framework.

Considerably more bulky, and working an even broader canvas, John Reader's *Africa: A Biography of the Continent* (Penguin, 1997) has met with universal praise as perhaps the most readable and accurate attempt yet to capture the sweep of African history for the general reader.

Several books document specific periods and/or regions in African history. Good coverage of the coastal Swahili, who facilitated the medieval trade between the gold fields of Zimbabwe and the Arab World, is provided in J de Vere Allen's *Swahili Origins* (James Currey, 1992). Among the better popular works on the early era of European exploration are Hibbert's *Africa Explored: Europeans in the Dark Continent* (Penguin, 1982) and Alan Moorehead's peerless classics of the genre history-as-adventure-yarn *The White Nile* and *The Blue Nile*, published in 1960 and 1962 respectively and available in Penguin paperback. An excellent biography pertaining to this era is Tim Jeal's *Livingstone* (Heinemann, 1973, recently reprinted). For an erudite, compelling and panoramic account of the decade that turned Africa on its head, Thomas Pakenham's gripping 600-page tome *The Scramble for Africa* was aptly described by one reviewer as '*Heart of Darkness* with the lights switched on'. For a glimpse into the colonial era itself, just about everybody who sets foot in east Africa ends up reading Karen Blixen's autobiographical *Out of Africa* (Penguin, 1937).

Field guides and natural history

If you have difficulty finding African natural history books at your local bookshop and you're not flying directly to South Africa (where you can pick them up easily) get hold of the Natural History Book Service, 2 Wills Road, Totnes, Devon TQ9 SXN; ☎ 01803 865913 or Russel Friedman Books in South Africa; ☎ 011 702-2300/1; f 011 702 1403.

Mammals

Dorst and Dandelot's *Field Guide to the Larger Mammals of Africa* (Collins) and Haltennorth's *Field Guide to the Mammals of Africa (including Madagascar)* (Collins), were the standard mammal field guides for years, but have been rendered obsolete by several newer and better books. The pick of these, especially if your interest extends to bats and other small mammals, is Jonathan Kingdon's *Field Guide to African Mammals* (Academic Press, 1997), which also contains a goldmine of information about the evolutionary relationships of modern species.

Chris and Tilde Stuart's *Field Guide to the Larger Mammals of Africa* (Struik Publishers, 1997) is better suited for space-conscious travellers who are serious about putting a name to all the large mammals they see. For backpackers, the same authors' *Southern, Eastern and Central African Mammals: A Photographic Guide* (Struik Publishers, 1993) is far lighter and still gives adequate detail for 152 mammal species. The Stuarts have also written the coffee-table format *Africa's Vanishing Wildlife* (Southern Book Publishers, 1996), an outstanding book of its sort and highly recommended as advance reading or as a souvenir.

Not a field guide in the conventional sense so much as a guide to mammalian behaviour, Richard Estes' superb *The Safari Companion* (Green Books UK, Chelsea Green USA, Russell Friedman Books South Africa, 1992) is well organised and informative but rather bulky for casual safari-goers.

Birds

Zimmerman, Turner, Pearson, Willet and Pratt's *Birds of Kenya and Northern Tanzania* (Russell Friedman Books, 1996) is a contender for the best single-volume field guide available to any African country or region. I would recommend it to any serious birder sticking to northern Tanzania, since it provides complete coverage for the northern safari circuit, the Usambara and Pare mountains and Pemba Island, and although it stops short of Dar es Salaam and Zanzibar, this wouldn't be a major limitation. Unfortunately, it's too bulky, heavy and expensive to be of interest to any but the most bird-obsessed of backpackers, and the gaps in its coverage would limit its usefulness south of Dar es Salaam or in the Lake Victoria and Lake Tanganyika region.

For any birding itinerary extending to parts of Tanzania west of the Serengeti or south of the Usambara, the best option is the brand-new *Field Guide to the Birds of East Africa* by Williamson and Fanshawe. Published in early 2002, this field guide provides comprehensive coverage for the whole of Tanzania, as well as Kenya, Rwanda and Burundi, and based on limited field usage to date it seems excellent, with accurate plates, good distribution maps, and adequately detailed text descriptions.

Another quality field guide that provides full coverage of east Africa is *Birds of Africa south of the Sahara: A Comprehensive Illustrated Field Guide* by Ian Sinclair and Peter Ryan (Struik Publishers, 2003), which describes and illustrates the 2,100-plus species recorded in the region. Should you already own it, or be planning more extensive travels in Africa, then this guide will more than suffice for northern Tanzania. But if your African travels will be restricted to east Africa, you are probably better off buying a more focussed field guide.

Ber Van Perlo's *Illustrated Checklist to the Birds of Eastern Africa* (Collins, 1995) is a useful, relatively inexpensive and admirably compact identification manual describing and illustrating all 1,488 bird species recorded in Eritrea, Ethiopia, Kenya, Uganda and Tanzania. Unfortunately, however, the distribution maps and colour plates are often misleading, and the compact format means that descriptions are too terse and pictures too cluttered to allow identification of more difficult genera. It is, however, far more useful than John Williams' pioneering but now obsolete *Field Guide to the Birds of East Africa*, also published by Collins and still referred to in many brochures and guides.

National parks

Bernhard Grzimek's renowned book *Serengeti Shall Not Die* (Collins, 1959) remains a classic evocation of the magic of the Serengeti, and its original publication was instrumental in making this reserve better known to the outside world. Iain Douglas-Hamilton's *Amongst the*

Elephants (Penguin, 1978) did much the same for publicising Lake Manyara National Park, though the vast herds of elephants it describes have since been greatly reduced by poaching.

About ten years ago, Jeanette Hanby and David Bygott wrote a series of excellent booklets covering Serengeti National Park, Tarangire National Park and Lake Manyara National Park. These were published by TANAPA and can still be bought for US$5 at many bookshops in Arusha, and possibly at some safari lodges. The same authors have written an equally informative and widely available self-published booklet covering the Ngorongoro Conservation Area. These older guides have now been formally superseded by a series of glossier booklets covering each of the four major reserves, published by the African Publishing House in association with TANAPA. These newer booklets are more up-to-date and colourful than the older ones, but they are also twice the price, and are not substantially more informative.

Giovanni Tombazzi's lively, colourful and accurate maps covering (among other places) the Serengeti, Lake Manyara, Tarangire and the Ngorongoro Conservation Area are probably the most user-friendly maps I've seen anywhere in east Africa. Each of these maps shows details of the appropriate conservation area in both the dry and wet seasons, and is liberally dotted with illustrations of common trees and other points of interest. Giovanni has also produced a map covering the whole northern safari circuit, useful to those who don't want to splash out on the whole series of more detailed maps. The maps are produced in collaboration with Hoopoe Adventure Tours (see *Safari operators*, page 110, for contact details) who also distribute them in northern Tanzania. As with the booklets mentioned above, these maps are widely available in Arusha and at the national park lodges, but vary in price depending on where you buy them.

Travel literature

Bradt also publishes the dedicated *Zanzibar: The Bradt Travel Guide*, the most useful book for those who are travelling to the islands in isolation. For people combining a visit to Tanzania with one or other of its neighbours, there are also Bradt guides available to Kenya, Ethiopia, Uganda, Mozambique, Malawi, Rwanda and Zambia. Two reasonably modern travelogues that touch on Tanzania are Dervla Murphy's *The Ukimwi Road* (John Murray, 1993) and Shiva Naipaul's *North of South* (Penguin).

Coffee-table books

The best book of this sort to cover Tanzania as a whole is Paul Joynson-Hicks' *Tanzania: Portrait of a Nation*, which contains some great down-to-earth cultural photography and lively anecdotal captions. Also recommended is *Journey through Tanzania*, photographed by the late Mohammed Amin and Duncan Willets and published by Camerapix in Kenya. Both of the above books are stronger on cultural, landmark and scenic photography than on wildlife photography, for which M Iwago's superb *Serengeti* (Thames and Hudson, 1987) has few peers. Also worth a look is John Reader's definitive *Kilimanjaro*. Javed Jafferji's atmospheric photographs are highlighted in *Images of Zanzibar*, while *Zanzibar – Romance of the Ages* makes extensive use of archive photographs dating to before the turn of the century. Both were published by HSP Publications in 1996, and are readily available on the island.

Travel magazines

The TTB produces a quarterly magazine called *Tantravel*, which normally includes a few gushing but interesting articles as well as plenty of ads, and can normally be picked up at Air Tanzania and Tourist Board offices. Far better is the quarterly magazine *Kakakuona: African Wildlife*, which is produced by the Tanzania Wildlife Protection Fund, and frequently includes several good articles about conservation in Tanzania: e kakakuona@africaonline.co.tz.

For readers with a broad interest in Africa, an excellent magazine dedicated to tourism throughout Africa is *Travel Africa*, which can be visited online at www.travelafricamag.com.

Recommended for their broad-ranging editorial content and the coffee-table standard photography and reproduction, the award-winning magazines *Africa Geographic* (formerly *Africa Environment and Wildlife*) and *Africa Birds & Birding* can be checked out at the website www.africageographic.com.

Health

Self-prescribing has its hazards so if you are going anywhere very remote consider taking a health book. For adults there is *Bugs, Bites & Bowels: the Cadogan Guide to Healthy Travel* by Jane Wilson-Howarth (2006); if travelling with the family look at *Your Child Abroad: A Travel Health Guide* by Jane Wilson-Howarth and Matthew Ellis, published by Bradt in 2005.

Maps

A number of maps covering east Africa are available. The best is the Austrian-published Freytag-Berndt 1:2,000,000 map. By far the most accurate and up-to-date dedicated map of Tanzania is the 1:400,000 *Tanzania Travel Map* published by Harms Verlag (www.harms-ic-verlag.de). For most tourists, the map of Tanzania produced by the TTB and given away free at their offices in Arusha or Dar will be adequate.

A series of excellent maps by Giovanni Tombazzi covers most of the northern reserves, as well as Kilimanjaro, Mount Meru and Zanzibar. Colourful, lively and accurate, these maps are widely available throughout northern Tanzania. Also recommended are the new Harms Verlag maps to Ngorongoro Conservation Area, Lake Manyara National Park and Zanzibar Island.

Fiction

Surprisingly few novels have been written by Tanzanians or about Tanzania (even a friend who has studied African literature failed to come up with one indigenous Tanzanian novelist). An excellent novel set in World War I Tanzania is William Boyd's *An Ice-cream War*, while the same author's *Brazzaville Beach*, though not overtly set in Tanzania, devotes attention to aspects of chimpanzee behaviour first noted at Gombe Stream.

A Tanzanian of Asian extraction now living in Canada, M G Vassanji, is the author of at least one novel set in Tanzania and the Kenyan border area, the prize-winning *Book of Secrets* (Macmillan, 1994). This is an atmospheric tale, with much interesting period detail, revolving around a diary written by a British administrator in pre-war Kenya and discovered in a flat in Dar es Salaam in the 1980s. Vassanji is also the author of *Uhuru Street*, a collection of short stories set in Dar es Salaam.

Novels set elsewhere in Africa, but which may be of interest to visitors to Tanzania, include the following:

Brink, A *An Act of Terror* or *A Dry White Season*
Cartwright, J *Maasai Dreaming*
Conrad, J *Heart of Darkness*
Dagarembga, T *Nervous Conditions*
Gordimer, N *July's People*
Kingsolver, B *The Poisonwood Bible*
Lambkin, David *The Hanging Tree*
Lessing, D *The Grass is Singing, Children of Violence* (5 volumes)
Mazrui, A *The Trial of Christopher Okigbo*
Mungoshi, C *Coming of the Dry Season*
Mwangi, M *Going down River Road*
Naipaul, V S *A Bend in the River*
Okri, B *The Famished Road*
Theroux, P *Jungle Lovers*

Thiong'o, N *Petals of Blood* or *A Grain of Wheat*
Slaughter, C *Antonia saw the Oryx First*
Van der Post, L *A Story like the Wind*

Websites
The following offer information on northern Tanzania and Zanzibar:

www.ntz.info
www.intotanzania.com
www.allaboutzanzibar.com
www.africatravelresources.com

THE ULTIMATE TRAVEL MAGAZINE

Launched in 1993, *Wanderlust* is an inspirational magazine dedicated to free-spirited travel. It has become the essential companion for independent-minded travellers of all ages and interests, with readers in over 100 countries.

A one-year, 6-issue subscription carries a money-back guarantee – for further details:

Tel.+44 (0)1753 620426
Fax. +44 (0)1753 620474

or check the *Wanderlust* website, which has details of the latest issue, and where you can subscribe on-line:

www.wanderlust.co.uk

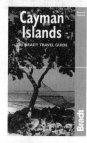

WIN £100 CASH!

READER QUESTIONNAIRE

**Send in your completed questionnaire for the chance to win
£100 cash in our regular draw**

All respondents may order a Bradt guide at half the UK retail price – please
complete the order form overleaf.

(Entries may be posted or faxed to us, or scanned and emailed.)

We are interested in getting feedback from our readers to help us plan future Bradt
guides. Please answer ALL the questions below and return the form to us in order
to qualify for an entry in our regular draw.

Have you used any other Bradt guides? If so, which titles? . . . .
. . . .

What other publishers' travel guides do you use regularly? . . . .
. . . .

Where did you buy this guidebook? . . . .

What was the main purpose of your trip to Northern Tanzania (or for what other
reason did you read our guide)? eg: holiday/business/charity etc. . . . .
. . . .

What other destinations would you like to see covered by a Bradt guide?
. . . .

Would you like to receive our catalogue/newsletters?

YES / NO (If yes, please complete details on reverse)

If yes – by post or email? . . . .

Age (circle relevant category) 16–25   26–45   46–60   60+

Male/Female (delete as appropriate)

Home country . . . .

Please send us any comments about our guide to Northern Tanzania or other
Bradt Travel Guides. . . . .
. . . .
. . . .
. . . .

Bradt Travel Guides
23 High Street, Chalfont St Peter, Bucks SL9 9QE, UK
✆ +44 (0)1753 893444 f +44 (0)1753 892333
e info@bradtguides.com
www.bradtguides.com

CLAIM YOUR HALF-PRICE BRADT GUIDE!

Order Form

To order your half-price copy of a Bradt guide, and to enter our prize draw to win £100 (see overleaf), please fill in the order form below, complete the questionnaire overleaf, and send it to Bradt Travel Guides by post, fax or email.

Please send me one copy of the following guide at half the UK retail price

Title	Retail price	Half price
... .	....	....

Please send the following additional guides at full UK retail price

No	Title	Retail price	Total
...	....	....	....
...	....	....	....
...	....	....	....

	Sub total	....
	Post & packing	....
(£1 per book UK; £2 per book Europe; £3 per book rest of world)	Total	....

Name . . . .

Address . . . .

Tel . . . .   Email . . . .

☐ I enclose a cheque for £ . . . . made payable to Bradt Travel Guides Ltd

☐ I would like to pay by credit card. Number: . . . .

    Expiry date: . . . / . . .   3-digit security code (on reverse of card) . . . . .

☐ Please add my name to your catalogue mailing list.

☐ I would be happy for you to use my name and comments in Bradt marketing material.

Send your order on this form, with the completed questionnaire, to:

Bradt Travel Guides/NTAN
23 High Street, Chalfont St Peter, Bucks SL9 9QE
✆ +44 (0)1753 893444   **f** +44 (0)1753 892333
e info@bradtguides.com   www.bradtguides.com

Bradt Travel Guides

www.bradtguides.com

Africa

Africa Overland	£15.99
Benin	£14.99
Botswana: Okavango, Chobe, Northern Kalahari	£14.95
Burkina Faso	£14.99
Cape Verde Islands	£13.99
Canary Islands	£13.95
Cameroon	£13.95
Eritrea	£12.95
Ethiopia	£15.99
Gabon, São Tomé, Príncipe	£13.95
Gambia, The	£12.95
Georgia	£13.95
Ghana	£13.95
Kenya	£14.95
Madagascar	£14.95
Malawi	£12.95
Mali	£13.95
Mauritius, Rodrigues & Réunion	£12.95
Mozambique	£12.95
Namibia	£14.95
Niger	£14.99
Nigeria	£15.99
Rwanda	£13.95
Seychelles	£14.99
Sudan	£13.95
Tanzania, Northern	£13.99
Tanzania	£14.95
Uganda	£13.95
Zambia	£15.95
Zanzibar	£12.95

Britain and Europe

Albania	£13.99
Armenia, Nagorno Karabagh	£13.95
Azores	£12.95
Baltic Capitals: Tallinn, Riga, Vilnius, Kaliningrad	£12.99
Belgrade	£6.99
Bosnia & Herzegovina	£13.95
Bratislava	£6.99
Budapest	£7.95
Cork	£6.95
Croatia	£12.95
Cyprus see North Cyprus	
Czech Republic	£13.99
Dubrovnik	£6.95
Eccentric Britain	£13.99
Eccentric Edinburgh	£5.95
Eccentric France	£12.95
Eccentric London	£12.95
Eccentric Oxford	£5.95
Estonia	£12.95
Faroe Islands	£13.95
Hungary	£14.99
Kiev	£7.95
Latvia	£13.99
Lille	£6.99
Lithuania	£13.99
Ljubljana	£6.99
Macedonia	£13.95
Montenegro	£13.99
North Cyprus	£12.95
Paris, Lille & Brussels	£11.95
Riga	£6.95
River Thames, In the Footsteps of the Famous	£10.95
Serbia	£13.99
Slovenia	£12.99
Spitsbergen	£14.99
Switzerland: Rail, Road, Lake	£13.99
Tallinn	£6.95
Ukraine	£13.95
Vilnius	£6.99

Middle East, Asia and Australasia

Great Wall of China	£13.99
Iran	£14.99
Iraq	£14.95
Kabul	£9.95
Maldives	£13.99
Mongolia	£14.95
North Korea	£13.95
Palestine, Jerusalem	£12.95
Sri Lanka	£13.99
Syria	£13.99
Tasmania	£12.95
Tibet	£12.95
Turkmenistan	£14.99

The Americas and the Caribbean

Amazon, The	£14.95
Argentina	£15.99
Cayman Islands	£12.95
Costa Rica	£13.99
Chile	£16.95
Chile & Argentina: Trekking	£12.95
Eccentric America	£13.95
Eccentric California	£13.99
Falkland Islands	£13.95
Peru & Bolivia: Backpacking and Trekking	£12.95
Panama	£13.95
St Helena, Ascension, Tristan da Cunha	£14.95
USA by Rail	£13.99

Wildlife

Antarctica: Guide to the Wildlife	£14.95
Arctic: Guide to the Wildlife	£14.95
British Isles: Wildlife of Coastal Waters	£14.95
Galápagos Wildlife	£15.99
Madagascar Wildlife	£14.95
South African Wildlife	£18.95

Health

Your Child Abroad: A Travel Health Guide	£10.95

Index

Entries in italics indicate maps